A Death of the World

SUNY series in Contemporary Continental Philosophy
Dennis J. Schmidt, editor

A Death of the World
Surviving the Death of the Other

Harris B. Bechtol

SUNY
PRESS

Cover credit: "And Jesus Wept" © 2024 Richard F. Ebert, Encircle Photos.
Published by State University of New York Press, Albany
© 2025 State University of New York
All rights reserved
Printed in the United States of America

All rights reserved.

Portions of the introduction appeared previously in "A Hermeneutic Phenomenology: The Death of the Other Understood as Event," *Journal of Applied Hermeneutics* (2017): 1–14. Portions of chapters 1 and 8 appeared previously in "The Gift of Mourning," *Journal of French and Francophone Philosophy* 31, no. 1/2 (2023): 85–105. Portions of chapter 3 appeared previously in "Event, Death, and Poetry: The Death of the Other in Derrida's 'Rams,'" *Philosophy Today* 62, no. 1 (2018): 253–68.

No part of this book may be used or reproduced in any manner whatsoever without written permission. No part of this book may be stored in a retrieval system or transmitted in any form or by any means including electronic, electrostatic, magnetic tape, mechanical, photocopying, recording, or otherwise without the prior permission in writing of the publisher.

Links to third-party websites are provided as a convenience and for informational purposes only. They do not constitute an endorsement or an approval of any of the products, services, or opinions of the organization, companies, or individuals. SUNY Press bears no responsibility for the accuracy, legality, or content of a URL, the external website, or for that of subsequent websites.

EU GPSR Authorised Representative:
Logos Europe, 9 rue Nicolas Poussin, 17000, La Rochelle, France
contact@logoseurope.eu

For information, contact State University of New York Press, Albany, NY
www.sunypress.edu

Library of Congress Cataloging-in-Publication Data

Names: Bechtol, Harris B., 1984– author.
Title: A death of the world : surviving the death of the other / Harris B. Bechtol.
Description: Albany : State University of New York Press, [2025] | Series:
   SUNY series in contemporary continental philosophy | Includes bibliographical
   references and index. Identifiers: LCCN 2024042450 | ISBN 9798855801880
   (hardcover) | ISBN 9798855801897 (ebook) | ISBN 9798855801873 (paperback)
Subjects: LCSH: Death. | Other (Philosophy) | Bereavement.
Classification: LCC BD444 .B357 2025 | DDC 113/.8—dc23/eng/20241112
LC record available at https://lccn.loc.gov/2024042450

One of us, each says to himself, the day will come when one of the two of us will see himself no longer seeing the other and so will carry the other within him awhile longer, . . . the world suspended by some unique tear, each time unique, through which everything from then on, through which the world itself — and this day will come — will come to be reflected quivering, reflecting disappearance itself.

— Jacques Derrida, *The Work of Mourning*

Surviving — that is the other name of a mourning whose possibility is never to be awaited. For one does not survive without mourning. No one alive can get the better of this tautology, that of the stance of *survivance* — even God would be helpless.

— Jacques Derrida, *The Politics of Friendship*

Always prefer life and never stop affirming survival.

— Jacques Derrida, *"Final Words"*

Contents

Abbreviations	ix
Preface	xiii
Introduction: The Question of Death, Event, and Survival	1

Part One — Symptoms of an Event

Chapter One: The Unexpected, Im-possible Event	23
Chapter Two: The Secretive Event without Reason	43
Chapter Three: The Transformative Event	65

Part Two — Spatial Transformations of the World

Chapter Four: Unexpected Loss and Life: The Presence of the Other's Absence	91
Chapter Five: Excess and the Death of the Other: Life/Death, Materiality, and Reason	107

Part Three — Temporal Transformations of the World

Chapter Six: Memories and a Past That Won't Stay Put	127
Chapter Seven: Lost Possibilities and a Fractured Future	149
Chapter Eight: The Gift of Mourning in a Present Out of Joint	167
Conclusion: The Afterlife	189
Notes	193
Bibliography	227
Index	241

Abbreviations

Works by Jacques Derrida

A *Aporias*. Translated by Thomas Dutoit. Stanford, CA: Stanford University Press, 1993.

AF *Archive Fever*. Translated by Eric Prenowitz. Chicago, IL: University of Chicago Press, 1996.

AR *Acts of Religion*. Edited by Gil Anidjar. New York: Routledge, 2002.

BS1 *The Beast and the Sovereign.* Vol. 1. Translated by Geoffrey Bennington. Chicago, IL: University of Chicago Press, 2009.

BS2 *The Beast and the Sovereign.* Vol. 2. Translated by Geoffrey Bennington. Chicago, IL: University of Chicago Press, 2011.

C *Cinders*. Translated by Ned Lukacher. Minneapolis: University of Minnesota Press, 2014.

DE "Une certaine possibilité impossible de dire l'événement." In *Dire l'événement, est-ce possible? Seminaire de Montréal, pour Jacques Derrida*, edited by Gad Soussana, Alexis Nouss, and Jacques Derrida, 79–112. Paris: L'Harmattan, 2001.

DP2 *Death Penalty*. Vol. 2. Translated by Elizabeth Rottenberg. Chicago, IL: University of Chicago Press, 2017.

DT2 *Donner les temps II*. Edited by Lara Odello, Peter Szendy, and Rodrigo Therezo. Paris: Éditions du Seuil, 2021.

EO *The Ear of the Other: Otobiography, Transference, Translation*. Translated by Peggy Kamuf. New York: Shocken Books, 1985.

F "*Fors*: The Anglish Words of Nicolas Abraham and Maria Torok." Translated by Barbara Johnson. In Nicolas Abraham and Maria Torok, *The Wolf Man's Magic Word: A Cryptonymy*,

	translated by Nicholas Rand, xi–xlviii. Minneapolis: University of Minnesota Press, 1986.
G3	*Geschlecht III: Sex, Race, Nation, Humanity*. Translated by Katie Chenoweth and Rodrigo Therezo. Chicago, IL: University of Chicago Press, 2020.
GD	*The Gift of Death*. 2nd ed. Translated by David Wills. Chicago, IL: University of Chicago Press, 2008.
GT	*Given Time: 1 Counterfeit Money*. Translated by Peggy Kamuf. Chicago, IL: University of Chicago Press, 1992.
H	*Heidegger: The Question of Being and History*. Translated by Geoffrey Bennington. Chicago, IL: University of Chicago Press, 2016.
LD	*Life Death*. Translated by Pascale-Anne Brault and Michael Naas. Chicago, IL: University of Chicago Press, 2020.
LLF	*Learning to Live Finally*. Translated by Pascale-Anne Brault and Michael Naas. Brooklyn, NY: Melville House, 2007.
MP	*Margins of Philosophy*. Translated by Alan Bass. Chicago, IL: University of Chicago Press, 1982.
MPM	*Memoires for Paul de Man*. Translated by Cecile Lindsay et al. New York: Columbia University Press, 1989.
OG	*Of Grammatology*. Translated by Gayatri Chakrovorty Spivak. Baltimore, MD: The John Hopkins University Press, 1997.
OH	*Of Hospitality: Anne Dufourmantelle Invites Jacques Derrida to Respond*. Translated by Rachel Bowlby. Stanford, CA: Stanford University Press, 2000.
P	*Points: Interviews, 1974–1994*. Translated by Peggy Kamuf et al. Stanford, CA: Stanford University Press, 1995.
PF	*The Politics of Friendship*. Translated by George Collins. New York: Verso, 2005.
R	*Rogues: Two Essays on Reason*. Translated by Pascale-Anne

Brault and Michael Naas. Stanford, CA: Stanford University Press, 2005.

SM   *Specters of Marx.* Translated by Peggy Kamuf. New York: Routledge, 1994.

SQ   *Sovereignties in Question: The Poetics of Paul Celan.* Edited by Thomas Dutoit and Outi Pasanen. New York: Fordham University Press, 2005.

VP   *Voice and Phenomenon: Introduction to the Problem of the Sign in Husserl's Phenomenology.* Translated by Leonard Lawlor. Evanston, IL: Northwestern University Press, 2011.

WA   *Without Alibi.* Translated by Peggy Kamuf. Stanford, CA: Stanford University Press, 2002.

WD   *Writing and Difference.* Translated by Alan Bass. Chicago, IL: University of Chicago Press, 1978.

WM   *The Work of Mourning.* Edited by Pascale-Anne Brault and Michael Naas. Chicago, IL: University of Chicago Press, 2001.

Works by Martin Heidegger

BT   *Being and Time.* Translated by Joan Stambaugh and Dennis J. Schmidt. Albany, NY: SUNY Press, 2010.

PR   *The Principle of Reason.* Translated by Reginald Lilly. Bloomington, IN: Indiana University Press, 1991.

PRL   *The Phenomenology of Religious Life.* Translated by Matthias Fritsch and Jennifer Anna Gosetti-Ferencei. Bloomington, IN: Indiana University Press, 1995.

TB   *On Time and Being.* Translated by Joan Stambaugh. New York: Harper & Row, 1972.

Works by Jean-Luc Marion

BG   *Being Given: Toward a Phenomenology of Givenness*. Translated by Jeffrey L. Kosky. Stanford, CA: Stanford University Press, 2002.

GWB   *God without Being*. Translated by Thomas A. Carlson. Chicago, IL: University of Chicago Press, 1991.

IE   *In Excess: Studies of Saturated Phenomena*. Translated by Robyn Horner and Vincent Berraud. New York: Fordham University Press, 2002.

ISP   *In the Self's Place: The Approach of Saint Augustine*. Translated by Jeffrey L. Kosky. Stanford, CA: Stanford University Press, 2012.

NC   *Negative Certainties*. Translated by Stephen Lewis. Chicago, IL: University of Chicago Press, 2015.

RG   *Reduction and Givenness: Investigations of Husserl, Heidegger, and Phenomenology*. Translated by Thomas A. Carlson. Evanston, IL: Northwestern University Press, 1998.

VR   *The Visible and the Revealed*. Translated by Christina M. Gschwandtner et al. New York: Fordham University Press, 2008.

Works by Jean-Luc Nancy

BSP   *Being Singular Plural*. Translated by Robert D. Richardson and Anne E. O'Byrne. Stanford, CA: Stanford University Press, 2000.

IC   *The Inoperative Community*. Translated by Peter Connor, Lisa Garbus, Michale Holland, et al. Minneapolis: University of Minnesota Press, 1991.

Preface

When I first started teaching undergraduate students, I quickly learned that while my students who were much more inclined toward philosophical thinking did not need much motivation to engage with the material in the course, the majority of my students needed an impetus to find interest in the material. I found that one such helpful hook is the topic of death and how we can live in the face of it. While the idea of getting about thirty eighteen- to twenty-five-year-olds to think about death for fifteen weeks during the semester may sound like madness, for who thinks of death during those ages, I have found this approach to be really helpful for the students. Many of my students over the years in this course on death have found unexpected interest in philosophy because while they thought philosophy to be just a bunch of abstract thoughts that have nothing to do with them, they began to realize that philosophy can be a helpful way of getting them to think through the Sisyphean stones in their life — those difficult aspects of life that never seem to go away and always rear their ugly heads around every corner of life, often when we least expect them.

So I tell my students on the first day of class that while fewer and fewer universals remain in our world, one such universal is unavoidable across cultures: death. For each of us has an encounter with death, whether through an existential crisis of our own mortality or through the death of someone or, heaven forbid, both. Regarding the death of someone, to paraphrase the philosopher Jacques Derrida, the unavoidable and inflexible law of life is that each of us will experience or live through the death of someone. Or as I will call this experience throughout this book: the death of the other. Each of us will have experienced the death of the other. This is the unavoidable and inflexible law of life. And I aim in the following pages to think through this experience by providing an interpretation of what happens to someone who undergoes this death of the other.

This experience of the death of the other first became a problem for me, a Sisyphean stone, when a dear friend and mentor of mine died tragically in front of not only my own eyes but also the eyes of roughly two hundred other people while I was an undergraduate at Baylor University. In the aftermath of this death over the many years between now and then, I have witnessed the collapse of communities, marriages, faiths in God as well as the rise of new directions for communities, the building and flourishing of new relationships, and reinvigorations of faith in a new God all of which centered around this experience. I experienced firsthand what I will call later in this project *life/death* as the interweaving of life with death in the aftermath of the death of the other. And this got me to thinking about what exactly happens to us human beings when we manage to survive such a death of the other. As I explored this question, I learned that what I had experienced was not entirely unique to me as I began to read philosophical, theological, psychological, literary, and personal accounts of the experience of death. I found in all of this that an interesting relationship gets forged between the world understood as spatial and temporal and those who survive such a death of the other. So I set to unpack this relationship between the survivors of the death of the other and their spatiotemporal world. In the first iteration of this project in my dissertation for my PhD degree at Texas A&M University, one of the members of my committee died about eight weeks before I defended the dissertation, and, then again, three years after my defense as I began rewriting the initial project, another member of my committee, who had replaced the member who died, also died while I was helping him teach his last graduate seminar at Texas A&M. Now, many years after that first death of the other that shook up the world for me, a few graduate degrees, marriage, children, other deaths of the other, and a touch with my own death in the form of open-heart surgery, the book in your hands or on your tablet or screen had finally been given the chance, the grace, or the gift of life.

This chance of life for my book has happened through the help of many people, both in the academic world as well as outside of it. Many thanks go to Ted George, Kristi Sweet, Jack Caputo, Brady DeHoust, Jen Gaffney, Michael Naas, Steven DeLay, Dan Conway, the late John McDermott, the late Scott Austin, Michael Portal, Kyle Bennett, Billy Daniel, and Jeff Vidt as well as the many people who had to deal with me talking about death and mourning while riding bikes on beautiful roads in Texas, Colorado, New Mexico, Montana, and Vermont: Will and Cheryl Brown, Dwight Hirsch, Bill Garrett, John Flynn, Mike Record, Deb Barton, Brad Wilcox, Ed Vargo, and the late Ken Spence. Additionally, I would like to thank the editors and assistants to the editors at the journals where editions of parts of this book first appeared. I would also like to thank the anonymous reviewers at SUNY and Dennis Schmidt for pushing me to bring out my argument and originality in this project. A big thanks also goes out to my team at SUNY who helped bring this project to completion. And, lastly but surely not least, I would like to thank my wife, Jen, and three children, Avery, Sutton, and Jude, for showing me daily what surviving looks like and why affirming it is an imperative.

Introduction

The Question of Death, Event, and Survival

We are, at present, swimming in a sea of grief. . . . Given the loss-filled waters we inhabit, how to better navigate through them, and without drowning?

— Cindy Milstein, *Rebellious Mourning*

On June 11, 1983, Eric Wolterstorff, son of philosopher and theologian Nicholas Wolterstorff, died during a climbing accident at the age of twenty-five. Nicholas Wolterstorff describes life after the death of Eric in the celebrated *Lament for a Son* in terms of the loss of "inscape."[1] Drawing from the poet Gerard Manley Hopkin's use of this word, Wolterstorff writes, "Eric put inscape on things: the way he dressed, the way he cooked, the way he shook hands, the way he answered the phone."[2] This inscape is the particular character or the particular meaning that Eric had imbued on the world through and with those around him. And when Eric died, this meaning remains in the world but now exiled without home, a refugee wandering from which it came, only to be carried, offered hospitality, and kept alive through the memories of those, like his father, who remember him. Wolterstorff poignantly describes this exile of meaning with the loss of Eric: "Everything in his room spoke of him — light and airy, prints on the walls, art books and mountaineering books on the table, Indonesian spices in the cupboard, everything neat. Inscape. But where is the person who arranged these things? Where is the life that gave them *meaning*? His clothes hang limp."[3] What Wolterstorff describes is, on the one hand, a most exceptional experience because the loss of a child goes against our expectations for life. Parents ought not bury their children; children bury their parents. And yet, what Wolterstorff describes is, on the other hand, the most normal of experiences because if any universal truths are left, the one truth about life is that we will all experience loss. As Jacques Derrida says, life adheres to a "fatal and inflexible law: one of two friends will always see the other die" (SQ 139). In a different register, the birth cry of even a newborn child need only remind us that the child comes into the world experiencing loss, namely, the loss of home in the mother's womb, but, as I explore below, life itself is often gained only through loss. The most exceptional yet entirely normal experience, the most expected yet unexpected experience, this "at once ordinary and extraordinary"[4] experience — such is the death of the other. *C'est la vie*. And such is life as we always find our being-*with* one another.

I offer here a phenomenological exploration of what Wolterstorff and many of us have already experienced in life and that all of us will experience one day. This book is a phenomenological exploration of the experience of death. Not the experience of death dealing with one's own death, which is often enough the focus in philosophy, but the experience of death dealing with the death of the other. At its most basic level, this book is about loss, but the particular form of loss on which I focus is the death of the other. Through my description I argue that the death of someone is more than just the loss of the other because this loss brings with it a death of the world. And the world dies with the other, I further argue, because the death of the other alters the spatiality of the world and the temporality of the world for those who survive this death of the other. My description falls into three parts, but before laying out the roadmap of these parts, a few preliminary matters need to be addressed in order to clarify how I describe this death of the other: (1) this is a radical hermeneutics of the death of the other that (2) aims to show that the death of the other is what continental philosophers have called an *event* in (3) their post-Husserlian developments of phenomenology, and (4) why I am focusing on the death *of the other* specifically.

Extending Radical Hermeneutics

First, as part of the phenomenological tradition in philosophy, I offer a radical hermeneutics of surviving the death of the other. In this, I follow John D. Caputo's description of radical hermeneutics in his eponymous book: "This new hermeneutics would try not to make things look easy, to put the best face on existence, but rather to recapture the hardness of life before metaphysics showed us a fast way out the back door of the flux. . . . [This is] hermeneutics as an attempt to stick with the original difficulty of life, and not to betray it with metaphysics."[5] With Caputo setting the terms for such a hermeneutics, I extend the scope of this hermeneutics by looking at the death of the other through this hermeneutical lens. Accordingly, I look at survival of the death of the other itself *as* radical hermeneutics by focusing on the messiness of life at its end in order to interpret what is happening in these experiences of death without trying to cover up the difficulty of this situation with concepts and ideas that push someone to look past them, ignore them, suppress them, and so on. Instead, my approach is related to Friedrich Nietzsche's attempt not to negate life or miss the happening of life by inventing concepts that make the unfamiliar, uncomfortable parts of life familiar and comfortable but to return to the singularity of life in an effort to affirm life itself. My hermeneutical approach to the death of the other is to look at this phenomenon in its happening in order to describe the multiple facets of death and life taking place for those who survive a death of the other. Consequently, I describe how the death of the other infuses the familiarity of the daily status quo with the unfamiliar in order to affirm the unfolding of life at the end of life. In this, I aim not to make the discomfort surrounding the death of the other comfortable but to let this discomfort show itself in its uncomfortability. In my radical hermeneutical approach to the death of the other, I develop beginning in chapter 3 what I call the worklessness of mourning as the way to mourn the death of the other because this approach to mourning is itself radically hermeneutical insofar as it does not try to cover up the discomfort of mourning but to embrace it and engage with it. While I will say more about this worklessness of mourning in a moment, I want to address the second preliminary matter, that of the event in continental philosophy.

The Death of the Other as Event

Wolterstorff's experience, and others similar to it, of going into the dead other's apartment and seeing his or her clothes hanging limp, almost devoid of the meaning given them by the one now deceased, is an experience that requires a particular approach and description in order both to carry responsibly this experience and to let that experience mold and shape those who undergo it. In other words, to approach the death of the other in a radical hermeneutics, caution must be exercised as to what ideas are employed in the description so as not to betray the difficulty of mourning but to understand this difficulty in its difficulty. To this end, I employ within my radical hermeneutics of the death of the other the term of art that has gained much popularity in continental philosophy: the event.[6] The event as a term of art became popular around the middle of the twentieth century when philosophers in phenomenology and hermeneutics began exploring post-Kantian ontologies whose aim is to engage facticity. The resulting ontologies attempt to resist the main thrust in the history of philosophy from at least Plato to Hegel that emphasizes the mastery of the human subject over the objects that stand over against it. To illustrate, these ontologies are *post*-Kantian because they seek to approach the meaning of being and the meaning of the subject both with the conceptual framework provided by Kant but also against this framework. Philosophers of the event, then, follow a Kantian approach to ontology with a focus on the meaning of things while resisting Kant's approach to subjectivity by arguing that the human being does not remain the sole source and controller of the meaning of things. For philosophers of the event, the human being undergoes an experience in which he or she is no longer the sole constitut*ing* subject. Regarding this shift in ontology and subjectivity, Kant's *Critique of Pure Reason* is an important starting point for these philosophies of the event in not only setting the parameters by which thinking can understand itself but also in setting the parameters that an event deconstructs, irrupts, saturates, or surprises. Hence, these philosophers of event develop ontologies *after* Kant. The shortcoming of such substance metaphysical approaches as Kant's, according to these philosophers, is that they have been unable to engage with the most important aspects of facticity, which can be gathered under the heading of degrees or modes of givenness.[7] These philosophers of the event are concerned with whatever exceeds the conceptual and linguistic horizons of subjectivity by either an excess of givenness or a givenness of recess. And the name offered for such givenness is *the event*.

As a result, the ontologies developed by philosophers of the event rethink the subject in light of the subject's experiences that prior to the subject constitute, in part, who the subject is. In other words, the human being finds that things in their world already have meaning upon their arrival due to the bequest of history, heritage, and tradition. With this, the idea of factical experience or facticity points to the richness of our belonging to a world, where *world* does not mean the earth on which we live but the meaningful context in which we find ourselves. The German *die Umwelt* captures this sense of world nicely because it denotes the world (*Welt*) surrounding (*Um-*) us. Thus, living on the earth, we find ourselves in many worlds, the pluralized world as I will call it, in which things and people have meaning. This pluralized world opens various possibilities to us but also closes other possibilities to us. In this way, facticity constitutes, in part, who the subject is by imposing limitations on him or her. And this experience of limitation motivates these philosophers of the event. They are attuned to the limitations imposed on and by the human being through facticity, and this experience of limit engenders their interest in what exceeds — either as excessive givenness or as givenness of recess — the intentionality of the subject or what exceeds our attempts to give things meaning. And they are interested in this excess of things because this excess indicates something that first and foremost constitutes the human being rather than the human being constituting it. In other words, facticity's limitations engender their interest in what exceeds human subjectivity. They explore this interest in excess through their accounts of the event. So the event, in most general terms, then, marks what always exceeds language and knowledge. Thus, the philosophers of the event retain the Kantian focus of meaning-giving or the constitution of the world in our experience with it. However, they introduce a new timbre to this focus with their interest in event as excess.

Nevertheless, the diverse group of philosophers concerned with the event[8] provides no universal definition that would capture the nature of an event. As Jean-Luc Nancy aptly says, "[T]here is no event 'as such'" (*BSP* 169). Nancy and others resist any definition of an event because an event is understood to be an experience of possibility, contingency, and singularity itself. All we ever have in terms of our experience of an event are our experiences of *particular* events. We can have many experiences of events, in this sense, but we never experience the event as such. Thus, no universal, transcendent form of the event exists. Only a plurality of singular events exists. Moreover, as Claude Romano argues, an event always strikes someone in their particularity, thereby effecting and affecting them uniquely in their particularity.[9] Attempts to universalize the singularity of any event are, then, resisted. However, these philosophers often use similar language to describe what experiencing a particular event entails. For example, an event concerns a transformative moment when the "unexpected and unpredictable [disrupt] the normalized, neutralized, and forcibly pacified status quo."[10] And this disruption of a "singular occurrence" introduces "an element to our world or our situation that could not have been thought or predicated in advance and that, as soon as it has arrived, reconstitutes the previous relations between beings in a world because it interposes itself among them. Thus, it changes and reconfigures the world."[11] This similarity of language to describe singular events means that an experience of an event has a "symptomatology" (DE 105): we know when an event has disrupted the norms of everyday life because such a disruption carries common symptoms with it. This notion of symptom comes from what Derrida thinks about "verticality" (DE 105) insofar as the arrival of an event is an arrival that "falls on me" (DE 97). He insists "on the verticality of this matter because the surprise [of an event] can only come from on high" (DE 97). Without such verticality, an event could be seen coming on the horizon. We could expect an event. But an event is precisely that which surprises and that which is an exception or without law. Thus, the symptomatology of an event suggests that an event's arrival "can only give rise [*donner lieu à*] to symptoms" that befall us after the event's occurrence (DE 106).[12] As an adaptation of the Freudian idea of *Nachträglichkeit*, an event manifests itself only in the aftermath of these symptoms: without horizon, surprising, unexpected, aleatory, excessive, transformative, and so on. Thus, if an event comes — a technological invention, a gift of forgiveness, a historical moment, a novel virus, a death of the other, for instance — it happens as a singular surprise, as "always exceptional" and "without rule" (DE 106). Through its exceptional happening, an event as other enters the realm of experience with a kind of "transcendental violence"[13] insofar as it ruptures the current conditions of possibility by inventing a new set of conditions of possibility. An event is, then, the impossible becoming possible before our very eyes. And an event arrives in such a way that we can say something about the symptoms that have befallen us with its arrival.

My radical hermeneutics of the death of the other draws on this symptomatology of an event to argue that when another person dies, this death of the other is an *event* because such death is at the very least a radical transformation of the world and things in it for those who survive this other. I describe this death of the other in terms of an event because an event is a disruption of the world to the extent that the world prior to the event and the world engendered by the event are dramatically if not radically different. In this, I understand the world to be what it is, to have the being that it has, or to have the meaning that it has on account of the relations formed with others in it. So when one such other dies, what is lost is not only the physical presence of the other but also what the world has meant to and with that other.[14] Consequently, after establishing the contours around the philosophical understanding of an event in part 1, I focus in parts 2 and 3 more directly on describing the death of the other as such an event by following these contours. Parts 2 and 3, then, focus on the phenomenological significance of the death of the other by showing how such death transforms the spatiality and temporality of the survivors who live on after this death. Through the loss of meaning that attends the loss of the other's presence in the world, I describe the death of the other as a transformation of a survivor's spatiality where I understand spatiality as the context in which things, places, and the self come to meaning as a result of the relations we have with others. When the other dies these things, places, and the self harbor the present absence of the now dead other and the meaningfulness that she provided while living. This present absence accompanies the transformation of a survivor's temporality as well because after the death of the other, a survivor's relation to her past, her future, and her present becomes fraught with the absence of not just the presence of the other but also the meaningfulness with which the world had been constituted with the other. At times this loss of meaning is permanent, especially when the meaning lost concerns unactualized, future possibilities, while at other times, as with Wolterstorff's loss of his son, this loss of meaning is exilic, especially when the meaning lost concerns the past. Consequently, I argue that the death of the other is an event because when the other dies the pluralized world as constituted in, by, and with this other dies with him or her, that is, the meaningfulness of the spatiality and temporality of the world that has been constituted through a relationship with this other has been lost entirely or transformed.

I focus primarily throughout this project on the deaths of those others who are deeply important to us because, as Saint Augustine shows after the death of his mother, Monica, the death of someone close to us causes "the habit formed by our living together, a very affectionate and precious bond suddenly [to be] torn apart."[15] And this loss of habit and bond is what makes, in part, the death of the other an unexpected event that challenges our rationality and transforms life as we know it because the habit and bond is the phenomenological world formed with the other. Yet this raises two important questions about my description: what about the deaths of those who are not close to us, and what about the deaths of nonhuman animals? I address both concerns further in the body of my description, but, for now, I aim for the scope of my description to account for the deaths of others, human and nonhuman animal alike, who are intimately interwoven with our lives through what I call the relational, existential difference of the death of the other. I use this idea to sharpen the phenomenological quill of Derrida's idea that "every other is wholly other" (*tout autre est tout autre*) insofar as the death of the other, human or nonhuman animal, broaches an important distinction between modalities of otherness based on the relational involvement that we have with the other in our lives. Such a relational, existential difference within the otherness or alterity of others spans from the others with whom we have little relation to the others whose relation structures our understanding of the world. My claim, then, is that we can learn about and find some of the abiding structures of the death of *any* other by looking first at the deaths of those others, be they human or nonhuman animal others, who are deeply important to us. The existential difference that the other had played in a survivor's life while the other was living, will directly affect the impact of this death as a death of the world on the survivor. Part of the work of workless mourning, as I discuss especially in my final chapter, is to understand better and better that any death of the other is a death of the world. Thus, the deaths of others with whom we have deep existential and relational, that is to say ontological, connection give us insight into what is happening when any other dies, even if all deaths do not touch us equally.

A Post-Husserlian Phenomenology

And, to address the third preliminary matter, this radical hermeneutics of the death of the other understood as an event follows the approach to phenomenology that has been developed in the appropriations of Edmund Husserl's founding ideas for phenomenology as first articulated by Heidegger's understanding of phenomenology and further developed by Emmanuel Levinas's notion of the other; Jacques Derrida's notions of the gift, the event, and the im-possible; Jean-Luc Marion's notion of givenness; and the notions of the event in both Nancy and Romano. Each of these philosophers, in their own way, approach the thrust of phenomenology in terms of focusing on the very happening of phenomena, that is, on the givenness of phenomena as they unfold. As François Raffoul argues, phenomenology, "in its most authentic sense, ought to be reconsidered in terms of the event and recast as a phenomenology of the event."[16] Consequently, a return to the things themselves with phenomenology implies a return to things not as given, static substances but as events or happenings that unfold and constitute relational contexts of meanings or worlds. The specific thing in itself that I am turning to in order to consider it phenomenologically as an event is the death of the other. Accordingly, this phenomenology of the death of the other aims to describe this phenomenon as an event, that is, aims to describe it in its very happening by looking at how the death of the other spatially and temporally constitutes and transforms our worlds. In this regard, I disagree with Raffoul when he writes, "One might be tempted to say . . . that death is the event *par excellence*, except for the fact that unlike events, which as noted generate time and constitute a world, death closes time and shuts down the world."[17] While he is not incorrect to associate death with the closure of time and world, as will become obvious below, in this very closure, the death of the other also opens time and the world by transforming the meaningful relations of things, which are our worlds, and by transforming our relation to the flow of temporality so that we see ourselves related to time not linearly but circularly.

So I am, on the one hand, considering the death of the other from the perspective of it being an event that falls upon us, transforming the meaningful relations in which we find ourselves in ways that are unexpected, surprising, and outside the bounds of calculative rationality. As such, this phenomenology treats the death of the other, understood as an event, as an unfamiliar, unexpected guest come to disturb the orderliness of the familiar. In considering this disturbance of the guest of death in the home, the aim is not to make the unfamiliar familiar or to control the uncontrollable but to help us to be more welcoming of the unfamiliar into the orderliness of the home, that is, to drop our need to control the chaos of life. As a radical hermeneutics, instead of trying to avoid such chaos or messiness in life, my phenomenological description aims to be hospitable to this messiness. Accordingly, the attendant ethics of hospitality toward an event, which is especially developed in part 3, aims to develop what Derrida calls being ready not to be ready for an event to break into the status quo and to disrupt and transform the order found there.[18] In learning to be ready not to be ready for the in-breaking of the unfamiliar death of the other, I argue that we learn, in turn, how to be ready for the familiar faces of the other around us.

On the other hand, in addition to describing the death of the other as an event and the kind of ethics that attends it, I am also approaching the death of the other as a particular instance in which we experience the eventiality of an event itself. Though death, and in particular the death of the other, is not the only phenomenon that can expose us to the happening of an event, the death of the other is an important phenomenon for doing so because when we experience the death of the other, we are granted access to, if only momentarily, the constitutive flow, movement, or happening of life itself. At the border where life ends and death begins, we catch a glimpse of how the meaningfulness of life happens through the transformations of the spaces we embody and of the temporality through which our life finds itself structured. Accordingly, this is a text on death and survival, on the survival of the tremendous event of the death of an other. As such, I offer a phenomenological description of what is happening for those who *live-on* after the death of the other. And as a phenomenology, I aim to unfold the abiding and prevailing structures of what happens to those who survive the death of the other.

Why the Death of *the Other*?

As can be seen already, and will become much more so the case throughout this project, Derrida's work is enormously helpful in understanding the symptoms of an event as well as the symptoms of the event of the death of the other. Nevertheless, important differences in the philosophical approaches to the event remain. One such difference concerns the contrasting temporalities of an event: "following the event" and "awaiting the event in its imminence."[19] Some figures, for example, Hannah Arendt, Alain Badiou, Marion, and Romano, orient the temporality of an event around a *past* occurrence whose givenness causes us to return repeatedly to this occurrence in an effort to understand and mine its depths. Consequently, these philosophers use *birth* as their primary inflection of an event. Marion claims, for example, that I *continually* aim at my own birth "intentionally" by "wanting to know who and from where I am, undertaking research into my identity" (*IE* 42). Our life is "solely occupied . . . with reconstituting [our birth], attributing to it a meaning and responding to its silent appeal" (*IE* 42).

And yet other philosophers, such as Heidegger, Levinas, Derrida, and Nancy, orient the temporality of an event around the advent of what is to come. *Death* has, consequently, become an important figuration of an event for these philosophers.[20] Yet the predominant approach to death has been through personal death or personal mortality. Since at least Plato, if not further back with Heraclitus's ruminations on the relation among the bow, life, and death,[21] the history of philosophy has been preoccupied with the death of the self or one's own death. While Plato's oeuvre likely grew out of his own experience of mourning the death of his teacher, Socrates, Plato's most celebrated dialogue about death, the *Phaedo*, focuses not on the experience of mourning but more on what happens to the soul when someone dies. Plato's dialogues, then, focus on personal death rather than what happens in the aftermath of the death of someone for those who survive the death. Heidegger's existential analytic of Dasein's being-toward-death in *Being and Time* has made this focus on personal death especially important. For he argues that anxiety over one's own death is the originary experience of death that exposes the human being to the meaning of its own being, to its relation to temporality, and to its responsibility to become a self. Adhering to Heidegger's analysis, one's own death can be understood as an event because anticipation of this end can engender new interpretations of one's own being and of the meaning or being of things in the world.[22] This approach by Heidegger has led to a veritable thanatology as found in many philosophers who develop the intersection of one's own death with the event. For example, Françoise Dastur recognizes that the death of the other is the only death that humans experience, but it remains derivative of the originary experience of death found in one's own mortality. Moreover, the death of the other only serves as a reminder of this more originary relation to death as found in our own mortality for Dastur.[23] Likewise, Santiago Zabala and Michael Marder have indexed the transformative aspect of the event to "the realization of one's impending mortality."[24]

However, in the works of both Levinas and Derrida this focus on personal death finds important philosophical objection. Levinas and Derrida agree that our own death is not our most fundamental experience of death because the death *of the other* is more fundamental. As Levinas says, "The death of the other: therein lies the first death."[25] In *Aporias*, Derrida shows that even if the Heideggerian being-toward-death remains the focus, what is found originarily in "my death" is the death of the other because the only relation to death that we have is to the perishing of animals, the medical demising of our own self, and "the death of the other" (*A* 76). Thus, the death of the other, "this death of the other in 'me' [in the experience of mourning], is fundamentally the only death that is named in the syntagm 'my death'" (*A* 76).[26] For Levinas and Derrida, this movement toward the originary death of the other has important ethical, and for Derrida at least, political implications. Levinas and Derrida maintain that the self is constituted first and foremost through its responsibility to the other. Consequently, for Derrida, the death of the other is the "more originary experience" of death because it "institutes responsibility . . . in the ethical dimension of sacrifice" (*GD* 48). And for Levinas, my "right to be" a self, then, "is already my responsibility for the death of the Other."[27] Thus, Derrida and Levinas substitute for Heidegger's *sum moribundus ego sum*,[28] that is, *I am mortal therefore I am*, the idea that what gives the *sum* or the *I am* its meaning is not the mortality of the *sum* but the mortality of the other. Such substitution leads Derrida to say, "I mourn therefore I am" (*P* 321). In this tradition following Levinas and Derrida, mourning is originary insofar as "mourning for the other is the unchanging form of our lives."[29] Following Levinas and Derrida's arguments, then, the death of the other is no longer "a marginal phenomenon on the fringe of authentic finite existence. Instead, it opens the space of historicity and of the historical as a social ontological . . . problem of how humans are with those having-been."[30]

The stakes of the experience of the death of the other and what is done with such death could not be higher, then, because they entail our authenticity. And our authenticity concerns our very existence in the world with one another. So in order to more authentically be in the world and be-with the living, learning how to be-with the nonliving is necessary. And this means that our being-with one another in the worlds in which we find ourselves requires understanding how this being-with is a matter of survival, a matter of *surviving* the death of the other. Learning to live means to inhabit the shared space with both the living and the dead and to do so in "a responsible way" because life is always a matter of "life after, as inheritance, ancestry, legacy, and fate."[31] Life is always *survival* in this regard because life is a matter of living on after those who have been lost. Derrida never ceases to remind us of this with his notion of life as *survivre* or *survivance*. This survival or living on can mean "a reprieve or an after life, 'life after life' or life after death, more life or more than life, and better [life]."[32] He even goes so far as to suggest that "resurrection" is a possible interpretation of *survivre*,[33] with the result that this idea of *survivre* can be a resource for thinking through the afterlife not as an other-worldly, transcendent phenomenon but as a this-worldly, immanent phenomenon.[34] Surviving the death of the other concerns the afterlife in this life after the death of the other. Such an afterlife would mean that learning to live occurs through "the other and by death" because life is only ever lived with the other and in the aftermath of death and loss (*SM* xvii). Thus, learning to live comes "from the other at the edge of life" (*SM* xvii). Death becomes, then, "the 'limit-experience' that defines life."[35] Accordingly, at this Jaspersian limit-experience on the edge or border of life and death, relief is given to how life can be practiced and cultivated with the living.

Moreover, at this limit-experience relief is given to the reality that life entails struggle. In this regard, Elizabeth Rosner's memoir about her inherited trauma from her father, a first-generation survivor of Buchenwald during the Holocaust, reminds us that life understood in terms of the German *Überlebende* entails that "to survive you really had to struggle, you had to *do* something."[36] Life understood as survival, life *as* survival, or life as life after death, is going to entail the struggle of what to *do* when the other dies. This is what Kas Saghafi calls "the survivor's condition."[37] For being a survivor pertains to "anyone who is mourning, of all work of mourning . . . regarding the originary guilt of the living as surviving the death of the other" (*AR* 383). Considering that people do many different things with their mourning in the wake of the death of an other, living on after the death of the other can be done well, badly, and a myriad of ways in between. And what is done in the aftermath of death can even involve the actions of an entire nation, as when the US responded to the attacks on 9/11 by launching a war on Iraq based on inaccurate information regarding weapons of mass destruction. Survival can be done well and poorly on an individual scale as much as on a national scale. The works by Athena Athanasiou[38] and Cindy Milstein, which appear in the second and third parts, show that individual mourning and political mourning done on a broader scale are both sites where a *responsibility* to mourn can develop. And this idea of the responsibility to mourn serves as a reminder that often the life after death in survival or the more life through survival does not always mean a *better* life after the death of the other. Nevertheless, survival can mean a struggle against the actions and decisions made in the wake of the death of the other so that the life after death, the afterlife here and now, can *become* a better life and not a worse one. Consequently, life as surviving the death of the other is a matter of "shared finitude" and "shared vulnerability"[39] as we inherit a past that continues to haunt us and work on us in the present. What we will have learned in this being-with both the living and the dead, in our survival, is that this sharing means that our being-with is not "in full possession of itself."[40] Our being-with as and through survival is a matter of *partage*, that is, of both sharing and separation. Hence, this is a matter of the *partage* of finitude and vulnerability making this as much about what is in our ability to share with one another and what remains out of our control in this sharing. And through this sharing in surviving the death of the other, we can move toward authentically being-with one another. After all, *survivre* is parsed by Derrida, in part, to mean "better [life]."[41]

Thus, what remains to be done in this history of the event and its relation to death is to provide a phenomenology of the death *of the other* that helps to understand this ordinary yet extraordinary experience as an event for those who survive it. In this vein, I offer the following description of the death of the other according to the symptoms of an event and following the contours of these symptoms in the phenomenon of the death of the other itself. Consequently, in what follows I describe the unexpected, im-possible arrival of the death of the other, the excessiveness of this arrival beyond our conceptual and linguistic horizons of rationality, and its transformative potentiality through the way the death of the other disrupts spatiality and temporality in our survival. The following description, then, falls into three major parts.

Part 1, "Symptoms of an Event," limns the symptoms of an event by connecting the expositions on the event in the works of Derrida, Levinas, Heidegger, and Marion with the death of the other. Throughout, Derrida's important work on the event leads the way because his writings most accurately fit the phenomena of events in life and provide a nice outline of the symptoms that tend to befall us after an event. He enumerates numerous aspects of the experiences of events: surprise, exposure, unforeseeable (*inanticipable*), without horizon, unpredictable, unplanned, not decided upon, unexpected, singular, impossible, and secretive. I summarize these themes under three major symptoms of an event, with each of the first three chapters focusing on one of these symptoms: impossibility, secrecy, and transformation. The impossibility of an event acts as the condition from which the other aspects flow. For Derrida says, "This experience of the impossible conditions the eventiality of the event [*conditionne l'événementialité de l'événement*]. . . . What happens, as event, can only happen there where it is impossible" (DE 96). I argue that this impossibility does not mean that an event is a logical impossibility. Rather, the condition of an event's possibility is found only in its metaphysically determined impossibility, that is, there where the occurrence of an event, the breaking in of an event into the status quo, does not accord with our horizons of expectation for an experience. An event is impossible in this sense because it cannot be anticipated: its occurrence exceeds or even resists our horizons of expectation through which phenomena ordinarily occur for us. An event suddenly breaks in and surprises us because it cannot be seen according to these horizons of expectation. Thus, Derrida says that we must speak of "the im-possible event" where the hyphenation of this word indicates "not only the opposite of the possible" but also "the condition or the chance of the possible" (DE 101). This im-possible event is not, however, "inaccessible," because it still "announces itself . . . swoops down upon and seizes me *here and now* . . . in actuality and not potentiality. . . . It is what is most undeniably *real*" (*R* 84; emphasis his). An event is possible there where it finds its limit in our various conceptual and linguistic horizons of rationality through which life becomes relatively predictable and stable. Yet this does not mean that an event never occurs. Rather, when an event arrives, its arrival disrupts the relative predictability and stability of everyday life. An event remains phenomenologically impossible to our expectations and known possibilities all the while bringing its own possibilities through which it appears. Only after an event, *après coup* or *après l'événement*, can what this event has made possible begin to be thought on account of the new conditions of possibility that attend its arrival.

Chapter 1, "The Unexpected, Im-possible Event," takes this description of the im-possibility of an event as its lead in order to describe the unexpectedness of an event in terms of its arrival outside of and through the shattering of our horizons of expectation. Drawing a through line from Derrida's early work on poststructuralism to his later thinking of the event by focusing on the *causality of rupture* through which an event occurs, I unpack the significance of this symptom of an event in order to begin showing how the death of the other occurs as unexpected and im-possible insofar as it follows the aspects of an event's causality of rupture. These aspects are what I identify as the catastrophic, monstrous or traumatic, and retemporalization of time.

With an event's possibility found in its im-possibility, Derrida points us to a second major aspect of an event: secrecy. An event is secret not insofar as it is hidden or clandestine but insofar as it "does not appear" in the way that we expect other phenomena to appear (DE 105). This nonappearance of an event removes it from any principle of sufficient reason or search for universal knowledge about the event. As such, an event remains "unexplainable by a system of efficient causes" (*GT* 123) because such a system belongs to our horizons of expectation through which life becomes relatively stable. Accordingly, Derrida says that if we can define an event with "one possible definition" it would be that "an event must be exceptional, without rule" (DE 106). An event obeys no rules or principles unless those principles are "principles of disorder, that is, principles without principles" (*GT* 123). In other words, considering that an event's occurrence exceeds or resists our horizons of expectation, the principles of its occurrence, like its causality of rupture, must be principles of *disorder* because its appearance disrupts our conditions of possibility for an experience. Consequently, an event is an experience of the other that resists the hegemony of subjectivity. Derrida utilizes this notion of the secret as a "way to let the other be, to respect alterity."[42] An event as other can happen in the realm of the same, the realm of phenomenology, but when it happens there, it does not appear according to our expected principles for phenomena. It irrupts into the same *as* the other. It appears as the correlate of an intention that cannot confine it. It surprises and exceeds us. As such, an event is a secret. Accordingly, chapter 2, "The Secretive Event without Reason," traces a line of thinking from Heidegger's reading of Leibniz's principle of sufficient reason in his lecture *The Principle of Reason* (*Der Satz vom Grund*) through Marion's phenomenology of givenness in order to explore how a phenomenon, in my case the death of the other, can be understood as an event because an event's appearing on the scene does not accord with the calculation of a cause-effect nexus. I utilize the connection between Heidegger and Marion, especially their shared reading of Angelus Silesius's poem on the blooming of the rose, to turn Marion's own description of these saturated phenomena against him in order to show how the death of the other can be understood as a saturated phenomenon insofar as its occurring is without why or in secret. In this way, chapter 2 sticks to the radical hermeneutics of my project to show how the death of the other cannot be confined to the principle of reason by which our mind tries "to make the unfamiliar familiar . . . and thereby increase our sense of control."[43]

Chapter 3, "The Transformative Event," concludes part 1 by rounding out the symptoms of an event in terms of how the world pre-event and the world post-event for a survivor remain drastically different due to the transformation of their world in the aftermath of the event. In this chapter, I develop four major ideas to show that this symptom of an event can be used to understand the death of the other as a transformative event. These ideas are poetic attestation, *a* death of *the* world, workless mourning, and the existential difference that attends different deaths of the other. I take as my guide in this chapter Derrida's interpretation of the poem by Paul Celan "Vast, Glowing Vault," in which Celan says, *Die Welt ist fort, Ich muß dich tragen* (The world is gone, I must carry you). And I situate my reading of Celan as a rejoinder to what Heidegger has to say in *Being and Time* about the death of the other. Through Celan's poetic attestation to the death of the other, I argue that his poem allows such death to be understood in its happening as an event that transforms the world because this poem shows us how such death is each time uniquely *a* death of *the* world in which we have a responsibility to mourn the other worklessly. In this, I trace an aporia around the meaning of *world* that develops in Derrida's reading of Celan. I argue, even though Derrida does not think fully in this direction, that *the* world that dies must be understood as the pluralized world so that each death can be *a* death of *the* world.[44] In the aftermath of this death, the ethical possibility-to-be for a survivor is what I call workless mourning. Such mourning is not about "getting over" the loss. It is about learning to live on with this loss and to bear or carry the responsibility of mourning the other. This kind of mourning is an interpretation of what Derrida calls half-mourning (*demi-deuil*) in response to Sigmund Freud's distinction between the work of *normal* mourning and the pathology of melancholy. Accordingly, as a person works through the loss in the aftermath of a death of the other, the work is never fully completed. I can work on mourning, but I am never fully done working on it despite my best efforts to get over the death of an other. The mourning process never lives up to the getting over of the death as described by Freud as normal mourning. The work of mourning remains *workless*, then, with a kind of nonpathological melancholy. Lastly, I use my idea of existential difference to explain that the death of the other includes more than just the deaths of human beings but also other nonhuman animals as well as, even, God. Moreover, I use this idea to explain why some deaths of the other, like those of people with whom we are intimate, affect us deeply, while other deaths, like those of people we only hear about once on the news, may not affect us deeply.

In the remaining two parts of the book, I expand on part 1 by describing how precisely a death of the other is, each time unique, a death of the world insofar as this death transforms the spatiality of the world and the temporality of the world. While Derrida suggests in his final seminar, *The Beast and the Sovereign II*, in a discussion about cremation, that such annihilation of the dead other causes the other to invade "the whole of *space* and the whole of *time*" (*BS2* 169; emphasis mine), I argue in my description that *any* death of the other involves this other invading all of space and time through the survivor's workless mourning. In this, the death of the other transforms the spatiality and temporality of the world for those who survive the other. The poet W. H. Auden poignantly describes such an invasion of the death of the other through its transformation of space and time in his poem "Funeral Blues."[45] Auden's poem points to the survivor's experience with the death of the other: the transformation of the meaning of things when the other dies. As he sings, the other now dead had been the survivor's moral compass and rhythm of their week, but now that the other has died the survivor cries out, "Stop all the clocks."[46] And this transformation of meaning occurs, I argue, through a transformation of the space through which things come to meaning. Such spatial transformation concerns how the death of Auden's lover entails the death of his cardinal heading. Moreover, and more noticeably perhaps in the poem, I argue how the death of the other transforms a survivor's lived experience of temporality. As Auden puts it, the death of the other involves the disruption of our weekly schedule, our daily routine, and even the cosmic placement of the sun and moon. The death of the other transforms how we find ourselves in the world temporally speaking.[47] Following along these insights, parts 2 and 3 deal with precisely answering the question that follows such a transformation of the world, "How do we live with the 'rupture' of time and space that was brought up by this event?"[48]

Part 2, "Spatial Transformations of the World," explores how the death of the other transforms the spatiality of the world by mapping the symptoms of the unexpected and without reason from part 1 onto the death of the other. Here I draw from and expand on Heidegger's notion of spatiality in his analysis of the worldliness of the world in *Being and Time*. Heidegger understands spatiality not in terms of the objective measurement of distance between things but, rather, as the condition for Dasein to draw out the meaningfulness of things in the world through its dealings with them. Spatiality is, then, to be understood as a condition of meaningful relationality among ourselves and things in the world. Spatiality is a condition of our being-with, in other words, insofar as we find meaning in the world through and with one another and other beings in the worlds in which we find ourselves. In short, the pluralized world itself and the things in it have meaning on account of the relations of the beings and things in that world. I extend Heidegger's analysis to argue that when the other dies, the spatiality through which meaning has been constituted in the world undergoes a transformation. Part 2 charts this transformation of the spatiality of things by examining how the meaningfulness of ourselves and the others with whom we are involved undergoes transformation. Through this, I bring a phenomenological edge to Celan's poetry from chapter 3, showing that Celan's insistence on carrying the other after death is quite literally a carrying of the dead other in things, places, and our bodies. In this description, I show that the death of the other is much more than just the loss of the person. The death of the other includes the exiled and lost meanings in the world that attend the loss of the other on account of the relationships through which she de-distanced and constituted the world. The death of the other affects, unexpectedly, the meaningfulness of everything in a way that exceeds calculative reason.

This analysis begins in chapter 4, "Unexpected Loss and Life: The Presence of the Other's Absence," through an exploration of how the loss of meaning that attends the death of the other is always unexpected. I extend beyond Heidegger's analysis of spatiality from *Being and Time* to argue that the death of the other transforms the self's ability to draw out the meaningfulness of things in the world because this meaningfulness carries the presence of the other's absence. Or, to say this differently, things carry the absence of the other's presence who had helped constitute their meaningfulness. I explore this relation of presence and absence in the death of the other through how the meaningful things of the now dead other continue to hold the presence of the other in them but only in an oddly absent way. The dead other is felt by us and even seems to touch us through his or her absence on account of the meaningfulness of the things and places that had been constituted with the other who is now dead. In the poetic words of Emily Dickinson, "Death sets a thing significant,"[49] by bringing the absence of the dead other into presence through the meaning that had been constituted through and with this dead other. What had been merely a book in his or her library is now a remnant of his or her absence brought into presence by the underlinings, notes, and earmarks that he or she left in the book. The meaningfulness of such things and such places opens us to the way the meaning of the world through the death of the other is transformed through the meaningful remnants carrying the meaning of the world before the death of the other into the world post-death-of-the-other. When Wolterstorff walked into his dead son's apartment, he walked into a space holding the present absence of his son. In this way, the death of the other transforms spatiality. As a result, the loss experienced in the death of the other always includes more than just the loss of the person. The loss of a person entails the loss of the meaningfulness of things constituted by and with the now dead other. While the death of the other is an end of the world through this loss of meaningfulness, I argue that such death can also open the world to reconstitution anew. The death of the other can open to new life. And we are never ready for how this loss of meaningfulness and reconstitution is going to strike us and affect us. Consequently, the death of the other is always unexpected even when we expect the other to die due to a medical diagnosis or the other's age.

Chapter 5, "Excess and the Death of the Other: Life/Death, Materiality, and Reason," continues to explore this analysis of the spatial transformation of the world by looking at how the death of the other arrives not just unexpectedly but also excessively insofar as the interweaving of life and death in it exceeds our conceptual and linguistic horizons of rationality. In describing this excessiveness of the event of the death of the other, I read together Derrida's 1975–76 lecture course *Life Death* in conjunction with stories from those who have survived the death of someone along with the epigenetic research on the intergenerational transference of trauma.

What these three sources reveal collectively is the *différance* of life with death that gets experienced in the material transformation of the body and the earth when the other dies. For example, I argue following recent research on epigenetics that while the death of the other does not change the sequencing of a survivor's genetic code, it does affect how this code gets expressed. Consequently, a survivor carries the death of the other literally in and along her body epigenetically. Following these themes, the lifedeath, survival, or afterlife beyond the death of the other "is marked by wounds but recreated through them."[50] Unexpectedly, then, the death of the other teaches that life must be open to and in contact with its other, death, in order to be life at all. As Geoffrey Bennington says, "[F]or a life that did not involve this openness would not be a life worthy of the name 'life,' at best a kind of suspended animation or living death."[51] Life is, then, always a matter of survival or living on after death insofar as life must be more than life, not merely life, but also be in relation to death in order to be life. Life and death: "each is haunted by the other."[52]

And this idea of haunting becomes especially important in part 3, "Temporal Transformations of the World." Whereas the spatial transformation of part 2 focuses on the meaningfulness of things and places that gets reconstituted through the death of the other, part 3, focuses on how the death of the other transforms who we are existentially by transforming how we relate to temporality's three ecstasies: the past, the future, and the present. In this, I explore the primordial temporality of the death of the other. The death of the other shows us how temporality itself unfolds in our lived experience through the way such death does not respect the boundaries between past, present, and future.[53] Drawing from what Raffoul calls an "eventful temporality" understood as a temporality that is "not a ruled sequence coming from the past to the present, but an eventful temporality, coming from the future, disrupting the causal networks, and transforming the entire complex of temporality, indeed transforming the past itself,"[54] I extend Raffoul's account to say that the death of the other occurs through such an eventful temporality. In his text, he only establishes this eventful temporality but does not make the further connection between it and the death of the other because death marks for him only the closure of time and world and not their opening. While part 2 shows how the death of the other does indeed mark the opening of the world, in part 3, I show particularly how the death of the other marks the opening of time.

Chapter 6, "Memories and a Past that Won't Stay Put," begins this analysis by expanding on my idea of workless mourning to say that such mourning involves a workless memory. I supplement Heidegger's notion of primordial time from *Being and Time* with Derrida's hauntology of the dead other from *Specters of Marx*. Though the death of the other occurs on a date in the past, the death of the other is never merely past or passed by because the actual dying of the other and/or the memories of the other continue to haunt the survivor in the present. Such a haunting precludes the unifying moment of what Heidegger identifies as Dasein's making-present through anticipatory resoluteness. I maintain that the being-with of the survivor is always already enmeshed with the absence of the other who has died, and this absence cannot be made present or unified with the present. Consequently, mourning the death of the other is best described as *workless* because as the survivor works through the loss that has been incurred, he can never fully be done with this work, which challenges any idea of *getting over* the death of the other. Workless mourning is best described, then, as a constant negotiation or a constant back and forth between what Freud calls normal mourning and melancholy because mourning involves carrying the ghost of the other that continues to come back and spook the survivor's present. In this haunting, the injunction from Celan, *Ich muß dich tragen*, gains further phenomenological purchase by understanding how we carry the death of the other in our memories. With our memories being one of the primary ways that we carry the other after her death, I follow Derrida's distinction in his work on Paul de Man to argue that in order to remember the other well, memory has to fail to a degree so as not to forget the other in her alterity. And I explore this workless memory through the being-with of memory called transactive memory. This memory is not only constituted by the other but also sustained by the other insofar as the other becomes an extension of the self's own memory. Thus, when the other dies, the survivor loses part of his own memory. The self loses part of itself. And now when the survivor remembers the other, her memory is itself fractured and recalls an absence of the other in her own memory. This memory-with after the death of the other requires, then, remembering the dead other as absent or as the ghost that continues to haunt the survivor's present. So rather than attempt to make the dead other present and efface the dead other's own alterity as absent, the survivor's memory must remain workless along with her mourning.

Chapter 7, "Lost Possibilities and a Fractured Future," extends the engagement on primordial time after the death of the other by thinking through the relation of the future and the idea of the impossible in Heidegger and Derrida. Here I make a distinction between the possible impossibility of personal death as covered in Heidegger's analysis of being-toward-death in *Being and Time* and the impossible possibility of the future to-come in Derrida. The notion of impossibility in Heidegger's analysis remains inadequate for engaging how the death of the other transforms the future for a survivor because the impossibility of personal death entails for Heidegger that death will and does come even though each person may not know when their death is coming. However, the impossibility of the future that attends the death of the other entails that the future once imagined through and by the other will never come. The fissures from the death of the other run through the future, causing those who survive to reconstitute their relation to their future on account of the lost possibilities that follow in the wake of the death of this other. Consequently, I turn to Derrida's thinking of the future to-come in order to discuss what I call the two tonalities of this to-come that are especially important for describing this fractured future after the death of the other. On the one hand, this future is full of impossible possibilities that never come to fruition or become actual. On the other hand, this future is full of im-possible possibilities insofar as these are possibilities whose absence in being actualized cause the present and future of the survivor to be restructured in and around them. Through this impossibility of the future to-come understood in these two tonalities, I argue that the present of the survivor is shown to be truly out of joint with a past that will not stay past but continues to haunt the survivor as if from out of their future.

In chapter 8, "The Gift of Mourning in a Present Out of Joint," I bring together the threads from, especially, the last two chapters to discuss how we can embody this spectral moment of the present haunted by the memories of the death of the other and directed toward a future fractured by the death of the other. Such an embodiment takes place under the name of what I call workless hospitality, as the third and final development of workless mourning. I argue that mourning the death of the other is the practicing of a responsibility to the dead understood as the *différance* of hospitality's two modalities that Derrida describes: conditional hospitality and unconditional hospitality. In developing this idea of mourning as workless hospitality that welcomes the dead by allowing this other to disrupt the spatial and temporal conditions of the home, I maintain that mourning opens our worlds to being more hospitable to the coming of an event in general. The gift of mourning through workless hospitality, I argue, is that it opens us to the Derridean notion of the gift. And while such an openness opens the world both to the promise of positive transformation and to the poison of negative transformation as a result of the coming of such event, this is the risk that must be taken so that we can become better at existing not only with those whom we have lost but also with those who are still alive. The gift of mourning is, then, fragile because it could open us to an excessive love of the other but also could be used, as Athanasiou shows, to reestablish unjust, oppressive political regimes. I draw from the ethico-political practices of agonistic and rebellious mourning to show how mourning's hospitality to and carrying of the world after the death of the other can help to make possible the coming of an event of justice for the living. By learning how to mourn the death of the other, we can learn how to exist better with the living.

Part One

Symptoms of an Event

Chapter One
The Unexpected, Im-possible Event

> The gift, like the event, as event, must remain unforeseeable. . . . It must let itself be structured by the aleatory; it must appear chancy . . . apprehended as the intentional correlate of a perception that is absolutely surprised by the encounter.
>
> — Jacques Derrida, *Given Time: I*

To begin my description, I establish that the unexpectedness of the death of the other allows this phenomenon to be understood hermeneutically as an event. Doing so requires diving into the depths of what can be some challenging ideas that cut across Derrida's and Heidegger's works. Yet understanding these ideas, sounding their depths so to speak, is crucial because they provide important language for letting the death of the other show itself as an event. This important language revolves around what I am calling the symptoms of an event.

At a 2001 conference dedicated to the theme of the event, Derrida lays out this language of the symptomatology of an event understood as the symptoms that befall us when an event irrupts into or interrupts everyday experience. I am crystalizing this symptomatology in the three symptoms that establish the structure of part 1 of my description: the event is unexpected and im-possible, the event is secretive or without reason, and the event is transformative. The first symptom gains special privilege because it is distinctly connected with the entire idea of symptomatology. For when Derrida explains what he means by a symptom, he says it must be understood through the idea of verticality as what falls on us from on high. And what befalls us in this regard does so as a surprise because we "cannot see it coming" (DE 97). This surprise or the coming of the unexpected "can only come from on high" (DE 97) insofar as to surprise us it must fall on us as if from above and not approach us head-on, thereby allowing us to see it coming. Without this verticality of the event, without this symptomatology in general, we could see the event coming on the horizon. We could expect the event. We could cancel the event's surprise and, thereby, the event itself. For the event is precisely that which surprises, that which is an exception, or that which is without law. Consequently, the event is symptomatological through its surprise and unpredictability. This unexpectedness of an event is indispensable, then, for knowing that an event has occurred. As Nancy says, "What makes the event an event is not only that it happens, but that it surprises" (*BSP* 159). Consequently, the surprise "constitutes the event."[1] Each time unique is the arrival of the event. As such, no structure can capture its coming so that we can prepare for it by seeing it coming in advance. When an event comes, it happens as a singular surprise, as "always exceptional" and "without rule" (DE 106).

I use this symptom of the unexpected to connect a few ideas from Derrida's earlier works — the event of poststructuralism and *différance* — with his later idea of the gift event. Just before his own death, Derrida says that he has been intrigued by this theme of the event throughout his writings but that "privileged attention to the event" has become "more and more insistent" throughout his writings, particularly in those about hospitality, the gift, forgiveness, the secret, and testimony.[2] I maintain that this increasing insistence of the event throughout his writings follows what I identify as an event's causality of rupture through which an event surprises in its occurrence. Through unpacking this causality of rupture, I establish how the death of the other occurs unexpectedly and im-possibly as an event because when a death of the other happens it follows the same causality of rupture. Through this causality, death can be understood as an event insofar as it follows the symptomatology of an unexpected event by being catastrophic, monstrous or traumatic, a gift, and a retemporalization of time.

Event and Poststructuralism

Derrida explores his interest in the event as an unexpected occurrence first through his writings that became important to the development of poststructuralism. Through his exploration of the *redoubling* of structurality within language and the attendant *rupture* of meaning that follows, the im-possibility and unexpectedness of an event can be traced. These two ideas of redoubling and rupture in conjunction with Derrida's understanding of *différance* provide the basis for understanding his early engagement with the theme of the event. His discussion of this begins importantly with his "Structure, Sign, and Play in the Discourses of the Human Sciences" (1966), *Of Grammatology* (1967), and "Différance" (1968).

He announces this interest in the event in the opening sentences of "Structure, Sign, and Play" when he writes, "Perhaps something has occurred in the history of the concept of structure that could be called an 'event'. . . . What would this event be then" (*WD* 278)? And he describes the "exterior form" of this event as "a rupture and a redoubling" of the semiological structure of language (*WD* 278). While this rupture and redoubling of an event goes beyond the context of the structuralist and poststructuralist debate, such an event in the context of the debate Derrida is having with the structuralists would be a repetition or a redoubling of structurality in the structure laid out by the structuralist theory of language. This repetition concerns specifically the status of *the sign*. According to structuralism, the *sign* consists of both a signifier, a particular word for instance, and a signified, which is this particular word's meaning. The signifiers are a play of differences in which each signifier is supplemented with other signifiers, all of whose definitions get determined through their differences with one another. However, each signifier points to or indicates a particular signified as its authorized meaning outside of this play of signifiers or differences. This signified is the stable, solidified meaning that is present to the inner voice as the *logos* of the signifier. Such a signifier is what Derrida identifies as the transcendental signified. The event that concerns Derrida in "Structure, Sign, and Play" is the redoubling of structurality in this structure, which means that this event aims to repeat the play of differences among the signifiers but on the side of the *signified* so that any signified itself consists also of a play of differences. Therefore, the *sign* for Derrida consists not of a signifier and its signified but of a play of signifiers all the way down. This is a play of meaning through difference through and through. Or, simply put, this is what Derrida calls a play of traces. The signifiers on Derrida's account of language, then, become a play of traces that point not to some transcendental signified outside of this play but to other traces caught up in this play. Thus, all language becomes through this open structure of signs, which is a structure without structure, a matter of supplementing one sign with another. All language is an infinite play of differences with no transcendental signified to stay the play or no present *logos* to the inner voice. This rethinking of language is an approach to language without any center or any center that could be "thought in the form of a present-being" (*WD* 280). Rather, the center of this rethinking of language is "a sort of nonlocus in which an infinite number of sign-substitutions [come] into play," thereby extending "the domain and the play of signification infinitely" (*WD* 280). Consequently, the stable, solidified meaning of things becomes, now, *relatively* stable, which means also *relatively* unstable, due to this play of differences through which meaning gets constituted.

Such is the repetition of this event, but what of its *rupture*? How is this event of the repetition of structure that gives rise to this open structure or to this play of traces also a rupturing? By the end of "Structure, Sign, and Play," Derrida writes, "[T]he appearance of a new structure, of an original system, always comes about . . . by a rupture with its past, its origin, and its cause" (*WD* 291). So this repetition is a break from, a modification of, or a transformation of what has come before. And he elaborates on this rupture by drawing on three metaphors in the closing pages of his essay: catastrophe, adventure, and monstrosity. Through these metaphors, he points this event toward the symptom of the unexpected.

This rupture of the event is understood first by Derrida based on "the model of *catastrophe* — an overturning of nature in nature, a natural interruption of the natural sequence, a setting aside of nature" (*WD* 292; emphasis mine). The origin of this model for understanding rupture is, for Derrida, both the structuralist theory of language that he is engaging in 1966 and the work of Jean-Jacques Rousseau. Drawing from Claude Lévi-Strauss to explore this metaphor of catastrophe, he says that language occurs not piecemeal but is "born in one fell swoop" (*WD* 291). The birth of a language is *catastrophic* in this sense because it marks a definitive *interruption* of the past sociological development of a people so that this people can have a meaningful or language-filled future. The day that everything possesses meaning for a people group is a day that comes catastrophically, suddenly, or unexpectedly. Derrida makes this connection between catastrophe and the unexpected more directly in his reading of Rousseau's account of the political transformation of human being from the precivil states of nature of "savage hunter and barbaric shepherd" to civil human being (*OG* 255). This transformation, on Derrida's reading, occurs according to a "causality of the rupture" understood as a "catastrophe" insofar as this transformation is "the effect of a strictly *unpredictable* force within the system of the world" (*OG* 256; emphasis mine). So catastrophe is a way to understand the causality through which an event ruptures with the past and has an effect on the world. The rupture from an event, then, has a particular causality to it understood in terms of this unpredictable effect on the world. Such is an event's causality of rupture.

While I develop this further in parts 2 and 3, an event's causality of rupture means that if the death of the other can be understood as an event, then a survivor of such death cannot be ready for what effect this death will have had. So while a survivor may expect their loved one to die due to a medical diagnosis of terminal cancer, for example, or simply of old age, what the survivor cannot expect in this is the effect that this death will have in its wake on the survivor's world. The death of the other may be expected and yet unexpected on account of this unpredictable effect because the death of the other adheres to the causality of rupture: the effect of the death of the other is unpredictable in terms of its impact on the survivor's world. Accordingly, this account of an event as an unpredictable catastrophe goes beyond just Derrida's work, as can be seen when thinking of other catastrophic phenomena involving the death of the other. The immediate experience of such a catastrophe is its unexpected unfolding. Think of, for example, the bombing of the Alfred P. Murrah building in Oklahoma City, Oklahoma, in 1995; the 9/11 attacks in New York City on the World Trade Center; the 2011 nuclear meltdown in Japan of the Fukushima Daiichi reactors after a tsunami, which we call a *natural* catastrophe, struck the banks of Japan; or the spread of COVID-19 throughout the world in 2020. Each of these catastrophes unfolded in such a way that people were *unprepared* for their unfolding. Had the world been prepared for these phenomena to occur, they either would not have occurred altogether or the effects of their occurrence would have been far less, as we say, catastrophic. Had the world seen these experiences *coming on the horizon*, the world would have been ready to stop these occurrences in their tracks. These national and worldwide phenomena show, in part, that the occurrence of a catastrophe entails that it will have been unexpected and without proper preparation. The rupture of an event as catastrophe occurs unexpectedly or without us being able to see it coming. A catastrophe occurs without horizon or *sans voir* because we cannot see it coming. In this way, the rupture of an event occurs unexpectedly.

Likewise, the rupture of an event is likened to the metaphor of adventure by Derrida in 1966. He makes this connection when he describes the affirmation of the play of differences that accompanies his poststructural account of language as the "*adventure* of the trace" (*WD* 292; emphasis mine). Recall that the trace is precisely what does the repeating in the event of the repetition of structure insofar as the trace redoubles the signifier so that even the signified itself is another signifier. This adventure of the trace is what transforms the *putative truth* of the transcendental signified that functions to stop the flux at play in the signs into the *myth* or *phantasm* of such a signified. The adventure of the trace, the adventure of poststructuralism, is to see what happens when the system no longer has such a transcendental signified, and this is an adventure precisely because what would happen had been unknown. Poststructuralism asks the questions: What would happen to sociology, ethnology, psychology, philosophy, religion, theology, and so on if the desires of passionate reason to have something at the center of these discourses assuring that they are grounded by something certain, stable, and explainable came up empty? How would the language and theories of each discipline go through a transformation? And the poststructuralists respond: Let's find out; let's take this adventure! For an adventure, any adventure, to take place, surprise must accompany what happens on the adventure. To take an adventure is to venture into the unknown. So to affirm an adventure, to agree to take an adventure, is to agree to the unexpected. The outcome or results of any adventure may be good or bad. The only way to know is to take the adventure and find out. The only way to know will occur after the fact, *après coup*. But with either a good or a bad outcome, the outcome of such an adventure will be catastrophic, unexpected, or something that could not be seen coming on the horizon. And, here, the final metaphor for the rupture of an event comes into focus. Derrida, lastly, describes the event of poststructuralism that repeats and ruptures structurality as occurring in "the terrible form of *monstrosity*" (*WD* 293; emphasis mine). The outcome of an event, what befalls us after an event, is monstrous, *ungeheuer*, tremendous, and, as I will discuss in just a moment, traumatic. What happens with the rupture of an event happens in an adventurously tremendous way. It happens unexpectedly but with tremendous, monstrous, traumatic outcomes, whether these outcomes be good or bad or both.

This monstrous transformation in the aftermath of an unexpected event has apparent connections with the death of the other. For the death of the other inherently brings with it a disruption in the life of those who survive the other. And such a disruption may be bad because of the sadness, depression, and longing for the other that the survivor experiences. Or this disruption may be good, for example, because the other while alive had been abusive or manipulative, and now the survivor is glad that they are gone. Or this disruption may lead to new relationships that lead to great happiness in the survivor's life that they had yet to experience. Either way, or, as we can see even in both ways, the death of the other is monstrous through the disruption that follows in its wake.

Event and *Différance*: On the Way to the Gift

Derrida deepens this description of this *event* of poststructuralism in his discussion of his neologism *différance*. For the rupture of the event in "Structure, Sign, and Play" occurs as a result of what is going on in the name of *différance*. After all, Derrida names this open structure without structure of his theory of language "arche-writing," and arche-writing is the "movement of *différance*" (*OG* 60) or inscribed by *différance* (*MP* 12). Through a closer reading of these dynamics, I argue that the causality of rupture as unexpected, catastrophic, adventurous, and monstrous that has concerned Derrida in his early career must be understood as the event of *différance* because *différance* is the means by which Derrida follows the repetition and rupture of structurality into a play of traces. Furthermore, these dynamics of *différance* understood as difference and deferral in his 1968 seminal piece "Différance" set the stage for Derrida's understanding of the symptoms of the event as they develop in his later thinking with the idea of the gift (*don*). For Derrida identifies *différance* as the name for the giving of meaning that occurs in language on account of the difference of the traces whose play defers any static meaning. In this matrix of giving named by *différance*, the Derridean gift event becomes possible. Consequently, *différance* marks the link between Derrida's early thinking of the event with the causality of rupture and his later thinking of the event through his understanding of the gift.

Différance is Derrida's neologism formed as a homonym of the French word for difference, *différence*. The spelling difference between these words, the neologism spelled with an "a" instead of the standard "e" in French, cannot be heard when spoken but can only be seen in the textual, written word. This textual difference of *différance* signals that Derrida's approach to thinking is guided by an understanding of language in which difference, understood as the play of traces, defers the ultimate meaning of our words. So *différance* signals textually, as I put it above, the *relative* stability and instability of language and the meaning of what we say through our words. *Différance* signals that meaning what we say with our words is much more difficult than we think. The meanings of our words are not as sure-footed as we suppose them to be because meaning contains a slippage through which the deferral of any purely stable meaning takes place on account of the play of differences or traces. Such relativity communicates not an anything goes kind of relativism but the *somewhat* stable nature of language as well as its *somewhat* unstable nature. Such relative stability and instability of the meaning of words in language is the result of the twofold meaning of *différance* that I am calling the dynamics of *différance*, namely difference and deferral.

When Derrida first explains this understanding of *différance* in the eponymous essay "Différance," he pits his thinking of difference through this neologism up against Heidegger's own thinking of difference. Considering the amount of scholarship that has been published on the relationship between Heidegger's and Derrida's thinking of difference, engaging fully in this debate would take us far afield from the project of my phenomenology of the death of the other. Yet three prefatory remarks about this conversation must be made. After these remarks, I can then make the connection from Derrida's early thinking of the event in terms of the causality of rupture and *différance* with his later thinking of the event as the gift. First, the nature of the debate that Derrida has with Heidegger concerns the relation of a few important terms and themes central to each thinker: presence with absence, sameness with difference, and gathering with dispersion. In this, Heidegger ostensibly favors the former in each pair while Derrida favors the latter.[3] Derrida emphasizes this at a roundtable discussion in 1994: "[O]ne of the recurrent critiques or deconstructive questions I pose to Heidegger has to do with the privilege Heidegger grants to what he calls *Versammlung*, gathering, which is always more powerful than dissociation or [dispersion]. I would say exactly the opposite."[4] Derrida's concern with Heidegger is that Heidegger's approach seems to point toward a kind of teleological gathering of meaning, a gathering that Heidegger names variously throughout his career: being itself, beyng, the event (*das Ereignis*),[5] *Austrag*, *Untershied*, and others. And the problem with such a kind of teleological thinking for Derrida is, as he says, "Once you grant some privilege to gathering and not to dissociating, then you leave no room for the other, for the radical otherness of the other, for the radical singularity of the other."[6] Yet the choice for each philosopher is not merely between one or the other but, rather, on which gets more emphasis.

Along this line of thinking, second, more and more Heidegger and Derrida scholars are showing that readers of Heidegger must come to understand this language of gathering in Heidegger's works as containing absence, difference, and dispersion.[7] Consequently, Heidegger and Derrida are more "fellow travelers"[8] than opponents on this path of thinking difference. So while Heidegger may have some "dehistoricizing gestures"[9] throughout his thinking where absence, difference, and dispersion perhaps get effaced, even if partially, by Heidegger's language of gathering, these moments of effacement are more often than not ostensible. So gathering for Heidegger includes dispersion, absence, and difference. Derrida himself saw the potential for such interpretations of Heidegger as he expressed in an interview to Dominique Janicaud in 1999: "It would be unfair and a simplification to say that Heidegger negates difference, dislocation, or dissemination: one could have a reading of Heidegger that would show that he does think dislocation."[10] And he himself put forth such an interpretation in his 1984–85 seminar *Phantom of the Other*, published as *Geschlecht III: Sex, Race, Nation, Humanity*. Derrida writes at one moment in this engagement with Heidegger: "If there were only gathering, sameness, oneness, place without path, that would be death. . . . And this is not what Heidegger wants to say, since he also insists on movement. . . . It must be, then, that relations be otherwise between . . . gathering and divisibility (*différance*), that a sort of negotiation and compromise be continuously underway that requires us to rework the implicit logic that seems to be guiding Heidegger" (*G3* 81). Even before this seminar course contained in *Geschlecht III*, in a 1978–79 seminar, which led to the book *Given Time: I* and the recently published *Given Time: II* (*Donner le temps II*), Derrida pays careful attention to the importance of "a certain withdrawal and a certain dissimulation" for Heidegger's own thinking of the gift within the German *es gibt* or "it gives" (*DT2* 117). Derrida goes so far as to say that such dissimulation for Heidegger's thinking of the gift is necessary so that "the very meaning of the *es gibt* can appear in its truth" (*DT2* 118).[11] So at important moments for Derrida's own thinking, he finds in Heidegger's own works that Heidegger resists turning to a simple presence or gathering of presence that effaces absence.

Third, as these quotations and readings of Heidegger from Derrida suggest and as I mentioned in my first prefatory remark, the choice is not between one or the other of gathering or dispersion but rather of the nuanced relation of the two. For, as Derrida says in *Geschlecht III* concerning his own thinking of difference, "To say that there is divisibility does not come down to saying that there is *only* divisibility or division either (that, too, would be death)" (*G3* 81; emphasis mine). Consequently, as the nuanced difference between Heidegger and Derrida continues to be clarified, I think a helpful approach to this difference is to see Derrida as wanting to avoid the possible moments of unclarity where difference and absence may get effaced in Heidegger's works. Thus, Derrida aims to offer a more consistent account of the *relation* of the binary pairings of presence-absence, gathering-dispersion, and so on. For throughout Derrida's writings, he resists choosing between a binary by showing that the terms involved in a binary are always in play or in relation with one other. Such is the nature of his understanding of language as well as his deconstruction of any thinker he engages. Yet he favors the language of dispersion or dissemination because he finds in this dispersion the condition for the possibility of a gathering that is complex enough to include absence and dispersion. As he says to Janicaud, "The difficulty is one of knowing whether one can think *Versammlung* [gathering] while including in it . . . the play of difference, of dislocation, of dissociation, or whether it is only to the extent that there is an *irreducible risk of dispersion* . . . that *Versammlung* can emerge."[12] Heidegger too does this, especially in his later thinking, but Derrida strikes me as more consistent in this way of thinking.[13]

I turn now to Derrida's thinking of *différance* with these prefatory remarks undergirding the reading of *différance* as it relates to Heidegger's understanding of the event (*das Ereignis*). For while Derrida sees himself as charting new territory in distinction from Heidegger, I want to temper this a bit so that Derrida's thinking of *différance* can be understood as resonating with Heidegger's understanding of the event.[14] Beyond this Heidegger-Derrida relation, though, I argue that Derrida develops his thinking of the event insofar as the dynamics of *différance* are the means by which a surprising rupture of an event becomes possible. This reading of *différance* leads to his later thinking of the gift because the gift develops Derrida's thinking of the causality of rupture further.

Much like Heidegger does with the idea of the event, Derrida uses *différance* to distance his thinking from the history of metaphysics in which everything has a static, solidified meaning as its transcendental signified. In this regard, Derrida says that *différance* "is not," "is not a present being," and has no "proper essence" (*MP* 21, 26) — all of which Heidegger could agree with regarding *Ereignis*. Like Heidegger's event, then, *différance* belongs not to the history of metaphysics because *différance* is not a being with a particular essence. For this reason, what Derrida says about the ontological status of an event near the end of his career applies here to *différance*. For he refuses to say in 2001 that an event *is* or that it *is not*, but he does affirm an event with his notion of may-be (*peut-être*). As a "category . . . between the possible and the impossible" (DE 106), the may-be points to the lack of metaphysical essence belonging to an event insofar as an event belongs not to the reign of being and non-being. The idea of the may-be, like Derrida's symptomatology, is an attempt to think the occurrence of an event without in this thinking reducing it to preestablished, metaphysical categories that give an event a static essence. Consequently, an event may-be, or an event is *perhaps*. To bring the later and early Derrida together, I write: *différance* may-be or is *perhaps*.

Two further similarities with Heidegger help to show that Derridean *différance* must be read in line with the description of the event in "Structure, Sign, and Play" insofar as *différance* operates unexpectedly or without horizon. First, *différance*, much like Heidegger's event, functions as an organizing of the history of metaphysics while remaining different from this history. Derrida and Heidegger both read the history of philosophy as a history of various philosophers trying to solidify the meaning of beings in a static, unchanging essence. This is what Derrida calls "the ontology of presence" (*MP* 21) or the history of metaphysics. While the event for Heidegger organizes this history as the generation of the particular historical moments in which this ontology of presence occurs, *différance* for Derrida "organizes" (*MP* 21) this history by producing in various contexts (e.g., semiology, speech act theory, psychoanalysis, philosophy, literature, religion, etc.) a play of differences that interrogate the everyday understanding of the stability of these contexts. *Différance*, as this interrogation, amounts to a fracturing of these contexts' reliance on presence. Yet this interrogation is itself "without origin" and like a "bottomless chessboard" (*MP* 13, 22).

This lack of bottom or pure origin in a transcendental signified means two things for *différance*. On the one hand, although *différance* is the organizing of this history, its explanatory power on which it rests and depends is only its own movement through the differential play and deferral of present meaning. *Différance* is a ground without ground because it rests only on an infinite play of traces. On the other hand, this movement of *différance* can be understood as being without why because *différance* organizes through this production of traces. And traces are free from cause-effect thinking because each trace is like "an effect without a cause" (*MP* 12). *Différance* may organize the ontology of presence by traces, but traces give no answer to why. *Différance* acts as a kind of organizing principle of the history of ideas insofar as Derrida "designates" it as "the movement according to which language, or any code, any system of referral in general, is constituted 'historically' as a weave of differences" (*MP* 12). And yet *différance* is no normal principle because its organizing of these differences through which meaning is relatively stable and unstable does not follow cause-effect thinking. No plan, predetermined or otherwise, is being laid out or followed. *Différance*, then, is an organizing principle without principle because it organizes without why. And to organize without why means that the operation and effects of *différance* occur unexpectedly. The movement of *différance* is like the adventure of an event whose effects are, for good or bad, catastrophic and monstrous because *différance* adheres to the causality of rupture.

The second similarity with Heidegger concerns how *différance* functions as this organizing principle as an interplay of presence-absence, clearing-concealing, gathering-dispersing, or, as Heidegger would also put it, appropriation-expropriation. For Derrida describes *différance* as the "*opening* of the space" in which the history of philosophy and the systems of philosophy are produced (*MP* 6; emphasis mine). In opening this space, however, *différance* exceeds this same opening "without return" (*MP* 6). *Différance* is an opening for philosophy to develop through the play of traces that develop from the difference and deferral of presence under the name of *différance*. However, *différance* is irreducible to this play of traces because it, as the dynamism of difference and deferral, can be found in and along, that is, concealed in this history of philosophy as an interrogation of it. *Différance* names the interrogating, reassembling, or soliciting (Lt. *sollicitare*) of the metaphysical thinking of this history that regards being as presence (*MP* 21). In this, Derrida's deconstruction of the history of philosophy with *différance* seeks a similar path of thinking as Heidegger's destruction of this history with the event because both seek to keep the tradition open and to show that in and along this tradition can be found the very opening as a play of differences that organizes it but to which this opening cannot be reduced. In this history of historicity or account of the origin of history, each moment in this history becomes an event, or what Michael Naas calls a "hyperbolic moment"[15] understood as a moment within the game of history that opens history itself to the coming of the other or the new that engenders foundational transformations of this history through rupturing what reason expects to occur. To read the history of philosophy through such hyperbolic moments means that this history of philosophy "would then be the history of the forgetting and reactivation of these various hyperbolic moments within particular historical structures."[16] In this understanding of the movement of the history of philosophy, we must stay attentive to what Derrida calls "the *différance* of the absolute excess" (*WD* 62) found in and along this history that is the opening of it up to what exceeds it. Drawing from Naas, then, I maintain that the work of *différance* is this history of historicity where each moment of a play of differences that opens meaning, in which *différance* remains concealed, is an evential, unexpected rupture of history.

These two similarities show how close Derrida and Heidegger are in their approaches except, insists Derrida, that the evential ruptures of history through *différance* give not gifts of presence but *traces* to emphasize absence more so than Heidegger does. *Différance* is the differencing and deferring that produces meaning through its unexpected play of traces. These dynamics of *différance* operate similarly to the Heideggerian event insofar as they mark the unfolding of meaning through the various gifts of meaning that arise from it. Yet Derrida is rethinking the history of being not as the gifts of present meaning, as he sees Heidegger doing with the event, but as the effects or play of traces happening under the name of *différance*. In this approach, Derrida returns to his assessment of Heidegger in *Of Grammatology* where he identifies Heidegger's understanding of "the meaning of being" as "a determined signifying *trace*" of *différance* (*OG* 23). As he writes in "Différance," if Heidegger's understanding of the history of being is an effect of *différance*, "then *différance*, in a certain and very strange way, (is) 'older' than the ontological difference or than the truth of Being" (*MP* 22), where "the truth of Being" is one of Heidegger's circumlocutions for the event. Consequently, Derrida tries to keep his thinking different from Heidegger by saying that *différance* is more "originary" or "older" than Heidegger's event to say that Heidegger's own thinking arises on account of the dynamics of *différance*. Yet in marking graphically the terms originary and older in scare quotes he indicates that the origin of this thinking with *différance* is not the pure origin that metaphysics hopes for in the transcendental signified. The trace for Derrida is not secondary or provisional. Rather, the trace is an originary supplement, which means that at the ground of the bottomless chessboard of *différance* are traces or signs upon signs that disrupt the expected, status quo of certain, solidified meaning in a transcendental signified. *Différance* is not one such trace, though, because it is a name for this play of traces developed through the dynamism of the difference and deferral of purely present meaning. Under *différance*, we have traces or a play of differences all the way down. Inscribed in and along this chessboard are gifts that are never gifts of presence but gifts of traces.

Accordingly, fourteen years after "Différance," Derrida returns to this reflection on the gifts of *différance*. But now, in 1982, he uses cinders or ash as "the best paradigm for the trace" (*C* 25). The cinder is what remains of meaning in the play of *différance*. We do not have meaning in its presence for Derrida. Rather, we always already have "what remains without remaining" of such meaning (*C* 25). We have its cinders or ashes. Thus, Derrida says that what is given in the play of *différance* is not beingness or the present meaning of a thing, as in Heidegger, but rather ashes or cinders. No longer do we have the "it gives [*es gibt*] Being" (*TB* 12) of Heidegger's event but the "*es gibt ashes*" (*C* 55) of *différance*. *Différance* is the name for this giving of ashes, this play of traces, that serve as reminders of what remains when starting from a thinking of dissemination so that presence is always brought into relation with absence. For ashes remain, are present, but their own presence points to the absence of what had been but has now been burned up. In this way, the dynamics of *différance* through a play of cinders marks where the unexpected unfolds, that is, where an event happens without gifts of presence.

And such giving, says Derrida back in "Différance," is to be understood "as expenditure without reserve, as the irreparable loss of presence" that "interrupts every economy" (*MP* 19). In this idea of the giving of *différance* as an unexpected interruption of economy, Derrida's early explorations of an event that unexpectedly repeats and ruptures linguistic structurality connects with his later writings on the gift. Through this later theme of the gift, Derrida develops a deeper understanding of how an event befalls us unexpectedly by identifying two more aspects of an event's unexpectedness: its im-possibility and temporalization of time anew. The themes of event and gift in Derrida's writings develop and enrich one another to the extent that his understanding of the gift becomes a paradigm for his understanding of the event. For he says at the aforementioned 2001 conference dedicated to the theme of the event, "There is not an event more eventful than a gift that breaks up the exchange, the course of history, the circle of economy" (DE 93). The gift "should be an event" because in breaking up the circle of economy, the gift "has to arrive as a surprise" (DE 92). The gift is the gift event.

Gift and Event

The gift is a paradigm for understanding Derrida's account of an event because the gift elaborates on the symptoms of an event through the logic of the *sans* by which the gift occurs. With this, a gift occurs for Derrida *sans voir*, *sans savoir*, and *sans avoir*.[17] This logic of the *sans* develops the idea of an event occurring unexpectedly because through this logic, the event's causality of rupture gains a temporal element through which an event conditions its own occurrence. Such conditioning of itself is what Derrida calls its im-possibility. In disrupting an economy of exchange by interrupting it in a transformative instant, a gift is given unexpectedly or without being able to see it on the horizon (*sans voir*), is given in secret outside the realm of calculative rationality (*sans savoir*), and is given without any person possessing what is given (*sans avoir*). Through this logic of the *sans* a gift is given unexpectedly and im-possibly as it conditions its own possibility. And I maintain that the death of the other appears as such a gift event because of its own temporalizing and im-possible structure.

How the gift for Derrida is this paradigm of the event becomes evident by understanding the conditions for its possibility as well as its impossibility. These conditions are the economy of exchange that occurs with everyday gift giving. When one person has the intention of giving something to another person who receives it, gift giving is made possible. In other words, "A gives B to C" (*GT* 11). These are "the conditions for the possibility of the gift" because "for there to be gift, gift event, some 'one' has to give some 'thing' to someone other, without which 'giving' would be meaningless" (*GT* 12 and 11). Without a giver, a givee, and the given, we could not speak about giving and the gift at all. Therefore, the gift for Derrida occurs as a *dissymmetrical* or asymmetrical event of giving insofar as A gives, C receives, and B is the gift.

However, as experience teaches, everyday gift giving is *not* dissymmetrical. What normally occurs in everyday gift giving is a circular cycle of giving, receiving, *and* returning. And this return constitutes the circular economy that nullifies the gift on Derrida's understanding. In this reciprocal economy, the giver puts the givee in a place of debt on account of the given. So the givee is obligated to give something in return. A "Thank you very much," perhaps, which effectively completes the circle of exchange. Of course, a further thank you gift from the givee might be given, which would complete the circle while possibly effecting another circle of exchange. Economy, then, always "implies the idea of exchange, or circulation, of return" (*GT* 6). And this return nullifies the gift by ridding of its dissymmetry. The economy causes the initial giver to become an *expectant* givee insofar as he or she expects something in return. Similarly, the initial givee becomes an *indebted* giver insofar as he or she is expected to give something back as a sign of appreciation for what has been given. Such an economy gives rise to a calculated generosity in which the gift (*don*) becomes a present (*cadeaux* or *présent*) according to Derrida. And the giving of presents is, in turn, a profitable giving. Person A gives presents in order to receive something in return; Person B receives presents with an indebtedness to give something back. In this way, the three conditions of the possibility of the gift — the giver, the given, and the givee — "designate simultaneously the conditions of the impossibility of the gift" (*GT* 12). Thus, if the gift is to remain possible, the very conditions of its possibility are also the conditions of its impossibility. Thus, the conditions become the conditions that ultimately constitute the economy that the gift event disrupts. The gift *as an event* must surprise, exceed any horizon of expectation, resist the confines of static, conceptual construction, and exhibit singularity. The gift must occur *sans voir* and *sans savoir* in this regard. The gift, then, must break out of the economy of exchange between giver, givee, and the given because this economy reduces any surprise to an expectation that arrives on a determined, expected, and economic horizon.

Nevertheless, Derrida maintains that the gift and the economy that it makes possible, which in turn makes the gift impossible, must always remain in concert together. Much like *différance* must be understood as the play of presence and absence, the trap of metaphysical thinking that would pursue the *pure* gift as a transcendental signified apart from economy must be resisted. The gift needs the economy as much as the economy needs the gift. Accordingly, Derrida has no qualms, per se, with economy. After all, he says, "[G]ive economy its chance" (*GT* 30) and, "[G]ive consciously and conscientiously" (*GT* 63). Yet even while we give economy this chance to do what it does, we must also know how the gift disrupts it because for the event to be possible, for the gift to be possible as the unexpected disruption of the economy, this economy must be there to be interrupted and transformed. The gift *as an event* must surprise and exceed any horizon of expectation, including the rational, profitable calculation within the economy. This disruption of the economy occurs through an excessive generosity and the temporality of the instant that attends the event. So rather than the calculated, profitable generosity of the economy, the gift operates according to an "excessive generosity," that is, a giving that gives not for profit but without return (*GT* 82). In such excessive generosity, the gift then becomes a "dissemination without return" (*GT* 100). The gift as gift is given without any need for something given back. The gift, then, "must not circulate, it must not be exchanged. . . . If the figure of the circle is essential to economics, the gift must remain *aneconomic*" (*GT* 7).

And this aneconomy of the gift follows a peculiar kind of temporality. In the circular economy of presents, the temporality at play is itself the present. This economy deals with presents that present presence. A present is always presented in the present. Derrida's image for this is "time as [a] circle" (*GT* 9). Though a present is present, a gift operates according to an aneconomic temporality of the to-come. This is the unexpected, surprising in-breaking or irruption of a future into the present that breaks and enters based upon its own conditions of possibility and not those of the economy at play. And this temporality of the gift that fractures or keeps out of joint the presence of the present means that a gift event breaks into and out of the presence of the economy of exchange. For this reason, Derrida says that the gift happens "at the instant" (*GT* 9).

Plato and Levinas each help us to understand the significance of this instant for Derrida. Plato's discussion of the sudden or the instant (τὸ ἐξαίφνης) in his *Parmenides* dialogue is illuminating for this idea of the instant because Plato connects this instant with *death* by exploring, even if briefly, the temporality of transformation or change specifically in relation to the death of the other. As a person changes from life to death, "from being to ceasing-to-be" (157a),[18] *when*, writes Plato, does this change occur? This change occurs in the temporality of *the instant*. He says, "The instant seems to signify something such that changing occurs from it to each of two states. For a thing doesn't change from rest while rest continues, or from motion while motion continues" (156d). The instant of change is an inter-ruption between one state and another state that allows for the transformation from the one to the other to occur. And in order to operate between these two states involved in the change, Plato writes that this instant is a "queer thing . . . lurk[ing] between motion and rest [between being and ceasing-to-be] — being in no time at all" (156e). This instant is an inter-ruption of the temporally present economy of motion and rest, which is the economy of exchange at play in this context. This instant of transformation is not happening in the now of presence in which movement and rest occur, but outside of the present altogether. Yet, nevertheless, this instant remains related to the present by giving rise to the change from one state to another in the present.[19] This means that the instant occurs outside any horizons of temporality other than the horizon through which it makes its own occurrence possible.[20] When the death of the other understood as an event occurs at the instant, then, its occurrence is a retemporalization of time on account of this instant's relation to time.

Reading this idea from Plato with Derrida's notion of the instant, Derrida similarly says that "this instant of breaking and entering [*effraction*] (of the temporal circle) must no longer be part of time" (*GT* 9; translation modified). This instant of a gift event is "paradoxical" because it breaks into and out of time all the while retaining a relation with time (*GT* 9). In other words, to borrow an idea from Levinas, this instant of the gift is *never lived-through*.[21] Levinas develops this idea that "[t]he great 'experiences' of our life have properly speaking never been lived"[22] by contrasting two kinds of temporality that he calls synchronic temporality and diachronic temporality. With synchronic temporality, the past, present, and future get reduced to the rule of the present now. As such, the past and the future have being only insofar as they are defined as being a series of past-nows and future-nows. The past becomes understood only in terms of being a time that *once was present* while the future becomes understood only in terms of being a time that *will be present*. Thus, in synchronic temporality, time consists of the past-*present*, the present-*present*, and the future-*present*. And the time through which experiences are lived is defined through these three accounts of the present. Accordingly, such synchronic temporality "is the linear order that allows events in the past, present, and future to be gathered into the present moment by consciousness."[23] This idea of synchronous time means for Levinas that when a phenomenon gets experienced, its otherness or alterity gets reduced to the conditions of possibility as defined by the lived, temporal experience of consciousness through the primary modality of the present. Consequently, the rule of the present attempts to prevent the coming of an other set on disturbing and rupturing the order of the present. Despite synchronic temporality, the *diachronic* temporality of an event ruptures this rule of the present over temporality by being irreducible to the present in any of the iterations of the past-present, present-present, or future-present. The movement of an event, then, "does not lend itself to the contemporaneousness that constitutes the force of the time tied in the present because it imposes a completely different version of time."[24] Consequently, Levinas says that all of "the great 'experiences' of our life have properly speaking never been lived"[25] because these moments are events that disrupt the rule of the present so that these moments are not lived through in the present-*present*. An event, therefore, temporalizes time differently. An event is temporalization anew and unexpectedly. This, in turn, means that these events are not *experiences* per se because only experiences are put through the economy of the present. Hence, Levinas names these events "experiences" with scare quotes to mark graphically that though they are important moments in life, they are never lived through in the presence of the present.

The question arises when reading this line from Levinas: what experiences does he have in mind when referencing these great experiences in life? He does not provide a list outside of the obvious one for him: the call of the other to responsibility. However, as I make more evident in part 3 below, the death of the other must be considered as one such great experience on account of the way that it breaks into experience, disrupting a survivor's relation to temporality as part of its own unexpected rupture. Levinas himself may even have the death of the other in mind, as well, because for him the "question of philosophy" amounts to "the question of my right to be which is already my responsibility for the death of the Other."[26] Instead of being worked through the economy of the present, the death of the other approaches from out of a future and passes by into a past leaving a trail of symptoms that befall the survivors. And these symptoms are the traces of this event's having come. This trail of symptoms is, moreover, the trace pointing to the present absence or absent presence of this event's having come.[27] For something presently takes place when the other dies, but this something remains only through its absence: the absence of the living other and the way things in the world signify the other's absence through the presence of their clothes hanging limply on the chair or their notes scribbled in the margins of books, and so on. And in the wake of its having come, a survivor's relation to time gets reconfigured or temporalized anew. Her past, future, and present are no longer the same but now disrupted by this death of the other. In this way, the instant through which the event of the death of the other occurs, an occurrence understood through the Derridean gift, both opens and transforms time by *rupturing* it unexpectedly in order for something new to happen. However, this coming of this gift can either be something good or something bad. Death as such a *catastrophic* event or gift can be the promise of something good or, in German, *ein Gift* — poison. Or this death can be both. Either way, as promise/poison the irruption of this gift into the status quo of the economy opens the circle of exchange.

Moreover, such an interruption or rupture of the economy at this temporality of the instant must be understood, once again, as monstrous or *traumatic* insofar as this event deformalizes time through "its interruptive force."²⁸ An event's relation to temporality, and thereby the death of the other's relation to temporality, is important for understanding any event as traumatic. Psychologists have argued that trauma has an inherent relation to temporality. For example, Bessel van der Kolk defines trauma in his celebrated work in psychology as not just something "that took place sometime in the past; it is also the imprint left by that experience on mind, brain, and body. This imprint has ongoing consequences for how the human organism manages to survive in the present."²⁹ An event is a rupturing that exceeds linear temporality by leaving unexpected traces on a survivor's relation to her past, present, and future. Derrida even goes so far as to maintain that any event on account of this unexpectedness is traumatic: "[E]ven when it is a happy event: an event is always traumatic, its singularity interrupts an order and rips apart . . . the normal fabric of temporality or history" (*WA* 135–36; cf. 139).³⁰ In this, I understand trauma to be this disruption of temporality, specifically of the relation of the past, present, and future, for the person who has been affected by this trauma. Accordingly, the event's causality of rupture can be understood as having a traumatic effect on those who experience it because of how it unexpectedly disrupts temporality. And while any event's occurring can be traumatic, I am focusing specifically on this trauma in relation to the death of the other. I am arguing here, and further in part 3 below, that the causality of rupture through which the death of the other impacts a survivor must be understood as traumatic. And this trauma from the death of the other creates grief in a survivor understood as the impact of this death on the survivor to which the response from the survivor is what I am calling mourning.

And as such a traumatic rupturing of temporality, a gift event, such as the death of the other, remains irreducible to any past, present, or future modality. It exceeds time all the while relating to time. This instant of the gift event that breaks into the temporality of the economy of exchange is what happens when a gift event arrives. Temporality fractures at the instant of the arrival of a gift event. In order for the gift *instantly* to do this, according to Derrida, the gift must operate, then, according to the *im-possible*. The giving and receiving of the gift must operate outside the order of knowledge and being known because the gift becomes possible there where the giver does not give with any intentions of giving and the givee does not receive with any recognition that she has received. The gift must, thus, occur *sans savoir* and *sans avoir*. He writes, "At the limit, the gift as gift ought not appear as gift: either to the givee or to the giver. It cannot be gift as gift except by not being present as gift" (*GT* 14; translation modified). The gift operates in the order of secrecy insofar as the parties involved cannot know that a gift has been given. If this gift enters the order of knowing, then it enters the circle of exchange and can no longer surprise, interrupt, and transform this circle. This secret operation of the gift that removes it from the realm of consciousness allows for the gift to surprise, to break in at the *instant*, and to interrupt the economy of exchange according to its own conditions of possibility and not those of the economy. In other words, the gift event can arrive, but its arrival must appear unexpectedly as im-possible where impossible is written with a hyphen to show that this does *not* mean "that there is no gift."[31] The impossibility of the gift with no hyphen would mean no gift is possible or that a gift is an impossible possibility that will never occur. However, the im-possibility of the gift with a hyphen means that the coming and inter-ruption of a gift event would resist the current conditions of possibility all the while bringing its own conditions of possibility. For example, in writing about the event of friendship that Derrida names *aimance* in his *Politics of Friendship*, he writes:

> It may be, then, that the order is other — it may well be — and that only the coming of the event allows, after the event [*après coup*], perhaps, what it will previously have made possible to be thought. . . . [I]t would be only the event of revelation that would open — like a breaking-in, making it possible after the event — the field of the possible in which it appeared to spring forth, and for that matter actually did so. (*PF* 18)

For an event to occur, in other words, the event must *seem* impossible to the current conditions of possibility. The occurrence of an event is something that is possible only to think *until* the event itself occurs because through its occurrence, an event makes the impossible both possible and actual. What once was possible only in thought is now possible in experience *after the event* because the event's own unexpected breaking into the status quo makes itself possible. An event is its own possibilization because an event transforms the current conditions of possibility through its own conditions of possibility that before the event seemed impossible. A gift event is phenomenologically impossible only until it breaks into phenomenality, transforming phenomenality itself through its rupture. In order for the gift to surprise, break in at the instant, and operate im-possibly, the gift must, then, "keep its phenomenality" (*GT* 14) because phenomenalization of the gift would annul the gift by making it a present that enters the economy of exchange in the expected conditions of possibility in the economy. Thus, to paraphrase the epigraph of *Given Time: I*, phenomenality takes all gifts, making them presents; we give the rest of our gifts to the instant, to whom we would like to give all of them.[32] The coming of a gift event, then, must be one that comes unexpectedly, without us being able to see it on any horizon. An event must be *sans voir*, *sans savoir*, and *sans avoir*.

Therefore, we give economy a chance by keeping the economy of exchange open, trembling, a little uncertain, or a little off-center. We must keep the circle loose in order "to create an opening for the *tout autre*,"[33] for the coming of the wholly other, of the event, of the gift event, that is, "of an alterity that cannot be anticipated" (*SM* 81). Giving economy a chance by knowing how such an economy works and how the gift disrupts it according to its causality of rupture is precisely what will have helped keep the circle open to the coming of an event. What is needed, then, for us to prepare for the gift event is an openness to its eventiality, that is, to its unexpected rupturing at any instant. Hospitality toward this coming of the event is, then, needed. And this hospitality consists of an ethos of welcome to the surprise of the event. Such would be, says Derrida, a "hospitality invented for the singularity of the new arrival, of the unexpected visitor" (*OH* 83). And such "hospitality without reserve" or unconditional hospitality is "the condition of the event" (*SM* 82).[34] To conclude, if the death of the other can be described and understood as such an unexpected event without horizon insofar as it adheres to a causality of rupture, the question arises, what can we do as survivors of the death of the other to offer hospitality to this surprising, unexpected adventure of such an event? I can say for now, though I develop this further below, that mourning, namely what I call workless mourning, can be the kind of hospitality for the coming of this unexpected event.

Chapter Two

The Secretive Event without Reason

> The parting [*partage*] between reason and its other, the calculable and the incalculable . . . is not a parting with two parts. If it is not a parting — a division into shares, or a distribution into parts — then *the space of rationality* can be totally invaded by or surrendered to what we call the incalculable, chance, the other, the event.
>
> — Jacques Derrida and Maurizio Ferraris, *A Taste for the Secret*

When an event befalls us, the im-possibility of this event causes its arrival to be unexpected, as has been shown. But this is not the only symptom of such an event. In addition to the im-possible arrival of the event is its *secret* arrival. The secret, Derrida says, "belongs to the structure of the event" (DE 105). Yet this does not mean that the event is hidden or clandestine, thereby precluding the arrival and possibility of the event. The arrival of the event is *not* absolutely impossible. Rather, the event as secret follows the may-be (*peut-être*), which means that the event always already remains an impossibility according to the established conditions of possibility even in its arrival. I argue in this chapter that one way to understand this secretive event that may-be is to understand that an event remains outside of the principle of sufficient reason. For example, the gift event remains "unexplainable by a system of efficient causes" (*GT* 123). The arrival of an event occurs in secret because this arrival exceeds the causal nexus that would usually operate to help us understand *why* this event is about to occur or has occurred. Furthermore, Derrida says that if we can define the event with "one possible definition" it would be that "an event must be exceptional, without rule" (DE 106). The event obeys no rules or principles unless those principles are "principles of disorder, that is, principles without principles" (*GT* 123). The event must be the other, alterity, that resists the hegemony of principles coming from a sovereign subject. The secret here is, then, a "way to let the other be, to respect alterity."[1] The event as other can happen in the economy of the same, the economy of phenomenology, but when it happens there, it does not appear according to the expected conditions of possibility. It irrupts into the same *as* the other. Thus, the event is irreducible to our phenomenological horizons that it disrupts and keeps open according to its causality of rupture from chapter 1. It appears without appearing. It shows up. But it shows up as the correlate of an intention that cannot confine it because it exceeds the confines of consciousness. It surprises us, and as such, the event is a secret.

As this explanation shows, these first two symptoms of an event — the unexpected and the secretive — are integrally wedded to one another to the extent that each symptom is a consideration of the aftermath of an event's occurrence but from two different trajectories. The secrecy of an event is the im-possible, unexpectedness of an event considered differently. After all, the primary reason for how an event exceeds the causal explanations for its happening is that an event surprises our horizons of expectation. And the primary horizon through which we prepare for any phenomenon is the principle of sufficient reason, which says, in short, that everything has a reason for its existence where this reason is the causal explanation for its existence. Or as Leibniz states, "Our reasonings are based on two great principles, that of contradiction . . . [a]nd that of sufficient reason, by virtue of which we consider that we can find no true or existent fact, no true assertion, without there being a sufficient reason why it is thus and not otherwise."[2] And, especially as an event would be considered by Leibniz a contingent truth or a truth of fact, the reason for any such existence would concern its *cause*.[3] As Marion explains regarding Leibniz's principle, "This principle posits that every fact, proposition, and therefore phenomenon too must have a reason that justifies its actuality; . . . and this can happen only if a term other than it comes, as cause or reason, to make intelligible this transition [of a phenomenon from possibility to actuality]" (*NC* 107). To follow the principle of reason, then, is "to explain effects through their causes."[4] This principle demands that reasons be rendered for the existence of any phenomenon. Thus, if an event exceeds our horizons of expectation so that it arrives unexpectedly, then an event exceeds this principle of reason by its surprising arrival. The event occurs without reason. Additionally, the trauma that attends any event in its occurrence disrupts the mind's ability to explain an event with causality because, as neurological research on trauma has shown, trauma affects our ability to fit experiences into logical sequences, with the result that "we can't identify cause and effect."[5] Trauma is, once again, a disruption of temporality. In this way, an event is excessive insofar as it is without reason or in excess of a causal nexus that explains *why* this event has occurred. An event occurs, then, in secret.

We have already seen preliminarily this integral connection among an event's unexpectedness and an event's exceeding of the principle of sufficient reason in the previous chapter. We have seen this connection prefigured in at least two ways. First, an event's causality of rupture is unexpected due to its being catastrophic, which also means that this causality is without reason because it breaks from "its past, its origin, and its *cause*" (*WD* 291; emphasis mine). Thus, in *Of Grammatology*, Derrida repeatedly describes this catastrophic rupture as "outside of historical and philosophical reason," "nonrational," "irreducible to logic," "inconceivable to reason," and "cannot be understood according to the patterns of rational necessity" (*OG* 257). An event's occurrence is unexpected because an event breaks into the confines of rational, causal thinking and exceeds these horizons with its own occurrence. An event is unexpected *and* without reason. Second, I argue in chapter 1 that the poststructural play of meaning and language signaled under the name *différance* is the means by which the history of metaphysics gets itself organized through traces. And this organization exceeds the principle of sufficient reason because as "an effect without a cause" (*MP* 12), a trace gives no answer as to *why* something occurs. So the movement of *différance*, that is, the means by which meaning is differential and deferred, is described as an event that occurs without reason because this movement occurs outside of cause-effect thinking.

This chapter explores in more depth why an event is understood to occur outside the confines of reason by looking at Heidegger's discussion in *The Principle of Reason* of Leibniz's articulation of the principle of reason. Through this discussion, an event cannot be explained exhaustively through a causal account as to why it occurred. However, this excessiveness of an event beyond any *why* does not preclude us from saying something about an event. Even though we may be able to say *how* a rose is able to bloom if provided with the right amounts of water, nutrient-rich soil, and sunlight, this does not explain *why* a rose blooms, instead of doing something else, when receiving such provisions. We may be able to explain *how* an event occurred, but this does not explain *why* it has occurred. Indeed, understanding an event through its causality of rupture, as I have done in chapter 1, or according to the symptoms that befall us in the aftermath of an event's occurring, is precisely an understanding of *how* an event disrupts the current conditions of possibility by introducing its own conditions of possibility. And this how of an event's occurrence is itself not a causal explanation as to *why* an event occurred. Moreover, the aspects of this causality of rupture (i.e., catastrophe, monstrosity, retemporalization of time) from chapter 1 show, as well, how an event adheres to a principle without principle for its own occurrence because if this causality of rupture is a principle, it operates without making an event predictable and confining it. This causality of rupture describes that an event is unpredictable through its own occurring. The secretive symptom of an event continues, then, along these lines to describe how an event occurs without explaining causally why it has occurred.

Heidegger's *Principle of Reason* is surprising, however, because his approach to thinking through Leibniz has a fascinating phenomenological implication. His focus on Leibniz continues Heidegger's concern to rethink the history of philosophy through his understanding of the event (*das Ereignis*), as mentioned in chapter 1, and is often called his being-historical thinking. But contained in his reading of Leibniz, he has the rich phenomenological description of the blooming of the rose from Angelus Silesius's poem through which Heidegger describes this blooming as operating outside of the principle of sufficient reason. While Heidegger's being-historical thinking and his phenomenological thinking can be in tension with one another,[6] tracing this tension in his course on Leibniz is beyond the scope of my project. Instead, I am concerned with following Heidegger's reading of the blooming of the rose in order to discuss how a phenomenon, such as the death of the other, grounds itself through its own occurring. Consequently, I move in this phenomenological direction by using Marion's understanding of givenness and the saturated phenomenon to further elucidate how the death of the other can occur without reason or without why. Yet Marion's helpful phenomenological approach errs by ignoring the import of the death of the other. Through this discussion of the second major symptom of an event — the secretive event without reason — from Heidegger, through Marion, and beyond, I begin showing how the death of the other occurs without reason insofar as when considered in its occur*ring*, such death can be interpreted as a saturated phenomenon without reason.

The Leap from Reason

Heidegger's 1955–56 lecture course on Leibniz's formulation of the principle of reason, titled *The Principle of Reason* (*Der Satz vom Grund*), belongs to the later Heidegger's approach toward the question of the meaning of being (the *Seinsfrage*) where Heidegger investigates the meaning of being through an investigation of the history of philosophy. At this juncture of his thinking, what he finds in the thoughts of other philosophers is the history (*Geschick*) of being understood as an underlying, almost subterranean, unthought essence of the history of philosophy. As Heidegger says in 1955–56, this history of being means that "being proffers itself to us, but in such a way that at the same time it, in its essence, already withdraws" (*PR* 65). In this being-historical thinking, Heidegger argues that in and along the history of how the meaning or beingness (*Seiendheit*) of beings has been thought can be found the unthought occurrence of being itself (*Sein*). In and along the history of metaphysics, in other words, Heidegger believes a space is opened or cleared for being itself, rather than the being of a particular being, to be experienced through thinking. And this clearing for being itself is the clearing of what he also calls the event, that is, being itself as the event (*Ereignis*). Thus, the event, being itself, being as being, the event as being, and beyng (*das Seyn*) become homologous terms that Heidegger uses during this time to name the abiding *Sache* of his thought: the meaning of being. In Heidegger's 1962 lecture *On Time and Being* mentioned in chapter 1, he maintains that this event is operative in the *es gibt* that gives beingness (*Seiendheit*) at different temporal junctures. These temporal junctures are the epochs of being itself that constitute the history of metaphysics where beingness has been thought in various ways. So, for example, when Plato says that a particular being finds its ultimate meaning in its form (ἰδέα or εἶδος), the event is not the particular being nor this form but is, rather, the generation of this coming to meaning at this particular historical juncture. This generation of meaning is what Heidegger calls the appropriating of the event from which the event expropriates itself because the event is not identifiable with the beings or being (e.g., form for Plato). The event is this movement of appropriation-expropriation.

This event is withdrawn or in and along this history because the event is not one of the beings in this history nor any of the particular meanings for the being of such beings. Thus, in and along, which is to say concealed in, the history of being is the giving or the event of being understood as a generative giving of beingness at these particular historical junctures. What is unconcealed as the beingness of beings (e.g., Plato's form, Aristotle's actuality [ἐνέργεια], the Plotinian One, the *substantia* of the Middle Ages, Nietzsche's will to will, etc.) are the *gifts* of meaning from this event of *giving*. Each beingness in the history of being is a gift of the event of giving. What Heidegger calls in *On Time and Being* these gifts of being he calls in his 1955–56 lecture course the "shapes of ground/reason" (*PR* 110). The principle of sufficient reason is one such gift from or shape of being. Accordingly, *The Principle of Reason* explores Leibniz's formulations of the principle of sufficient reason in an effort to find in and along Leibniz's principle the unthought occurring of the event. Heidegger's reading of Leibniz provides helpful resources for understanding how an event can be without reason and, thereby, appear through the symptom of the secret. While his analysis is primarily about the meaning of being, his analysis opens the door to understanding particular phenomena as events. In this, his reading of Leibniz centers around three main ideas: the two tonalities of the principle of reason, Angelus Silesius's blooming rose, and the distinction between the terms *why* (*warum*) and *while* (*weil*).

To begin, Heidegger's attempt to hear the two tonalities of this principle of reason is based on the shorthand version of Leibniz's principle, which states, "Nothing is without reason." Heidegger hears two ways of emphasizing this version of the principle that give rise to the two tonalities. The first way to hear this is with the emphasis on the "nothing" and the "without" so that we read, "*Nothing* is *without* reason" (*PR* 40; emphasis his). This hearing amounts to saying, in a positive sense, that "everything has a reason" (*PR* 40). This is the tonality that we have when referring to the principle most of the time when talking about the reasons or the grounds for a particular phenomenon being one way or another. Such a reason *or* ground, which are two ways to translate the German *Grund*, must be rendered in order for our mind to be able to understand a phenomenon. In rendering such a reason upon which our understanding of any phenomenon can be grounded, a phenomenon is aligned with calculability, that is, according to Derrida, "with the blinding or blind calculating drive of a calculation that passes itself off as reason itself" (*DP2* 139).[7]

This calculating machine called reason operates according to the principle of reason by demanding that any phenomenon be an object of our cognition. As such, the principle of reason reduces everything that must have a reason to an object of our own calculation. The reasons rendered for a being, says Heidegger, require that "the object itself always be a founded — which means securely established — *object*" (*PR* 28; emphasis mine).[8] *Nothing* is *without* being the "calculable stuff" of cognition (*PR* 56). The principle of reason places the particular phenomenon under question into the orbit of the calculable or calculability so that we can cognize it as an object. Heidegger helpfully elaborates on this first tonality in his 1956 Bremen lecture of the same title as his lecture course, "Whatever happens to be actual has a reason for its actuality. Whatever happens to be possible has a reason for its possibility. Whatever happens to be necessary has a reason for its necessity" (*PR* 117). This first tonality brings the phenomenon into the purview of our understanding and reasoning capacity so that we can calculate what this phenomenon *is* as actual, possible, or necessary. So this first tonality says to us that everything that is, from a true proposition to a phenomenon, has some reason that can be rendered or given for why it is the way it is and not some other way. Such is reason's economy of exchange by which it attempts to calculate experience. According to this tonality of the principle of reason, the death of the other would be completely calculable. We could understand not only how the other dies but also why the other dies when she dies. But such complete calculability of the death of the other does not fit how this phenomenon occurs when someone loses someone close to them be it a human or nonhuman animal. If the death of the other could be completely calculable in this way, then people would not say things such as "I can't believe he is gone" or "It just doesn't seem right that she is dead." Yet survivors of the death of the other give these kinds of testimonies frequently. Such testimonies, then, make questionable the relationship of the death of the other to this first tonality of the principle of sufficient reason.

In contrast, the second tonality of this principle of reason resounds with the emphasis on the "is" and "reason" so that we read, "Nothing *is* without *reason*" (*PR* 40; emphasis his). This hearing amounts to saying, in a positive sense, "every being (as a being) has a reason" (*PR* 40). Or, perhaps more simply put, any phenomenon *is* on account of a reason. Whereas the first tonality is "a supreme principle about *beings*" for Heidegger, the second tonality is to be heard as "a principle of being" with regard to the *Seinsfrage* (*PR* 68; emphasis mine). In this, the second tonality names being itself, that is, being understood as event, and with this second tonality, he develops his thinking of this event in his lecture along three fronts. First, the second tonality reveals the intimate relation among being and the ground itself. For this second tonality indicates that the being of a phenomenon, named by the emphasized copula, is associated with the reason for the phenomenon. The being of the phenomenon is in some sense *given* — here is the *es gibt* once again — by reason or ground. This second tonality for Heidegger brings being (*Sein*) and ground (*Grund*) together so that being is itself the reason for a phenomenon insofar as being occurs as ground. In other words, a phenomenon is ground*ed* or found*ed* upon being as its reason for being at all. Therefore, being itself (*Sein*), according to the second tonality of the principle of reason, occurs as ground/reason (*Grund*). In this, being turns out to be an occurrence of "grounding" (*PR* 49) so that "ground/reason and being ('are') the same" (*PR* 50).

This leads Heidegger to his second front for thinking of the event with this second tonality: the intimate relation among being and groundlessness or the abyss (*Abgrund*). For while all beings have a ground or are founded upon being for their reason, being itself is not a being but the grounding of all beings and is, thereby, not founded or grounded upon anything. Being itself, that is, the event, is the active, unfolding ground*ing*. Being as this occurring of grounding is, therefore, without ground or without reason because such a happening is not a particular being or beingness. All beings (S*eiendes*) have a ground. Being (*Sein*), however, is not a being and thereby is groundless (*Abgrund*). As Heidegger writes, "[B]eing can never first have a ground/reason which would supposedly ground it. Accordingly ground/reason is missing from being" (*PR* 51). Consequently, being itself does not fall into the orbit of the first tonality of the principle of sufficient reason because only beings have a ground or reason for being. Outside of the first tonality of the principle of reason, being, then, is no longer an object. Being itself is "ob-jectless [*Gegen-standlose*]" (*PR* 33). This means that being itself has no ground or reason *but not* because being "founds itself" (*PR* 111). Being is not even onto-theologically the ground/reason of its own grounding. Any notion of ground, foundation, "even and especially self-founded ones," and "foundability" itself remain inappropriate to being because these ideas stem from the first tonality of the principle of reason and degrade being to *a* being (*PR* 111).

This means, now following the third front of Heidegger's thinking, that being itself, the event, "is" not. Being itself as groundless is now the nothing named by the principle of sufficient reason in its first tonality that is precisely without ground/reason. Being, the nothing, as the groundless grounding is precisely without reason. So whereas the actual, the possible, and the necessary phenomenon have a *Grund* for being what they are, being itself appears as the impossible that is without *Grund*. Being is *Abgrund* or without ground. Whereas the principle of reason in its first tonality places beings under the banner of calculability and the calculation of our rational faculties, being as *Abgrund* is no longer calculable but incalculable. Yet, as Derrida points out, this incalculability is not to be read in the sense of in excess of our finite ability to calculate, which would make being still "homogenous with the calculable" (*DP2* 140). Rather, being as *Abgrund* is incalculable in the sense of "noncalculable" or in excess of calculability altogether (*DP2* 140). The second tonality concerns, then, "singularities that exceed a calculable economy."[9] Just as being is nonfoundable or nongroundable — being is not even the ground of itself[10] — so too is being noncalculable. As such, being as *Abgrund* is without reason or without why; being, the event, is the nothing that is without reason. In this, Heidegger turns to Silesius's poem about the blooming of the rose to illustrate the grounding that is being in this second tonality of the principle of reason. For both being and the blooming rose are occurring without why. Both are operating in the incalculable or in excess of the calculable altogether. Considering that the common testimonies after the death of the other regarding the interminable disbelief regarding the other's death makes such death not fit with the first tonality of the principle of reason, like Silesius's rose, then, the death of the other, I argue, occurs following this second tonality of the principle of reason. The death of the other occurs without reason or without why. Understanding the death of the other in this direction helps elucidate why when the other dies so many questions from survivors get posed concerning why the other has died. While they may be able to explain *how* the other died (e.g., electrocution, car crash, old age, cancer, COVID-19, etc.), the *why* of their death still remains.

This question of why is the question that gets asked when looking for reasons to be rendered for something. The principle of reason asks, particularly in its first tonality, for such reasons to be rendered. So this principle can be reformulated in its first tonality to read as "nothing is without why" (*PR* 35). Any phenomenon must have a reason; any phenomenon must have a why. And yet, Heidegger turns to Silesius's poem about the blooming of a rose to show that the *occurring* even of a phenomenon, the blooming of a rose, can operate outside the orbit of this tonality of the principle of sufficient reason. By turning to the phenomenon of the rose's blooming and describing it as without why, I maintain that Heidegger's description of the second tonality of the principle of reason can be expanded to include not just his idea of the event in his being-historical thinking but other phenomena themselves. This interesting move within Heidegger's lecture course happens in his analysis of Silesius's poem: "The rose is without why [*warum*]: it blooms while [*weil*] it blooms." It pays no attention to itself, asks not whether it is seen (*PR* 35; translation modified).

This is not to say that reasons cannot be given for *how* the rose blooms: botany and our experience of the growth of plants tell us of the "chain of causes and conditions for the growth of plants" (*PR* 36). Given the right soil, enough water, and enough sunlight, a rose will bloom. This is calculable. But the deeper question that Heidegger and Silesius are pointing to here is that given all of these conditions and causes, the question remains: *why* does the rose bloom rather than do something else? Even given the right causal chain of events, the causes do not help to answer *that* the rose blooms as the effect of this causal chain. The blooming itself operates outside the orbit of the rendered calculation of the causal chain. The blooming is, then, *without why*. The blooming is incalculable. Likewise, when speaking in the medical field, we can raise the question as to why cancer occurs, why heart valves fail, why aneurysms occur, and so on. And reasons can be rendered: genetic markers, congenital valve issues, overworking of the heart, age, et cetera. Yet given all of these calculative grounds for the medical issue to arise, the deeper questions persist: Why does this gene give rise to this? Why congenital issues? Why did the overworking of the heart give rise to the aneurysm? Why now? Why at all? *How* the other dies and from what he dies is calculable; *that* she dies remains incalculable. And when the other dies from such issues or a myriad other possible issues, as Derrida raises, why do we cry when we are sad rather than something else? He writes: "Even if one knows why one weeps, in what situation, and what it signifies (I weep because I have lost one of my nearest and dearest . . .), but that still doesn't explain why the lachrymal glands come to secrete these drops of water which are brought to the eyes rather than elsewhere, the mouth, or the ears" (*GD* 56). All such phenomena, like the rose, are without why despite the reality that causes can be rendered and calculated for the how of these phenomena. And Heidegger notes that Silesius is even sensitive to this, as evidenced by the second half of the first line: the rose "blooms *while* [*weil*] it blooms" (*PR* 36; emphasis mine). So the blooming of the rose occurs "without why [*warum*] and yet not without while [*weil*]" (*PR* 36; translation modified). This distinction between the *why* and the *while* is a crucial one whose difference makes all the difference.

The issue that distinguishes the why from the while is not the presence of reasons or grounds, especially in the form of causes, themselves. Rather, the concern is with the relation to such reasons, grounds, or causes. The *why* "seeks grounds" (*PR* 36) insofar as the why is the question that we pose in our subjectivity that must be answered in order for us to understand, especially objectively speaking, the phenomenon at hand. Considering that Kant calls cognition thinking according to concepts,[11] to understand a phenomenon in this way means that the mind desires to conform the phenomenon to our own concepts so that we know the phenomenon as an object of our cognition. Heidegger comments, "The 'why' unfolds itself in the questions: How? When? Where? It asks about the law, the time, the site of what happens" (*PR* 126). The why asks for a calculation. In contrast, the while "conveys grounds" (*PR* 36) insofar as this while does not go in search of the grounds but allows the grounds themselves to manifest in relation to the phenomenon's own active occurring or happening. This while frees thinking, then, to "let the matter be what it is" in relation to its grounds (*PR* 42). Whereas the *why* seeks the grounds to fit the phenomenon to our own cognition and concepts, the *while* lets the phenomenon's own grounds manifest in the arising of the phenomenon itself. The reason or ground when following the while "is a reason that belongs to the thing itself: it is as if the meaning of the thing was entirely contained in the thing itself."[12] The rose blooms for the simple fact that it blooms. The rose does not need the causal chain of reasons to be rendered to it in order to bloom. Rather, the rose's blooming, *that* it blooms, "is a simple arising-on-its-own," and the while seeks to point to this happening of the blooming itself from itself (*PR* 38). Consequently, whereas the *why* seeks out the foundations that found a being, the *while* "guards against . . . investigating foundations" (*PR* 127). The *while* is uninterested in finding the grounds that found and calculate the phenomenon in its being based upon the first tonality of the principle of reason, which claims that *nothing* is *without* reason; every phenomenon must have a reason for its being what and how it is. Rather, the while looks to the occurring of the phenomenon itself, the bloom*ing* of the rose, and understands that this *event* is occurring not according to the causal nexus that our understanding calculates but according to its own occurring outside of calculation. The rose takes a leap (*Satz*) from the principle (*Satz*) that demands for reasons (*Grund*) to be rendered for its blooming. The rose's blooming leaps from the principle of reason (*der Satz vom Grund*) and blooms for it blooms. The *while* names this event of the rose's blooming by pointing to this blooming as the "pure arising-on-its-own" (*PR* 57). The blooming is, then, without why just like the grounding of being itself is without why. Being understood as event and the blooming of the rose are without why — each grounds or blooms while it grounds or blooms. This occurring of being itself and the blooming of the rose point for Heidegger to the event being without why and exceeding calculability. As such, the event and the phenomenon of the rose expose reason to the incalculable.

Through this connection between being understood as an event and the rose, we find a way or a path for understanding phenomena themselves as events that Heidegger, quoting Goethe, says, "[S]tick to the *while* and ask not *why*" (*PR* 127; translation modified; emphasis his). Phenomena understood in this way ask us "to leave the why (the cause) for . . . the event."[13] Such an understanding of phenomena allows for the occurring of these phenomena to be outside the orbit of the first thinking of the principle of sufficient reason. And this description would allow for these phenomena to arise on their own and occur without reason or without why, which would mean, as I am investigating, that their arising occur not only im-possibly but also *in secret*. In order to unfold phenomenologically how a phenomenon, particularly the death of the other, can be without why further, I turn to Marion's phenomenology because Marion remains more consistently focused on developing these phenomenological insights from Heidegger without attempting to rethink the history of philosophy on a grand scale. In this, Marion calls such phenomena, whose occurring are without reason or without why, saturated phenomena.[14]

Saturated Phenomena and/as Events

While Marion's discussion of saturated phenomena is ostensibly simple in the initial presentation of it in his 1992 essay "The Saturated Phenomenon," rehearsing this presentation can lead to missing his insights for why these phenomena exceed, like Silesius's rose, the principle of reason in its first tonality. In order to follow these insights, his broader phenomenological project needs to be situated in the context of his critical appropriation of Heidegger's phenomenology through which Marion turns to the theme of givenness as the ground of his discussion of saturated phenomena. With this ground settled, the saturated phenomenon can be understood as part and parcel of the degrees of givenness in his phenomenology through which he develops his fuller description of these phenomena and the "intrinsic character" (*BG* 150) of their phenomenality. Through this, I argue that understanding the death of the other as a saturated phenomenon shows that the occurring, like Silesius's rose, of such death happens in secret as without why. Marion's phenomenological approach concerns, then, letting phenomena occur without why or by *sticking to the while and asking not why* by focusing on the occur*ring* of phenomena. Marion attempts not to explain this occurring away with causal thinking but to allow this occur*ring* to give itself from itself. For these reasons, Marion's approach to phenomenology picks up where Heidegger's reading of Silesius leaves off, namely with a phenomenological approach guided by a thinking of phenomena as events.

His overall aim with saturated phenomena is to free the givenness of phenomena from any limits so as to let it play even against the limits of our rational faculties. In order to free givenness, Marion, in part, critically appropriates Heidegger's "phenomenology of the inapparent."[15] For Marion, the reduction and phenomenological method "lets manifest itself what has the right to do so" (*BG* 10). So phenomenology is required where phenomena "remain dissimulated or still invisible" (*IE* 110) in order to make such phenomena visible that would otherwise "remain inaccessible" (*BG* 68). The phenomenological task, then, is to let what is invisible or nonmanifest become visible or manifest from out of itself — to let the phenomenon *give* itself from itself. In this, Marion returns to Heidegger's famous saying in *Being and Time* that the "lett[ing] be seen" that occurs through phenomenology is primarily of what conceals or hides itself.[16] Marion agrees that what must be the focus for phenomenology is what primarily conceals itself, but he retorts to Heidegger that what conceals itself with any phenomenon is its givenness. In this direction, Marion says that a phenomenon can show itself only if it first gives itself (*BG* 5). More specifically he claims that Heidegger never develops his phenomenology of the inapparent beyond his initial statement of it in *Being and Time* because Heidegger never approaches "givenness as such" (*BG* 38) insofar as his attempts remain bound to a horizon of being and not to givenness.[17] Heidegger, and Husserl for that matter too, on Marion's reading limits how givenness gives itself. Givenness can give itself only as either an object of consciousness for Husserl or as that which has to be for Heidegger. Thus, Marion's phenomenology revolves around what he identifies as a reduction to givenness that aims not to limit givenness. So his concern is no longer with the being of beings but with their givenness as givens. He is concerned with givenness in and along "the incident"[18] understood as the "first moment" when a phenomenon "crashes," "explodes," or "fall[s] on" us (*BG* 156, 151). Accordingly, he writes, "Being [*être*] should henceforth be thought according to the determinations of the incident" (*BG* 156). In other words, his concern remains ontological only insofar as the focus is on *being given*, that is, on the unfolding of givenness in and along a particular given. This phenomenology of givenness remains a phenomenology of the inapparent because the givenness in and along a given "remains withdrawn, held in reserve, in the background, dissimulated by its given; it thus never appears as such, therefore especially not as a being, a substance, or a subject" (*BG* 60).

Furthermore, Marion names this giving of a phenomenon, the giving of itself, with various names: the givenness, the arising, the upsurge, the birth, and the *eventiality* of the phenomenon. This giving of itself before it shows itself, that is, the givenness of a phenomenon, characterizes every phenomenon as an event. Consequently, Marion develops his account of the event first and foremost by indexing it to givenness.[19] All phenomena, insofar as they give themselves, are events for Marion because the event marks the self of these phenomena that are given. And only through givenness can the phenomenon be encountered on the phenomenon's terms and not on the terms of a sovereign subject gazing at it. He focuses not on how we perceive an appearance or phenomenon but on the very apparition of this appearance. To use Heidegger's distinction from *The Principle of Reason*, Marion focuses not on the *how* or *why* but on the *that* or *while* of phenomena. He wants to let "appearances appear in such a way that they accomplish their own apparition, so as to be received exactly as they give themselves" (*BG* 7). In other words, the phenomenon's showing of itself rests on the very apparition or eventiality of the phenomenon. While Heidegger has said that the blooming of the rose is a "pure arising-on-its-own" (*PR* 57), Marion names this arising of the phenomenon "anamorphosis" to emphasize that the giving of the phenomenon occurs without any subject limiting it through calculative conditions. Instead, the phenomenon assumes its own form as it rises into visibility (*BG* 131). Through anamorphosis, then, a given phenomenon arising of its own accord "modifies my field (of vision, of knowledge, of life)" (*BG* 125). As an anamorphosis, a phenomenon is an event that inter-rupts the status quo by arising unexpectedly through the causality of rupture. Through this explanation, the terms *givenness*, *phenomenality*, *eventiality*, and *the event* become homologous for Marion across his writings.[20] So the term *event* names the apparition of a phenomenon that requires not "seeing what [the given] is, but of seeing it coming up into visibility" (*BG* 48). Accordingly, I argue that the death of the other can be understood as an event following Marion's phenomenological approach through this reduction to givenness. In following him further with his phenomenology of givenness, I show how the eventiality of the death of the other can be understood as a saturated phenomenon even if Marion himself does not, for reasons explained below, take his description in that direction.

Marion deepens his phenomenology of givenness by showing that this event of givenness in and along each phenomenon arises according to degrees or different modalities.[21] All phenomena may give themselves, but "all does not give itself in the same way" (*BG* 178). Drawing from an important distinction grounded in Kant's *Critique of Pure Reason* and Husserl's phenomenology, these degrees of givenness concern the relation among the *intuition* or givenness of a phenomenon and the *concepts* of the subject who intends and seeks to understand this intuition. These modalities of givenness engender Marion's classification of phenomena into three kinds: poor phenomena, common phenomena, and saturated phenomena. While these three degrees of givenness or eventiality are distinguishable by the amount and intensity of their intuition, these degrees of givenness are really a determination of whether or not the subject engaging them allows the phenomena to give themselves fully. The distinction in these degrees, it seems, has a hermeneutical dimension. Accordingly, following his idea of the banality of saturation, all phenomena can be understood as saturated phenomena when understanding their givenness, but their being poor or common phenomena is a result of a relation to this givenness through the confines of calculative rationality that aims to fit phenomena into the principle of sufficient reason. Phenomena become poor or common, then, when a description or use of them submits them to the confines of conceptual, calculative thinking. Poor phenomena are those phenomena regarded by the subject as not needing much more for their intuitional givenness than the concept that the subject has for the phenomenon. These could be, says Marion, the phenomena of mathematics and logic (*BG* 222). They have "no accomplished phenomenality" (*BG* 222) insofar as if we know that a triangle is a three-sided figure whose interior angles add up to one hundred eighty degrees, then we have all the intuition needed to calculate, literally, a triangle. The phenomenon gets contained in the confines of its concept. Common phenomena could be the *objects* of physics, the natural sciences, and especially technology. These phenomena would then have their "givenness . . . cut to the size of objectification" by the subject (*BG* 223). With each, the subject calculates the intuition of the phenomenon according to the concept of objectivity to secure "the concept's mastery" (*BG* 223) over the meaning of the phenomenon. This assures that the concept remains sovereign over the phenomenon's intuition with the result that the intuitional givenness confirms the subject's conceptualized intention "without any surprise" (*BG* 224), im-possibility, or secrecy. Poor phenomena and common phenomena are phenomena, then, whose intuitional givenness is captured interpretively by the calculative rationality of the subject by submitting the phenomena in one way or another to the first tonality of the principle of sufficient reason.

In contrast to poor and common phenomena, saturated phenomena would be phenomena whose givenness is not confined by conceptual thinking. Saturated phenomena are phenomena considered in their givenness as events whose occurring is without why. Consequently, the intuition of these phenomena subverts any intentional engagement by the inquiring mind leaving these phenomena "absolutely unconditioned" or without horizon (*BG* 225, 189). The satur*ated* phenomenon, saturated with intuition, becomes satur*ating* because it gives more than can be received by intentionality (cf. *BG* 362n37). Marion elaborates on this mode of givenness that belongs to every phenomenon by inverting the function, power, and scope of the categories of understanding from Kant's *Critique of Pure Reason*.[22] Whereas a phenomenon for Kant must be conceptually determined according to the understanding's concepts of quantity, quality, relation, and modality, the intuitional givenness of saturated phenomena exceeds each of these conceptual calculations. By exceeding these concepts of the understanding, a saturated phenomenon's givenness can be described through four ideas — invis*a*ble, unbearable, absolute, and irregardable — each of which point to the incalculability of such phenomena in their givenness as events par excellence. As he argues throughout his essay, "The Banality of Saturation," phenomena become poor or common in their givenness when we presuppose that experience is univocally the experience of objects whose meaning is calculated and constituted by subjectivity rather than by the givenness of the phenomena themselves. He writes, "[T]he majority of phenomena that appear at first glance to be poor in intuition could be described not only as objects but also as phenomena that intuition saturates and therefore exceed any univocal concept" (*VR* 126). Accordingly, any phenomenon when allowed to give itself fully can, then, be a saturated phenomenon. I unpack each of these aspects of Marion's understanding of saturated phenomena by showing how the death of the other can be understood as one such phenomenon. In this, I maintain that the death of the other can be understood, like Silesius's rose, as occurring without why. To show this, I align the death of the other with the features of a saturated phenomenon.

First, saturated phenomena are "invis*a*ble" or "cannot be aimed at" according to the category of quantity (*BG* 199). In Kant's Axioms of Intuition, he shows that the mind uses the category of quantity to determine the extensive magnitude of all phenomena by organizing all phenomena through finite parts so that we can understand finite part by finite part a particular object of experience. Yet the excess of intuitional givenness in a saturated phenomenon cannot "be divided nor adequately put together again by virtue of a finite magnitude homogenous with finite parts" (*BG* 200). The extensive magnitude of a saturated phenomenon cannot be calculated according to its finite parts. A saturated phenomenon's modality of givenness gives more than the mind can aim at successively, which is to say that such givenness is quantitatively incalculable. Marion explains this saturation of the category of quantity in terms of the desire to find the cause or causes of such a phenomenon. He does not deny that a saturated phenomenon can, and likely does, have causes and antecedents. Such an event can be explicable and calculable in terms of *how* it happened. Yet the arising or arrival of an event, namely *that* it has happened or is happening, exceeds any such explanatory and calculative antecedents and precedents to the extent that the response to an event is, "'I've never seen [heard of, imagined, fathomed, etc.] such a thing'" (*BG* 172).

For example, when discussing world-historical phenomena as saturated phenomena, no amount of causal explanation can explain their happening. This does not mean, however, that such an event is without any causes. Rather, the happening of an event has a multiplicity of causes none nor all of which exhaust the significance of the event because "the information — here concerning what triggered World War I — is overabundant" (*BG* 167). An event can accept *many* causes. But this overabundance "forbids assigning it a [distinctive, sufficient] cause, and even forbids understanding it through a combination of causes" (*BG* 168). Such a phenomenon "cannot be accorded a unique cause or an exhaustive explanation, but demand[s] an indefinite number of them" (*IE* 36). This indefinite number of causes and explanations can come from historical and aesthetic disciplines. Yet an event remains ever inexplicable and incalculable. As Elie Wiesel has said about the Holocaust, "In spite of all the movies, plays, and novels about the Holocaust, it remains a mystery, the most terrifying of all times."[23] He says, elsewhere, "Auschwitz cannot be explained nor can it be visualized. Whether culmination or aberration of history, the Holocaust transcends history."[24] An event exceeds any assigning of causes because its givenness saturates any measure with which reason tries to calculate. Consequently, an event "saturates the [Kantian] category of quantity" (*BG* 228) because the occurring or the fact that an event has occurred exceeds any piecemeal explanation of *how* it occurred. Thus, the happening or occurrence of this singular, unrepeatable event that surprises us strikes us as an impossibility "with regard to the system of anteriorly indexed causes" (*IE* 37).

This invisability according to quantity with regard to the death of the other can be seen insofar as such death is much more than just the one moment when the other shifts from living to dead. Considering the death of the other as just this moment seeks to confine death to one finite part in order to make this death calculable. While, of course, including this moment, the occurring of the death of the other includes many other important moments after it. For example, every time the other gets remembered after her death becomes a further moment of the death of the other. The actions of going through the other's things in her absence and selling or keeping these things become a further moment of the death of the other. Surprising moments when a survivor thinks they see or hear or even smell the other now that he is gone become further moments of the death of the other. And such experiences are myriad if not infinite over the time following the other's death. So the death of the other considered in its givenness saturates according to this category of quantity because its occurring resists being confined to a finite moment.

Second, saturated phenomena are unbearable according to their quality. This concerns the *intensive* magnitude or intensity of a saturated phenomenon's intuitional givenness. In Kant's Anticipations of Perception, the intensive quality of intuition or intensity of givenness is what allows the mind to *anticipate* a phenomenon by limiting it to a predetermined intensity regarding what the mind *expects* to experience when encountering it. As a result, Marion maintains that Kant considers all phenomena as poor in intuition when assessing their intensive quality as what can be anticipated. A saturated phenomenon, however, has "an intensive magnitude without measure, or common measure, such that . . . the intensity of the real intuition passes beyond all the conceptual anticipations of perception. Before this excess, not only can perception no longer anticipate what it will receive from intuition; it also can no longer bear its most elevated degrees" (*BG* 203). So a saturated phenomenon's incalculable intensity of its intuitional givenness means that its occurring is *unexpected*. The death of the other understood as a saturated phenomenon in terms of its intuitional quality would appear, as described in chapter 1, according to the symptom of the unexpected and the im-possible insofar as it follows a causality of rupture.

Third, saturated phenomena are absolute or evade any analogy of experience according to the category of relation. Kant's Analogies of Experience are used to anticipate experiences in terms of substances and their accidents, causes and their effects, and commonality among substances. However, as absolute, saturated phenomena disrupt experience by not being assigned to a substance with accidents, a cause with effects, or a commonality that would relativize the uniqueness of each phenomenon (see *BG* 207). This means that saturated phenomena lack any analogy with an *object* of experience (*BG* 209). Consequently, each phenomenon remains "absolutely individualized, arrives only . . . once and for all . . . without sufficient antecedents" (*BG* 171; cf. *IE* 33). An encounter with a saturated phenomenon is, then, each time unique. Moreover, this uniqueness comes from each phenomenon's saturation of many horizons of expectation. In order to begin even describing the givenness of the phenomenon, an infinite number of horizons is required (see *BG* 210), and yet even with all of these horizons, the phenomenon remains unexpected and surprising. Thus, similar to its saturation of the category of quantity, a saturated phenomenon is without a definite cause or happens on account of innumerable causes, none of which can be identified as its *sufficient* cause.

Regarding a saturated phenomenon's relation to its cause or causes, the search for such causes comes not on account of the phenomenon itself or the givenness of the phenomenon but on account of an attempt to understand it metaphysically through the first tonality of the principle of sufficient reason. Marion insists that in terms of its givenness, an event arrives unexpectedly in its facticity as an effect (see *BG* 164–65). This arising of the phenomenon as its incidence is without cause, then, because as an arrival that has already happened, its causes are unimportant and not integral to its own arising as a given phenomenon. Causal inquiry as the search for the cause of this phenomenon is *after the fact of the phenomenon* and not part of the phenomenon's phenomenality or rising into visibility. For example, wars are "discovered once the fact of their effect has been accomplished" (*IE* 36). Even the pleasure from eating a piece of food invades our senses without any suggestion as to its cause (*BG* 169). Once the other has died and the effects of this death affect us, we then ask the question, "Well, how did she die?" For Marion, this search for a cause belongs to metaphysical reflection on the occurring of the event of a phenomenon. As Heidegger says regarding Silesius's rose, the question of *why* is after the happening of the blooming that occurs because it occurs. The blooming of the rose "does not need reasons rendered in which its blooming is grounded" (*PR* 37). Phenomenologically, then, an event "precedes" its cause(s) to such an extent that the search for a cause becomes an "effect of the effect" (*BG* 165).

The cause comes as a supposition after the effect in an effort to *understand* the event and make it calculable. Causally calculating an event arises out of our own subjective need or desire "to make the unfamiliar familiar . . . and thereby increasing our sense of control."[25] The search for a cause comes from the need for everything to have a reason. After all, reason tells us, "*Nothing* is *without* reason" in the first tonality of the principle of reason. Thus, insists Marion, attempts to calculate an event through causal thinking are misguided phenomenologically. The eventiality of saturated phenomena overcome this desire of reason or this measure of the understanding for everything to have a reason. The phenomenon considered phenomenologically as an event, then, remains incalculable and without reason. Consequently, causal inquiry occurs *after the fact*, after the effect, and not as part of the arising and arrival of this event itself. In this way, a saturated phenomenon's modality of givenness gives itself absolutely or without horizon according to the quality of relation.

Using this account with regard to the death of the other, in addition to the unexpectedness of the causality of rupture through which the death of the other disrupts what is expected, the uniqueness of each death of the other concerns not necessarily and not usually what caused the other's death. After all, more than one person dies of cancer and even the same type of cancer. Rather, the uniqueness of the death of the other results from the specific occurring of each death as this is understood in terms of the specific aftermath that each death brings with it for those survivors of the other. This would concern not the general statement of the death of the other's causality of rupture, as I outline it in chapter 1, but the specifics of the effects of this rupture with each death. An event befalls each person specifically.[26] And while the causality of rupture means that the death of the other is, in general unexpected, the specifics of each rupture with each death are certainly unexpected until their occurring is underway. Moreover, considering that multiple people usually become the survivors of a death of the other, even considering each person's unique expectation and experience of this death, these multiple horizons of experience do not comprehend this death of the other. The multiple horizons do not comprehend it but continue to add a richness to the experience even when such richness concerns death.

Fourth, saturated phenomena are irregardable in terms of their modality. A saturated phenomenon can be received on its own terms because of its excess of intuitional givenness, but it is not gazed at, guarded by an *ego*, or, which is the same thing, transformed into an object by the sovereign subject's calculation. Modalities for Kant, in the Postulates of Empirical Thinking, concern the fundamental relation of phenomena and their agreement with the "transcendental I" (*BG* 212) that determines their possibility to be and to be known. Modalities make phenomena calculable. Yet a saturated phenomenon "annuls all effort at constitution," does not "'agree with' or 'correspond to' the power of knowing of the I" (*BG* 213). Therefore, a saturated phenomenon "cannot be looked at, regarded" (*BG* 214). As irregardable, the *ego* or "eye without gaze" sees "the superabundance of intuitive givenness" but not clearly or precisely (*BG* 215).

So the subject experiences the saturated phenomenon, but experiences it as a counterexperience that is incalculable because the subject cannot constitute it through calculation. This "counter-experience of a nonobject" (*BG* 215), then, is an experience of the phenomenon that occurs according to the symptom of the secret because it exceeds not just the calculating confines of the *ego* but, in this, exceeds calculation entirely. The saturated phenomenon is, then, noncalculable or without why.

According to this saturation of the category of modality, the death of the other can be understood as im-possible once more insofar as the occurring of the death of the other determines the conditions of its own possibility. For when the other dies, the actual way that she died may be unexpected, but the aftermath of this death is always already unexpected or incalculable. This is, once again, why people often respond to the death of someone with, "I just cannot believe that he is gone." Such statements are even made years after a person has died, suggesting that even if a survivor knows how the other has died or from what she has died, *that* she has died or the fact of her dying, the *while* of the death, continues to be without why. Consequently, as invisable, unbearable, absolute, and irregardable in their givenness, saturated phenomena like the death of the other are incalculable and, as Silesius's rose, stick to the while and ask not why.

While I have shown how Marion's description of saturated phenomena can be useful for understanding the death of the other as such an event, Marion resists understanding such death in this way. So in order to conclude how the death of the other can be understood as incalculable and without reason with regard to the second symptom of an event as secretive, I address why Marion does not engage the death of the other but, instead, turns toward birth.

Events, Birth, and Possibility

Marion's preferred example to illustrate the saturated phenomenon understood as an event is birth. In this, Marion follows in a tradition going back, at least, to Arendt's notion of natality, but this tradition may even go further back to Augustine's *Confessions* and *City of God*, considering that Arendt begins developing her notion of natality in her dissertation on Augustine's *Confessions*. For Marion, unlike Arendt and Augustine, birth is how he articulates the importance of givenness in general because givenness is the way phenomena give themselves to us at the birth of their arising. Birth "implements the eventiality that supports and sets off every phenomenon as an event that passes (of) itself" (*NC* 193; translation modified). Birth exposes the eventiality of all phenomena, thereby making birth the event par excellence for Marion. Similar to Marion, Romano prioritizes birth as the event par excellence because this "original event"[27] inaugurates any other events or makes possible the possibility for other events in someone's life insofar as birth is "the opening of possibility in general."[28]

Beyond this connection of birth and givenness, Marion uses personal birth to counter the Heideggerian preference of personal *death* so that birth, not death, is seen as existentially and phenomenologically most important. Following Heidegger's description of being-toward-death in *Being and Time*, Marion says that death for Heidegger gives itself as the "'possibility of impossibility'" (*BG* 56).[29] As such a possibility, personal death "fixes the event of an ultimate impossibility" (*BG* 57), namely, an ultimate impossibility that Heidegger describes as the absence of any projection toward future possibilities, that is, the absence of what Heidegger calls existence (*Existenz*). Marion calls this ultimate impossibility "the experience of finitude as an unsurpassable existential determination" (*BG* 58). Personal death as the possibility of this impossibility is given insofar as it gives me to myself as "the possibility par excellence" (*BG* 57) of projecting toward future possibilities. I am exposed to my own intentional projections on account of the givenness of death. Yet Marion remains critical of this focus on personal death because, he says, in Epicurean fashion, "[I]f death passes in me . . . as I die with it, I can never see the event in it" (*IE* 40). For what is given in death "we do not know" until we have received "the gift of death" (*IE* 40), which means that we are unable to know what happens in death until we die, but then we are dead. We remain ignorant, in this way, of what happens in death. And this ignorance marks the excess of the event of personal death over our intentionality, thereby making personal death "inaccessible" (*BG* 40). Consequently, I cannot receive my own death to effect an existential impact on me in the way that my own birth can, according to Marion.

Marion understands birth to be given as an event insofar as it is without cause, unrepeatable, excessive, and possibilizing. Personal birth, then, occurs as an event. Undoubtedly, my biological birth is a this time, once and for all. While I could point to the cause for how I was born, namely the sexual act of my parents, Marion's point is that birth as an event exceeds any such determination of a cause because personal birth, though "always past," is "never surpassed" (*IE* 42). We continually aim at it "intentionally" by "wanting to know who and from where I am, undertaking research into my identity" (*IE* 42). Our life is "solely occupied . . . with reconstituting [our birth], attributing to it a meaning and responding to its silent appeal" (*IE* 42). So personal birth overcomes our attempts to understand and come to terms with it because it exceeds all such attempts by opening innumerable possibilities to the self. Marion explains that personal birth "renders possible an indefinite, indescribable, and unforeseeable series of original impressions to come. . . . In this way, birth opens the course of life to innumerable temporal intuitions, for which I will seek without end . . . meanings" (*IE* 43–44). The intuitional givenness of my own birth as I repeatedly return to it exceeds my intentional engagements with it. Thus, my origin at my birth remains "originally inaccessible . . . because the first phenomenon already saturates all intention with intuitions" (*IE* 44). In this way, personal birth opens many possibilities to us as we continually reconfront this event.[30] Personal birth gives more than we can measure or calculate with our reason.

Moreover, quite simply, personal birth happens, accomplishes itself, imposes itself on us as a fact "without and before me ... without my knowing or foreseeing anything" (*BG* 289). So we repeatedly come back to personal birth in order to come to know ourselves more and more. And yet this search is interminable because "I cannot ... see this irrefutable phenomenon directly" (*IE* 42). Personal birth gives itself as an event but never shows itself *directly*. We never see our own birth there in its incidence because our birth is simultaneously our own incidence. Personal birth "happens as an event *par excellence* ... from the fact that it gives me to myself" (*IE* 43). Marion's analysis implies that we must rely on eyewitnesses, birth certificates, photographs, and videos in order for this event to show itself *indirectly*.

But what about the death of the other? When Marion addresses this question, he maintains that the death of the other "appears in that it happens" (*IE* 39). The death of the other does show itself insofar as it happens before us. And yet "the passage ... from the state of being alive to the state of being a cadaver" does not show itself (*IE* 39). The death of the other is *merely* "the instant of a passage. ... The death of the other person only shows itself in a flash and only gives itself in being withdrawn — withdrawing from us the living other" (*IE* 40). This instant in which the death of the other happens, thus, remains inaccessible or, as I described in chapter 1, without horizon, because it exceeds us. In a way, then, Marion agrees with Heidegger when Heidegger says regarding the death of others, "We do not experience the dying of others in a genuine sense; we are at best always just 'near by'" (*BT* 230). What we know is that our loved one had been living and is now dead. But the instant that marks the passage of this movement is unknown. So death, according to Marion, whether as personal death or as the death of the other, may give itself as an event, but it remains too inaccessible to show itself if even indirectly through memories, hearsay, and photos.

Now this analysis of the death of the other from Marion and Heidegger should give us pause even in these preliminary moments of my description of the death of the other. For both Marion and Heidegger argue that the death of the other does not disclose anything to those who survive it. And while showing fully why such an account of the death of the other remains inadequate is my focus in this book, I must pose some questions to their analyses of the death of the other that I will answer in the coming pages. For why would the death of the other be reducible to this instant of transformation from living other to cadaver that remains inaccessible to those who survive the other? Of course, this instant of the death of the other is important, as discussed in chapter 1 and further in part 3, because this instant is part of the causality of rupture of this death through which it retemporalizes time for the survivors after this death. Moreover, as I argued above and further in part 2, the death of the other extends beyond merely this finite moment because through this moment a new understanding occurs regarding the meaningfulness of things in the world for the survivors of it. After all, the death of the other strikes a survivor most vividly when returning to those places that mean the most to her on account of the moments she had shared there with the one who is now dead. Moreover, how often do we hear of a person or family moving houses after a husband, wife, partner, or child dies? Why would this be such a common occurrence if the death of the other is, as Marion claims, reducible to this moment when the other becomes a cadaver? Wolterstorff's loss of his son seems to attest that the death of the other is more than just this fleeting moment when he writes, "What does it mean, Eric dead, removed from our presence, covered with earth, inert? Or is such shattering of love beyond meaning for us, the *breaking of meaning*?"[31] In the aftermath of this death of the other, meaning itself, the meaning of the world, is broken. So we may be able to say that the death of the other also repossibilizes the world. While Marion misses this point in his discussions of birth and the death of the other, Romano perceptively notes that the death of the other happens as an event insofar as the world understood as a "*universum* of possibilities" gets "redrawn" by the happening of the death of the other.[32] While birth remains the original event for Romano, as with Marion, this opening of further possibilities for Romano is an opening to understand the death of the other, unlike Marion, as an event insofar as this death marks a transformation of the meaning of the world, thereby signaling "the advent of a new world,"[33] for those to whom this event befalls.

Moreover, while we may never gain access to that instant of passage that occurs between life and cadaver for the other, this instant of passage is no more inaccessible than the instant of passage that occurs at *our own* birth or even the birth of the other. For all three events remain accessible only through memory, hearsay, certificates, and technological archives. And all three events are happenings to which we return repeatedly in an effort to glean something from them. In this reception of the death of the other, *pace* Marion, we experience the final symptom of an event in the way it transforms the world through the arising of new possibilities from it.

Chapter Three

The Transformative Event

> It [the event] does not happen in a world — it is, on the contrary, as if a new world opens up through its happening.
>
> — Françoise Dastur, "Phenomenology of the Event"

In the first two chapters, I have argued that when an event occurs, the conditions for what is possible get redefined on account of the im-possibility and secretivity of the event because an event conditions its own possibility through which it challenges the principle of reason. In happening without cause or reason, the event's "essence . . . is, from a metaphysical point of view, impossible" (*BG* 172). The event "imposes itself as the very effectivity of that which our thought, until that moment, took to be impossible."[1] What is impossible according to metaphysics, is for an event its "very possibility" (*BG* 173). A metaphysical impossibility becomes a phenomenological possibility with the occurring of an event. Thus, an event can be called possibilizing on account of its potential to redefine what is possible through which "everything is articulated and organized" around it (*BG* 169). This possibilizing of an event is why many philosophers of the event agree, as Marion states it, that an event "provokes . . . the arising of a world, the world" (*BG* 170). Accordingly, an event concerns nothing less than the world itself. To draw from the examples at the end of chapter 2, then, through the blooming of the rose, the birth of a phenomenon, one's own birth, the death of Dasein, or, as I am arguing, the death of the other, the world itself is at stake. With this, the symptoms of an event are, once again, integrally connected. With the happening of an event in its im-possibility and secrecy, the world gets transformed or repossibilized.

To explain this final symptom of an event, I turn to Derrida's engagement with the poetry of Paul Celan as my guide for unpacking this transformative symptom of an event through the death of the other. I focus, particularly, on his reading of Celan's poem "Vast, Glowing Vault" at the 2003 commemoration of the one-year anniversary of Hans-Georg Gadamer's death as found in Derrida's essay "Rams: Uninterrupted Dialogue — Between Two Infinities, the Poem." With Derrida's reading as a guide, I develop three ideas to show how an event, particularly the death of the other, is transformative of the world. These three ideas are what I call poetic attestation, a death of the world, and the responsibility of worklessly mourning the other. I argue that an *ethos* or comportment[2] of poetic attestation provides access to an event's potential to be transformative, namely, the transformation of the world with the death of the other, through the loss of being that occurs when the other dies. Such loss is an absence not only of the person but also of the world as a whole. And, in this loss, the event carries with it an originary call of responsibility for remembering and commemorating the other — a responsibility that, much like Levinas argues, precedes the responsibility we have to ourselves as individuals.[3] I articulate this responsibility as a disclosure of the survivor's ethical possibilities-to-be after the death of the other in what I call workless mourning. Through this, I argue that the death of the other involves a death of the world but also a possible birth of the world because in the presence of the other's absence or the absence of the other's presence with death, a new world can come to be with the loss of the world insofar as the survivor of the other chooses to carry or bear this world into the future.

Poetic Attestation, Event, and Death

Poetry plays an important role when discussing events because it uniquely allows a glimpse into the givenness or arising into visibility of a phenomenon. This occurs through poetic attestation. To illustrate this, I turn to Derrida's understanding of poetry, particularly the poetry of Celan, to show how Celan's poetry attests to the eventiality of the death of the other as a transformation of the world. I argue that Derrida's reading of Celan's poem "Vast Glowing Vault" reveals this poetic attestation to the death of the other as a transformative event through the ontological and ethical implications of this event. And I maintain that these implications must be understood as a rejoinder to Heidegger's engagement with death in *Being and Time*.

This poetic attestation to the event of the death of the other follows what Derrida has called the performative, rather than constative, form of speech. I maintain that his reading of Celan's poetry as such a performative speech allows us to see the particular structure of the arrival of the death of the other understood as im-possible, unexpected, nonrepeatable, singular, and secretive, which, as I have discussed, are the symptoms that will have befallen us with an event. Only a performative saying of this event for Derrida grants access to its happening, because such a speech does not attempt to disseminate knowledge about the event, as would a constative saying of the event, which misapprehends the event as a general, repeatable occurrence. Rather, a performative saying consists "in making the event . . . happen" through speech (DE 91). Poetic attestation is a way to approach an event, allowing it to rise into visibility of its own accord by allowing an event, to borrow from Heidegger and Goethe, to stick to the while and ask not why. For this speech is cut for granting access to the limit or im-possibility of the event, thereby granting access to its possibility, because as "a speech on the unique, on the instance, on the exception," this speech "agrees with this value of eventiality" (DE 106). Such speech lets the im-possible appear as a surprise and secretively by presenting the event before us without constatively saying anything about it that attempts to explain its *why*. Poetic attestation is presentation that the event is occurring without trying to causally explain why it is occurring or has occurred.

Poetry, says Derrida, is "the only place propitious to the experience of language, that is to say, of an idiom that forever defies translation and, therefore, demands translation" (*SQ* 137). As with language itself for Derrida, the poem is transcendent not because of the failure of a finite discourse to say enough about the poem's overabundance of meaning. Rather, in poetry the transcendence of language gets experienced for what it is: a groundless, originless field of infinite substitutions that defies any interpretation but engenders many. Derrida maintains, in this regard, that the poem "remains an abandoned trace. . . . It wanders . . . from one referent to another . . . destinally abandoned, cut off from its origin" (*SQ* 146). And in its wandering — in and on its abandoned traces — the poem provides access to that which appears as im-possible, secretive, and transformative, namely to "repetitions of singular, unique, unrepeatable events" (*SQ* 146). As such, poetic attestation performs itself as a password or a *shibboleth* to an event. The significance of a *shibboleth* has nothing to do with the definitional, constative content of the word, but only with how it is performed. In the Jewish-Christian tradition, *shibboleth* recalls the story from their shared scriptures where the Gileadites use this word *shibboleth* as a password for distinguishing between their own people and those of their enemy, the Ephraimites. The Gileadites could pronounce the "sh-" in *shibboleth*, while the Ephraimites could say only "sibboleth." For the Gileadites, the significance of *shibboleth* has nothing to do with the definitional, constative content of the word, but only with how it is performed. The significance of *shibboleth* lies solely in its sound. The sound of the "sh-" in *shibboleth* becomes the safe keeping of the Gileadites and the certain death of forty-two thousand Ephraimites (see Judges 12). For Derrida, the poem, then, is "nothing but *shibboleth*" (*SQ* 33) or a "performativity" (*SQ* 47) that grants access to the event by showing "that there is something not shown, that there is ciphered singularity: irreducible to any concept, to any knowledge" (*SQ* 33). The poem presents *that* there is an event, it presents the event, points to it, but seeks not to confine the event in calculative rationality. The poem lets the event rise into visibility without why.

In Derrida's commemorative speech "Rams," then, the "overabundance of meaning" (*SQ* 160) in Celan's poem is the performativity granting access to the death of the other. In his reading of this poem, Derrida presents the death of the other that happens "each time singularly" (*SQ* 140) as an event. I maintain that what Celan's poem attests to in the death of the other is the interweaving of presence and absence that attends the death of the other. For, in one sense, the death of the other exposes us directly to death because in the loss of the other, her absence, an absence to which I will return, is made present. In another sense, however, death remains absent in the death of the other because the instant of death in that of the other remains inaccessible to the survivor. As Heidegger and Marion both agree, as I have discussed in chapter 2, the instant of passage from living to cadaver is an instant to which survivors of the death of the other have no access. By granting access to the absence made present when the other dies, the poem attests to the im-possibility, secrecy, and transformativity of this strange instant. Drawing on Derrida's reading of Celan's poem, I show that this relation of presence and absence in the death of the other can especially be seen through the ethical implications for the survivor in the aftermath of this death. Consequently, I maintain that Derrida's reading of Celan's "Vast Glowing Vault" leads to two implications for how the death of the other is disclosive in the poem. First, by granting access to the loss of being, the absence, when the other dies, Celan's poem shows that when the other dies we see not only this event's transformativity through the death of the world but also through the origin of the world, the source of its birth, in our relations with others. Second, this loss of being becomes a call to responsibility for those who survive. This twofold disclosivity of the death of the other takes place through Derrida's interpretation of the last line of Celan's poem:

> *Die Welt ist fort, ich muß dich tragen.*
> [The world is gone, I must carry you.][4]

He focuses on the last line of this poem because, following Gadamer, the last line is what "carries the meaning of the whole poem" (*SQ* 144).

Yet before I turn to my reading of Celan through Derrida, I want to emphasize the importance of this reading by discussing how it is a rejoinder to Heidegger's account of death in *Being and Time*.[5] As discussed briefly in chapter 2, Heidegger settles on personal death, namely the dying of Dasein, as *the* modality of death for disclosing Dasein's understanding of its own being and possibilities-to-be. Yet his chapter on this idea of being-towards-death is curious because it opens with the insight that the death *of the other* may actually be the disclosive modality of death for which he is searching. He begins this initial move toward the death of the other by rewriting the Epicurean problem from Epicurus's "Letter to Menoeceus." To paraphrase Epicurus's famous saying: while we are present, death is not, and when death is present, we are not. In other words, says Epicurus, we are not present for our death. When Heidegger begins his seminal chapter on death in division 2 of *Being and Time*, he reworks this insight from Epicurus by stripping it of its dependence on Epicurus's atomism and hedonism and situating this insight in his own existential analysis of Dasein from division 1. He opens this chapter in division 2 with his version of the Epicurean problem: "When Dasein reaches its wholeness in death, it simultaneously loses the being of the there. The transition to no-longer-Dasein lifts Dasein right out of the possibility of experiencing this transition and of understanding it as something experienced. This kind of thing is denied to each and every Dasein in relation to itself" (*BT* 229). When Dasein dies, rather than maintaining its meaning of being (*-sein*) there (*Da-*) for the disclosure of being, Dasein loses this being-there because Dasein is no longer *Da* but lost (*fort*). In death, Dasein has no there in which to be because it is no more. Moreover, on account of this no-longer-being-there, Dasein has no experience of its own death. Dasein is not present for its own death because while Dasein is, death is not, but when death is, Dasein is not. The obvious conclusion that Heidegger draws from this is that if Dasein cannot experience its own death, then the death *of the other* seems to be the modality of death that discloses Dasein's being to itself. Thus, he writes: "The death of others, then, is all the more penetrating. In this way, an end of Dasein becomes 'objectively' accessible. Dasein can attain an experience of death all the more because it is essentially being-with with others" (*BT* 229). And Heidegger proceeds momentarily with his analysis as if the death of the other will lead him to his intended goal, even going so far as to identify the death of the other as part of Dasein's own ontological structure from his existential analysis in division 1. For the now dead other is part of the being-with of taking care (*Besorge*) and concern (*Fürsorge*) of other beings in the world not only through the "funeral rites, burial, and the cult of graves" but, more importantly, through the "mourning and commemorating" that honors the dead (*BT* 229).

All of this suggests that Heidegger's own analysis could be helpful, along with Levinas and Derrida, for understanding the importance of the death of the other. Heidegger even seems to prefigure what Levinas and Derrida develop in their own approach toward the dead when he writes, "In such being-with with the dead, the deceased himself is no longer factically 'there'. . . . The deceased has abandoned our 'world' and left if behind. Nonetheless, it is in terms of this world that those remaining can still be with him" (*BT* 230). Heidegger is already wrestling with the relation among presence, absence, and world with the death of the other and doing so along the lines limned by Celan's poem: the world now lost. Heidegger goes part of the way to begin developing an "intersubjective ontology of a being with the dead."[6] However, he moves from this helpful analysis of mourning the death of the other to argue that the death of the other is not ultimately disclosive of Dasein's own being. His reasons for saying this revolve around two concepts: mineness (*Jemeinigkeit*) and existence (*Existenz*). Death is never something that can be taken from someone. Someone may sacrifice him/herself for the other and die at that moment in the other's stead, but the other saved at this moment will die at another moment.[7] Each other must die its own death. And this means that the individual's death is always characterized by mineness insofar as my own death is only ever my own to die and no one else's. As Heidegger says, "Insofar as it 'is,' death is always essentially my own" (*BT* 211). The death of the other, however, is not marked by this mineness because only the other can die his or her own death. So, according to Heidegger, personal death over the death of the other has more existential weight as a result of its *Jemeinigkeit*. Furthermore, personal death discloses how Dasein finds its essence (*Wesen*) through its existence (*Existenz*), that is, through how Dasein finds itself in its own future projects or possibilities-to-be. Heidegger writes, "And it [personal death] indeed signifies a peculiar possibility of being in which it is absolutely a matter of the being of my own Dasein" (*BT* 231). Consequently, for Heidegger, Dasein's anxiety over its *own* death reveals Dasein's own *Wesen* as something that only Dasein can determine through its possibilities-to-be. Anxiety, then, singularizes Dasein as the individual that it is and for which it is responsible. In other words, the fact of my own mortality or that I can die is what gives my own being its ultimate meaning. Or as Heidegger says elsewhere, "The *moribundus* first gives the *sum* its sense."[8] Moreover, the ethical impetus of anxiety for Heidegger is "that I alone am answerable for myself."[9] For these reasons, Heidegger says that the death of the other is nondisclosive. The death of the other, experienced in the mood of mourning, does not reveal this *Wesen* of Dasein. Instead with the death of the other, death is revealed "as a loss [*Verlust*], but as a loss experienced by those remaining behind. However, in suffering this loss, *the loss of being* [*Seinsverlust*] *as such* . . . does not become accessible. We do not experience the dying of others in a genuine sense; we are at best always just 'near by'" (*BT* 230; emphasis mine). The loss experienced in the death of the other does not, for Heidegger, reveal anything to us about who we are and our possibilities-to-be.

I maintain in the following two sections that Celan's poem guided by Derrida's reading of it must be understood in contrast to Heidegger's analysis of the death of the other in *Being and Time*. For whereas Heidegger finds the death of the other to be nondisclosive of our possibilities-to-be and the loss of being in the death of the other to be inaccessible, I argue that Celan's poetic attestation to the death of the other in the last line of "Vast, Glowing Vault" — "The world is gone, I must carry you" — provides access to this loss, which, in turn, opens us to our possibilities-to-be that arise from out of this event. Celan's last line in this poem shows that Romano is correct when he writes, "Death . . . hands over the task of interpreting it to those who survive it."[10] This line carries the meaning of the poem in two phrases. The first phrase, "The world is gone," discloses the loss of being when the other dies. The second phrase, "I must carry you," discloses our possibilities-to-be opened up by the death of the other.

Die Welt Ist Fort ...

With his reflections on this first phrase, "The world is gone," I argue that Derrida helps to show how Celan's poem grants access to the loss of being that happens in the event of the death of the other because this line shows how the death of the other is both the death *and* origin of the world. Derrida's question near the end of his text is programmatic for how I understand his interpretation of this first phrase. He asks, "Isn't it the very thought of the world that we would then have to rethink, from this *fort*" (*SQ* 163)?

He begins his reflection with an attempt to bear witness to his "melancholy" over Gadamer's death (*SQ* 135). The root of his melancholy is the hermeneutical and existential fact that all dialogue, relations, and life are marked by "a sad and invasive certainty," namely the "fatal and inflexible law: one of two friends will always see the other die" (*SQ* 139). All of life is marked by the "ultimate interruption" and "ineffaceable incision" of this inflexible law (*SQ* 139). And when this ineffaceable interruption happens, when the other dies, "each time singularly," this death "is nothing less than an end of *the* world" (*SQ* 140; emphasis his). The world is *fort*, gone, lost, departed, far off, annihilated, and dead with the death of the other (see *SQ* 149, 160). Derrida seeks to emphasize and think with Celan the strange arithmetic of this event insofar as each death is each time a singular, nonrepeatable end of the one and only world. Yet this unique death is also repeatable with each death of the other.[11] In order to trace this strange arithmetic and repetition of the death of the world with the death of the other, I want to trace Derrida's insights across the claims that he makes in his thinking of the world from this loss. For Derrida's various engagements with this line from Celan raise a number of questions regarding how exactly we are to think the world in relation to this *fort*.[12] Or more simply: what does "the world" mean for Derrida in his reading of Celan and in relation to the death of the other? Answering this question is no easy accomplishment because Derrida offers many different meanings of "the world" in his reading of Celan both in "Rams" as well as the last year of his final seminar at the École des hautes études en sciences sociales in the volume *The Beast and the Sovereign II*. Across these two texts, I see Derrida developing at least six important claims regarding the death of the other and the world in its aftermath.

The first four claims come from a dense passage in "Rams" where two meanings of the world seem to come into focus:

> Death puts an end neither to someone in the world nor to *one* world among others. Death marks each time, each time in defiance of arithmetic, the absolute end of the one and only world, of that which each opens as a one and only world, the end of the unique world, the end of the totality of what is or can be presented as the origin of the world for any unique living being, be it human or not. (*SQ* 140; emphasis his)

First, this death is not merely the death of someone in the world. This death is also the death of the world.[13] Second, this death is also not the death of one world among a plurality of worlds. This meaning of *world* understood not as *the* world but a world among a plurality of worlds is a meaning to which Derrida seems to return, as I point out in just a moment. Instead, third, this death is each time "in defiance of arithmetic" the death of "the one and only world" (*SQ* 140). Connecting this meaning of the world with his discussion in his final seminar helps clarify this third claim. For in his last seminar, he acknowledges that one way we can understand the meaning of the world is as the shared habitat of humans and other nonhuman animals (see *BS2* 8). This would be the "common world" in which humans and other nonhuman animals, as well as plants perhaps, live, suffer, and die (*BS2* 264). In "Rams," the one and only world that dies with the death of the other may just be this "common world" for two reasons. On the one hand, at the end of the passage I am closely reading from "Rams," he seems to refer again to this one world as "the totality of what is" or also what "can be presented as the origin of the world for any unique living being" (*SQ* 140). On the other hand, if this common world is such an origin of the world for any being "be it human or not" (*SQ* 140), then this one world seems to be the world that each being opens onto or exposes through its own existence. This last claim is precisely what I see Derrida saying in the fourth claim from this passage.

Fourth, this one and only world, this common world perhaps, that dies each time the other dies in defiance of arithmetic is the world "which each opens as a one and only world" (*SQ* 140). Here the world would be the unique opening that each being "be it human or not" (*SQ* 140) becomes for this one and only world. To clarify what Derrida may mean here I am going to utilize a phenomenological idea that may or may not be in the background of Derrida's own thinking of the world in relation to Celan and the death of the other at this point. This is the idea that a world is a context of meaning or the meaningful context in which we find ourselves with others and with things. Using this idea, the world in this fourth claim would mean the unique context of meaning that each being opens onto the common world. So while the *world* can mean, as in the third claim, the world shared with others, now *world* can also mean the perspective, angle, or context of meaning that each living being uniquely opens to the world shared with others. Perhaps the next words in the "Rams" passage are even Derrida's name for this world that each opens onto as a one and only world: "the unique world" (*SQ* 140). So now the world seems to mean, on the one hand, the common world but, on the other hand, the unique world understood as the opening onto this common world that each being is. If so, then, each being opens *the* world as *a* world, as his or her world. Through the various worlds or meaningful contexts in which the other finds herself, she enlarges the meaningful relations of *the* world. The ways that each person chooses to live his or her life make of the one world to which we all belong what he or she wants. By constituting each of these meaningful contexts, each person contributes to the meaningful whole of the one world. In this way, each other opens the one world as a world. So when the other dies, the death of her world marks, on account of their relation to the one world, the death of *the* world each time in defiance of arithmetic.

Obviously, the meaning of the sign "world" has become complicated and aporetic in this fourth claim, because while he wants to say, as I noted in his second claim, that what ends with the death of the other is not *one* world among a plurality of worlds, now a plurality of worlds seems to be upon us. For if each being opens the world "as a one and only world," then this passage seems to have stumbled into a plurality of worlds. Perhaps, though, the thinker of the principle of sufficient reason, Leibniz, offers a way to think this strange arithmetic of the world that each opens without leading into a plurality. For Leibniz explains similarly the relation of the various monadic points of view with the *one* universe: "Just as the same city viewed from different directions appears entirely different and, as it were, multiplied perspectively, in just the same way it happens that, because of the infinite multitude of simple substances, there are, as it were, just as many different universes, which are, nevertheless, only perspectives on a single one, corresponding to the different points of view of each monad."[14] This parallel with Leibniz does not mean that the other for Derrida is a Leibnizian monad. Far from it. For we shall soon see that the other for Derrida is anything but windowless.[15] Nonetheless, the relation between a point of view and the universe in Leibniz may be instructive in helping to see the relation of the world that dies with the other in relation to the opening that each other has uniquely offered to this one world.

Fifth, Derrida returns once again to the idea of the common world or "the community of the world" (*BS2* 8) in his final seminar when he develops the idea of the "prostheticity" of this idea of the common world (*BS2* 88), that is, the idea that *the* world is really not anything other than a prosthetic or phantasm created by us. "Perhaps," says Derrida, "there is no world" (*BS2* 266). What the death of the other would reveal about the world, in light of this claim, would be that such a death shows that no such world common among humans as well as common among other living beings ever existed. The death of the other would be the death of the world understood as this common world insofar as now this common world is shown to be merely a phantasm or fabrication. The death of the other would reveal that the world is "the name of a life insurance policy for living beings losing their world" that we fabricate through language and social convention in order to better assure "the longest survival" (*BS2* 267). Instead of having this common world between human beings as well as between humans and other nonliving animals, perhaps even plants, "there are only islands" (*BS2* 9). Without any bridge to build "between my world and any other world," what would exist would be only "an infinite difference" and a plurality of such isolated, unbridgeable islands (*BS2* 9). Perhaps, then, this idea or phantasm of a common world is precisely what dies each time the other dies. Furthermore, this idea of a common world could also be the common idea that each being, be it human or nonhuman animal, opens as its unique island. If all of this is so, then, once again, a plurality of a "solitude of worlds" (*BS2* 266) has appeared once more but this time more deliberately.

Sixth, despite this common world's prostheticity that gets revealed each time the other dies, Derrida insists that with the death of the other or with this death of the world we have two options, "one or the other," of not having any common world (*BS2* 268). On the one hand, we can affirm the phantasm of this one world as well as the solitude of the plurality of worlds and then carry the other "in the void" of not having any common world (*BS2* 268). On the other hand, and this is the option that Derrida seems more interested in developing if we consider the amount of time he spends thinking about it both implicitly in "Rams" as well as at the end of his final seminar, we can affirm the phantasm of this one world and yet "make *as if* there were just a world, and to make the world come to the world" (*BS2* 268; emphasis his). In other words, while the death of the other marks each time uniquely the death of the idea of a common world — understood phenomenologically, once again, as some kind of shared context or even contexts of meaning — this second option after their death affirms, nevertheless, a "refined utilitarian nominalism" (*BS2* 267) of the sign "world" within which the survivor of the now dead other continues to live mournfully with the other.

And so where exactly does Derrida leave us in his thinking of the world out of what is lost (*fort*) when the other dies? He leaves us in a complex terrain that may contain some inconsistencies or just *aporiai*, regarding whether or not we are left, or have just always had, a plurality of worlds as a plurality of contexts of meaning that we agree upon in various linguistic, cultural, societal, religious, political, and other contexts of meaningful constitution. This is the direction, despite Derrida's second claim above, to which I take this thinking of the world from out of the *fort* in Celan's poem. And I argue that Derrida's thinking points in this way because this direction of thinking is not only the most helpful direction for understanding what is happening when the event of the death of someone occurs but also this direction of thinking makes the most phenomenological sense in general.

For, on the one hand, the idea that *the one world* understood as this common, ordered world shared by inhabitants of earth is a phantasm is not something that only the death of the other shows us. For example, the phantasm of *the one* world understood in this sense can be seen by looking at the many divisive topics of conversation, especially those that have been occurring during the outbreak of COVID-19, across the globe regarding the importance of vaccinations and the decision to wear or not to wear a mask. That no one context of shared meaning upon which all beings involved can agree or disagree does not exist anymore, if it ever did, comes with little surprise if someone looks outside of the communities to which they belong and identify at other communities to which they do not belong, do not identify, and with which they likely disagree. Consequently, what now is prevalent across the globe are communities of likeminded people with likeminded goals through which each person and the community together tries to find its way in life. And calling these communities "worlds" makes phenomenological sense because these communities are contexts of meaning through which further meaning gets added to the places people inhabit. Heidegger's own thinking of such a plurality of worlds during his early Freiburg years is instructive for understanding how this plurality of worlds can relate (see *PRL* 8–10). For many of these contexts of meaning are embedded within one another. Accordingly, my own unique way of understanding the places I find myself can be called my self-world (*Selbstwelt*). Yet this self-world is intimately related to and affected by the many communal worlds (*Mitwelten*) to which I belong, be that my immediate family, a political group, a religious group, a group of people who gather around a common hobby, a university, a course I take or teach, and so on. Moreover, these communal worlds are embedded within even larger, expansive contexts of meaning that can be identified as the surrounding world (*Umwelt*), be this the country to which a person belongs or a religion they follow or many other things. And this relation of worlds is nonhierarchical (*PRL* 10), for each is embedded in or contains the other so that each ultimately defines and affects the others. So the idea of *the* world is certainly a phantasm. Accordingly, even if Derrida is right when he says that such worlds are linguistic, cultural constructions as various life insurance policies helping with our survival (*BS2* 8–9, 266–67), these worlds are precisely what rise into visibility in our relations with others. So that, much like Leibniz above, this plurality of unique worlds that each being, and now group, constitutes as a unique take on the shared place of inhabitance called Earth is precisely what we could now call *the* world. But *the* world would, then, just be a name for this plurality of worlds with the result that the sign "world" has a meaning that is relatively stable yet unstable on account of the many worlds teeming within it. Such is what I call the *pluralized* world.

On the other hand, drawing from Derrida, the death of the other marks each time uniquely a death of the world understood as this phantasm of the one world insofar as each death of the other serves as a reminder of the death of this phantasm. In this, I say that the death of the other is *a* death of *the* world to emphasize that each death of the other marks uniquely the death of this idea so that this idea can die many times insofar as each death of the other reminds us of this one death but in a unique way each time. Moreover, through this each time unique death of the world, I want to think further what is happening phenomenologically to the world for those who survive such a unique death of the world. In other words, I am thinking through what is happening to the survivors in the absence of this one unique world or one unique opening that the other was while living when the other dies. For this absence of this one unique world is precisely what rises into visibility with the death of the other each time uniquely. And this rising into visibility of the absence of the world understood as this opening from the other is what I am calling the transformation of the world as the final symptom of the event of the death of the other.

Therefore, this understanding of the plurality of worlds is precisely, even if Derrida does not want to think completely in this direction, the direction I take my understanding of world with him and Celan. Accordingly, every person opens the one and only world through his or her perspective on this world, and each unique perspective contributes to the being of the one world. So when the other dies not only would her presence as a lived body be lost to those who survive her but so too would be lost her worlds that she has constituted as the various meaningful contexts to which she belonged and helped constitute.[16] Beyond this, though, her death can also be understood to mean not only the end of *a* world of the other but also an end of *the* one world of which the person has a unique perspective and to which she has provided access because her death marks uniquely the death of the idea of the one world. In this way, the death of the other marks each time singularly *a* death of *the* world. So when the other has died, his or her perspective of the one world that has added to the meaning and significance of the world has now died too. Consequently, those who survive this death of the world remain in the pluralized world but now without the other who has imbued the house, the park bench, the car, the bike, the jacket, and so on with significance. Such innerworldly things whose significance or meaning came from the dead other while he lived now remain in the world without this other. Their meaning is now outside that world in some sense on account of the other no longer being a living part of the world. The dead other's absence is made present through this lack that things in the world now have on account of the death of the other. These things remain present, but their meaning remains exiled or even dies with the other.[17] And this presence makes present the other's absence because the other's absence is felt in the world through the presence of these things.

This scar or wound that the death of the other leaves on the world can be seen poignantly and pointedly in two expressions of mourning: one personal and one collective. On the personal level, Wolterstorff evidences this present absence of the death of the other in relation to the world when discussing the loss of his son:

> There's a hole in the world now. In the place where he was, there's now just nothing. A center, like no other . . . which once inhabited this earth is gone. Only a gap remains. A perspective on this world unique in this world which once moved about within this world has been rubbed out. Only a void is left. . . . A person, an irreplaceable person, is gone. Never again will anyone apprehend the world quite the way he did. . . . The world is emptier. My son is gone. Only a hole remains, a void, a gap, never to be filled.[18]

In a different context and on a quantitatively larger scale, this void or gap left and felt in the world with the death of the other is remembered and carried on a collective level every year in Israel. On Yom HaShoah, at exactly ten in the morning, two minutes of sirens commemorate the death of the six million victims of the Holocaust. And this moment of mourning is expressed by the masses: freeways crowded with slow-moving cars slowly come to a standstill, and with engines off and many drivers out of their cars, people honor the death of the others during this moment; trains come to a halt in honor of the dead; people bustling about in subway stations, schools, stores, and so on all come to a standstill to mourn the dead during these two moments. Why? Rosner comments: "Because wherever you are is where the dead can be found, and where the consequences of their losses persist. . . . When the sirens fade all the way to silence, people resume their suspended activities. Drivers climb back into their cars and trucks. Forward motion begins again. Life is restored to the appearance of normalcy, though you know . . . this *world* has been *permanently marked. Scarred.*"[19] And Celan's poem provides the occasion to explore this loss of being, this absence made present, that arrives as the event of the death of the other. The death of the other is disclosive here because it shows the absence that is made present when the other dies. Not only is the other no longer present, but her worlds as constitutive of *the* world remain absent, no longer here. The world gets transformed after this event, *après l'événement*.

Derrida's reading of Celan further pushes my thinking in this direction of the pluralized world when he says, "This poem says the world, the origin and the history of the world . . . how the world was conceived, how it is born and straightaway is no longer" (*SQ* 162). In granting access to the absence made present in the other's death, we also are granted access to the birth of the world because the presence of the other's absence in and through the loss of the world shows that the world is brought to being always as a with-world. In other words, the death of the other shows that the world has meaning only on account of our relations with others. The death of the other marks the origin of the world insofar as the idea of any world whatsoever is shown through the death of the other to be what it is on account of the meaningfulness of things constituted with and through others. For this reason, the death of the other is more than just the closure of a world. The death of the other is also an opening of the world.

Accordingly, I maintain that when Derrida says the death of the other shows us the origin of the world he means that the death of the other discloses the relational ontology of the human being that has been described by many philosophers including Heidegger, Derrida, Nancy, and Romano.[20] For example, Heidegger maintains that Dasein is always Dasein-with or being-with and that the world is, consequently, always a with-world where we explore our possibilities-to-be with others. He defines the being of Dasein as care (*Sorge*) understood as "being-ahead-of-oneself-already-in (the world) as being-together-with (innerworldy beings encountered)" (*BT* 186). In other words, Dasein is always already in a world with others with whom Dasein gives meaning to other things in this world as these things disclose themselves as tools useful for Dasein to actualize its projected possibilities-to-be.[21] Dasein is ontologically a being-with others with whom Dasein pursues its own possibilities-to-be in the future. And this being-with includes both the living and the dead even though, as we have seen, the ethical impetus in Heidegger's project focuses on the singularity of Dasein's individual responsibility arising from its own death and in separation from those with whom Dasein has its being-with. Heidegger fails, in large part, to develop the significance of the world as this with-world. Accordingly, Nancy seeks, in part, to reexamine Heidegger's existential analytic through the notion of being-with in order to explore a different fundamental ontology that unfolds from being-with as the orienting idea. To this end, Nancy writes, "[I]t needs to be made absolutely clear that Dasein . . . is not even an isolated and unique 'one,' but is instead always the one, each one, with one another" (*BSP* 26). This approach brings ontological ramifications because the "minimal ontological premise" becomes: "Being cannot *be* anything but being-with-one-another, circulating in the *with* and as the *with* of this singularly plural coexistence" (*BSP* 27 and 3; emphasis his). Only through our relations with others does being have meaning or is being meaning for Nancy. Being is always and only being-with. And this *with* also "is the measure of an origin-of-the-world as such" (*BSP* 83). In his own reworking of Heidegger's *Being and Time* in what he calls his evential hermeneutics, Romano maintains that "an original dimension of the human adventure is a constitutive relation with others" insofar as the possibilities opened by one's own birth "are entwined with another's possibilities."[22] Moreover, Romano, like Derrida, maintains that the death of the other is an event that "opens the playground of possibilities [*l'aire de jeu et de possibles*] from which our world is articulated as a shared or common world."[23] I argue that Derrida's statement regarding the death of the other showing us the origin of the world can be understood as drawing on Nancy's developments of being-with in order to show that the death of the other discloses this relational ontology to us. The trauma of this unexpected, im-possible, secretive, and transformative event of the death of the other shows to us the interdependence of the ontology of the self, other, and world.[24] The world *is* only on account of our relations with the other, with others. We are always *with* others, and our world is always a with-world, including those who are now dead.

My reading of Celan's phrase "The world is gone," guided by Derrida has, thus far, accomplished three things. First, this line from Celan grants access to the event of the death of the other by showing *that* this death is disclosive. Second, Celan's line shows *that* this death is disclosive in terms of the access that it provides to the loss of being in the presence of the other's absence who has died. And this absence made present in the death of the other includes not only the loss of the other but also *the* pluralized world with her. Third, this loss of the world that Celan grants access to is also a disclosure of *the* pluralized world as always a with-world. And this with-world has ethical implications following Derrida's continued reading of Celan. Consequently, Derrida's reflections on the second phrase, "I must carry you," extend his account of death's disclosivity by presenting the call to responsibility that arises out of the realization that the with-world itself is lost with the other or, alternatively, that the with-world for which we are responsible includes the now dead other. The world persists after a death of the world through "the responsibility that I have in relation to the other and the world itself that he or she opens up when this world comes to an end with his or her death."²⁵ This call to responsibility from out of the other's death shows that such death does disclose possibilities-to-be for us. The death of the other does disclose our *Existenz*. As Derrida draws out in his reading of Heidegger's *Fundamental Concepts of Metaphysics*, this possibility of carrying the other is a "finite force that defines existence (*Existenz*, this time)" (*BS2* 107). Consequently, for Derrida, the *sum moribundus* does not open me to my *I am* because "[b]efore I am, I carry. Before being me, I carry the other" (*SQ* 162).²⁶ Or, as Derrida says elsewhere, "I mourn therefore I am" (*P* 321). While the death of the other can be the end of the world for a parent, a sibling, a friend, and so on insofar as the survivor refuses to go on living after the death of the other, in choosing to continue living without the other, the ethical possibilities-to-be disclosed in the death of the other provide further warrant for understanding this death as a transformation of the world for the survivor.

. . . Ich Muß Dich Tragen

By following Derrida's readings of this last phrase of the last line of Celan's poem, I show that the death of the other carries a call to an originary responsibility for remembering the other through workless mourning. I see in Derrida's reading of Celan and in Celan's poem itself a call for responsibility to the other that extends beyond the living other. Accordingly, Derrida's reading of Celan becomes an extension and expansion of Levinas's ethics of the face and responsibility to the other even though this call from the other is a call not of presence but of the absent other. This expansion of Levinas can be seen by following how Derrida wants to rethink the "*fort* itself from the '*ich muß dich tragen*'" (*SQ* 163). I trace this rethinking of the lostness through the carrying in two ways. First, this absence engenders a responsibility to mourn. Second, when taking up this responsibility, we run a risk inherent to responsibility. These two lines of thinking follow the two ways that he writes Celan's last line in order to weigh the charge, accusation, price, or "verdict" of Celan's poem (*SQ* 151).

First, how the absence of the other in death engenders this responsibility to mourn can be seen in Derrida's reading of Celan's line just as it has been written: "The world is gone, I must carry you." As Derrida says, "When the world is no more . . . when the world is no longer near, when it is no longer right *here* (*da*), . . . but gone far away (*fort*), perhaps infinitely inaccessible, then I must carry you, you alone, you alone in me or on me alone" (*SQ* 158; emphasis his). He takes the loss of the world's nearness when the other dies as an opportunity to reflect on the call to responsibility to the other that this loss engenders. When the world dies with the other, I become responsible for carrying this other. And we carry the other, we practice this responsibility, by mourning the other who has died. The event of the death of the other contains an imperative — I *must* carry you — because I am the one who survives the other and the world without the other, the "world after the end of the world" (*SQ* 140). As a human being whose response to the call of the other is "irrecusable,"[27] the response to the other for a survivor or one who lives on after the death of another now includes the dead other. The death of the other expands a survivor's ethical possibilities-to-be to include the responsibility to mourn this loss and, thereby, to carry this other. The writer and activist Harmony Hazard puts this point perfectly after the death of her friend and fellow activist Brad Will: "To the world, his death becomes a brief international headline; to his friends, his death is the world."[28] His death becomes their world because now their context of meaning gains significance on account of this loss. The absence of the with-world is made present precisely as the world that is to be carried after Brad's death. In surviving the other, the survivors are responsible for remembering the other so that the world-with-him is not forgotten. These survivors must retain the memory of the world-with-him, of what the world had meant to and with him, even though this world has died with him. This carrying of the other and of the other's unique perspective or opening to the pluralized world is precisely what I think Derrida means when he says in his final seminar that in carrying the dead other "what I must do, with you and carrying you, is make it that there be precisely a world, just a world . . . or to do things so as to make as if there were just a world, and to make the world come to the world, to make as if . . . I made the world come into the world" (*BS2* 268). My responsibility in mourning the death of the other is to reconstitute the world, to fill the world with meaning, by remembering the other who has died and the world that has been lost with her. The world will have been lost with the death of the other, and in the aftermath of this, the world needs reconstitution by carrying the unique opening that this other had been onto the pluralized world.

Yet Derrida insists, with and against Freud, that in this carrying of the other in mourning, "a certain melancholy must still protest against normal mourning" (*SQ* 160). I interpret such melancholic mourning, or "half-mourning [*demi-deuil*]"[29] as Derrida sometimes calls it, through my idea of *workless* mourning.[30] This workless mourning is how a survivor can make their own grief their own when the other dies.[31] I adopt this idea of worklessness (*désouvrement*) from Nancy and Maurice Blanchot. For example, Nancy argues that if the work (*oeuvre*) of a community is its "fulfilled infinite identity" (*IC* xxxix), which the history of philosophy identifies as an essence, then a community for Nancy must be identified by what it "does not do and that it is not" (*IC* xxxix) because the community does not have such a static, universalizable essence. Therefore, community lacks a work. Hence, the title of Nancy's book on community: *The Inoperative* [désoeuvrée] *Community*. Additionally, Blanchot's surrealist literature shows the worklessness of literature insofar as "it is impossible for language to fulfill its ambition to bring the world into immediate, full presence."[32] Following these notions of worklessness, I am making four claims about mourning in calling it workless. First, I am adapting the logic of the *sans* in Derridean deconstruction, and other French thinkers such as Blanchot, to explore the idea of work *without* work in relation to mourning. Second, mourning lacks a fulfilled identity, essence, or work as Nancy has said with regard to community. Mourning is, then, a work because the survivor is doing something when she mourns. However, this work is *without* work insofar as mourning has no static essence but is a dynamic process always underway. Third, the work of workless mourning remains nonteleological insofar as the mourning process cannot be brought to any ultimate fruition. This would mean that the work of mourning remains infinite and interminable, never brought to full presence, or workless because it is interminably a back and forth between what Freudian psychoanalysis calls the successful mourning of getting over the loss and the melancholy of never recovering from the loss. In this, workless mourning becomes a *negotiation*[33] or back and forth between mourning and melancholy that is without end or without leisure. Accordingly, this worklessness is not to deny, fourth, as any survivor of the death of the other who has had to struggle through their loss can attest, that mourning *is work*. It takes time, effort, and often suffering. Yet often this work is also something that seems to overtake a survivor so that the survivor is not always the active agent of the work taking place in mourning the loss but sometimes the passive recipient of the mourning suddenly overcoming them. Moreover, a third option also occurs where the survivor is no longer agent nor passive recipient but caught up in the mourning process in what some classical languages call the middle voice between activity and passivity. In this middle-voiced space, the mourning process remains underway, something is being done, some working is going on but much more in the sense that mourning is how the survivor finds herself in her own world. This would be, to apply a Heideggerian term, her *Befindlichkeit* or moodedness in the world. Such a mood of mourning that colors a survivor's entire relation to her own world remains a kind of work but one *without* active work on their part. So mourning can be a work *without* work or simply workless.

I want to unpack these four claims about the worklessness of mourning understood as a work *without* work further by tracing the relation that Freud first sets up between the norm of mourning and the pathology of melancholy. The *work* of normal mourning, Freud explains, consists of two steps. First, the recognition that "the loved object no longer exists."[34] This loss is a recognition that "the world . . . has become poor and empty."[35] This is the moment of mourning where the absence of the loved object is made present, which indicates an emptiness and, as I have argued, a death of the pluralized world. Second, Freud says that a demand is made to withdraw "all libido . . . from its attachments to that object."[36] This second step of the work of mourning requires focused attention on each of our individual "memories and expectations in which the libido is bound to the object."[37] Through the retelling of stories about the loved object and going over the ways in which that object had been significant, the detachment is accomplished. Derrida comments, "According to Freud, mourning consists in carrying the other in the self. . . . I must carry the other and his world, the world in me: introjection, interiorization of remembrance (*Erinnerung*), and idealization" (*SQ* 160). Through this interiorization, the work of mourning is finished and "the ego becomes free and uninhibited again."[38] Melancholy, in contrast, is a pathological form of mourning on Freud's account for at least one reason. In melancholy, the mourner experiences the loss and emptiness as in normal mourning. However, instead of the world becoming poor and empty as in mourning, in melancholy *the ego itself* becomes poor and empty. Freud explains, "The patient represents his ego to us as worthless, incapable of any achievement and morally despicable."[39] With this, the work of mourning remains incomplete and pathological because the object of love is not interiorized by the ego, and the ego remains inhibited by the loss.[40] While much of Freud's theories get challenged in psychology today, the current language of psychology still seems to consider normal mourning as optimal insofar as the proper goal of mourning is "to exclude the 'other-from-self.'"[41] Moreover, while current psychology no longer uses the word "melancholy," what Freud describes under this name seems to go under the name now of "prolonged grief disorder," understood as "a pervasive grief response to a loved one, characterized by symptoms of intense emotional pain and yearning or pre-occupation with the deceased person" over a minimum of six to twelve months after the death of the person.[42] While the norm of mourning, rather than prolonged grief disorder as another way to understand a protracted, pathological mourning, is the major voice in psychology, voices can be found who adhere closer to what I am calling workless mourning in their practice of helping others manage their mourning rather than getting over it.[43]

Following these distinctions by Freud, workless mourning not only finds its meaning through the difference between normal mourning and melancholy but also through the deferral of each in its other. Workless mourning, then, is mourning brought under the dynamics of *différance*. Normal mourning can never be brought into full presence, but neither, for that matter, can melancholy. Workless mourning suggests that we never have *pure* mourning or *pure* melancholy. As Derrida says using the related terms of introjection and incorporation, "There is no successful introjection, there is no pure and simple incorporation" (*P* 321). Thus, the work of mourning as workless is nonteleological insofar as the mourning process as this negotiation between mourning and melancholy is impossible to bring to an end fully. Workless mourning is, then, our Sisyphean task.[44] And workless mourning remains such a task because of the alterity of the other who is dead. Melancholy's failure to interiorize the other in the self is precisely why Derrida says that carrying the other in me in an act of mourning must be accompanied by a certain melancholy. And he understands this melancholy not as pathological but as an ethical requirement because melancholy preserves the alterity of the other while normal mourning does not. Workless mourning is always a negotiation between normal mourning and melancholy because the other as the mark of difference and alterity par excellence is inappropriable.

The other *as* other cannot be made part of me and my ego. In his 1976 forward to Nicolas Abraham and Maria Torok's *The Wolf Man's Magic Word: A Cryptonomy*, Derrida maintains that in refusing to forget the dead other precisely as *other*, the psyche develops, adapting his idea from Abraham and Torok, a crypt. This crypt keeps the other *as* other safe from the process of normal mourning that aims to introject the other in making her merely a part of me, thereby forgetting the other in her alterity. This "cryptic enclave, between 'the dynamic unconscious' and the 'Self of introjection,' forms, inside the self, inside the general space of the self, a kind of pocket of resistance, the hard cyst of an 'artificial unconscious'" (*F* xix). This crypt allows the other to be other in me. This crypt is *where*, so to speak, I carry the other in workless mourning. The other has died, but she lives on in me *as other* through the crypt and on account of my melancholic, workless mourning that refuses to forget this other as other.[45]

In contrast, the norm of mourning, with its interiorization or introjection of the other, is "nothing other than the good conscience of amnesia. It allows us to forget that to keep the other within the self, *as oneself*, is already to *forget* the other" (*SQ* 160; emphasis his). As Derrida puts this in 1976, this process of introjecting in normal mourning "adopts [the object of love] as part of his Self" (*F* xvi). The other is no longer other with normal mourning but has been forgotten in becoming part of the ego. Such forgetting of the alterity of the other in normal mourning is twofold. First, in normal mourning we forget that before I am, I must carry the other. Normal mourning forgets that the bond or relation with others precedes individuality and that responsibility is first and foremost to these others. Normal mourning means that we forget that before *I am*, I am responsible to the other whom I must carry. Second, normal mourning forgets the structure of alterity that makes the other *other*.

Consequently, Derrida says that the responsibility to carry the other when the other dies is "a question of carrying without appropriating to oneself" (*SQ* 161). The call of responsibility when the other dies is a call to carry the other as other, that is, a call not to forget the other in her alterity. This is a carrying of "the infinite inappropriability of the other . . . its absolute transcendence in the very inside of me" (*SQ* 161). Even in our mourning the other, the other remains singular and, thereby, inappropriable. Thus, mourning must include melancholy insofar as the ego fails to interiorize and appropriate the other. The other always remains other even when mourning his death and the death of the world with him. The work of mourning must, then, always remain *workless*.[46]

Through this idea of workless mourning, I, once again, am challenging Heidegger's reading of the death of the other by questioning whether or not anxiety is the fundamental mood toward death. If the world is always a with-world and my responsibility to carry the other precedes and constitutes my own self, then my originary relation to death, that is, the fundamental mood (*Befindlichkeit*) of my being-toward-death, is through mourning and not anxiety.[47] Therefore, when "the world is gone, I must carry you," the you remains always other in his/her singularity even in the mournful carrying of this you.

I must carry the dead other, but I will always fail to carry him because he is always other, and, thereby, I am unable to make him part of me in remembering him mournfully. The process of introjection fails. And yet to carry the other as other, incorporating the other in and along myself in the crypt, the mourning cannot occur normally but must fail. The you can be carried in the crypt, on the body, much like warriors during war carry their injured and dead comrades on their body, but the you cannot be made part of the *ego* through interiorization. The *ego* cannot make the you its own even when the you has died. In this regard, the possibility-to-be that gets disclosed with the death of the other is that the responsibility to mourn must be worked through *différance* so that this mourning is different from normal mourning by its deferral through melancholy. Mourning must always be mixed with melancholy and thereby workless.

But then Derrida rereads the last phrase of Celan's poem by rewriting it inversely: "If I must carry you, then the world is gone" (*SQ* 158). Responsibility to the other, which always precedes the *cogito sum* and the *sum moribundus*, means that I assume all responsibility in carrying the other. When I carry, I assume all of the risk of responsibility. No "world can any longer support us, serve as mediation, as ground, as earth, as foundation, as alibi" (*SQ* 158).[48] In this, I am "without world (*weltlos*)" (*SQ* 140). To assume the responsibility of carrying the other when the world is lost means that we run the risk of forgetting the other as other, of mourning too well. Beyond this risk, however, we run another risk that is inherent to responsibility. All responsibility on Derrida's account involves choosing to carry one other, which is always a choice over and against our responsibility to carry different others. And we make this choice without any external justification. To carry one other means also to sacrifice another other. As Derrida reminds us in his reading of Søren Kierkegaard's reading of the binding of Isaac (Genesis 22), "every other (one) is every (bit) other; everyone else is completely or wholly other" (*GD* 69) — *tout autre est tout autre*. Consequently, the "if I must carry you" in Derrida's second reading means that I have an absolute responsibility to any modality of otherness. Each modality of otherness has the same structure as Abraham's absolute responsibility to God. Abraham's honoring his absolute responsibility to his wholly other God means that he must sacrifice his son Isaac. Likewise, writes Derrida, "I can respond to the one (or to the One), that is to say to the other, only by sacrificing to that one the other" (*GD* 71). To expand this to the context of mourning, in choosing to mourn the death of *this* other and *the* world with her, even doing so with the desired dose of melancholy, I simultaneously deal gifts of death to all those deceased others to whom I have an absolute responsibility to carry. And these gifts of death come in the form of either mourning these others too well, thereby, forgetting them, or failing altogether to mourn them. If "I must carry you," then I run the risk inherent to responsibility: to choose to carry is also to choose to sacrifice. If "I must carry you," I must do so without ground or alibi for my responsibility outside of my own choosing to carry this other over anyone else.[49]

Yet I want to sharpen this discussion of the risk in responsibility with regard to mourning. For when considering a few different kinds of deaths of the other based *not* on who or what dies but on the relational impact that each has on a survivor's with-world, an existential difference between these deaths develops that shows that while every other is wholly other, each other impacts a survivor's world with different intensities. With this, I am not refuting Derrida's problematization of responsibility as just discussed in his *Gift of Death*. Rather, I am attempting to sharpen its phenomenological quill. I use this existential difference to show why a survivor can feel this responsibility to mourn others in different degrees. For if every other is wholly other, how do we account for the differences in how the death of the other affects a survivor? One death may leave me mostly unaffected while another death *solicits* me entirely. Why is this?

To begin with, recalling Romano's insight, when an event befalls someone, thereby transforming their world, this event always occurs personally to this survivor. Accordingly, the death of the other understood as an event is something that befalls a person in their particularity.[50] My description of the death of the other as event, then, focuses on the way that the death touches someone personally in order to follow the symptoms that befall the survivor to whom the event occurs. The focus on the personal event of the death of the other allows the fullest intensity of the event to come into focus from which the other lower intensities with which an event affects someone can then be understood. In addition to an event occurring personally to someone, each modality of alterity brings with it a difference that follows the impact or intensity with which each other has played in constituting the meaning or reality of a person's world. Accordingly, when an other dies, this event of their death occurs along a spectrum of intensity that follows this relational role that the other had played while alive for the now survivor. Through this personal nature of an event that follows the relational impact of each modality of the other, the existential difference for the death of the other gets determined. Consequently, the death of the other understood as an event occurs with a degree of eventiality or degree of how much a survivor experiences the death as an event depending on this *existential difference*. In short, then, this difference is the difference that each other makes for our experience on account of our relations with the other. And this existential difference affects how significantly the death of the other touches a survivor as an event.

Using this idea of existential difference, I follow Derrida in his expansion of the responsibility that we have to the other to include humans, nonhuman animals, and even God whether living *or* dead.[51] In this expansion of responsibility, "I must respect the first comer, *whoever* it be" (*BS1* 239; emphasis mine). Each modality of alterity — be it humans, nonhuman animals, or God — remains different in degree and not of kind, because if every other is wholly other, the only way to differentiate one other from another would be through a difference of degree. And the criteria for this difference concerns different intensive qualities of relationality. So this difference concerns not who or what the being *is* but the role they play or intensive quality they have in a person's being-with or with-world. Depending on how we are-with a particular other determines the difference in the degree of alterity. This difference is an existential difference.

Paying attention to the deaths of an other who is intimately close to the survivor helps us to learn what is happening, nevertheless, when *any* other dies. And this other who is intimate to the survivor can be another human, nonhuman animal, or even the God someone believes in because we constitute the meaning of our worlds through many different relations with many different others. For some people, their pets are as significant to them as another person's child. For some, God is the most important relation to have, while for others their children play this most significant role. The death of the other includes many different modalities of alterity. When an other who has played a significant role in a survivor's being-with dies, the impact of this death sheds light on what happens when any other dies, even the ones we learn about through the news and social media that have little to no *impact* on our world. Much of the time, the deaths we learn of on the other side of the globe through social media have little to no impact in terms of the survivor experiencing their eventiality behind the computer screen as a death of the world. Other times, however, the technologies of social media and global media allow a more intense impact from these events to affect people across the globe who would not have otherwise been affected by it so that such deaths rise into visibility as *events* (see *BS1* 36–39). Even these deaths of the other with whom a survivor may have little or no being-with remain a death of the world even if their impact or experience of their eventiality is less intense for one survivor over another. Each death would then be an intense event for someone, for some survivor, but this intensity of the event need not be the same for each survivor depending on the existential difference that the other had played while alive in the survivor's life. So while a death of the other may be an anonymous death[52] for me or a group of people insofar as I do not know this other who has died at all, which means that their death has little impact on me on account of the little relational impact this other has had on me and my worlds, such a death is not anonymous for everyone. And in learning about these others who have died for me anonymously can allow their death after the fact to begin having more of an impact on me and my world.

This existential difference does not absolve us from our responsibility to mourn the death of any other who is wholly other. The little to no relation to an other who has died does not mean that I am off the hook from mourning this loss. Whether I feel the loss in a significant way or not, my description of the death of the other through this existential difference is an exploration of why we do not feel this responsibility in the same way when every other dies. And yet we are still responsible to mourn the death of the other regardless of the existential difference he or she has made in our with-world. The aporetic nature of responsibility from Derrida's *Gift of Death*, then, carries over to the nature of mourning. With this, I maintain that each death of the other, be it God, humans, or other animals, is each time a death of the world and, thereby, an event. And for each, I am responsible to carry mournfully the loss that irrupts into and disrupts the world.

Derrida has sought to engage the verdict of Celan's poem by reflecting on the injunction to carry in its last line, an injunction that I have used to rethink the absence (*fort*) in death alongside Derrida. We can now see that Celan grants access to the event of the death of the other insofar as the absence made present in this event discloses a call to responsibility, an ethical possibility-to-be of mourning worklessly. And in our response to this imperative, we carry the other as other, thereby committing ourselves to the danger of ethics. Even when mourning with melancholy, even when our mourning is workless or a negotiation between mourning and melancholy, the choice to carry this other is concomitantly the choice to deal death to other others. Freud is right. We remain guilty in melancholy, but this, Derrida reminds, is the nature of responsibility: "No one in the world is innocent, not even the world itself" (*SQ* 157). The ethical impetus or call to responsibility when the event of the death of the other happens is risky business, but necessary nonetheless. And it remains necessary even if never complete, that is, even if this ethical possibility-to-be remains workless.

The World after the Death of the Other

I have shown how the poem can be a type of performative speech that grants access to how an event transforms the world without attempting to explain constatively anything about it. The poem performs the event's rising into visibility or givenness. For this reason, Derrida's reading of Celan's "Vast Glowing Vault" has been my guide to grant access to the givenness of the event of the death of the other in its own transformation of the world. Accordingly, I have argued that Celan's line — "The world is gone, I must carry you" — shows how the death of the other is disclosive not only of the absence made present when the other dies but also of the ethical impetus that attends the other's death. When a person dies, not only is *her* presence gone, but *the* pluralized world itself dies with her. On account of this absence of the other and *the* world with her, we come to see that the world *is* what it is or has the meaning that it has only through our relations with one another. Moreover, this with-world that gets disclosed when the other dies entails that the survivor has a responsibility to carry the other in workless mourning. Therefore, poetic attestation has become the *ethos* or attitude that allows a relation to the transformative, unexpected, im-possible, and secretive occurring of an event, namely the event of the death of the other, out of which our responsibility to the other gets disclosed. Insofar as the death of the other as event is a "fatal and inflexible law: one of two friends will always see the other die" (*SQ* 139), I am showing the existential side of the aftermath of this law. This existential lathe of the event of the death of the other is the focus of the next two parts of this project that aim to deepen and expand the description of the death of the other as an event that arrives im-possibly and secretively as it transforms both the spaces in which the world and the things in it come to meaning and the survivor's relation to the past, future, and present in her lived experience of time. For considering, as I have maintained in these first three chapters, that any event strikes "at its roots . . . the configuration-of-possibilities that articulates the world and that, consequently, determines its meaning,"[53] in the following chapters I articulate how exactly the death of the other as an event transforms the pluralized world for a survivor. In this, I take the reading of Celan that I have offered in this chapter further by describing more precisely what the world remains to be or how it rises into visibility anew with the occurring of the death of the other in addition to what carrying the other in this world can mean.

ns of the World

Chapter Four

Unexpected Loss and Life

The Presence of the Other's Absence

[D]eath takes from us not only some particular life within the world... but, each time, without limit, someone through whom the world, and first of all our own world, will have opened up in a both finite and infinite — mortally infinite — way.

— Jacques Derrida, *The Work of Mourning*

He had *expected* the death that caught him here by *surprise*.

— Jacques Derrida, *Aporias* (emphasis mine)

I have argued in part 1 that an event occurs *après coup* symptomatically as unexpected or im-possible, secretive, and transformative, and I began to show how the death of the other can be understood according to these three symptoms of an event. The purpose of the next two parts of this phenomenology of the death of the other is to deepen this description of how the death of the other occurs as an event insofar as it occurs unexpectedly, without reason, and as transformative of the world. Parts 2 and 3 show how the death of the other rises into visibility according to these symptoms because such death is transformative of the spatiality and temporality of the pluralized world in which we find ourselves. In particular, part 2 focuses on the death of the other appearing both as im-possible and secretive through its transformation of the spatiality of the survivors' worlds. In order to accomplish this description, a more helpful and robust understanding of spatiality as more than merely the distance between objects must be developed so that I can show how the death of the other transforms the spatiality in and through which the meaningfulness of our worlds gets constituted. I adapt this notion of spatiality from Heidegger's account of the worldliness of the world in *Being and Time*. Such spatiality is a condition of meaningful relationality among ourselves and things in the world. Spatiality is a condition of our being-with because, as covered in chapter 3, the pluralized world's meaningfulness occurs through and with other beings in the worlds in which we find ourselves. The world itself and the things in it have meaning on account of the relations of the beings and things in that world. Spatiality concerns this relational meaningfulness of things.

Consequently, I argue in part 2 that when the other dies, this spatiality through which meaning has been constituted in the world undergoes a transformation because now the meaningfulness of things, places, and the self harbor the present absence of the death of the other. This meaningfulness of the world ostensibly concerns the *presence* of such meaning in and through others so that things, places, and the self can have any meaning. However, surviving the death of the other shows that such presence always harbors absence with it as well because the other, who is now dead, had been while living integral to the constitution of the world's meaningfulness understood as its spatiality. And her absence marks such spatiality now with absence as well, namely the other's present absence in things, places, and the self. This spatial transformation of the world in surviving the death of the other unfolds, then, the physical and material aspect of mourning. Physical places and material things are constant or occasional reminders of the world that has been lost when the other dies. Consequently, mourning carries with it a physical, material, and bodily characteristic. So I turn now to describing this transformation of the world's spatiality by looking at how the death of the other is much more than just the loss of the person. The death of the other includes the exiled and lost meanings in the world that attend the loss of the other insofar as these meanings are carried in the things that once belonged to the now dead other, in the places in which she dwelled, and in the bodies of those who survive her.

Here, in this chapter, I argue specifically that the loss of meaning that attends the death of the other is always unexpected because in the aftermath of his death, the other's absence gets carried in the presence of things. And how such absence touches the survivor remains always unexpected. By extending beyond Heidegger's analysis of spatiality, I argue that the death of the other transforms the self's ability to draw out the meaningfulness of things in the world because such meaningfulness had been constituted previously both with and by the now dead other. In the absence of the other who is now dead, this constitution of the meaningfulness of things gets transformed. In this way, the death of the other transforms space. Consequently, the loss experienced in the death of the other always includes more than just the loss of the person because this loss includes the loss of the meaningfulness of things constituted by and with the now dead other. With the death of the other, the world calls for reconstitution insofar as the meaningfulness of places and things to the now dead other is exiled. Things continue to carry the meaning that they had in relation to the one who is now absent. This continuation of life in the things and places connected with the dead other surprises the survivors insofar as this continuation makes the presence of the other's absence or absence of her presence palpable in ways the survivor could not foresee. Surviving the death of the other becomes, consequently, a matter of carrying this present absence or absent presence in the world after the death of the world. Such carrying brings unexpectedly, in turn, a possible continuation of life with it. Like a Derridean gift, the death of the other may be the poison that spells the end of the survivor, or it may be the promise of a new world and more life, survival, through carrying the world after the death of the other. The death of the other occurs, then, not merely as a closing of the world but also as an opening of the world even if the world opened through the death is vastly different.[1] For the world "is a function not only of the other's nativity . . . but also of the responsibility that I have in relation to the other and the world itself that he or she opens up when this world comes to an end with his or her death."[2] With this responsibility, the death of the other never ends but continues disrupting unexpectedly the survivor's world on account of the presence of the other's absence in things and places. The death of the other sends waves throughout life affecting the meaningfulness of everything in a survivor's various worlds. The death of the other affects, unexpectedly, the meaningfulness of everything.

Spatiality in and beyond Heidegger

In order to understand how the death of the other transforms space, I need to develop a more phenomenologically rich understanding of space that delves deeper into the understanding of space as the three-dimensional place that an object occupies. Heidegger maintains that considering space three-dimensionally in terms of the location, position, or amount of space occupied by something that exists with extension is to understand space not in terms of the way that Dasein experiences it in its everyday existence but in terms of an abstract and uninvolved, that is, objective, position (*BT* 109). While Heidegger's analysis seems to pose against one another his account of space and the more scientific account of space in terms of three-dimensions, I do not see these accounts as opposed to one another as Heidegger does. Rather, the understanding of space within everyday lived experience is a further, more phenomenologically rich description of space outside of a scientific context. Furthermore, to push Heidegger's understanding beyond his own intentions, his understanding of space can also be seen as even shedding more light on even the scientific understanding of space as well. For the lived experience of the scientist *as scientist*, space is, perhaps, three-dimensional. Regardless of how this relationship between phenomenology and science is taken, I take as the starting point for this understanding of space the *everyday experience* of space in lived experience in order to see how the death of the other transforms such experience of space. For without this understanding of space, to say that the death of the other transforms the three-dimensional place that an object occupies will seem odd at best. Once we come to understand what space is within lived experience, though, to say that the death of the other transforms space will shed light on the experience of such death. In order to begin rethinking the lived experience of space, I turn to Heidegger's analysis of the worldliness of the world and the distinction between the objective presence (*Vorhandenheit*) of objects and the handiness (*Zuhandenheit*) of Dasein's tools. In this much celebrated chapter that begins the existential analytic of Dasein in Heidegger's *Being and Time*, he describes his account of space with regard to his analysis of tools or handy things (*Zuhandenes*), Dasein, and the world.

Heidegger takes as his point of departure the idea of the work-world of Dasein, that is, its surrounding world (*Umwelt*) of the toolshed or place of work. The world is understood first and foremost from out of the phenomenologically experienced contexts of meaning in which Dasein explores its own projects or possibilities-to-be with the things or tools discovered in this exploration. Heidegger's starting point is important because his understanding of the world and space begins and ends with the lived experience of Dasein. While this Dasein-centric understanding of all of these terms may be problematically humanistic or anthropocentric, his starting point is important nevertheless when expanding his analysis to include the death of the other because in such death the focus is on the human experience of surviving the death of the other. These challenges to Heidegger notwithstanding, his analysis of spatiality begins with a recalibration of the meaning of space from its historically determined meaning in the history of philosophy. Thus, his analysis moves from a traditional, Cartesian definition of space understood through the *res extensa* "enclosed by the extended boundaries of something extended" (*BT* 99) to an understanding of spatiality centered around the meaningful constitution of the world and things used in it. This is a shift from understanding space as a container of things to space understood as spatiality or the context in which things come to meaning.

The first things that come to meaning within the world for Dasein are the tools used by Dasein in reaching toward or avoiding its various possibilities-to-be. Beings encountered in the world as tools "do not simply have a place in space, objectively present [*vorhanden*] somewhere, but as useful things are essentially installed, put in their place, set up, and put in order. . . . The actual place is defined as the place of this useful thing for" accomplishing Dasein's projects (*BT* 100). Dasein provides the various ends or *teloi* — named by Heidegger the "in-order-to" and "what-for" of the tools — in larger, significant contexts of relations of these tools through which the space of these tools gets experienced.

Such a significant context or place becomes the basis through which everyday experience defines the space of things in terms of the constitution of a thing's meaning. Heidegger calls such places of significance a "region" (*BT* 100). And these regions "are assigned to what is at hand in the circumspection of taking care of things. . . . The where of their handiness is taken account of in taking care and is oriented toward other handy things" (*BT* 101). These meaningful contexts are the places or spaces where tools come to have their meaning for Dasein. These meaningful contexts constituted by Dasein's use of tools provide the basis for the everyday experience of space understood as the place of a thing in its usefulness. Heidegger says that we come to recognize this everyday understanding of the space of things in terms of their place when something is out of place or not in its place. In this, he echoes his earlier analysis in *Being and Time* regarding the ontology of the tool. Dasein becomes aware of the tool's being as handy in Dasein's own future projects only when this tool breaks down or does not work the way it is supposed to work. When a thing is out of place, likewise, we recognize that space "belongs to beings themselves as their place" (*BT* 101). For example, when the car keys are not *where* I put them or *where they are supposed to be*, this space of the keys is shown to be constitutive of the keys when they are not in use. Or, to push this analysis beyond Dasein's tools toward something closer to my project here, when a person is no longer there, lost, dead, or *fort*, the space of the person is shown to be constitutive of the other's significance as part of the world. Her space is where she comes to be who she is in relation with others and things. The space of something is, then, where a thing or a person comes to a specific meaning.

Consequently, the space of a thing is directly connected to the meaningfulness that it plays for the surrounding world (*Umwelt*) of Dasein. The worldliness of the world articulates "the relevant context of a totality of places that have been circumspectly assigned" through Dasein (*BT* 102). And this means that the space of the world is organized around how Dasein itself is *in* the world. Dasein's lived experience constitutes the space of the world and the place of things in the world. And Heidegger delineates how Dasein is *in* the world according to what he calls "de-distancing" and "directionality" (*BT* 102). Dasein's own being is organized around and as an active de-distancing of things insofar as Dasein is the being that "lets beings be encountered in nearness" (*BT* 102), that is, as the handy things that allow Dasein to accomplish its own possibilities-to-be. In this, Dasein is "essentially de-distancing" (*BT* 102). De-distancing names how space understood as the meaningful context of a thing gets constituted by Dasein through its dealings with things and others. In Heidegger's language, Dasein de-distances beings in the world through its "circumspect, heedful everydayness" (*BT* 103). To de-distance means that Dasein through its own being as being-in-the-world constitutes the place of a thing. Dasein puts things in their place, thereby giving things their meaning. And such de-distancing by Dasein is, furthermore, always "directional" because this activity occurs in regions that have already been constituted as part of Dasein's own exploration of who it is.

Consequently, Dasein's own being-in-the-world is organized spatially insofar as when Dasein makes its way through its various meaningful contexts by throwing itself at its possibilities-to-be, Dasein does so by putting things in their place via directional de-distancing. Space as spatiality is a matter of Dasein's "giving space [*Raum-geben*]" (*BT* 108) to things that puts them in their place of meaningfulness. Space as spatiality is, then, understood as a region, that is, a context in which things have been directionally de-distanced (cf. *BT* 107). In this, Dasein draws out the specific meaningfulness of things in the world through its dealings with them.

In moving beyond, or perhaps deeper within, the understanding of space as the three-dimensional location of something, Heidegger shows that spatiality is better understood in our lived experience as a condition of meaningful relationality among Dasein and the things in its worlds. Where Heidegger's analysis falls short is precisely the place where Nancy and Romano push beyond Heidegger's existential analytic of Dasein, namely with regard to a matter of being-with. For Heidegger's analysis of spatiality focuses singularly on Dasein's individual dealings in the world and not with the deeper reality that Dasein is never alone in this world but always dealing with tools *and* with others. So I expand beyond Heidegger's analysis in order to say that spatiality is not just a condition of Dasein's dealings with *tools* as Dasein seeks its own future projects. Spatiality is even more so a condition of our *being-with* insofar as we find meaning in the world through and with one another and other beings in the worlds in which we find ourselves. The world itself and the things in it have meaning on account of the relations of the things *and* others in that world. Spatiality concerns the meaningfulness of others, places, and things. And with these others, the meaningfulness of the world gets *co*-constituted or *co*-de-distanced. With these others, things and places are given space, put in place, given meaning, or directionally de-distanced. While *Being and Time* has moments of acknowledging such co-constitution, the analysis is in the end about Dasein in its singularity and less about Dasein's being-with. Considering that the de-distancing that occurs in the world is done *with* the other, when the other dies, the spatiality through which meaning has been co-constituted in the world necessarily undergoes a transformation. The social effects of mourning on survivors provides evidence of this co-de-distancing of the world in the aftermath of the death of the other because "the meaning people give to the more ordinary and everyday objects, spaces, and practices associated with daily living" become how "material culture" carries life after the death of the other.[3] The mundane, everyday objects of life can, in the aftermath of the death of the other, "symbolise our link to our dead and come to embody the feelings of care and protectiveness we feel towards them."[4] Such "materialisation"[5] of mourning that accompanies death indicates the interdependence of the meaningfulness of the world on the self as always *with* the other. The death of the other exposes the survivor to such interdependence in a relational ontology. And how the death of the other exposes this interdependence is always surprising because it occurs like waves rolling onto a beach: repeatedly and each time differently.

The Unpredictability of the Death of the Other

For those who survive the death of the other, the world is given space, put in its place, or de-distanced differently because this death transforms the meaningful contexts that have been co-constituted with the now dead other. In this transformation, the death of the other shows itself to be not merely the loss of the other but also a loss of the meaningfulness of the pluralized world on account of the being-with this other. The death of the other is, then, a death of the world. And while the person may have died suddenly, out of nowhere, or according to an expected time-frame from a medical diagnosis, for example, how the world dies with her and calls for de-distancing anew remains always unexpected. As Mark C. Taylor writes, "Even when anticipated, the end arrives unexpectedly — like a thief in the night."[6]

Such unpredictability is rather obvious in the case of tragic deaths. For example, when parents must live on after the death of their own child, they are "experiencing the *unimaginable* and *never expected* experience of being a bereaved parent."[7] As a bereaved parent, the natural flow of life has been brought to a halt: children are supposed to bury their parents — not the other way around. The natural flow of one generation to the next has unexpectedly been reversed. After the death of their twenty-one-year-old daughter, Maia, to a car accident, Lori and Brian McDermott comment that their past experiences of losing their own parents, grandparents, uncles, and cousins "provided little preparation for what [they] were now experiencing."[8] The tragic loss of their child was unexpected and surprising, and their past experiences of death could not prepare them for this singular event. Additionally, I could cite the many examples during the worldwide COVID-19 pandemic of someone speaking with a loved one on the phone one day, and the next they are dead due to complications from the virus. Though her father died from kidney infection complications, and not due to COVID-19, the mourning of Chimamanda Ngozi Adichie after the death of her father during the pandemic is instructive. She writes, "It was so fast, too fast. It was not supposed to happen like this, not like a *malicious surprise*, not during a pandemic that had shut down the world."[9] The COVID-19 pandemic heightened or highlighted the unexpectedness of death to almost unbelievable heights because of how many suddenly died. Such sudden deaths surprise us because we did not see them coming, literally, and we could not have imagined them happening and especially in the way that they happened. Sudden deaths remind us that the death of the other happens like an event in and at the time of an event: the instant.[10] Joan Didion, in her memoir about the death of her husband, John Dunne, to a widow-maker heart attack while eating dinner with her on the night of December 30, 2003, at their home in New York City, goes so far as to emphasize, "Life changes in the *instant*. The ordinary *instant*."[11]

So while tragic deaths obviously occur unexpectedly, the more planned, predicted, or *imminent* deaths of the other seem not to be unexpected but foreseen or even predicted. These deaths do not seem to be unpredictable, especially when we consider the instances of death where the other plans her own death on a particular date — as, for example, Brittany Maynard controversially did on November 1, 2014 — or when a doctor declares that a patient has a limited number of months left to live. This important difference between different ways that the other dies notwithstanding, all deaths of the other, even if imminent, remain *unpredictable*. After all, as I have discussed in chapter 2, the death of the other cannot be limited to some finite moment. The focus with the death of the other is as much about the inception of this event when the other moves from a living body to cadaver as it is about *living on* after this death, that is, *surviving* the other. Whether the loss of the other was sudden or expected, one factical element pervades all of these experiences: those who survive the death of the other must live on in the world without this other. And this experience of survival is always unexpected because we can never be prepared for how the de-distancing of the world from the loss of the meaningfulness of things in our worlds will touch us after the other is gone. While theoretically the distinction can be made between the moment the other dies and the aftermath of this moment, in our lived experience of this moment and its aftermath, they get experienced together. So the death of the other includes both the moment the other dies and its aftermath. And while the moment the other dies does not necessarily have to be unexpected, the aftermath is always already unexpected. Therefore, in this lived experience of death, the death of the other is always unexpected. In other words, how the death occurs may not be surprising, but the death of the world that remains part and parcel to the occurring of the death of the other will have touched the survivor in unpredictable ways. Didion describes this unexpectedness of survival in her memoir: "Grief turns out to be a place none of us know until we reach it. We anticipate (we know) that someone close to us could die, but we do not look beyond the few days or weeks that immediately follow such an imagined death. We misconstrue the nature of even those few days or weeks."[12] Despite our abilities to anticipate that others will have died insofar as life adheres to the inflexible law that one of two people will see the other die, the occurring and aftermath of such death ends up touching the survivor as an unexpected event. What specifically touches the survivor unexpectedly in the death of the world with the other is the presence of the other's absence in the world after the death of the other. De-distancing the world amid this present absence is, then, surprising. Didion highlights this present absence as "the unending absence that follows, the void, the very opposite of meaning, the relentless succession of moments during which we will confront the experience of meaninglessness itself."[13]

This unexpectedness is especially evident when the other's absence is given or made present when we return to those places that mean the most to us on account of the moments we have shared there with the one who is now dead. For example, when a loved one dies and the survivor visits what used to be *their* favorite restaurant, now that he or she is dead, everything seems off, uncomfortable, or strange. "It just doesn't feel the same without him/her," survivors often say in these situations. The food, though it is the same chef, ingredients, dish, and recipe, may even taste different. This alteration arises on account of the absence of the other that is made present at the restaurant. For we experience the world as a with-world as de-distanced collectively, and when a survivor returns to such co-de-distanced worlds after the death of the other, she simultaneously experiences "the situation as a member of a 'we'" while also "recognizing painfully that 'we' no longer exists in fact."[14] This place calls for another de-distancing in the absence of the other with whom it had been de-distanced. Wolterstorff, after the death of his son, describes this experience as the world looking "different now. . . . Something is over. . . . Especially in places where he and I were together this sense of something being over washes over me."[15] In this, we can understand why when a loved one dies, we often hear of the survivor moving houses after his or her husband, wife, partner, or child dies. The absence of the other is so present that it becomes deafening in the house, making the house uninhabitable. Through the silence in the home a survivor often "really feel[s] her absence — a real silence."[16] What Didion remembers most, in fact, about returning home after the death of her husband "was its silence."[17] The absence is present through the experience of a silence that says more than words. This effect of the presence of a place in connection with the dead other in which a geographical location can remind the survivor of the significance of the variously de-distanced worlds in connection with the dead other is what Didion calls the "vortex effect."[18] The presence of the other's absence in places whose significance had been de-distanced with the dead other can draw the survivor into its vortex where the survivor is bombarded by memory after memory of experiences with this other. Mourning can draw a survivor worklessly into such a black hole in which the survivor can lose herself for a time both working through her mourning yet refusing to forget or let go of the dead other.

Similarly, the presence of the other's absence surprisingly strikes the survivor when encountering meaningful things that had been de-distanced with the now dead other. Gabriel García Márquez illustrates this effect of the presence of the dead other's absence on the meaningfulness of things when he describes, in his *Love in the Time of Cholera*, Fermina Daza's return to her home after the death of her husband, Dr. Juvenal Urbino. Márquez writes, "Everything of his made her cry: his pajamas under the pillow, his slippers that had always looked to her like an invalid's, the memory of his image in the back of the mirror as he undressed while she combed her hair before bed, the odor of his skin, which was to linger on hers for a long time after his death."[19] Though fictitious, Márquez's story illustrates how the absence of the dead other bathes over the presence of the world after the other's death. And while Marion is not describing this effect of the death of the other, this bathing of the world in the other's absence recalls Marion's own words that when what we love is lacking, "[t]he one who loves sees the world only through the absence of what he loves, and this absence . . . flows back on the entire world. . . . [T]he world has not disappeared; it remains present . . . but this disappearance [of what is loved] nevertheless strikes the appearance of the world with vanity" (*GWB* 136). Marion's fitting description here is prefigured in Saint Augustine's mourning of the death of his friend Nebridius. Augustine confesses after Nebridius's death that everything on which he set his gaze "was death. My hometown became a torture to me; my father's house a strange world of unhappiness; all that I had shared with him was without him transformed into a cruel torment. My eyes looked for him everywhere, and he was not there."[20] The pluralized world, in other words, gets de-distanced differently in the aftermath of the death of the other. And such de-distancing is how a death of the world occurs or rises into visibility with the death of the other. Moreover, in this de-distancing of the world anew, the pluralized world gets reborn. This is the survival of the survivor's world. As if in response or continuation of Celan, we could say, "As it was in the beginning, is now, and ever shall be, world without end."[21] The world is still there because life continues on after the death of the other. However, the world means differently on account of the way in which the death of the other calls for a de-distancing of the world differently. Wolterstorff reflects this de-distancing anew in his own mourning: "Now he's gone, and the family has to *restructure* itself. . . . We have to live differently with each other. We have to live around the gap. Pull one [child] out, and everything changes."[22] And the gap that they live through is one in which the absence of their son is "as present as our presence, his silence as loud as our speech. Still five children, but one always gone."[23]

Moreover, the McDermotts evidence this death of the world marked by the vanity or meaninglessness of things in their own experience of the death of their daughter. They describe this death as a "shattering [of] our world" in which they have been "left behind . . . to adjust and find meaning" in "a most unwelcome new world."[24] After their loss on February 20, they awoke to "a totally upended world" that they name "the post-220 world" and "the post-220 journey."[25] But when they return to Maia's room and experience the presence of her absence through the things in her room, they recognize in this not only the end but also the birth of their world: "When we opened the door and saw all of her things arranged as if in a state of permanent suspended animation, tears fell from our eyes and our hearts filled with sorrow. The still incomprehensible reality of it all hit us again: Maia's not coming back to finish reading that book by the bed, or go to the next class on her schedule, or use her computer to send us an email, or cuddle with all those pillows."[26] Wolterstorff calls what the McDermotts recognize in the book, the computer, the pillows, and the entire room *inscape*, which I have been characterizing phenomenologically in terms of the meaning that these things have on account of their relation with one another. Such inscape is the way that the world has been de-distanced through someone; inscape is the contextualized nexus of meaning that people give things.[27] These are the "details in which the former world gleams with a sudden intensity, as though we were transported there anew."[28] With Maia's death, the meaningfulness of these things is now exiled or without a home because the one through whom they were given place is now gone. And surviving the death of the other concerns carrying this meaningfulness with us as the survivors of the other. In this carrying, survivors recognize that "[d]eath sets a thing significant"[29] because when the other has been lost do we often only then recognize that things like a book, computer, or pillows have the meaning or significance that they have on account of the relation of these things with the other who has now died.[30] Similarly, Wolterstorff recounts that his son was "a gift to us for twenty-five years. When the gift was finally snatched away, I realized how great it was."[31] Much like Heidegger's analysis shows that the meaning of the tool or the space of a thing is recognized only when the tool does not work or the thing is out of place, so too the death of the other understood as the other no longer being in his or her place shows that the pluralized world has been co-de-distanced with this other. And now this world must be co-de-distanced anew in the presence of the other's absence. Our ontological being-with others includes being-with the de-distanced things that hold meaning on account of our relations with others.

In this, the death of the other marks, once again, both the death of the pluralized world as well as the birth of this world as a *with*-world. The death of the other shows that we are not "self-contained social atoms," or windowless monads, "impermeable and invulnerable, and truly independent."[32] Rather, the other who is now dead shows herself to have been "integral" to our ability "to experience and engage with the world, to perceive things in structured ways that reflect a coherent system of projects, cares, concerns, and abilities."[33] And now that this other who had been so central is gone, so too is this coherent system with her. Thus, the meaningful context of Maia's room and all of the things in it had been de-distanced and constituted *with* Maia — it is a with-world. With Maia's death, one focal point of this de-distancing has been lost, and now her things carry the presence of her absence in their meaningfulness. Her death marks a death of this world so that when her parents experience this post-220 world, they are experiencing the presence of Maia's absence through the recess of meaning or the meaninglessness of the things in their with-world without Maia. As a result, "[t]hings in general lack the significance they once had — everything appears strange and unfamiliar."[34] To experience the death of the other, to undergo this event, is to survive a death of the world, and this survival, as we can see, extends beyond the finite moment in which the person is actually lost. And due to this extension, the death of the other, which always includes surviving it beyond its inception or the moment that the person is lost, remains always unexpected. We never know when or how the loss of the other is going to touch us as we move through the world without the other and have to begin de-distancing the world differently as a result.

Consequently, this description of the death of the other shows that this event is not merely the inaccessible instant of passage from life to death to which Heidegger and Marion reduce it because the death of the other understood as a saturated phenomenon includes living on after the other is gone. The death of the other includes the aftermath, the shock, and the mourning of the loss of the person and the loss of what the world has meant to and with that person. The death of the other includes a death of the world. After all, this loss of the world with the other is happening, for instance, in the instant that the funeral is being prepared and happening or that tours of new houses are being given. Thus, when the death of the other happens, occurs, breaks in, interrupts, or disrupts, it marks a transformation of the pluralized world. The pre-event world and the post-event world are radically different insofar as the meaning of the world, the world itself, has been lost. A "new order of [the] world" is at play when the other dies.[35] Therefore, when a husband, wife, partner, or child dies, those who survive this person often move houses because the presence of the other's absence is suffocating now that the survivor of the other must carry on with life in the house that he or she helped establish as the home, as the pluralized world for the family. For the loss that is experienced is the loss of what the world had meant to that person and what the world had meant to us, or to a group, on account of our relation with the now deceased. The being-with of the restaurant, the food, the house, and so on includes the now dead other. So when we revisit those places where he or she used to be or were meaningful on account of that person, we experience this absence. And such de-distancing clearly requires dealing with "objects and places that once evoked positive feelings" but are now "painful to encounter."[36] Dealing with such places and things is, most often, done in the de-distancing of the world after the death of the other through a literal reworking of physical space in memorials.

Presence and Absence in Memorials

One of the most powerful ways to mark the transformation of the spatiality of the world in the aftermath of death is through the construction of both personal spaces as memorials for the dead as well as national, cultural memorials. Personal memorials erect "a space" in the lives of survivors "for dead loved ones" that allows the survivors "to go on living in the everyday world."[37] Such "memorial spaces" become a "material focal point for evoking presence" amid the absence of the dead other insofar as they provide a place for repeated visitation as "an enduring symbol of the deceased person's presence."[38] Particularly, personal spaces of mourning provide a place for "carrying on without" the dead other while "at the same time maintaining them as a presence" in the survivor's everyday world.[39] The personally de-distanced space is erected in an effort to carry the presence of the other's absence or absence of her presence in the survivor's life. And through this de-distancing, the death of the other and her world is carried by the survivor while the survivor carries on with life. These personal remembrances of the other, whether in "a picture on the mantel-piece or ashes on the cabinet in the living room, or anything really,"[40] are ways that we carry the other by putting things in their place anew that, in turn, bring the other's absence into the present as a reminder. These personal remembrances constructed by various items in a survivor's life "memorialize mourning" for the survivor because these things operate as "melancholy objects"[41] through which survivors both work on their mourning and find their own mourning deferred. For these things are both a "means of holding on *and* letting go" of the memorialized other.[42] These de-distanced things constitute sites of workless mourning. The work of mourning through these personal memorials remains always workless because in them "you never let them [the dead others] properly go."[43] While these spaces of meaning are not unrealistic denials that "the other has died," they are, rather, material refusals "to let the inimitable singularity of the other be effaced from reality."[44] These personal memorials are material ways to carry the other and her world worklessly after the unexpected death of the world.

While personal memorials operate this way for a survivor or small group of survivors, national memorials operate in this way on a much larger scale for both those who are directly affected by a national tragedy as well as those who are indirectly affected. National memorials become sites for workless mourning to occur not merely on a personal level but also on a collective level so that an entire city, state, nation, or nations can work through remembering the tragedy that occurred. In this, the many deaths of the other that occurred in addition to the death of what the city, state, and entire nation had been before this tragedy can be mourned through national memorials. Thus, national memorials can be ways for the pluralized world to mourn worklessly and carry the world that has died. For example, in the aftermath of the bombing of the Alfred P. Murrah Building in Oklahoma City at 9:02 a.m. on April 19, 1995, the Oklahoma City memorial is a way for the absence of the others who died as well as the world that died with them to be collectively brought to presence. And in this collective remembering, survivors for whom this death of the world had little existential impact are brought into the presence of the absences of the 168 others who died in this bombing in 1995 so that the eventiality of this event can rise into visibility. The memorial materially carries the death of the other in the world in a twofold way. On the one hand, the memorial is a literal reworking of the earth and the three-dimensional space in which the remembered tragic event occurred. On the other hand, through this reworking of materiality, the spatiality of the world is itself de-distanced by reconstituting the meaning of the world as a reminder of what occurred on the date of the tragedy as well as a reminder of the carrying on of life and the world in its aftermath.

Furthermore, the memorial is on a large scale workless as well because it allows all survivors across the existential difference of this event both to hold on to what occurred and to let go. The cultural memorial is caught in the *différance* of both mourning and melancholy. It is caught in workless mourning. The Oklahoma City memorial is specifically caught in this dynamic in a number of powerful ways. First, to prefigure a theme that I return to in part 3, the entire memorial is a reworking of, a retracing of, or perhaps, even, a restitching together of the time of the tragedy. For the entire memorial is contained within what are called the Gates of Time. On one end of the memorial is the Gate of Time marked by the time of 9:01, which represents the time of innocence in the world before the bombing occurred while on the other end of the memorial is the Gate of Time marked by the time of 9:03, which represents the time of survival after the bombing occurred. The unspoken, absent *instant* when the bomb was detonated, 9:02 a.m., the time of the event of terrorism, is the occupied time of the survivors who enter the memorial. The entire memorial is frozen in this instant both inside and outside time when the death of the other occurred on a scale that at the time of this attack was the most deadly and devastating terrorist attack on US soil. The memorial both remembers the time of the event and reworks the time of the present, bringing the survivors back into the presence of the absence of this event. And when survivors enter this reworked space-time continuum of the memorial, they are greeted by two visually captivating features: a large reflection pool and the field of empty chairs. Both of these features are two more ways that this memorial enacts a workless mourning.

The reflection pond operates on two fronts to bring the absence of the death of the other into the present. On the one hand, the reflection pool has a dark gray, almost black bottom to it with only a few inches of water suspended, motionless, within it. The black bottom and motionless water de-distance this world as reminders of the death that occurred. On the other hand, the shallow, motionless waters with a black bottom serve to reflect the world around it: those who peer into it, the gates that stand on either end of it, the surrounding buildings, the Survivor Tree, and so on. The reflection pool reflects this de-distanced world and in so doing, the pool reflects the world upside down. The pool reminds the survivors of how the pluralized world was transformed at 9:02 a.m. on April 19, 1995, and how this world is transforming in its aftermath. In these ways, the reflection pool reflects back the workless mourning occurring in the aftermath of this tragedy. The reflection pool reminds the survivors that the absence that entered the world on that day in 1995 remains present if only through its absence.

Likewise, the field of empty chairs marks the world through their presence with the absence of those who were lost in the bombing, both adults, represented by large chairs, and children, represented by small chairs. For these chairs, though present, are always empty. They carry the absence of the others lost and the world with them. The chairs are for those killed to sit in their absence so that the survivors who experience them are reminded of this absence palpably. This presence of the other's absence is especially stunning at night because the chairs are illumined from beneath, allowing the absence of those lost to light up and shine forth amid the darkness of the memorial shrouded in night.

As survivors walk through the 9:03 gate into the time of survival back into the world after the death of the world that is remembered by the memorial, the thought cannot help but be raised silently or audibly: What then are we to do? As if in response to this question, standing outside of this 9:03 Gate of Time, standing in the time of survival, is a memorial smaller in scale and funded by the Saint Joseph's Old Cathedral just across the street. For what you find across the street facing away from the main memorial is a statue of Jesus weeping that recalls Jesus's response to the death of his own friend Lazarus (John 11:35). And while Jesus faces away from the large memorial, he faces a wall reminiscent of the Wailing Wall in Jerusalem. Yet this wall toward which the statue weeps contains 168 niches where the stones for the wall are missing. These absences bring into the present the deaths of all those who died in the bombing. So in the presence of the others' absences, the response in carrying the world after the death of the world is through tears of mourning, tears of never forgetting, tears of carrying on, that is, tears of workless mourning.

Whether in a personal memorial or large, national memorial, memorials de-distance the world anew in the aftermath of the death of the other, thereby transforming "the experience of absence . . . into one of highly personalized presence by creating spaces that [represent] focal points for continuing contact between the living and the dead."[45] These cultural memorials or "memoryscapes"[46] are especially potent places for de-distancing the world anew not only for people who are direct survivors of victims of terrorism or oppression but also for those who live in the world after events of terrorism, be this a city, state, nation, or number of nations. For these specially redesigned and reconstructed places understood as "trauma landscape[s]" are "powerful trigger[s] for traumatic associations that remain embedded" in the consciousness of survivors.[47] Memoryscapes as landscapes of trauma allow the series of survivors to de-distance the world anew insofar as these spaces serve as "interactional webs where meanings are constructed by the families of survivors"[48] but also by cities, states, and nations. In this way, memorials help to deepen "the descendant's role as *carrier* of the memories and traumas"[49] that have been affected by the event of the death of the other. Consequently, personal and national memorials as well as cemeteries become newly de-distanced spaces "set apart from the hustle and bustle and routine of daily living"[50] as reminders of the continual presence that the absence of dead others can have in life that continues with and after the death of the other.

By following the transformation of the spatiality of the world that occurs in the death of the other, I am revealing how the topic, broached by Celan in chapter 3, of carrying the other now that the pluralized world is gone with the other's death can unfold in a few different ways. A survivor carries the other by mourning this loss. A survivor carries, as well, the meaningfulness of the world to the dead other as the survivor lives on after this death. And a survivor, perhaps in a way that carries the other two notions of carrying the other with it, carries on, lives on, or survives this death of the other by de-distancing the pluralized world anew in the aftermath.[51] Such carrying on in this world after the death of the world is how mourning the dead occurs as an act of continuing to live with the dead as life carries on. What we find with the death of the other is the world transforming event of loss *and also* the pluralized world calling for reconstitution of its meaning. We find the world in our mourning in need of de-distancing. We find, in other words, that life with its business of de-distancing finds itself inescapably bound to a survival of the death of the other. After all, the *tragen* of Celan's poem means not simply to carry but specifically to carry an unborn child in hopes for her live-birth and in preparation for her arrival (*SQ* 159).[52] Thus, to carry the other and the newly de-distanced world after his death means not just to carry the memory of this other but also to carry "a promise of novelty"[53] into the future for the life after this death. Surviving the death of the other through mourning exposes us to this inescapable relation among life and death.

Chapter Five

Excess and the Death of the Other

Life/Death, Materiality, and Reason

> And you, O tree, ...
> let your fruit forever be dark
> as a token of mourning.
>
> — Ovid, *Metamorphoses*

While the previous chapter described the im-possible, unexpected, and transformative power of the death of the other as it calls for a de-distancing of the pluralized world anew so that the presence of the other's absence or absence of her presence is carried in this world as the survivor lives on after the death of the other, this chapter deepens this analysis by looking at the excessiveness of the death of the other in terms of how it directly transforms the materiality of the survivors and the earth itself. In this, such death's excessiveness comes from two interrelated sources. First, the death of the other exceeds the separation of life from death. By looking at Derrida's understanding of the relation among life and death in his lecture course *Life Death*, I argue that we see this relation of life death quite clearly in the death of the other. When the other dies, a survivor finds all around them that in order for life to be life it must be more than life, that is, it must be inherently connected with its other — death. Surviving the death of the other reveals that life is always a matter of life/death. How the death of the other exceeds the separation of life and death in this way is evidenced by the stories of those who are living on after the death of the other as well as by the research in the field of epigenetics concerning the intergenerational transference of trauma. This first source of the excessiveness of the death of the other is found, then, in the materiality of mourning and survival. Mourning carries with it a physical or bodily characteristic insofar as it brings the relationship of life and death together in a significant sense so that in mourning, we must see existence as caught up in the difference and deferral, that is, *différance*, of life and death rather than seeing existence as merely or purely life. Second, the death of the other as a saturated phenomenon, as I have argued in chapter 2, resists calculative rationality. In defying the principle of sufficient reason, to paraphrase Blanchot,[1] the death of the other ruins everything, all the while leaving everything intact. The death of the other exceeds calculative rationality as it exposes us through our survival to not just death and not just life but the relation among death in life and life in death. For in our mourning we carry in our bodies, quite literally as we shall see, the others who have died, while the earth itself carries this death in its materiality.

By exploring these two sources of the excessiveness of the death of the other, I continue to expand Heidegger's analysis of spatiality to argue that the death of the other transforms the self's ability to draw out the meaningfulness of things in the world because the survivor carries the trauma of the death in their body and even, perhaps, in their genes. Moreover, by returning to the landscapes of trauma under the guise of what are called survivor trees, we see how the death of the other is carried not just in and along the human body but that even the earth itself carries materially the death of the other.

Derrida on Life and Death, Life or Death, or Life/Death

The relation of life and death gets carefully explored by Derrida in his 1975–76 lecture course at the École normale supérieure on the themes of life and death. This course helps highlight what a survivor undergoes in the aftermath of the death of the other. He begins his entire course by remarking on the absence of the "and" in his title for the course, *Life Death*, the absence of which becomes a deconstruction of the exam program set by the university for that year's entrance exam to the philosophy program on the theme "Life and Death." This removal of the "and" was not to suggest a lack of difference between the words but, rather, to present the idea that he explores throughout: life and death are related not through opposition to one another — as may be commonly thought and suggested by our tendency to think of life *and* death or even life *or* death — but as *belonging together*. As he says, "I am neither opposing nor identifying life and death . . . I am neutralizing, as it were, both opposition and identification" (*LD* 6; cf. 219–20).[2] Instead, Derrida aims throughout his course to limn the lines of a "différ*a*nt" logic of life and death (*LD* 234), that is, an understanding of how life and death are what they are through their difference from and deferral in one another. In reading this course alongside the stories of people who are carrying their dead others and carrying on with life, I show that the lived experience of the death of the other not only gives evidence to Derrida's ideas but also indicates how such death is an event on account of its excessiveness beyond this traditional opposition of life *and* death.

Derrida's deconstruction of both life and death's opposition takes place primarily through two lines of thinking. He begins by and spends the majority of the course on deconstructing the definition of life and living in the genetic theory of the French biologist François Jacob as found primarily in Jacob's *The Logic of the Living*. Derrida couples this reading with a different yet closely related reading of Freud's pleasure principle and death drive.³ The focus of Derrida's deconstruction in both lines of thinking concerns "[t]he relation to the outside," that is, the relation of two *supposedly* opposed systems to one another. He shows that this supposed opposition is the wrong interpretation of the relation because the "relation to the outside is more complex" (*LD* 14). He maintains that the inside is always open to its supposed outside so that life exposes itself in itself to its outside of death and vice versa for death in relation to life. While showing this complexity in his readings of Jacob and Freud, Derrida drives home his deconstruction of the binary thinking of life *and* death. Life is not, on Derrida's reading, outside death nor death outside life, but life and death are exposed to one another. Each "differs from itself and defers itself in its wholly other" (*LD* 272). This is his différ*a*nt logic of lifedeath.

These themes of life and death and inside and outside as well as their relation to *différance* are not new themes for Derrida to be discussing in 1975. For these three themes figure large throughout his 1968 monumental work *Of Grammatology* in connection with the famous relation that Derrida argues for in this text between speech and writing. One way of reading this relation among speech and writing in his *Of Grammatology* would be to trace this as a relation of life and death. For Derrida repeatedly identifies the putative pure speech that metaphysics dreams and longs for as *living* speech while writing is defined by metaphysics as the *death* of such pure speech (cf. *OG* 39, 71, 141). The supplement that writing is to speech, then, "threatens with death" (*OG* 155; cf. 313, 315). And the aim for Derrida in *Of Grammatology* is not to follow metaphysics in this opposition of speech and life with writing and death but to bring life and death into relation with one another as he is bringing speech and writing into relation with one another so that writing is seen as both a principle of life and principle of death where "life (is) death" (*OG* 246; cf. *OG* 229). My reading of *Life Death* in what follows aims to show how this seminar is, in part, a rereading of *Of Grammatology* with emphasis on this bringing of life and death into relation through *différance*.⁴ What remains especially unique in his lecture course, which he only alludes to twice in *Of Grammatology*,⁵ is his explicit turn to biology in exploring these themes. Drawing on these important themes in his work at the time, then, Derrida's deconstruction in his seminar begins with unfolding Jacob's attempt to define living based on the distinction that Jacob *wants* to make between two kinds of memories in the body: mental and genetic. While mental memory plays an important, indispensable role in the living of an organism, Jacob maintains that the essence of living is to be found in the genetic code or message. Thus, genetic memory becomes the more important kind of memory for Jacob. Following Jacob's opposition between mental and genetic memory, he maintains that while the mental memory of an organism has a relation to its outside, its genetic memory has no such relation. The mental memory or mental program "has a relation to its outside and registers its effects; it is porous, susceptible to the influences of history and of the politico-economic field" (*LD* 14). So mental memory allows an organism "to learn from experience" and even "be transformed" by its experience (*LD* 18). However, the genetic memory or program "is completely closed off to all of this" (*LD* 14) with the result that "the genetic program forms a closed, deaf system, *purely* endogenous, impervious to" deliberate change from its environment (*LD* 18; emphasis mine). While mental memory is capable of transmitting "acquired characteristics" from environmental, cultural, and societal sources, which could be thought collectively under the name *outside* influences, genetic memory "prevents such transmission" on Jacob's theory (*LD* 17).[6] Derrida shows that Jacob's desire for this *purely* interior system of genetics is based on a metaphysical approach that presupposes not only that such a *pure* system exists but exists insofar as its *pure* inside aims to keep the threat of the outside from infecting the inside understood as the true origin of biological essence. Accordingly, any changes that occur in an organism's genetic makeup and program would not be deliberate because the organism itself nor its environment has any direct control on such changes. Any genetic changes are, in this sense, contingent to the organism or environment. But while contingent in this way, such changes are determined by "a logocentric teleology" (*LD* 20). Genetic changes for Jacob occur due to "a preestablished design, a plan, without any subjective psychical intention" (*LD* 21). This logocentric model is, it seems, a latent theocentric model as well because, after all, God is often understood as the omniscient and omnipotent being *preestablishing* everything. However, Jacob's logo-theocentric model begins to deconstruct itself once Jacob maintains that the way genetic heredity is passed down is *textual* in nature. Derrida, quoting Jacob, maintains that the genetic program according to this plan is "copied, *sign by sign*, from one generation to another" (*LD* 22; emphasis mine). With the discovery of the double helix deoxyribonucleic acid (DNA), the passing along of heredity is determined by the reproduction of the sequences of guanine, cytosine, thymine, and adenine. Such are the *signs* of genetics. With this, genetics is transformed into a field determined by the language and metaphorics of textuality. The genetic *code* is itself a text. As Derrida says, "The text is not a third term in the relation between the biologist and the living; it is the very *structure* of the *living*" (*LD* 81; emphasis mine). And the moment that textuality enters the picture with the genetic program being constituted as a text or "textual in its structure" (*LD* 78), the metaphysical presuppositions of Jacob's logocentric teleology can no longer hold.

For textuality brings with it the idea of the supplement and the breakdown of the opposition between the inside and outside, that is, between the *purely* inside and the *purely* outside. As Derrida argues in *Of Grammatology*, the logic of the supplement or supplementarity means that the outside already is inside or "that the other and the lack," which are considered outside of the subject or the organism, "[take] the place of a default in the thing, that the default, as the outside of the inside, should be already within the inside" (*OG* 215). Whereas the notion of a *pure* inside maintains that any addition from outside would pervert or contaminate the purity of the inside, the logic of supplementarity shows that such an addition is neither a perversion nor a purification because the outside has always already found itself in the inside. Moreover, the idea of a pure inside, then, is just a fiction as an effect of the supplement itself. As Derrida says, "Is the concept of origin . . . anything but a function, indispensable but situated, inscribed, within the system of signification? . . . Within the play of supplementarity, one will always be able to relate the substitutes to their signified, this last will be yet another signifier" (*OG* 266). So any idea of an origin or pure inside is but another trace or another signifier in a play of signs rather than being the true origin or signified that stays the play between signifiers and their signified. In other words, the signified of the pure inside is but another signifier or effect of supplementarity. Due to supplementarity, the pure inside cannot be a signified or transcendental signified because the outside is always already inside. Thus, supplementarity is a "structure" through which oppositions such as inside and outside, signifier and signified, or even life and death find their meaning through their difference from one another and whose meaning is deferred through the other. And Derrida names this structure of supplementarity "originary *différance*" (*OG* 167; translation modified). To say this differently, Derrida writes, "The supplement is always the supplement of a supplement. One wishes to go back from the supplement to the source: one must recognize that there is *a supplement at the source*" (*OG* 304; emphasis his). *Différance* or this logic of supplementarity shows, in this, that rather than separation through opposition as the heart of language we find relation through difference and deferral as its heart. Consequently, no longer can any pure inside or pure outside be sustained and maintained. The logic of the supplement shows that the supplement conditions what "supposedly, putatively, came before it — the pure inside, the realm of ideality."[7] The outside is always already inside.[8] Consequently, as Derrida shows in his reading of Jacob, death as the supplement to life in the organism means not that death contaminates life but death is always already found with life. Where we find life, we find death and vice versa.

Derrida does not, in his reading of Jacob, introduce this idea of supplementarity into Jacob's theory. Jacob's own text, notes Derrida, introduces this idea in its claim that genetics is structured textually. Thus, in a classic move of Derridean deconstruction, Derrida shows that Jacob's *own* text is auto-deconstructive. The pivotal moment of this automatic and self-deconstruction occurs when Jacob identifies death as a *supplement* to the normal reproductive process of passing the genetic code down from one generation to the next (*LD* 91). I have discussed already that Jacob identifies the genetic program with the essence of the living organism, that is, as the origin of the organism. So for death to be a supplement to this program means that death is a supplement to the essence of living itself or to this origin. Accordingly, following the logic of supplementarity, the essence of life is now no longer opposed to death. The supplement itself alters the purity of the idea of origin so that the supplement itself becomes originary in the idea of origin. In this, the outside or supplement becomes coeval with the inside or the origin so that no origin remains simply originary. The origin is not the pure essence of the living organism understood as the genetic code passed down from generation to generation. The essence of life is no longer purely or merely living but now living and death together — lifedeath, life death, or life/death as Derrida variously writes it. The supplementarity of death supervenes on the life of an organism "bringing inside, in inscribing as an internal law, the very thing that comes from the outside" (*LD* 109) with the result that any opposition between inside/outside or life/death breaks down. Life must be thought, then, as "a detour (*Umweg*) of the inorganic toward itself, toward the inorganic, a race to death" (*LD* 271). In this, we hear the ancient echoes of Heraclitus, who says that "death is everything I see awake" (B21) and that the work of life, much like the work of the hunting bow, is death (see B48). To think about life and its essence, death must be taken as part and parcel of this thinking and of this essence. Death must be considered as what gives life "its impetus, its very breath."[9] For "death (the end toward which life tends) is inscribed as an internal law and not as an accident of life" (*LD* 271).

While Derrida does not turn to studies in biology to show that this is the case, I want to note that his insights align with recent studies in biology and oncology showing that each cell adheres to its own programmed cellular death through which the life of the entire organism gets secured.[10] An organism lives through the cycle of the death of some cells that become the sustenance for the life of other cells. On this cellular level, life is always already bound up with death. However, some cells eschew this apoptosis in an effort to attain *pure* life, that is, in order to attain immortality. These "immortal" cells are what often develop into cancer in the body. This cellular "desire" for nothing but life is an act of "autonomous 'rebellion'" that "brings death to its host along with the tumor."[11] Consequently, life must always be more than life. Life can never be just *pure* life. Pure life or life purified of death, its other, would be life devoid of *différance*, of the play among life and death. And such "life without *différance*" is just another name for "death" (*OG* 71; translation modified). In other words, to separate life from death is to just be talking about a corpse. Life must always be in relation with death in order for living to occur. Only when life and death are understood according to this différ*a*nt logic that eschews opposition in favor of relation can we see that life and death are what they are by differing and deferring themselves through their wholly other (cf. *LD* 272). Accordingly, to return briefly to the Heidegger-Derrida relation from chapter 1, life must consist of both gathering and division. Just as pure gathering means death so too does pure divisibility (*G3* 81). Thus, *différance* is never purely one side of any binary but the relating of the two. Derrida is concerned, then, in *Life Death* with the différant logic of lifedeath.

And, as I am arguing, what Derrida is describing and deconstructing in his course is not merely about the practice and effects of a deconstructive philosophy. This is not merely about textual hermeneutics but is also a kind of hermeneutic realism. For this différant logic finds a phenomenological edge in the experience of surviving the death of the other. Derrida himself is aware of this relation of lifedeath and mourning the dead. For he writes four years after his *Life Death* course in his eulogy of his friend Roland Barthes, "Neither life nor death, but the haunting of the one by the other" (*WM* 41). Other examples abound pointing to this relation of life and death through mourning. For example, Didion describes this closeness of life and death in her survival of her husband's death by translating the first line — *media vita in morte sumus* — of an old Gregorian chant from the *Book of Common Prayer*: "In the midst of life we are in death."[12] Additionally, Adichie comments that, especially during the COVID-19 pandemic, "The layers of loss make life feel papery thin."[13] And in accord with my argument through Derrida's *Life Death* course, this papery thinness of life makes perfect sense because what survivors experience in the aftermath of the death of the other is the deferral of life in death. So life feels papery thin because such death exposes us to the integral relation of life and death to one another that is operative all the time but which we notice only sometimes due to experiences, like the death of the other, that exceed the opposition of life and death. Carrying on while the death of the other is carried by the survivor exposes the survivors palpably to this différant logic about life's papery thinness. The experience of mourning and the trauma attending the death of the other suggests that "death and life are coterminous rather than sequential, entangled rather than clearly delineated."[14]

Lifedeath, Epigenetics, and Survivor Trees

We see this entanglement or *différance* of life and death with the death of the other in the recent epigenetic research focused on the intergenerational transference of trauma.[15] For this research is indicating, slowly but surely, that mourning is quite literally *embodied* or, in the language of workless mourning, incorporated genetically. In crossing Derrida's readings of Freud's distinction between mourning and melancholy with the related distinction from Abraham and Torok between introjection and incorporation, as I have explained them in chapter 3, epigenetics can help to see the important linguistic shift from the introjection of the dead other in what Freud calls normal mourning to the incorporation of the dead other in and along the body of the survivor in workless mourning. Derrida's work on mourning highlights the embodiment of mourning with his deconstruction of introjection and incorporation by saying that mourning is a matter of "the completely other, dead, *living in me*" (*WM* 42; emphasis mine). To mourn is to carry the other in me in some bodily way. The shift to the term *incorporation* highlights this bodily carrying insofar as the body, *corpus* in Latin, can be seen and heard in the name in*corp*oration. Derrida develops this idea by saying that we incorporate or carry the other in our *corpus* through what he calls a crypt. This crypt in which the dead other is housed for safekeeping is "inside the general space of the self, a kind of pocket of resistance" to the forgetting of Freudian normal mourning or introjection (*F* xix). Such a crypt is "a topographical arrangement made to keep (conserve-hidden) the living dead" (*F* xxxvi). This crypt holds the dead other as other in me as the space of what I have been calling workless mourning. And I argue that such an embodied crypt in the self can be read not just psychoanalytically as Derrida has done but also epigenetically. So to carry on or survive the dead other in mourning them worklessly is, then, a matter of carrying the other in our genetic code.[16] Beyond the dead other continuing to be present through her absence as found in memories, the gravesite,[17] and co-de-distanced material things as discussed in the previous chapter, the dead other can even be with the living through the effect that their death has on the epigenetics of the living self.

The burgeoning field of epigenetics focuses on how the environment of an organism can affect the *expression* of an organism's genetic code or genome in the organism's behavior, physiology, susceptibility to illness, and mental health. With this, epigenetics shows, contra to Jacob, that genetic memory is always already open to its outside on account of the epigenome. The study of epigenetics began in the 1940s with Conrad Waddington, who wanted to explain how the cells in the body, which all have the exact same genome or genetic code, can end up becoming different cells and having different functions. In an effort to avoid charges of epigenetics just being another version of Jean-Baptiste Lamarck's idea that the behavior and environmental effects on an organism can change *directly* the *genetic* code of an organism, epigenetics first theorized and has now shown that an organism's behavior and environment affects not their genome directly but *how* this genome gets expressed. Rachel Yehuda, a leading scientist in the study of epigenetics, says, "The term 'epigenetics' refers to a set of potentially heritable changes in the genome that can be induced by environmental events. These changes affect the function of genomic DNA, its associated histone proteins, and non-coding RNAs, collectively referred to as chromatin, but do not involve an alteration of DNA sequence."[18] To take as one example of how epigenetics affects the genome, the environment can affect the genomes *expression* by altering the proteins, called histones, that closely surround every chain of DNA in the organism. The presence and absence of these histones affect not the sequence of the DNA but the activity of the DNA in the organism by telling the DNA strands to be active or to be repressed in the copying phase of cell reproduction. The histones affect the transcription of the genes so that each gene gives rise to a particular kind of cell for a particular part of the body depending on which part of their genetic code is activated by the histones. The genome remains the same, but *how* the genome is used by the organism changes based on the epigenomic presence and absence of histones. And these changes to the histones are *inheritable* and, thereby, open to the outside. Histones are, in short, where the outside is always already inside genetically. The inheritability of these changes has given rise to the field of behavioral epigenetics that studies how experiences, especially traumatic ones, effect these epigenetic changes.

One of the first indications that trauma in one generation is inheritable in the second and third generation came from the chronic health issues and higher morbidity rates among survivors of the *Hongerwinter* in the Netherlands during World War II. Scientists found that children and grandchildren of survivors of the *Hongerwinter* had the same chronic health issues and the same higher morbidity rates as their parents and grandparents who lived through the *Hongerwinter*. Furthermore, even before the developments in the field of epigenetics, therapists were aware of the intergenerational transference of trauma from first-generation survivors of the Holocaust to the second generation. They were considering this transference as an abnormal version of "transposition," that is, "the psychological process of unconscious cross-generational transmission of massive trauma."[19] Such transposition describes a normal psychological process in which parents unconsciously pass on their own "wishes, desires, fantasies, ideals and experiences"[20] to their children. However, this transposition was abnormal on account of what was being absorbed by the child: the parent's personal, massive trauma. The mode of this transposition of trauma was, at the time in the early 1970s, considered unconscious through the "caregiving *gestures*" of parents to their children.[21] While this consideration of transposition had yet to be influenced by the field of epigenetics, the mode of transposition was still considered bodily insofar as the *gestures* of parent to child communicated the trauma to the child. Since the first study of these survivors of the *Hongerwinter*, a number of important studies about this intergenerational transference of trauma have been conducted that begin to argue that rather than trauma being passed down through the conscious and unconscious parenting gestures, trauma is passed down *epigenetically* from generation to generation. Within this development of epigenetics, the material and bodily element of the intergenerational transmission of trauma becomes especially pronounced because trauma is now seen as carried directly on the body through the epigenetic effects on the expressions of DNA. Perhaps the most famous study conducted, in this regard, concerns the physiological transformation of the olfactory bulbs in the brains of second- and third-generation mice whose male parents were conditioned to associate the smell of acetophenone, which smells like cherry blossoms, with being shocked. These male mice who were first conditioned in this way developed a more pronounced part of their olfactory bulb that allowed them to be more sensitive to the smell of acetophenone in an effort to avoid it. They, in turn, passed this genetic marker for sensitivity to the odor down to the next generation, which passed it to the third generation. The scientists conclude that the genetic activation for this same part of the brain to be overly developed in the second and third generations of the mice was passed epigenetically through the sperm of the male mice.[22] This study has shown that trauma can have an epigenetic effect on the physiology of the body.

Of course, this study was done on mice and was not about the effect of mourning on humans. However, scientists have been studying and continue to study the effect of death and loss on human beings and how effects from such trauma are passed down epigenetically from generation to generation. Though more studies need to be done to connect the effects of mourning more directly to epigenetics, rather than behavioral conditioning of children from the effects of their parent's mourning on the home life,[23] studies that have been done suggest that the effect of mourning the death of the other not only alters epigenetically the genetic expression of the one who experienced the death of the other but also this survivor's progeny. One study has shown that grief can, indeed, have an epigenetic effect on the genetic expression for fighting diseases in the body. This immunological effect occurs based on the intensity and duration of a survivor's grief.[24] Van der Kolk also notes that research in neuroscience, psychopathology, and neurobiology has shown that "trauma produces actual physiological changes, including a recalibration of the brain's alarm system, an increase in stress hormone activity, and alterations in the system that filters relevant information from irrelevant."[25] The disruption of temporality understood as trauma, including the trauma attending the death of the other in mourning, leaves an imprint on the body, says Van der Kolk, through its myriad effects on the brain. Furthermore, Yehuda's work on the transmission of the effects of PTSD on Holocaust survivors to the second and third generation has shown that the cause for being affected by PTSD is a lower level of cortisol levels in the body. And she has shown that this biological propensity for lower levels of cortisol is passed down all the way to the third generation. Moreover, in a study conducted beginning in 2002, Yehuda and her team of researchers have shown that women who were pregnant while they experienced directly the attacks on 9/11 and developed PTSD, as shown through their low levels of cortisol after 9/11, passed this low level of cortisol along to their babies who were in utero on 9/11, thereby making their children more susceptible to PTSD in the future.[26] The trauma experienced by people in the Holocaust and other disastrous events, such as the treatment of Native Americans and Black and African Americans throughout history,[27] the terrorist attack on 9/11, and, perhaps time will tell, even the effects of all of the death due to and during COVID-19, are having profound impacts on generations of survivors. While I am not flattening out the differences of the events that have led to such trauma in their various survivors, what I am pointing out is that the death of the other is each time uniquely traumatic on account of how it disrupts a survivor's embodied existence. Moreover, drawing from the research done on the effect of such trauma across generations, I am claiming that the trauma from the death of the other leaves its imprint on the epigenome of its survivors in direct relation to the existential difference that the other who has died played in the co-constitution of the pluralized world for the survivor while this other was alive.

While the practice of mourning the death of the other through "an embodied signifier" such as a tattoo is popular, especially among the children and grandchildren of Holocaust survivors who get their ancestor's camp number tattooed on their body in honor and memory of the now dead other,[28] perhaps the epigenetic effect of mourning can also be read as such a signifier. For if remembering can mean "[t]o bear witness on one's own skin,"[29] then perhaps remembering can also mean to bear witness in one's own epigenome. The dead other will have then been carried as a sign in the body through the effect of his or her death on the survivor. And the passing down of this information, *sign by sign*, would constitute the life/death of these survivors. And such an embodied signifier would heighten the Levinasian and Derridean idea that the self becomes a self only through its responsibility to the other — whether she be living *or* dead, human, nonhuman animal, or divine. The loss and absence that attend the death of the other remain inscribed in our bodies and materiality so that the death of the other becomes an event that transforms even the space of the body itself.

Such an embodied signifier in and along the survivor's body can also be seen in the material transformation of the earth that can attend the death of the other. We see this most poignantly in what are called "survivor trees." As I have argued in chapter 4, the death of the other is transformative of the spatiality of the pluralized world insofar as the survivors have to de-distance the world anew without the other who has died. Such de-distancing can also occur, though, on account of the earth itself carrying the death of the other in its own material transformation. To illustrate, following the nuclear attacks on Hiroshima and Nagasaki, the Japanese language underwent a transformation as a result of the material transformation that attended this event. For example, the idiomatic name for people who survived these attacks is *hibakusha*, that is, "bomb-affected people."[30] Moreover, in order to retain the transformative power of this tragic, horrendous death of the other on the physical landscape of Japan, the Japanese also call the trees that survived the bombing *hibakujumoku*, which can mean "survivor tree" or more literally "a-bombed-tree."[31] These trees are marked by "yellow tags . . . worn like humble medals on the trunks" of several species of trees that survived surprisingly the blast of the bomb.[32] Here the Japanese language goes through a transformation in order to adapt to the transformed world in the aftermath of the death of the other. While this transformation of the Japanese language may be unique, the turn to trees as evidence for how the materiality of the earth can be itself transformed or de-distanced directly by the death of the other is a common theme both in literature and in the lived experience of survivors of the death of the other.

In his *Metamorphoses*, the epic poet Ovid weaves a myth about the transformation or metamorphosis of the mulberry tree as a response to the death of the other. The setting of this transformation is the forbidden love of Pyramus and Thisbe. The two lovers, much like Shakespeare's own later story of Romeo and Juliet, belong to two families whose fathers disapprove of their marriage. Though prevented from marrying, Pyramus and Thisbe fall deeply in love by merely exchanging whispered messages to each other through the crack in the stone fence separating their two estates. One evening they decide to meet under the large mulberry tree outside of the walls of both of their estates, where they will, then, be able to satisfy their desires for one another. Thisbe, on the designated night, arrives at the tree first but flees to a cave in fear of a lioness drinking water from the nearby stream. In her haste, Thisbe leaves behind her mantle at the base of the tree, which the lioness finds and mauls "inside her gory mouth" that had been "besmeared with the blood of the cattle she'd newly slaughtered."[33] When Pyramus arrives at the tree to see the blood-soaked, torn mantle of his lover Thisbe, he thinks that Thisbe has been killed by an animal. Overcome with guilt for the death of Thisbe at the hands of a beast, Pyramus commits suicide by falling on his own sword. In the process of killing himself, his blood not only soaks the roots of the tree but also splashes on some of the white berries hanging on the mulberry tree, dying them "to a red-black colour" and providing them "with a purplish hue."[34] Returning to the tree from her haven in the cave, Thisbe finds Pyramus dying at the foot of the tree. Assessing that he had died by his own sword due to their forbidden love and her delay in getting to the tree, she too grabs his sword and stabs herself through the heart so that she can share death with her lover if she cannot ever share her body with him. But before dying she cries out:

> And you, O tree, whose branches already are casting
>   their shadows
> on one poor body and soon will be overshadowing two,
>   preserve the marks of our death; let your fruit forever be
>   dark
> as a *token of mourning*, a *monument* marking the blood
>   of two lovers.[35]

In this, as a memorial to this death of the other as if carrying in its own body or materiality the death of the other, the mulberry tree comes to bear red instead of white berries. Such a metamorphosis suggests that the earth itself can be materially transformed by the death of the other. This story of a survivor tree or, as Rosner calls them "trees of witness,"[36] shows that the death of the other and the world remain integrally bound so that the loss of someone can de-distance the earth itself. The earth can carry this death through *tokens of mourning* or embodied signifiers.

While a myth, Ovid's narrative is much more than myth, as evidenced by the presence of survivor trees in the landscapes of trauma. Both the 9/11 Memorial in New York City as well as the Oklahoma City National Memorial have famous survivor trees. Both of these trees were at ground zero for the terrorist attacks that each city experienced, and both trees represent the excessiveness of the death of the other through the *différance* of life with death. While still carrying the wounds of the explosion on April 19, 1995, the Survivor Tree, as it is named, is a central feature of the Oklahoma City bombing memorial. This elm tree, alive since 1920, sits at the highest geographical point of the memorial overlooking the memorial itself as if to remind those who enter that while the memorial remembers the death of the other, the tree represents a symbol of life amid death. And this tree, as the low wall around it says, is a reminder to those who visit the memorial that "our deeply rooted faith sustains us." As such, the tree represents "the endurance of the city, the endurance of the country, the endurance of democracy, of freedom, of dignity, in the face of terror."[37] This tree itself, along with the wounds it still carries from the explosion, is a token of mourning and memorial that the earth itself carries the world after this death of the other. In this way, the earth itself gets transformed in its materiality by the death of the other. These survivor trees are further indications that life and death are not in opposition to one another but rather are bound up with one another, making existence into what we experience it to be: lifedeath.

So regardless of the future findings in the field of epigenetics on the *incorporation* of the death of the other, mourning challenges, as we have seen, the separation that has traditionally been placed between life and death. Derrida's reading of Jacob in *Life Death* helps to highlight precisely what gets experienced materially with the death of the other. For in the mourning process, the other who is now dead continues to have an enduring "social bond that continues beyond the life-death boundary."[38] To recall the focus from the previous chapter, the dead continue to have a presence through their absence in the life of the living. And this present absence has a material effect on existence for the survivor. This excessive *différance* of life with death that attends the death of the other can be seen, additionally, in how such death exceeds calculative rationality.

The Death of the Other and the Principle of Reason

The death of the other as an event exceeds the expectation and calculation of reason insofar as such death marks "the breaking of meaning"[39] itself. Accordingly, the death of the other follows the symptom of an event that I have called the secret. The following examples where survivors of the death of the other find this death to exceed questions of why the other died are instructive in this regard. With the death of the other, the survivor is, like Didion, needing "more than words to find the meaning" of the death.[40] No matter how much factual information a person may have about when and how the other has or will have died, the survivor continually comes back to the question, in one form or another, of *why* the other has died. In the wake of Maia's death, the McDermotts express that "there is no *reason* for a loss that hurts this much."[41] Adichie grieves, "[W]e do not *know* what to do with this rupture."[42] When Tommy Givens, "a Baptist pastor's kid, lifelong Christian, former missionary and [Christian] seminary professor," survived his father's death from Lou Gehrig's disease, he maintains, "We were groping for what might help us navigate something very profound . . . something that would shape us for the rest of our lives."[43] Regardless of the answers that Tommy's own faith had to offer him in this experience, he continued to grope for something that would *make sense* of it. Belief in seeing the deceased again in the afterlife may assuage some worries in the survivor, but this belief does not help explain *why* the other has been lost. No exhaustive account or reasonable explanation placates the trauma and pain that accompanies this loss. To the easily abused line of Paul's theology in the New Testament, "Where, death, is your sting?" (1 Cor. 15:55 NRSV), a survivor can point to the material conditions of their differently de-distanced world in the wake of the death of a loved one as where that sting can be found. As already mentioned in chapter 4, even Jesus — whom Christianity claims to be both human and God and would, thereby, know more assuredly than others the bliss that one of his followers would experience in the afterlife — weeps when his friend Lazarus dies. The death of the other breaking in to experience as an event resists any principle of sufficient reason, that is, resists this horizon of expectation, as to why the other has died. A survivor may certainly know what caused the death: heart failure, cancer, overdose, respiratory failure, police brutality, COVID-19, and so on. Often these medical explanations can alleviate some of the pain, but none of nor all of them can cause us to stop asking why the other has died. These reasons cannot explain away the pain and trauma of this loss. Suddenly, the survivors find themselves in the world of Voltaire's *Candide*, where the principle of sufficient reason has been reduced to a "pitiable state" unable to explain why *this* state of affairs "is for the best in this world."[44] So like Silesius's rose, once again, the death of the other is without why because its occurring saturates what the mind is capable of understanding and knowing about it. The death of the other sticks to the while and asks not why.

This excessiveness of the death of the other beyond calculative rationality is, to conclude, succinctly described by Blanchot. For the irruption of the death of the other is one that, as Blanchot says, "ruins everything, all the while leaving everything intact." This quotation is, of course, an adaptation of the first line of Blanchot's *The Writing of the Disaster*, where he writes, "*The disaster* ruins everything, all the while leaving everything intact."[45] Though Blanchot speaks specifically about the disaster and not about the event by name nor the death of the other,[46] in this one sentence his text can be pushed to offer a phenomenologically fitting description of this event of the death of the other because he helpfully unpacks three aspects of it as I have described it thus far. First, his account is sensitive to the transformative symptom of death insofar as the spatiality of the world is transformed in this disaster of the death of the other. Second, his account puts in precisely paradoxical terms how the death of the other exceeds the principle of sufficient reason. And, finally, he explores in this one sentence the inseparable relation of life with death. And he manages to do all of this with just one sentence taken in three parts: with ruination, with the temporality of "all the while," and with a strange, almost tragic, sense of restitution. The death of the other ruins everything, all the while leaving everything intact. This sentence even seems to say more than what a language can say. For how can everything *instantaneously* be ruined and yet intact? And this ruination and restitution are held together by nothing more than a comma, an instant, or a mere pause. I can even take out the *stated* temporality of this event, the "all the while," to emphasize the strangeness and paradoxicality of the death of the other: death ruins everything, leaving everything intact.

In an effort to unfold these three parts of Blanchot's statement, I take them in the order in which we read them in the sentence: ruination, the instant, and restitution. The death of the other ruins the pluralized world because this death calls for a new spatiality or differently de-distanced world in which the meaningfulness of the world to the now dead other is carried by the survivors as they themselves carry on with life. As a result, for example, when a loved one dies "the zest" in life is gone. Wolterstorff writes: "I remember delighting in . . . trees, art, house, music, pink morning sky, work well done, flowers, books. I still delight in them. I'm still grateful. But the zest is gone. The passion is cooled, the striving quieted, the longing stilled. . . . I've become an alien in the world. . . . I don't belong any more. When someone loved leaves home, home becomes mere house."[47] His words evidence once again that the loss or ruination he is experiencing is, as we have seen in the previous chapter, the loss of what the world had meant to that person and what the world had meant to you, or to a group, on account of your relation with the now deceased. The event of the death of the other ruins everything because with this death, a death of the world too has happened.

And yet everything is left intact with this event of the death of the other. Despite the fact that you have just lost a loved one, a friend, belief in God, a beloved pet, a mentor, or whoever, the sun continues to rise, the weather continues to change. When life seems like it should stop on account of the loss that has happened, life continues despite the death that has just ruined your world. Adichie reflects, "How is it that the world keeps going, breathing in and out unchanged, while in my soul there is a permanent scattering?"[48] Such continuation of life after death is precisely what Derrida and others have redefined the afterlife to be. The afterlife is not just about the life after death *for the dead* but also the life after the death of the other *for the living*. This is what *survival* or living on after the death of the other is all about. This survival can even be renamed "the afterlife within life."[49] Such life after death is a way of understanding the afterlife, survival, and carrying on in terms that takes seriously the *différance* of life with death. This afterlife would not be a jettisoning of this world for another, as traditionally understood, but an embracing and affirmation of this world, of existence here and now, in the exigencies that the death of the other entails. Afterlife, then, would be an embracing of life with death or afterlife as carrying the other and carrying on after the death of the other.[50] And this is precisely Derrida's own definition of survival in his final interview in 2004 just months before his own death. In this interview, Derrida describes survival as not an addition to living or dying but as a "complication of the opposition life/death" (*LLF* 50, 26). Survival is a matter of living after death not for the dead but for the one who lives on, survives, the death of the other (*LLF* 26). Such survival is, says Derrida, "[T]he structure of what we call existence, *Dasein*, if you will" (*LLF* 50). And in this afterlife, the survivor now has myriad questions and problems to deal with: When will the funeral be? Who's the next of kin that we need to call? What do we do with the body? Cremation? Burial? What kind of music at the funeral? Who will speak at the memorial? What do I do about his car? How will our department recover from this? Who grades his students' papers? Am I okay? Should I see a therapist? The world continues intact, but am I intact? Will I recover? The *différance* of life and death is felt when the other dies because such death exceeds their separation.

In fact, the possibility that Blanchot's text recognizes, but only implicitly, with the death of the other, is that this afterlife is one in which the survivor's wholeness after the event may precisely be unwhole or fractured. When we get to the second clause of the sentence — "leaving everything intact" — we encounter this idea. This clause itself is not *intact* so to speak because it lacks a subject. To see this, I could rewrite Blanchot's sentence, saying, Death ruins everything, all the while *death* leaves everything intact. And, of course, this is how we understand the text even without the repetition of "death" in the second clause. We understand the subject to be death that is leaving everything intact, but without the presence of this subject in the clause, we get the sense that death may leave everything intact but only in some incomplete way. For a survivor might be irrevocably ruined, driven mad, or driven to their own death because of the death of the other. The death of the other as a gift event may be the poison that spells her end. The carrying on after the death of the other may be more than a person can handle. Afterlife, then, may be a living hell.[51] Or as Augustine says, "The lost life of those who die becomes the death of those still living."[52] This is always a possibility. After all, as I have been arguing, one of the things for which a survivor can never be ready is the aftermath of the death of the other. The survivor can never be ready for how they will respond to this death of the world. In this way, the death of the other in its very ruination remains unexpected *and* beyond reason. "She was too young to die." "We all knew he wasn't in good health, but I still cannot believe he is gone." "It just doesn't make sense." Or simply, "Why?" Beyond this surprise of the event in its very happening, the way in which everything is left intact may even surprise us. Your alarm goes off one morning months after she is gone and your first thought is, "Another day? Do I really have to get up? Why am I still like this?" This is why the restitution after the event of the death of the other may be a tragic one. And it may not be. Both are always live options here because, after all, we are dealing with an event that could be either a promise of good to come or even poison. Though life and death, as Derrida has argued, relate through a différ*a*nt logic, recognizing this existentially when someone dies can be a gift of poison or a gift of new, yet different life.

Yet I seem to have skipped the instantaneous temporality of the event: the "all the while." I said that I would take the adapted sentence from Blanchot as it gives itself to us in three parts: ruination, the instant, and restitution. I seem to have skipped its temporality though. Nevertheless, the instantaneous temporality of the event has been with us all along. With this, the phenomenality of this instant is one of surprise through an event's causality of rupture. The rupture or loss of the world surprises us. The restitution or continuation of the world surprises us. Moreover, the rupture surprises in the instant that the restitution surprises us, and the restitution surprises the instant the rupture surprises us. This simultaneity of rupture and restitution indicates "life resurrecting amid the ongoingness of death."[53] As Nancy Moules argues in her work on the hermeneutic experience of being a bereavement nurse, this life after the death of the other is a matter not of "'getting over,' resolving, or ending grief, but finding a way through [the] suffering and sorrow to make room for a relationship with grief that is livable, acceptable, creative, and for a *life* that may even be richer for its presence."[54] Drawing on this, the hope with mourning is not for a denial of the death and a forgetting of the other, but a transformation of the relationship with the dead other that opens life in its *différance* with death to new possibilities.[55] Such an approach to mourning the death of the other is about seeing mourning not as a way to get the same world and the same self back but as a "transformation . . . through which we can articulate and thus generate newly meaningful ways of living in response."[56] In short, the hope is for a differently de-distanced world. Certainly the death of the other is recorded as having taken place at a particular, temporal moment or now point: "The estimated time of death was . . ." or "She was pronounced dead at . . ." Time of death is codified on the death certificate. But the phenomenon of the death of the other as a whole is both inside time in this way while also outside of time. It is outside of time in the way that the rupture and restitution bleed into one another, overlap one another, or instantly take place with one another. To see this textually, I rewrite Blanchot's sentence one last time:

All the while, death ruins everything leaving everything intact.

The death of the other is never just the loss of the person. The death of the other includes a death of the pluralized world and *simultaneously* a continuation of life in and around mourning. This world may be lost, but I must carry the other in myself and in a freshly de-distanced world. And in this survival, I am responsible for the other who has died and for the world that has died with her. I must carry the other even when, or especially when, the reason for why the other has died exceeds the reasons that can be given.

Part Three

Temporal Transformations of the World

Chapter Six

Memories and a Past That Won't Stay Put

The past is never past.

— William Faulkner, *Requiem for a Nun*

In describing the death of the other as an event, I have argued that this death transforms the spatiality of the survivor's world because the regions through which the world comes to meaning require de-distancing anew after the death of the other. In this final part of my description of the death of the other, I argue that surviving the death of the other also involves a transformation of temporality. In this, the death of the other transforms not world time or clock time, which is the passing of time that pays us no mind. Rather, the death of the other transforms primordial time or *temporality* understood as the survivor's lived experience of time in his or her everyday life.[1] In this, the death of the other transforms a person's relation to time insofar as after the death of the other they begin to experience time no longer as the linear flow of past to present to future as we tend to represent time to ourselves. Instead, the survivor experiences time as an interrelational flow among past, future, and present: the past will not stay in the past but haunts the survivor's present, the future is full of fractured and lost possibilities, and the present haunted by this past and future in the aftermath of the death of the other is out of joint.[2] The death of the other, in this way, and not just through cremation as Derrida maintains (see *BS2* 169), invades all of temporality. When surviving the death of the other, "time doesn't work the way we think it ought to."[3] Consequently, the death of the other follows what Raffoul calls an "eventful temporality" where time after the event is not brought to an end but interrupted now as "an ecstatic, interruptive, and differential happening" experienced as "the arrhythmic beat of temporality."[4] This experience of time remains thoroughly solicited, fractured, and ruptured by the unexpected and excessive event of the other's death to the extent that the pluralized world, the with-world, will never be the same. The world may still be present, but its temporal presence is filled with the absence of the other who has died. The following three chapters take up one by one the transformation of each ecstasy of time, that is, the way that time gets stretched through our lived experience differently after the death of the other.

Accordingly, this chapter focuses on how the death of the other that occurs in the past continues to haunt the survivor in the present, thereby lending credence throughout to my epigraph from William Faulkner for this chapter. In this haunting, the lived experience of temporality in the topsy-turvy temporal relation described above comes to the fore. Heidegger's development of his notion of primordial or originary temporality in *Being and Time* becomes an important resource for understanding what occurs to temporality in surviving the death of the other. But this notion of originary temporality needs to be tempered, in the aftermath of the death of the other, with the hauntology of Derrida. On the one hand, I argue that the death of the other shows Heidegger to be correct regarding the relation of the past, future, and the present. For as we participate in our own temporalization, the death of the other transforms how we find ourselves in temporality insofar as in the present we find the past and the future out of place from a linear perspective. Thus, I describe the moment of the loss of the other, the inception of the event, as a past that will not stay put. This past moment returns or comes again — *revenir* — like a specter, ghost, or *revenant* come to haunt the present. On the other hand, I also argue that the death of the other shows contrary to Heidegger that we cannot *unify* our relation to temporality in the aftermath of the death of the other. Consequently, Derrida's notion of hauntology is necessary for adequately describing how the death of the other transforms a survivor's temporality.

Through this hauntological relation to the past after the death of the other, the survivor finds himself existentially transformed insofar as what is lost with the death of the other is the memory shared with and through the other as well. The death of the other is simultaneously, then, the loss of the other's physical presence, the loss of meaningfulness to and through the other for the pluralized world, as covered in part 2, and, now, a loss of memory. I argue that the specific loss of memory with the death of the other is the loss of social or transactive memory, as psychologists call it, and this loss deepens the death of the world that attends the death of the other because what is lost, in part, is the self's dependence on the other through their shared memory by which they navigated the world together, that is, by which they were a being-with. As the survivor carries the death of the other in his or her own memories, these are memories fraught with absence, the presence of the other's absence, not only because the other helped constitute the survivor's memory while living but also because the now dead other had been an extension of the survivor's own memory. The death of the other marks a loss of the survivor's memory — a unique kind of amnesia.

And I argue that this loss of memory develops further what I have called the workless mourning of the survivor because this mourning now involves what I call workless memory. In this, the unity of temporality, particularly the survivor's relation to the past, is irrecuperable or un-unifiable. The relation to the past is a relation with the specter or ghost of the other that continues, as a revenant, to return and haunt the survivor.

The Death of the Other and Temporality

The death of the other as specter or ghost is a returning theme at this point in my description. The ghost, who "begins by coming back" (*SM* 11), is already coming back. We have previously encountered the haunting and temporality that occurs with the death of the other in the idea of lifedeath. After the death of the other, we experience "[n]either life nor death, but the *haunting* of the one by the other" (*WM* 41; emphasis mine). Moreover, the death of the other in the instant, which as identified in chapter 1 is the time of the event's arrival in its causality of rupture, simultaneously ruins everything yet leaves everything intact. The haunting of life with death and death with life occurs in this instant of ruination and restitution. The death of the other arrives in this instant of surprise and excess to haunt the present with its absence. Thus, the entire phenomenon of intergenerational transference of trauma that I have discussed in chapter 5 can be recast as the haunting of the past in the epigenomic space of the body.

Yet this haunting of the death of the other and its transformation of temporality requires more careful description in order to understand how this haunting transforms a survivor's temporality. This haunting and attendant transformation has its phenomenological footprint in the cyclical nature of the mourning process. Similar to Marion's understanding of our own birth, a survivor repeatedly returns to the death of the other, perhaps even to its inception at the passage from life to corpse, in an effort to mine the depths of this event. Yet a survivor cannot reason their way through this event, as evidenced by repeatedly living through and beyond this moment itself in their workless mourning. In chapter 3, I have argued that workless mourning is nonteleological, and now that the temporality of mourning is coming into focus, this nonteleology of workless mourning gains further description. Mourning is itself workless in part because it does not adhere to a linear temporality of progress or a linear progression through stages. So rather than mourning heading toward a final goal or purpose, such as getting over the loss, the mourning takes place with a nonlinear temporality making this mourning a process or a task that is ongoing with various developments but not a onetime accomplishment. Accordingly, Julia Cooper says, "There is no timeline because the work of grieving is never done."[5]

This nonlinearity of mourning is related to the focus at the end of the twentieth century on the nonlinearity of suffering in survivors of trauma more generally considered on account of how trauma disrupts the relation to temporality of the one who experiences it. During this time, "trauma came to be identified as what does not get integrated in time and thus returns or remains, obstructing one's ability to engage the world as one did before. . . . [T]rauma marked a problem of living in the present, given that the past was still a 'living' and intrusive reality."[6] For example, C. S. Lewis describes the circularity and nonlinearity of his grief after the death of his wife, "[I]n grief nothing 'stays put.' One keeps on emerging from a phase, but it always recurs. Round and round. Everything repeats. Am I going in circles, or dare hope I am on a spiral? But if a spiral, am I going up or down it?"[7] Consequently, the death of the other is a traumatic event that "is not remembered per se, but recurringly relived."[8] Van der Kolk's definition of trauma from chapter 1 once again fits the experience of the death of the other because it remains not merely something that happened in the past but continues to leave traces as an "imprint left by that experience on mind, brain, and body" that have "ongoing consequences" for the survivor.[9] The experience of the death of the other is relived "'belatedly' in the form of intrusive and uncontrollable flashbacks."[10] The survivors of the death remain unable "to integrate the experience into ordinary systems of personal history and meaning" because this trauma "short-circuits" the brain.[11] The event "remain[s] stuck and never gain[s] access to the frontal lobes [of the brain], which is not only where language arises but is also the part of the brain that reasons and understands."[12] Moreover, MRI scans of the brain done during a survivor recalling their trauma shows that the parts of the brain having to do with sequencing and time are affected, thereby leading survivors to experience temporality nonlinearly.[13] Thus, survivors who have lost loved ones often say that they cannot believe he or she is gone. They are struck by the reality of the other's absence, by this absence's facticity, but they fail to "'believe in it,' or say what it is."[14] Didion has this experience after the death of her husband as she struggled with "truly believing it had happened, absorbing it, incorporating it, *getting past* it."[15] Consequently, survivors tell and retell the story of the death of the other along with the stories about the life lived by the other who has been lost. The survivors find themselves mourning the loss of the other but unable to work fully through this loss. Their past loss continues to haunt their present. Thus, their work of mourning remains, as I have been arguing, *workless* insofar as it is a *negotiation* between moving completely beyond their loss and a melancholy that never comes to terms with the death of the other. The McDermott family, after the death of their daughter Maia, experienced this worklessness because, as they say, "[F]inding the balance between the 'old normal' and the 'new normal' would probably be a constant challenge forever more."[16] The cyclical, workless nature of mourning is a process that attempts to appropriate the unexpected loss of meaning or the unexpected absence made present in the world when the other dies. Yet this appropriation fails, in part, because the past event of this death refuses to remain past but continually bleeds into and infuses the present experience of time with its absence. As survivors carry the other after the death of the other and the world that occurs with their death, they must do so in a present that is never fully present but always stretched into its past.

Accordingly, a more phenomenologically adequate description of time in the aftermath of the death of the other is required. For while time understood as a linear flow can be helpful for teaching various disciplines in academia, structuring our daily lives according to the datability of occurrences on our calendars, and understanding always in hindsight our own histories and history itself, our lived experience of time *especially* in the survival of the death of the other refuses to adhere to this linearity. The phenomenological tradition has provided some helpful ways for understanding our lived experience of non-linear temporality. While we typically think of time as just the way of passing or keeping track of the objective changes that occur during life, the phenomenological tradition has shown that time is much more than just this marking of the process of change. Phenomenology has shown that in our lived experience, time is an important way that we structure our own relation to this change and to the events and occurrences that take place over the span of our life. Such *temporality* comes down to the way that we structure our own lived experience of the world. And, more often than not, this lived experience of time is what refuses to obey the linear distinctions of past, present, and future especially when considering surviving the death of the other.

This phenomenological awareness of our own temporal structuring of experience begins to be developed systematically in 1781 and 1787 in Immanuel Kant's *Critique of Pure Reason*.[17] While not a book that is explicitly phenomenological, the development of Kant's transcendental idealism in the *Critique of Pure Reason* serves as a prolegomenon to much that will be developed in phenomenology, particularly in the works of Husserl and Heidegger. For Kant makes possible in his First Critique a rethinking of our relation to time. He shows that though material reality exists outside of the subject, the structure and meaning of this reality comes from the mind of human subjectivity. The conditions for the possibility of anything with material reality to have meaning at all arise from the human mind, particularly from what he calls the *a priori* forms of intuition and the twelve concepts of the understanding. This is, in broad strokes, Kant's bequest to us under the name of transcendental idealism. More specifically, he radically reshapes the philosophical understanding of time along the lines of what I am calling temporality. Though he does not make this distinction between time and temporality when he explains in the "Transcendental Aesthetic" how time, in addition to space, is an *a priori* form of intuition, he shows that when human subjectivity engages with material reality the reception of this reality in the mind through the faculty of sensibility structures the engagement according to a temporal sequence. Time, thus, becomes one of the primary ways through which we structure our reality. Kant's argument marks a shift from understanding time as an objective feature of the world to an understanding of time as the temporal way that the human mind structures its own experience of this world. This effectively makes time no longer *merely* external to our mind but also integral to how our mind understands and orders our own reality. Kant's arguments become revolutionary in causing a powerful transformation of intellectual life during the Enlightenment, which leads to many philosophical developments both during Kant's time and especially at the turn of the twentieth century with the development of phenomenology in the works of Husserl and Heidegger. While Husserl and Heidegger describe temporality tout court and not in relation to what occurs in surviving the death of the other, their descriptions begin to provide a helpful framework for understanding how the death of the other transforms the temporality of such a survivor.

Husserl and Heidegger both distinctively develop the Kantian insight regarding temporality, but Heidegger's development more adequately describes the lived experience of temporality in general. Husserl explores temporality through what he calls our inner awareness of time or internal time-consciousness. He makes a distinction between three notions of temporality: the empirical experience of things in "objective time," the "pre-empirical time" or "phenomenological time," and "the absolute time-constituting flow of consciousness."[18] The experience of time, following in the Kantian tradition, that interests Husserl are the latter two notions of temporality. Phenomenological time results from the time-constituting flow of consciousness understood as the internal structure of consciousness in three simultaneous, unified phases that Husserl calls retention, primal impression or presentation, and protention. This unity in consciousness of retention, primal presentation, and protention becomes the condition for the possibility of phenomenological time, which is the time through which we become conscious of our experiences of ourselves and objects as having a past, present, and future.[19] For example, an object has a relation to objective time in terms of past, present, and future, but we are aware of this only because retention is directed toward the past phase of the object, protention is directed toward the future phase of the object, and primal presentation is directed toward the present phase of the object.[20] The importance of Husserl's approach notwithstanding in this phenomenology of temporality, his understanding of time-consciousness is problematic for a few reasons. First, he is most interested, as with his entire approach to phenomenology, in our *consciousness* of temporality and less concerned about the relation among this consciousness and our experience in the world. Second, he never offers a definitive and complete explanation of his theory of internal time-consciousness. Third, following Levinas's critique of Husserl, Husserl's understanding of temporality is entirely too wedded to the present for my purposes considering that I am dealing with an experience of the presence of absence or the absence of presence. For while Husserl may have been sensitive to how retention and protention are directed toward absence and, thereby, absence is implicit to the synchronic simultaneity of the retention-primal presentation-protention structure of consciousness, his emphasis in his analysis of temporality remains not on describing the important role that this absence plays in our relation to temporality.[21] Rather, he is focused on "the 'width' or 'depth' of the presence" of this simultaneous unity of retention, primal presentation, and protention to our consciousness.[22] In other words, the absence of retention and protention always point to the presence of this simultaneous unity that constitutes internal time-consciousness.[23] Consequently, Derrida explains that for Husserl, then, "to respect the movement of temporization is to respect this *a priori* unconditionality of the Present" (*H* 140; cf. 136).

Considering these limitations in Husserl, Heidegger's description of primordial or originary temporality advances beyond these three limitations. For, to begin with, Heidegger's engagement with temporality is grounded firmly not in the consciousness of subjectivity but in a being-in-the-world. With this, Heidegger sees his notion of primordial time as a development of Husserl's internal time-consciousness, for Heidegger says a year after *Being and Time*, "That which Husserl still calls time-consciousness, i.e., consciousness of time, is precisely time, itself, in the primordial sense."[24] In this, Heidegger reworks "the standing-streaming of consciousness — Husserl's primordial temporality — into an existential manner in which Dasein has left itself behind in its own temporal self-manifestation as present to the world."[25] And, lastly, Heidegger focuses more prevalently on the constitutive role that absence plays in our experience of temporality even if, as I shall argue, his notion of the moment of anticipatory resoluteness continues to focus problematically on the unifying presence of this moment.

Heidegger sharpens Husserl's analysis of temporality through his distinction between vulgar time, world time, and primordial time. This distinction fits into Heidegger's aim in *Being and Time* to understand the meaning of being (*Sein*) based upon the understanding of being that Dasein has of its own being. And Dasein understands its being through how it relates to temporality, specifically through how Dasein relates to its own death. Death for Heidegger is understood as "the possibility of the impossibility of existence [*Existenz*] in general" (*BT* 251), which means that death is the possibility of the impossibility of Dasein having any further future possibilities-to-be that it can throw itself toward in anticipation of its future. This relation to its own death structures Dasein's relation to temporality, which results in Heidegger's three notions of time in division 2 of *Being and Time*: vulgar, worldly, or primordial time. In other words, Heidegger argues that our death structures our ontology based on how we understand our own death's presence in our past, future, and present. Authentic Dasein's relation to temporality results in primordial time while inauthentic Dasein results in time understood in the vulgar sense or in the worldly sense. To begin with, though primordial time is, to borrow Aristotle's distinction, first in the order of nature, we shall begin with what is first in the order of knowledge insofar as we "initially and for the most part [*zunächt und zumeist*]" (*BT* 16) relate to temporality inauthentically. Vulgar time treats time in a pre-Kantian sense as merely outside of us as an objectively present series of infinite nows. Vulgar time is an inauthentic relation to time insofar as it arises from Dasein's flight from how death structures its being through its relation to time (*BT* 403). Vulgar time thus fails to acknowledge how death structures our relation to time and refuses to give any credence to a modality of time outside of the presence of the present now.

While still a result of inauthentically relating to temporality, world time makes advances beyond vulgar time because world time is grounded in the public understanding of time based on the keeping of time on clocks, which is itself grounded in diurnal time. This public nature of world time allows for us to coordinate affairs with others through world time's "datability" (*BT* 388). Thus, world time is a result of Dasein's need in its being-with others to accomplish various activities in the world as it pursues its various projects. Such "circumspect taking care" is, then, reliant on an understanding of temporality "in the mode of making present that awaits and retains" (*BT* 387). The past is retained and the future is awaited all in service of accomplishing in the present what needs doing. The past and future find themselves moored to the making present insofar as the past and future are defined by world time as the "'*now* no longer'" and "'*now* not yet'" respectively (*BT* 387; emphasis mine). So even though world time exceeds the vulgar conception of time as an infinite series of nows because world time has a conception of the past and future, the presence of the present *now* still reigns supreme for world time. Heidegger writes, "[I]n measuring time, time gets made public in such a way that it is encountered in each case and at each time for everyone as 'now and now and now'" (*BT* 397). Moreover, this world time or clock time is effective for all kinds of activities in academia, medicine, athletics, economics, and so on by treating the topics and beings in these various activities as within time. Such a use of world time presents time as the linear arrow of time flowing from the past, through the present, and into the future. Through this, world time *estranges* Dasein from its own death by *tempting* Dasein to see death as only part of its future that is not yet now. While this understanding of time is effective in our dealings with one another in the world, Heidegger does not think that this efficacy of world time is the most originary relation to time that we as Dasein have. The keeping track of and dealing with time, the "time-reckoning" for which world time is so helpful, finds its "existential and ontological necessity" in the being of Dasein that Heidegger calls *care* (*Sorge*; *BT* 392). The ontological feature of care that Heidegger calls *thrownness* (*Geworfenheit*) is the ontological ground for any kind of "public time" (*BT* 392) because Dasein's thrownness consists of all of those ontic, particular features given to a human being upon birth in the world that he or she did not choose but for which he or she is now responsible. Such thrownness involves, then, being the type of being that is always a being-with both things and others in the world. Being attuned to its thrown past in this way, Dasein ontically must reckon with time in a public, datable way. World time finds its origin, then, in the structure of Dasein's being that is grounded in a more primordial temporality.

This primordial time is Heidegger's development of the Kantian and Husserlian idea for how we structure our own experience through temporality. And, in this, temporality becomes the ground of Dasein's being. Hence, in part, why

Heidegger's magnum opus is about being *and* time. In order to understand his idea of primordial time, the elements of the ontological structure of Dasein called care need to be aligned with the three "ecstasies of temporality" (*BT* 314) of having-been (*Gewesenheit*), the present (*Gegenwart*), and the future (*Zukunft*) in order to show the relation of each of these elements. The alignment of these elements and their authentic relation gives rise to the authentic disclosedness (*Erschlossenheit*) of Dasein called anticipatory resoluteness (*vorlaufende Entschlossenheit*). In order to understand what occurs with anticipatory resoluteness, the passage from *Being and Time* toward which I want to work hermeneutically is the following: "Temporalizing does not mean a 'succession' of the ecstasies. The future is not later than the having-been, and the having-been is not earlier than the present. Temporality temporalizes itself as a future that makes present in the process of having-been" (*BT* 334). When Heidegger defines the ontological structure of the human being, Dasein, as care, he already has in mind the temporalized nature of each element of this structure. He defines *care* as "being-ahead-of-oneself-already-in (the world) as being-together-with (innerworldy beings encountered)" (*BT* 186). To begin connecting this ontological structure with authentic temporality, the being-ahead of Dasein concerns Dasein's relation to the future through its existence or *Existenz*. Such *Existenz* concerns not the *mere* existence of Dasein, as existence is colloquially used, but specifically how Dasein throws itself toward future possibilities-to-be or future projects for itself based on Dasein's hopes and anxieties about the future. Dasein's primary ontological orientation is toward these future projects for itself, which means the future takes ontological priority for Dasein. Who Dasein *is*, in the sense of its active, unfolding being (*Wesen*), originates from the coming of these future projects. Yet this orientation to the future is always already grounded in Dasein's having-been. Thus, the "already-in (the world)" of care concerns Dasein's relation to its having-been or past understood through its thrownness in the world. Such thrownness orients Dasein to its future through some mood or attunement (*Stimmung*) in which Dasein finds itself thrown. Authentically, Dasein is attuned in its having-been through anxiety toward its future, specifically toward its death. Dasein's own death always already affects Dasein in its relation to its past and future. Its death is integral to its having-been as part of its thrownness. And its death is integral to its future in the sense of being the possibility of the *Existenz* becoming impossible. Though absent, then, Dasein's death plays a structural role with regard to how Dasein relates to its past and future. Moreover, this connection through death between Dasein's past and future means that being-ahead is never later than being-already-in the world, that is, the future is not later than having-been because Dasein's future remains always grounded in the attunement of a thrown having-been. In other words, the possibilities-to-be approaching Dasein from its future are opened to and closed for Dasein on account of Dasein's past. Furthermore, the having-been of thrownness in this opening and closing of possibilities-to-be is "still in the process of happening"[26] as Dasein anticipates its future.

And this connection of the future with the past comes to bear on the present in Dasein's ontological structure of care according to "being-together-with (innerworldly beings encountered)." Dasein, as discussed in chapter 3, is always a being-with both things and others through which Dasein pursues its future possibilities based on its having-been. Dasein's present does not come between a past that is no more and future that is not yet because in Dasein's present the past and future are coming to bear simultaneously. As Derrida explains, as if riffing on my epigraph for this chapter from Faulkner, "*Dasein* is its past: that means that its past is not passed by" (*H* 97). Consequently, Heidegger maintains that Dasein comes to see itself as distended or stretched (*erstreckt*) through time to the point that in the present Dasein is stretched into its having-been that grounds its future possibilities-to-be. Dasein's present is always already related to its past and future by working out in the present which possibilities to pursue and which to avoid in making them present or actual. Dasein remains in the present dependent on its having-been and its coming future through which Dasein is involved in the activity of temporalizing: of bringing the to come of its future from out of its past to the present. In this way, the past, present, and future never relate in Dasein's experience of temporality in a linear way because Dasein's "future . . . makes present in the process of having-been" (*BT* 334).

This authentic culmination of temporality that I have been describing occurs through Dasein's anticipatory resoluteness. Such resoluteness is Dasein's gathering of the moments of its being as care (i.e., being-ahead, already-being-in, and being-with) to decide to enact possibilities to be in the present while foregoing others. Such resoluteness occurs specifically through what Heidegger calls the moment or the instant (*Augenblick*). This moment is when Dasein resolves to be who it is in the present in relation to its future possibilities-to-be for itself that are grounded in its having-been. This moment is a "making present" (*Gegenwärtigen*) or a gathering into the present of who Dasein is on account of its future possibilities that arise from its thrownness of having-been (*BT* 311, 313). Such actualization of possibilities that have-been, or this weaving together in the present the past and future, allows Dasein to engage the temporalizing of temporality in Dasein's own being. Through this making-present, Derrida explains, Dasein constitutes "the present as the past of a future" (*H* 188). Such a moment allows Dasein to see that temporality is not a succession of the past, to the present, and to the future but to see the present's carrying of the past and future always already with it in and as the "unity" or oneness (*Einheit*) of its being. As Heidegger writes, "Dasein temporalizes itself in the unity [*Einheit*] of future and the having-been as the present. The present, as the Moment, discloses the today authentically" (*BT* 377).

This primordial temporality described by Heidegger is the experience of temporality that occurs with the death of the other *but* with a difference that makes all the difference. In the death of the other, Heidegger's understanding of primordial time finds its phenomenological evidence *except* with regard to this *Einheit* of the *Augenblick* in the presence of the present. While Heidegger acknowledges the importance of the absence of the past and the future, particularly the absence of Dasein's death, for the present, the authentic culmination of this absence seems to get effaced or at least loses prominence in the *making present* of the past and future by Dasein. This critique is not to ignore Heidegger's analysis that the wholeness or being-a-whole (*Ganzsein*) of Dasein is a matter of being unwhole. Such wholeness implies that the absence inherent to Dasein's having-been and future, namely the absence of its own death in both its past and future, plays an integral role in the structure of Dasein's being. In this regard, Derrida even comments that for Dasein "the past and the future are not simply left behind as past present or future present but *more than that*, are *still* or are *already*, but in a still or an already that no longer have the sense of presence" (*H* 148; emphasis his).[27] The present is always full of Dasein's having-been and future, but such fullness is not on account of the presence of Dasein's death but more of death's *absence*. Thus, Heidegger says that the structure of care "tells us unambiguously that something is always still *outstanding* [*aussteht*] in Dasein which has not yet become 'real' as a potentiality-of-its-being. A *constant unfinished quality* thus lies in the essence of the basic constitution of Dasein" (*BT* 227; emphasis his). This unwholeness (*Unganzheit*) of Dasein is structural because — to recall what I have named the Epicurean problem in Heidegger's analysis of Dasein's being-toward-death — to make real its own death, which is precisely what is "outstanding" for Dasein, means that Dasein becomes "no-longer-being-there" (*BT* 227) in the sense that its *Existenz* becomes impossible. So to eliminate "what is outstanding in its being is equivalent to annihilating its being" (*BT* 227). The wholeness of Dasein is, and must always already be if Dasein is to be Dasein, unwhole. The being of Dasein is marked in this by a structural absence whose presence would bring to an end Dasein as a whole. This structural absence notwithstanding in Heidegger's analysis and Derrida's early reading of it, the emphasis on the *unity* of the *Augenblick* in anticipatory resoluteness becomes problematic when placing this account of temporality in relation to surviving the death of the other.

For in surviving the death of the other, this past cannot be brought into a unity with the present. Mourning always remains workless and fails to make present the absence of the death of the other. Even when the death of the other is made present by things and places de-distanced with the now dead other, this making present, as I have argued, is a making present precisely of the dead other's *absence*. A present absence or absent presence is experienced in the newly de-distanced world after the death of the other as I have argued in part 2. In this regard, this lived experience of temporality through mourning is phenomenologically similar to the lived experience of temporality after trauma considered more generally, especially considering that trauma is the result not merely of a past experience but one that continues to leave traces on the present because trauma disrupts the linearity of temporality. For example, in her twenty years of working with survivors of sexual and domestic violence, Judith Harman's description of these survivors's experience of time after their trauma is similar to what I am developing here. She writes, "Long after the danger is past, traumatized people relive the event as though it were continually recurring in the present. They cannot resume the normal course of their lives, for the trauma repeatedly interrupts. It is as if time stops at the moment of trauma."[28] Yet I argue that with regard to the trauma of the death of the other that this being stuck in the past is a result not of the past being so present that it takes over a survivor's present. Rather, I argue that the past death of the other interrupts or haunts the present because the past cannot be made fully present and thereby moved beyond. Accordingly, the absence of the trauma in the present is the cause of this transformation of time in the survival after the past trauma of the death of the other.

To illustrate this further, one survivor whose descendants died during the Holocaust reports hating the Jewish celebration of Sukkoth (the Feast of the Tabernacles) every year because this tradition now brings with it "the persistent memory of who was *not there*, who would *not* be celebrating with us."[29] The absence of the now dead other is surely made present in the yearly celebration of Sukkoth, but this making present is not an effacement of the other's absence but a continual reminder of it. The repetition of this tradition blends the past with the present while preserving each in their alterity so that the temporality of this repetition is a kind of "purgatory between past and present tense."[30] In this and many other stories from survivors of relatives who died in the Holocaust, the dead other returns in a present yet absent way to the survivor at various moments in their life as they continue to work with the mourning. And in these stories the focus is never on the visitation of some ghost, as represented in so many movies, but of the presence of something that was at the same time *not there* in the way other things in the world are present.[31] Such is the absence of the other's presence or presence of the other's absence as I have been describing it, and now I am describing the temporality of this as a *différance* of the past and the present. With this, to recontextualize Van der Kolk's account of trauma, the death of the other is traumatic because it leaves traces in history, on culture, on families, in the mind and emotions, and "even on our biology and immune systems."[32] Consequently, the death of the other remains traumatic because the traces it leaves can be understood as a disruption of temporality in terms of the present absence of the other or, specifically, the dead other's absence coming back, as if from the future, as a revenant or ghost that, once again, "begins by coming back" (*SM* 11).[33] Such a ghost is a "non-object" because it is a "non-present present" or the "being-there of an absent or departed one" (*SM* 5). The being-there, Da-sein, or presence of the dead other is absence. And we have seen how the dead other returns and haunts the survivor with regard to how the brain deals with the trauma of the death of the other by turning and returning to the loss.[34] In this way, Derrida refers to the revenant as coming from the future because its haunting is a coming back or a returning, as if from the future, of a past or having-been that is unable to be unified or made present.

These turnings of trauma in surviving the death of the other are the haunting of the past and its refusal to stay in the past. The death of the other continues to invade the lived experience of the survivor through which the survivor's relation to temporality undergoes a transformation. Such a return of the revenant "is not identifiable, one cannot see, localize, fix any form, one cannot decide between hallucination and perception, there are only displacements" (*SM* 170). In other words, the dead other as past cannot be unified with the present because this other continually spooks the present with its absence. The ghost cannot be made present through the temporalizing process in our lived experience.

Therefore, the Heideggerian idea of primordial temporality captures our lived experience of temporality but not the lived experience of temporality in surviving the death of the other.[35] For, as Derrida says, "In *Being and Time*, the existential analysis does not want to know anything about the ghost [*revenant*] or about mourning" (A 60). Hans Ruin argues, in contrast to this claim by Derrida, that while Heidegger does not explicitly mention the dead as constitutive of Dasein's being-with in *Being and Time*, Heidegger makes an *implicit* inclusion of the dead in Dasein's ontological constitution as having-been (see *BT* §72).[36] While Ruin's argument is a challenge to Derrida's reading, Ruin does seem to agree with Derrida's reading nevertheless because this inclusion of the dead, Ruin emphasizes, is only *implicit* in *Being and Time*. Moreover, much as I have argued in chapter 1 regarding the relation of gathering and difference in Heidegger and Derrida, even if Heidegger's understanding of temporality in *Being and Time* can be understood as not effacing absence, getting this point across in Heidegger's text requires a significant amount of hermeneutical work throughout which no consensus has been made as to the role absence continues to play in Heidegger's authentic temporality.[37] Consequently, Derrida's understanding of temporality in response and relation to Heidegger's seems to emphasize more so than Heidegger does how absence permeates temporality and how temporality cannot be unified but remains fractured. Moreover, such an account of fractured temporality fits more readily with the experience of mourning in surviving the death of the other. Consequently, I want to develop such an understanding of time that confronts both ghost and mourning. This means that primordial temporality needs the supplement of the ghost or a hauntological supplement to its ontology.

The Death of the Other and Haunted Time

Derrida's introduction of the idea of hauntology in his 1993 *Specters of Marx* is a reworking or rewriting of the ideas of *différance* and iterability for which he became (in)famous in the late sixties.[38] As discussed in chapter 1, *Of Grammatology* and the essay "Différance" engage Heidegger's thinking of being and the ontic-ontological difference by always describing the trace, arche-writing, supplementarity, iterability, and *différance* as "more 'originary'" (*OG* 23) or "'older'" (*MP* 22). Each time in this engagement with Heidegger, Derrida uses scare quotes to signal that he means by *originary* and *older* something other than what would be expected because, à la his own poststructuralism, any putative or supposed origin is always already an *effect* of supplementarity. The origin that he refers to with *différance* is an odd kind of origin because in the origin can be found already the play of signifiers and supplementarity. The supposed origin is really just another trace and not the *pure* origin that metaphysical thinking hopes it to be. In *Specters of Marx*, Derrida says something similar with regard to hauntology along two fronts. On the one hand, he describes hauntology as "larger and more powerful than an ontology or a thinking of being" (*SM* 10). This description makes hauntology, like *différance*, more "originary" than such a thinking of being insofar as hauntology would be the condition of the possibility of any "ontology, theology, positive or negative onto-theology" (*SM* 63). On the other hand, hauntology is more than just "larger and more powerful" (*SM* 10) than any ontology because hauntology, as does *différance*, brings into question any "reassuring order of presents and, especially, the border between the present, the actual or present reality of the present, and everything that can be opposed to it: absence, non-presence, non-effectivity, inactuality, virtuality, . . . the simulacrum . . . and so forth" (*SM* 48). Hauntology brings into question any such binary logic (*SM* 78). And, as he emphasizes in both the late sixties and in 1993, by calling into question binary logic, he is not favoring the other side of the binary. He is not favoring absence over presence because he is trying to show that presence and absence are always already bound up together — that each haunts the other. Presence and absence are always brought under *différance*, then, just as I have shown that life and death are in the survival after the death of the other.

So rather than a binary logic, Derrida develops with his hauntology a "spectral logic" understood, in a direct connection with his earlier work, as a matter of a "deconstructive thinking of the trace, of iterability, . . . of supplementarity, and so forth" (*SM* 94). Thus, with the idea of hauntology, he rewrites or repeats his thinking of deconstruction to say that the binary, oppositional thinking of metaphysics that hopes for the presence of a *pure* origin is really a thinking haunted by the absence of such an origin. And he wants to, with this, introduce this idea of haunting to "every concept, beginning with the concepts of being and time" (*SM* 202). Thus, rather than a Heideggerian ontology of the syntagm *my own death* engaged through the being-toward-death of authentic Dasein in anticipatory resoluteness, Derrida proposes what I call a hauntology of the death of the other.[39] For the death of the other as event approaches as a ghost from a past that haunts the future of a survivor who remains unable to bring this ghost into the present presence of a unifying temporality. The event of the death of the other becomes, then, one of "the great 'experiences' of our life" that is never "lived through"[40] because this "experience" occurs im-possibly at the instant without passing through the full presence of the present. The temporality of an event, specifically here that of the death of the other, is a hauntological temporality. Derrida even suggests bringing together this thinking of the death of the other with the event and its temporality when he says that "the specter is of the event" (*SM* 125). The death of the other has-been and returns as if from the survivor's future to haunt her present. And in this return, the death cannot be made fully present, which means that the survivor cannot fully mourn this loss. Such is the arrival of event of the death of the other *at the instant*.

And this instant through which the death of the other haunts the survivor must be thought in distinction from the Heideggerian *Augenblick*. Accordingly, Derrida calls this instant that transforms the present of the survivor the "spectral moment" that does not belong to time understood as "the linking of modalized presents" (*SM* xix).[41] This moment becomes the phenomenological footprint of the time of Shakespeare's *Hamlet* that is out of joint because the death of the other would not be completely joinable to the present. The death of the other would make this not a broken or completely dysfunctional time but "a time without certain joining or determinable conjunction" (*SM* 20).[42] The temporality of surviving the death of the other is a temporality that continues but is punctuated by the ghost of the death of the other disjoining temporality at its joints unexpectedly and without reason. To say this differently, world time remains untouched after the death of the other insofar as the earth continues to orbit around the sun creating sunrise and sunset. However, the survivor may wish this were not the case because her relation to time has been disrupted. And this disruption of a survivor's time may be enough to turn this event of the death of the other into poison that spells the end of the survivor too. Or the survivor may work with this disruption for the promise of new yet different life in the aftermath of the death of the other. As the poet W. H. Auden says after his experience of the death of the other, "Stop all the clocks."[43] The death of the other disrupts the survivor's weekly schedule and daily routine. The survivor's primordial temporality or how she finds herself in time has been fractured by the haunting of the past death of the other that cannot be passed by or through. For the absence of the dead other cannot be brought to full presence and, thus, returns in a half-present/half-absent phenomenality. Accordingly, the worklessness of her mourning is a result of this inability to make the death of the other fully present. So rather than being able to calculate in a linear way the time that mourning may take, mourning does not obey any such "arithmetic of mourning."[44]

Often in surviving the death of the other, attempts are made, especially by media, social media, and the internet, to stitch time back together in a linear understanding of it in an effort to allow us to live and relive an event of the death of the other as it occurred according to world time. This certainly occurred with the 9/11 attacks in New York City as news outlets replayed repeatedly the various traumatic scenes during that day.[45] We see this even, in part, in the Gates of Time at the Oklahoma City bombing memorial. For by reinscribing this event into the clock time between 9:01 and 9:03 a.m., the memorial tries to make this event of the death of the other partially predictable, understandable, and measurable within a linear calculation of world time. While such efforts are part of the mourning process, especially when concerning such public deaths of the other, we must, as Mauro Carbone maintains, resist such "temporal therapy"[46] that can cause us to miss our more originary relation to temporality in surviving the death of the other through the spectral temporality of survival. For many of the survivors of the deaths that occurred in Oklahoma City, for example, their *temporality* is stuck at the world time of 9:02 a.m. because the other who died at this datable and measurable time refuses to remain past according to world time but haunts the *temporality* of the survivor's present infused with her own past. The now dead other's absence haunts the present of the survivor. Consequently, this hauntology of the death of the other serves as a way to redefine the being-with others and things of Heidegger's Dasein as part of its structural being-in-the-world understood as care into also always already a "being-with specters" (*SM* xviii). Existence understood as the *différance* of life and death, as lifedeath, is this "between life and death" (*SM* xvii) entangled with spectral others, that is, with the death of the other.[47] Such a self as being-with specters is a matter of "the lodging, the haunt of a host of ghosts" (*F* xxiii). Or as Derrida paraphrases Descartes's famous philosopheme, "I mourn therefore I am" (*P* 321). A survivor's being-with the ghost of the death of the other in this spectral moment can be seen especially in the effect that such death bears on memory as our access to the past. For ghosts "signal unsettled *memories* coming forward."[48]

Haunted Temporality and Memory

When the world is gone with the death of the other, the survivor carries the other in her memories. But in this carrying, the absence of the other haunts the survivor in both the recall of the memories themselves of the now dead other and also through the loss of memory that attends the other's death. In both cases, what comes back and haunts the survivor is the absence of the other's presence that constitutes, in part, the dead other's alterity. Memories are often a survivor's access to the now dead other, but through these memories the survivor is reminded not only of who the other had been but also that the other is now absent. For example, Adichie comments after her father's death: "Rather than succor, my memories bring eloquent stabs of pain that say, 'This is what you will never again have.' Sometimes they bring laughter, but laughter like glowing coals that soon burst aflame in pain. I hope that it is a *question of time* — that it is just too soon, too terribly soon, to expect memories to serve only as salve."[49] Derrida explores this relationship among the death of the other, memory, and temporality in his own work on and mourning of Paul de Man in *Memoires for Paul de Man*.

His reflection on de Man's work follows de Man's engagement with the distinction in Hegel's *Encyclopedia of Philosophical Sciences* between the two kinds of memory or remembering of *Erinnerung* and *Gedächtnis*. I argue that Derrida's deconstruction of this distinction deepens the description of what is happening in workless mourning because his deconstruction describes the memory at work in such mourning. For while workless mourning brings under *différance* the Freudian and psychoanalytic distinctions between mourning and melancholy *and* introjection and incorporation, the memory involved in this workless mourning brings *Erinnerung* and *Gedächtnis* under *différance*. Consequently, *Erinnerung* is related to mourning/introjection while *Gedächtnis* is related to melancholy/incorporation. Thus, Derrida reads *Erinnerung* in conjunction with the interiorizing of the other in Freudian normal mourning in an effort to call this "remembrance as interiorization" (*MPM* 35). And this memory is considered by the tradition as "good memory" or memory that has life in it (*MPM* 70). Nevertheless, Derrida maintains that this *Erinnerung* would be the remembering of the other that reduces the alterity of the other by interiorizing or introjecting the other as part of the subject's ego. Such remembrance would be, in turn, a forgetting of the other in his or her alterity. With *Erinnerung*, the ego takes the dead into itself interiorizing the dead totally so that "it is no longer other" (*EO* 58). For Hegel maintains that *Erinnerung* lifts the content of intuition "out of the particularity of space and time, the particularity to which the content, in its immediacy, is bound" and puts this content in the ego's "inwardness, in its own space and its own time."[50] The other remembered in this way would be "posited as mine" and "preserved unconsciously" in the "nocturnal pit [*Schacht*]" of the ego.[51] I would even go so far as to associate this memory with the unity of making-present in the Heideggerian anticipatory resoluteness of the *Augenblick*. For this memory, says Derrida, "is the name of what is no longer only a mental 'capacity' oriented toward one of the three modes of the present, the past present . . . present present and the future present. Memory projects itself toward the future, and it constitutes the presence of the present" (*MPM* 56–57). Such memory would be the making-present of the other. This kind of memory would be what psychologists call "normal memories" that have a beginning, middle, and end with logical sequencing.[52] In relation to mourning, this would be a preoccupation with making-present the death of the other from the past in an effort to remember her but through which her alterity or absence gets forgotten and effaced by presence. This would be a failure to allow the death of the other to remain other as ghost and absent. This would be a failure of workless mourning.

In contrast, Derrida reads *Gedächtnis* as "a thinking memory . . . linked to technical and mechanical hypomnesis" (*MPM* 35–36). He calls *Gedächtnis* a thinking memory because it is related to the process of memorization through all of the mechanical techniques by which memorization happens, most particularly that of writing. *Gedächtnis* is, then, "the mechanical or technical form of memory at stake in memorizing a poem or in the act of writing."[53] With this connection to writing and writing's own connection, as explored in *Of Grammatology*, to absence and death, in contrast to the "good memory" or living memory of *Erinnerung*, the tradition has treated this other memory as the "bad dozing memory" that can mark death to the life of good memory (*MPM* 70–71). This other memory, though "bad" as considered by the tradition, is considered in Derrida's own engagement as a remembrance of the other in a self-avowed failure to bring the other into full presence in the interior of the ego. This would be a remembering of the other that allows the other to remain in his or her alterity. Hegel's understanding of *Gedächtnis* even allows for this possibility when he explains that this kind of memory no longer deals with the interiorized image of *Erinnerung* but, instead, deals with "a reality that is the product of intelligence itself."[54] Consequently, *Gedächtnis* allows the other to remain other and exterior to the ego while also remembering the other within or interior to the ego. The other, then, says Hegel, becomes "a reality known *inside out* that remains enclosed in the inside of intelligence and is its outside, its existing side, only within intelligence itself."[55] As such, *Gedächtnis* would be integral to the remembering and memory of workless mourning that embodies the spectral moment. For these reasons Derrida says that the "power of *Gedächtnis* without *Erinnerung*" is a memory that is "pre-occupied by a past which has never been present and will never allow itself to be reanimated in the interiority of consciousness" (*MPM* 65). This memory or remembrance of the other would be, then, a recognition of, in the case of the death of the other, that such an event is never lived through or has never been brought into presence and, therefore, can never be fully present. Moreover, this would be a memory of the dead other that refuses to attempt to make-present the death of the other. Rather, it remembers the other in her alterity by allowing the presence of her absence or absence of her presence to haunt the survivor in the moment.

However, rather than maintain that *Erinnerung* and *Gedächtnis* are in a dialectical relationship, as Hegel says, Derrida wants to hold both ideas of memory together in a workless kind of memory. Such workless memory would not be the normal memory described as linear by psychology but a traumatic memory that remains "disorganized" and "dissociated"[56] because the trauma from the past death continues to leave traces on the present disrupting the linear flow of temporality as I have been arguing. Moreover, this workless memory that attends workless mourning revolves around the act of forgetting. Derrida says that the "law of mourning" maintains that for mourning to succeed "it would well have to fail, to fail well" (*WM* 144) because in order to interiorize the other *in her alterity*, mourning must fail to interiorize the other. In the process of interiorizing and introjecting the other in Freudian normal mourning, the other's alterity is forgotten. To put this in terms of memory, in order to remember, specifically *Erinnerung*, the other well and not forget her alterity, remembering, *Erinnerung*, must fail. And we can understand this failure along two fronts. On the one hand, mourning must fail because the death of the other as past cannot be made fully present. So the past cannot be fully interiorized or introjected because of the past's hauntology in surviving the death of the other. With this, I have shown, in chapter 4, that survivors often turn to melancholy objects as ways to memorialize the other and "signify the incompletion of mourning"[57] insofar as the survivor cannot go back to the past and make-present the now dead other. On the other hand, mourning must fail in the process of introjecting the other by becoming always bound with melancholy and *Gedächtnis*. For only through this relation can the other *as other* be carried in and along the body and incorporated in the crypt of the psyche. Only through *différance* with melancholy and *Gedächtnis* can the other's alterity be remembered well, that is according to her alterity and absence. Memory, *Erinnerung*, must fail so as not to forget the other's alterity. Yet memory must fail well in order to remember, *Gedächtnis*, the other's alterity. Through this failure or through this *différance* of memory's two sides, the survivor approaches what Derrida calls — and notice the scare quotes once more — "a memory already 'older' than *Gedächtnis* and *Erinnerung*" (*MPM* 71). Yet this kind of workless memory has never and will have never existed as a truly "older or more original 'third term'" (*MPM* 137) because workless memory is only possible through the differing and deferral of the two sides of memory in one another. Such is the *différance* operative in a workless mourning. And such is a hauntological memory — the memory of workless mourning.

To offer a phenomenological bite to this workless memory, I maintain that this kind of memory can be understood through the research being done on transactive memory. As first defined by David Wegner, transactive memory is a social or group memory that individuals form with one another, particularly those with whom they are close or intimate, according to the three primary stages of memory: encoding, storing, and retrieval.[58] Transactive memory is the memory that the self builds always with the other. Consequently, the being-with of the human being must be extended to include this transactive memory as a *memory-with*. After all, transactive memory is built or encoded through our engagements *with* the other, and the information within such memory is stored not only in the memory of the solitary ego but also in that of the other, which means that the self relies upon the other for retrieving such information. Wegner comments, "The bonds of intimacy bring with them a large degree of cognitive interdependence, a tendency for individuals' thought processes and structures to be mutually determined."[59] Consequently, this relation with the other for memory-with is not asymmetrical but reciprocal insofar as I would help encode, store, and retrieve the memory of the other as well. For in a relationship with the other, both the I and the other share a "circumstantial responsibility for the knowledge"[60] for, especially, storing and retrieving the information that pertains to their shared memory. Transactive memory reveals the socially constructed nature of memory, especially as this memory gets constructed through those with whom we are close. Such a development of who each person is through and on account of the other further shows that the idea of a pure self, of an *ipse*, is a metaphysical phantasm that aims to deny the relationality of the self. For the self is always a being-with, and, as Levinas, Nancy, Romano, and Derrida continually show, the self only becomes a self through the other.

And the self in its own memory, I am arguing, remains a being-with. While this term of transactive memory was invented in 1987 before the rise of the internet and, especially, social media, the idea of transactive memory has even wider resonance and reach now because of our connections across the globe with others and various virtual stores of information such as Twitter or X, Facebook, Instagram, Snapchat, TikTok, and Wikipedia. Our memory is more and more transactive with all of our technological advancements so that personal memory is more adequately understood as memory through and with the other.

Such socially constructed memory-with seems ostensibly more *present* or able to be made-present with the rise of more and new inventions of cloud-sharing. After all, knowledge in the age of the internet, the Cloud, and AI is less about what you know and more about knowing where to look and how fast you can find information. We are continually relying more on others for, especially, the storage and retrieval of memory. A limit-situation of this ability to make-present such transactive memory, though, is the death of the other. For here we come into contact with a loss of transactive memory because the other with whom a survivor has formed her memory is now lost. The now dead other had played an important role in the encoding of memory, but now the other is absent and with her the survivor's access to the storage and retrieval of the parts of their memory that the survivor relied upon the other for storing and retrieving. Moreover, the now dead other can no longer play a part in the encoding of any more of their memory-with. Consequently, the death of the other means that the survivor loses part of her self, namely her memory that was in the other. Perhaps this loss of memory through and with the other is partly why Augustine cries out after the death of his friend Nebridius, "I did not wish to live with only *half* of myself."[61] As if commenting on this line from Augustine, Romano maintains that mourning understood as "*mourir à autrui*," which he articulates as a dying to another that implies a dying to self, "[T]he suffering of bereavement lies especially in that, being stripped of a beloved, I no longer fully belong to myself, since the one in whose sight I was unique and irreplaceable no longer exists."[62] This death of the self that accompanies the death of the other can be understood, as I am arguing here, in terms of the shared (*partage*) memory with this other. For the survivor can no longer retrieve this memory-with that has been part of the survivor's own identity because now the storage space with the other has been lost. So when the other dies, the world shared with the other, namely the access to past encoded memory stored in the other, dies with the other too. Accordingly, Wegner says in relation to the loss of the other and its effect on the survivor that "the grief and disorientation that accompanies the dissolution of a close relationship can be traced to the loss of transactive memory capacities. . . . The loss of transactive memory feels like *losing a part of one's own mind*."[63] While this discussion is clearly directed toward relationships with others that are intimate, in connection with what I have called the existential difference that attends the death of the other, the effect of such death on a survivor relates directly to the relational difference that the other had played in the survivor's life while the other had been alive. One way to understand the existential difference of others on someone is to look at what significance the other had in someone's transactive memory. The more significant the role the other plays on someone's transactive memory, the greater the effect or impact of the death of the other on the survivor. With the rise of social media and continual globalization of the world through technology, the others who constitute a person's transactive memory are becoming much wider in scope. And with this so too is the wider scope of the effect of a death of the other across the globe.

In connection with transactive memory, the death of the other is, then, a death of the pluralized world insofar as this death affects our ability to relate to our past and the information that had been encoded, stored, and retrievable with and by the other. So the haunting of the death of the other is a haunting not merely of the absence of the other but also a haunting of this memory that had been encoded, stored, and retrieved with the now dead other. The death of the other transforms the survivor's relation to temporality insofar as he loses the ability to make-present the past that had been built with the now dead other. This transactive memory will never be able to be made present in the aftermath of the death of the other. This world, the world, is gone with the death of the other. In this, the death of the other transforms the survivor's relation to her past. So not only does the death of the other continue to haunt a survivor's present but also the access to memory shared with the now dead other haunt's the survivor as well.[64] Consequently, the death of the other as a death of the world transforms the survivor's relation to temporality insofar as the survivor carries the other in and through the present absence of this loss of memory.

Remembering the dead other becomes fraught with absence considering the transactive memory with and through the other. The survivor can remember what they shared with the other, but this remembering is a recalling of what is now absent. The survivor remembers, but she does not remember well because the other on whom the survivor would rely in order to remember fully in the present is gone, lost, *fort*. So the survivor remembers but fails to remember fully. Her memory remains amnesiac, hauntological, or workless. Her memory, *Erinnerung*, is now bound to and contains another, less reliable memory, *Gedächtnis*. And this remembering of the other through which the other haunts the survivor affects not just the survivor's relation to his past. This remembering also transforms his future. For, after all, the ghost returns as if from the future.

Chapter Seven

Lost Possibilities and a Fractured Future

[T]he thinking of the specter . . . signals toward the future. It is a thinking of the past, a legacy that can come only from that which has not yet arrived — from the *arrivant* itself.

— Jacques Derrida, *Specters of Marx*

Heidegger's idea of the *Einheit* or unity of the moment of authenticity understood through anticipatory resoluteness has become problematic for understanding originary temporality in the aftermath of the death of the other. In the previous chapter, I considered how the event of the death of the other as past and absent refuses to remain past but affects the survivor not as something present but through its present absence. This absence of the other refuses to be unified in the presence of any present moment. Consequently, the moment of the present in the aftermath of the death of the other must be understood as a *spectral* moment. In this chapter, I deepen the analysis of this spectral moment by looking at how the *future* of a survivor of the death of the other remains riddled with a recalcitrant absence that cannot be brought into any unity. This absence effects the survivor's present as the past death of the other twists "its branches all the way into the future."[1] The absence that fills a survivor's future in the aftermath of the death of the other is interminable insofar as the possibilities that had been viable with and through the living other are now after the death of the other impossible possibilities that cannot ever be actualized. To think through these possibilities that fracture the survivor's relation to his future, I want to think through their impossibility in this chapter.

To begin thinking the impossibility of these possibilities, I begin with Heidegger's understanding of the future's relation to the present through his analysis of possibility and impossibility in the context of Dasein's death in *Being and Time*. I argue, however, that the death of the other requires a different description of a survivor's relation to the future. For the possibility of Dasein's own death as Heidegger describes it is a possible impossibility whose occurrence is certain, even if indefinitely, to happen. Dasein's death is a possibility that marks the impossibility of Dasein continuing to be at all. And this impossibility occurs or comes to fruition. In contrast, the death of the other marks an impossible future that has an effect on the present but whose impossibility can never be brought to actuality. The fissures from the death of the other run through the survivor's future causing the survivor to reconstitute her relation to the future on account of the felt loss of possibilities that follow the wake of the death of the other. The future in the aftermath of the death of the other remains full of possibilities, but those possibilities connected with the now dead other are now dead too sending ripple effects through the survivor's relation to this fractured future. These impossible possibilities that attend the death of the other make the death of the other itself an impossibility unlike that of our own personal death. Consequently, I argue that the survivor of the death of the other experiences two modalities of the impossible. On the one hand, she experiences impossible possibilities or those future possibilities that will now never take place as had been the expectation while the other was living. On the other hand, the survivor experiences im-possible possibilities that never come into the present and through this absence restructure the present from out of the future. In these two ways, the death of the other has an effect on the future insofar as the future becomes full of possibilities whose occurrences are the ghosts of the past coming to haunt the future with their interminable present absence that cannot be unified in any moment but must be approached in the spectral moment.

The Possible Impossibility of Dasein's Death

I have shown throughout this description of the death of the other that Heidegger understands the ontology of the human being understood as Dasein through what he calls care. This ontological structure unfolds according to three primary, equiprimordial aspects: thrownness, projection, and falling prey or authenticity. Each of these aspects of care has a distinctive temporality. Thrownnness pertains to the having-been or past of Dasein, projection pertains to the future possibilities-to-be of Dasein, and falling prey or authenticity pertains to how Dasein embodies the present in relation to its past and future. In this temporalized, ontological structure, the future takes ontological priority because, as Heidegger says in the opening lines of his existential analytic of care, the "'essence' ['*Wesen*'] of Dasein lies in its existence [*Existenz*]" (*BT* 41). Dasein's essence is not a static whatness or thatness for Heidegger but is an active essence that is always already unfolding. Hence, Heidegger names this essence the *Wesen* of Dasein where *Wesen* is to be read in its verbal form as the active coming to be or coming to itself. This active essence finds its fullest expression in the *Existenz* of Dasein because such existence implies that Dasein determines who it is going to become as it strives for actualizing or avoiding the future possibilities-to-be or projects for itself. Dasein's future takes ontological priority because through these future projects, Dasein determines who it is, its *Wesen*, in the present. Consequently, the future is not just a later occurrence on Heidegger's understanding of originary temporality because this future unfolds in the present. As Heidegger has said, the future "makes present" (*BT* 334).

Moreover, these projects or future possibilities-to-be for Dasein are always already grounded in the having-been or past of Dasein's thrownness. Thus, Heidegger says that this future makes present "in the process of having-been" (*BT* 334). Dasein throws itself (*entwirft*) at its future possibilities-to-be. And these future possibilities are themselves already thrown (*geworfene*) possibilities. As I have shown in the previous chapter, this ontological "being-ahead" of Dasein through projection is a being-ahead that is "already-in (the world)" or already thrown into the world (*BT* 186). So Dasein's thrownness orients Dasein to its future by both opening certain possibilities-to-be for Dasein and closing certain possibilities-to-be. Accordingly, Dasein's past does not come sequentially before Dasein's future because its future remains always grounded in its having-been. The past is always already affecting and effecting Dasein's future projects that it pursues and avoids. Consequently, as I discussed in the previous chapter, the past of Dasein is never fully passed because the past is "still in the process of happening"[2] as Dasein determines its being through projecting or throwing itself towards these *thrown* possibilities-to-be. The past and future of Dasein remain integrally connected so that Dasein's past constitutes Dasein's future as Dasein in the present unfolds who it is by pursuing this future. Heidegger's primary example for how this works ontologically is, of course, his analysis of death and being-toward-death. By understanding how Dasein's own death is linked to a notion of the impossible, Heidegger's analysis shows how the absence of the future can affect the present. Through this, I can begin showing why this notion of impossibility is inadequate for understanding the impossibility of the future that attends the death of the other.

To begin, Dasein's death is integral to its having-been as part of its thrownness. Moreover, its death, as I have shown, is integral to its future in the sense of being the possibility of Dasein's *Existenz* becoming impossible or ending. For when Dasein's future death arrives — and it will arrive because Dasein's finitude means, in part, that Dasein will not exist forever — "this attainment becomes the absolute loss of being-in-the-world. It [Dasein] is then never again to be experienced as a being" (*BT* 228). Dasein's death plays a special, structural role with regard to how Dasein relates to its past and future insofar as its personal death constitutes both its thrownness and projection. Dasein's own death remains structurally part of its being from the moment that it is thrown into the world, and this finitude arising from the thrownness of death becomes the primary and pivotal possibility-to-be or project for Dasein's being.

Heidegger's description of this being-toward-death begins with his account for how Dasein's death reveals the wholeness of Dasein's being (*Ganzsein*) as always unwhole based upon what I have previously called the Epicurean problem that Heidegger develops in his analysis of death. This problem is, in short, the idea that as Dasein remains Dasein, its death remains outstanding (*aussteht*) or merely possible. Yet when Dasein dies and achieves the wholeness of its being through the actualization of this possibility of its own death, Dasein is no longer Dasein because it is no longer there to be the unfolding of its *Wesen* through its existence. So while Dasein exists, its death does not; when its death arrives, Dasein no longer exists. Heidegger elaborates on this Epicurean problem by calling Dasein's death "the possibility of the impossibility of existence [*Existenz*] in general" (*BT* 251).

The relationship of possibility and impossibility with regard to Dasein's death can be seen by first understanding how Dasein's death is a possibility. Death is one of the possibilities-to-be through which Dasein works out its own *Wesen*. Yet Dasein's death is a particular kind of possibility that sets it apart from any other possibility-to-be in Dasein's future because death marks Dasein ontologically as a "being-toward-death" (*BT* 236). In other words, Dasein's ontology as its relation to temporality arises through death structuring its being. The ontological-temporal structure of care results from Dasein's relation to its own death. Consequently, Heidegger calls death "the ownmost, nonrelational, certain, and as such, indefinite and insuperable possibility of Dasein" (*BT* 248). Through these four characteristics, death holds a unique place for Dasein as a possibility-to-be because death is disclosed as Dasein's own impossibility of being Dasein. The possibility of death reveals death to be the impossibility of any further *Existenz* for Dasein. In other words, Dasein's death is its impossibility of being able to be there for the disclosure of its own essence. Consequently, death is the *ownmost* possibility-to-be for Dasein not simply because death is marked by mineness (*Jemeinigkeit*) but also because death holds the trump card for Dasein being able to pursue any further possibilities-to-be. When Dasein's death arrives, and it will arrive, Dasein can no longer be Dasein by working out its being through its future projects. Furthermore, this ownmost possibility belongs structurally to Dasein as its *nonrelational* possibility-to-be. Death is nonrelational because no one can die Dasein's death for it. Dasein's death is always its own or colored through mineness. Even if someone sacrifices herself for me, for example, I may have not died in that moment, but my own death continues to be mine and only mine that I must undergo. As Heidegger says regarding such sacrifice, "Such dying for . . . can never mean that the other has thus had his death in the least taken away" (*BT* 231).

And Dasein's pursuit of this ownmost, nonrelational possibility of its being is *insuperable* because this possibility is always already imminent, underway, or in process. The insuperability of personal death means that death is structural to Dasein's thrownness and its projection. Regarding death and thrownness, Heidegger, quoting Georg Simmel, writes, "'As soon as a human being is born, he is old enough to die right away'" (*BT* 236). Dasein's death as thrown is insuperable because its death becomes structurally part of its own birth. Dasein's future death is a possibility set by its having-been. Moreover, in terms of projection, having been thrown as a finite being through death, Dasein from the moment it is born begins projecting or throwing itself ontologically toward this possibility of its being. As such, Dasein's being-toward-death allows Heidegger to distinguish between the *Ableben* of Dasein and the *Sterben* of Dasein. When Dasein comes to an end physiologically, biologically, or medically with death, this is a matter of Dasein's demise or *Ableben*. And Dasein's demise will occur whether or not Dasein authentically relates to its ownmost, nonrelational, and insuperable possibility-to-be through *Sterben* or dying. This *Sterben* concerns, then, authentically or inauthentically relating to its own death as Dasein's distinctive possibility-to-be. To die in the sense of *Sterben* is Heidegger's way of describing how Dasein's being gets constituted through its relation to its own death, that is, how Dasein is a being-toward-death authentically or inauthentically. In making this distinction between demising and dying, Heidegger maintains that only a being such as Dasein who is a being-toward-death can demise (*BT* 238; cf. *A* 39). Demising is the medical and biological death of Dasein, but such demising is possible only because Dasein can die (*Sterben*) in the sense of being the type of being (*Seiende*) whose being (*Sein*) is a being-toward-death. This means that Dasein can demise while inauthentically dying, or Dasein can demise while authentically dying. The possibility of demising holds only because of the possibility of dying either authentically or inauthentically. Other nonhuman animals cannot demise. Instead, they die in the sense of perishing (*Verenden*) for Heidegger. Most importantly, though, Dasein's death understood as dying (*Sterben*) is Dasein's being-toward-death or how Dasein relates authentically or inauthentically to its death.

Relating authentically to this death requires understanding, lastly, that Dasein's death is not just its ownmost, nonrelational, and insuperable possibility-to-be but also its *certain yet indefinite* possibility-to-be. Dasein's death is *certain* because when it arrives, and it will certainly arrive, it marks Dasein as no longer Dasein. Yet *the when* of this certain possibility-to-be makes Dasein's death simultaneously, in defiance of all logic, certain and *uncertain*. Dasein's death will come; Dasein just does not know when. When relating authentically to this "constant threat" (*BT* 254), Dasein allows itself to be attuned to this aspect of its having-been and projection through the fundamental mood of anxiety. For anxiety "hold[s] open the constant and absolute threat to itself arising from the ownmost individualized being of Dasein" (*BT* 254). Through its anxious attunement to its own death as certain *and* uncertain, Dasein's death as a possibility becomes understood also as its impossibility. Heidegger writes, "In anxiety, Dasein finds itself faced with the nothingness of the *possible impossibility* of its existence" (*BT* 254; emphasis mine). So this ownmost, nonrelational, insuperable, certain yet indefinite possibility-to-be is, as such, the impossibility of Dasein itself. Dasein's death is its possible impossibility.

And this makes sense because this possibility marks, once again, the impossibility of Dasein's own *Existenz*. Death is Dasein's impossibility because when it arrives, and this impossibility will arrive, Dasein will no longer be able to pursue its *Wesen* by projecting itself toward its having-been that is underway in and through its possibilities-to-be.

Consequently, Heidegger's existential analysis of death reveals how, from the perspective of originary temporality that has been guiding my engagement with time, the past effects the future as Dasein brings to fruition its own meaning in the present by pursuing its future possibilities-to-be. And part and parcel of this constitution of its own meaning through relating to temporality is the possible *and* certain actualization of its own impossibility through death. So death as a future event will not only just be a possibility of Dasein's future because this possibility is one that will be actualized and bring to an end Dasein as Dasein. Dasein's possible impossibility will come to fruition in the unity of the present. This understanding of impossibility in relation to the future cannot be used when engaging the death *of the other* because the impossibility attending the death of the other remains always and forever impossible. The impossibility that accompanies the death of the other does not arrive but remains always to-come. To describe the death of the other's relation to the future, a different understanding of the impossible is needed that is similar to Heidegger's, insofar as the impossible will continue to affect and effect the present, and yet different from Heidegger's. For the impossibility of the death of the other will never occur but will always remain to-come.

The Impossibility of a Future To-Come

In response to Heidegger's analysis of the possible impossibility of personal death, my analysis of how the death of the other fractures the future requires an understanding of an impossibility that cannot be unified or brought into a present moment. This would be a different thinking of the impossible that is adequate to the interminable, unactualizable impossibilities that come to a survivor of the death of the other. And this resource for thinking differently about impossibility can be found in Derrida's thinking of the future as to-come. As he writes, "[I]n French, I prefer saying this with the to-come of the *avenir* rather than the *futur* so as to point toward the coming of an event rather than toward some future present" (*AF* 68). As insightful as Heidegger's analysis of death is from an existential standpoint, his understanding of the possible impossibility that attends personal death does not fit the kind of impossibility that occurs with the death of the other. In fact, the idea of death as the possibility of my own impossibility, even if Heidegger's analysis of *dying* (*Sterben*) does not fall prey to this, can easily fall into the notion of the future understood as a future *present*. Such a future present implies that the future can be brought into the present or will be brought into the present, into that unifying moment of the present, but the character of when this future present will come is precisely unknowable. Even if we considered personal death according to this notion of a future present impossibility, anxiety could still remain as the fundamental mood of this future present. Yet as a future present, this future impossibility is certain to come; when it comes is just unknown. In contrast, the idea of the future understood through "the to-come of the *avenir*" or simply *l'à-venir*, the to-come, refers to a future that can occur, but this occurrence must be thought over and against occurring in the present.

Derrida even thinks this to-come in relation to Heidegger's analysis of being-toward-death in *Aporias*. In this context, though, Derrida covers over an important distinction between he and Heidegger's understandings of the future in relation to death. Derrida's engagement with Heidegger in *Aporias* reaches its climax near the end of Derrida's reading when he associates Dasein's death with the themes of love, the gift, the other, and the event in general, that is, with what Derrida calls "all that is only possible as impossible" (*A* 79). In this moment, Derrida reinterprets Dasein's death understood as the possibility of the impossibility of existence to be a version of something, like the gift, that is possible only as im-possible written with a hyphen. Dasein's death is, then, no longer merely the possibility of the impossibility of Dasein's existence but also "the simple possibility *of* impossibility" (*A* 71; emphasis his). Derrida makes this shift in his interpretation when he says that death for Heidegger is the "possibility *of* the impossible" and "the manifestation of the possible *as* impossible" (*A* 70; emphasis his). The result of this reinterpretation of Dasein's death is that Derrida understands Dasein's death as "the possibility of the impossible *as such*" (*A* 78; emphasis his). In other words, Dasein's death has become metonymy for these other figurations of what is possible only in being im-possible according to the future to-come. Raffoul has helpfully criticized this move by Derrida by showing that Heidegger nowhere refers to death as the impossible *as such*, and what Derrida is doing here in making this claim is imputing his own thinking of the impossible into Heidegger's understanding of death.[3] If we were to follow Derrida's interpretive move, an important difference between Derrida and Heidegger gets lost. Consequently, we have to exercise caution with Derrida's metonymy in *Aporias*. Such caution is necessary because the impossible that attends his notion of the to-come is importantly different throughout his work from the impossible that Heidegger utilizes in *Being and Time*. In order to maintain this important distinction between the two philosophers and allow for a different thinking of the impossible than Heidegger's, I distinguish between two tonalities of the to-come in Derrida's work.

To unpack this distinction between Heidegger's and Derrida's understandings of impossibility further, I want to think the to-come in Derrida simultaneously in relation to a useful distinction between impossible possibilities *and* im-possibile possibilities, though as the description unfolds this distinction will deconstruct itself. The to-come in relation to impossible possibilities refers to possibilities in the future whose coming will never occur. This side or tonality of the to-come must be considered in relation to the death of the other, as I shall show, even though Derrida does not focus much on this tonality of the to-come. He calls the kind of impossibility in this tonality of the to-come an "impossible impossibility" (*R* 77). I elaborate below on this timbre of the to-come because it is important for describing the transformation of temporality through the death of the other. The more important timbre of the to-come for Derrida is the im-possible possibility, written with a hyphen, which will prove to be *especially* important for understanding the future after the death of the other. Such im-possibility of the future to-come refers to an occurrence that is not merely or entirely impossible in the sense that it will never happen. Accordingly, this im-possibility of the to-come refers to the coming of a future, namely of what I describe as an event in part 1, that when it comes, we will not know in the present that it has arrived. Yet we will only know after the fact, *après coup* or *après l'événement*, that this future has come. Due to this second tonality of the to-come, the to-come must be spoken of not in terms of the grammatical future present — this future *will come* — but with the grammatical anterior future — this future *will have come*.

With these two tonalities of the to-come, a tension within Derrida regarding this idea of the to-come arises based on his wrestling with the possible coming of this future to-come. For example, in *Politics of Friendship*, as he discusses the possibility of an other politics that he calls the democracy to-come, he says that this politics would be like the coming of an unforseeable event that would resist the current conditions of possibility for a politics and would bring its own conditions of possibility upon its coming (*PF* 18). Such an event to-come would possibilize itself from out of the future and condition its own arrival over and against our horizons of expectation and rationality. Yet he ends *Politics of Friendship* by maintaining that "even when there is democracy, it never exists, it is never present, it remains the theme of a nonpresentable concept" (*PF* 306; cf. *SM* 81). So Derrida seems to leave us with a question over whether or not this democracy and its justice that are to-come, or any event in general to-come, will ever be able to arrive and effect or transform the world. To approach this question, I want to read these texts in light of Derrida's continual discussions of this to-come to show that the arrival of the to-come is not *merely* impossible. The to-come can certainly include such an impossible possibility. For the chance of an event to occur means that the event may not actually come. However, if an event happens to come and arrive, then this arrival will not take place in the present. In other words, we will know that the to-come has come but only after it has already arrived and transformed the pluralized world in which we find ourselves. And such knowledge will arise through the symptoms that befall us after this event. Such a to-come of the anterior future is the temporality of the event written as im-possible with a hyphen. And this im-possibility is, as I have discussed in chapter 1, how an event occurs unexpectedly according to the causality of rupture. This im-possible "can no longer be determined by the metaphysical interpretation of possibility or virtuality" (*WA* 234). The im-possible can arrive, might arrive, or will have arrived *"perhaps"* (*WA* 234). And if it does arrive in this aleatory modality, it will have transformed the world through arriving. Consequently, in contrast to the "impossible impossibility" above, the im-possible is "of the order of the possible, of the nonimpossible" (*R* 77). Thus, Derrida writes, "It is a possibility" (*R* 77). And more emphatically, "It is what is most undeniably *real*. And sensible" (*R* 84; emphasis his). Like Heidegger's impossibility, this im-possibility can arrive. However, unlike Heidegger's impossibility, the arrival of the im-possible occurs without any unity of the present of presence. For the possibility of such an arrival and the arrival itself of the im-possible to-come exceeds any subject or subjectivity having sovereign power over its coming. The coming of the to-come comes of its own accord. The to-come, like Silesius's rose, arrives while it arrives but not according to any causal, known, and/or predictive horizon. This im-possible to-come "comes over us like an absolute surprise."[4] Such an anterior future is what Levinas has referred to previously in saying that the greatest experiences of our life are never "lived through."[5] These events can occur, but they do so without any horizon of expectation so that we cannot see them coming. They are, in this regard, "structurally unknowable" or "structurally unforeseeable."[6] We recognize such events only after the fact. So these events are never brought into the present or unified in a unity of the moment. Rather, they leap right over the present and its *Einheit* but nevertheless transform the world around them in their leap. The im-possibility of what is to-come occurs, then, not according to ordinary time but according to a time out of joint.[7] This to-come of the *avenir*, then, remains a future that makes present by having-been. It comes from the future and effects and affects the present but by having been recognized only after its arrival.

By following these two tonalities of the to-come for understanding the future in relation to the aftermath of the death of the other, I argue that the death of the other and survival come to resemble important aspects of Derrida's analysis of the archive. For the death of the other like the archive are never just concerned with the question of the past but also with the question of the future. One of the major points of Derrida's *Archive Fever* is precisely to explain and motivate that an archive is never merely about the past but, more importantly, also about the future. After all, an archive attempts to save a unique moment in the past that is pertinent to the purposes of the archive. Yet in order to preserve this past, the archive must in the archiving moment make this unique moment from the past repeatable for the future. So Derrida writes, "The archivization process *produces* as much as it *records* the event" (*AF* 17; emphasis mine). Consequently, the archive is not "a question of the past" but "a question of the future, the question of the future itself, the question of a response, of a promise, and of a responsibility for tomorrow" (*A* 36; cf. 33 and 68–81). An archive preserves the past, and in doing so becomes a way of writing what is possible for the future.[8]

Similar to the archive, I maintain that the death of the other becomes not merely a question of the past but a question of the transformation of the future that is to-come with the result that the death of the other even like the archive "opens out of the future" (*AF* 68). Like the archive, then, the past that is engaged through the survivor's memories of the dead other in her mourning is bound to an "anticipation of the future to come" (*AF* 79) that results from this death of the other. In this, the workless memory of the past after the death of the other preserves this past as one "that has never been present . . . and always remains, as it were, to come — come from the future, from the *to come*" (*MPM* 58; emphasis his; cf. 138). The memory of the dead other in conjunction with the survivor's workless mourning becomes a memory not only of this past but also how the past has affected and is transforming the survivor's future. For the survivor's future is marked by the possibilities-to-be that had been connected with the now dead other, but such possibilities after the other's death now remain impossible *and* im-possible. Therefore, in order to describe fully how the death of the other transforms the survivor's relation and experience of the future, I argue that the death of the other occurs according to these two tonalities of this to-come. Both tonalities attend the future after the death of the other because the survivors find themselves relating to future possibilities that both are merely impossible or never arrive as well as im-possibilities whose absent arrival in the present transforms the present *après coup*. Through considering both of these aspects of the to-come, I argue that the death of the other, now a part of the survivor's thrownness and having-been, is still happening as the survivor continues to project herself into her future possibilities-to-be but now in the absence of the other who was once a part of these possibilities. Consequently, surviving the death of the other requires reckoning with "the future of the past."[9]

For example, the death of the other continues to take place in the planning of the funeral, the purchasing of a new house that the other had never lived in, the distributing of the other's students' papers that need to be graded, the community's hiring of a new pastor to fill the other's position, the visiting of the other's favorite restaurant but now without the other, and so on. In this, as discussed at the end of chapter 5, the rupture and restitution of the world after the event of the death of the other bleed into one another, overlap one another, or instantly take place with one another. The moment of the loss of the other, the inception of the event, becomes a past that will not stay put. This past moment of the event has returned, come again — *revenir* — like a specter, ghost, or revenant come to haunt the present by altering the survivor's future. And in its haunting, the survivor is reminded not only of the loss of the other and the loss of the meaningfulness that attended her relation with the other but also of the loss of the future. As the McDermotts attest after the death of their daughter, "[I]t is now time to emerge and face a totally upended world and *a future that had shifted 180 degrees.*"[10] The possibilities that once were hoped for in relation with the other are now no more. Such possibilities are, as futural, constituted by their absence that the survivor once hoped one day would become actual and present. Now, however, that hope for the actualization of these possibilities is lost, thereby redoubling the absence that constitutes them. And this absence cannot be brought into any unity in the moment because this absence fills the moment with the absence's own spectrality.

The Impossible and Im-possible Future with the Death of the Other

The death of the other can affect the future first by filling the survivor's future with possibilities whose actualization is merely impossible. This first tonality of the impossible future to-come of the death of the other can be seen most clearly in at least three scenarios. First, the impossible possibility of the future after the death of the other can result from what the other while living had been planning to do but will never do now that the other has died. And such impossibilities ripple into the future of those who survive this other. This impossibility results from future possibilities-to-be of the other becoming unactualizable with their death. So suppose a college-aged person's mother dies before her child's college graduation; suppose a soon-to-be wife or husband's father dies before the wedding; suppose an expecting mother's husband dies before the birth of their child. In all of these cases, the futures of the people involved in these scenarios gets significantly transformed: the mother will now not be at graduation, the father will now not be at the wedding, and the husband will now not be at the birth of their child, much less at the child's first birthday, first day of school, graduations, weddings, births of his grandchildren, and so on. The fissures from the death of the other run through the future causing those who survive to reconstitute their relation to their future on account of these lost possibilities that follow in the wake of the death of this other. Romano's notion of *mourir à autrui* is helpful here insofar as he explains that the death of the other is a death of the self because the death of the other marks "a collapse of my possibilities that were only possible for me by 'existing' for the sake of the other and thanks to her presence."[11] So when the other dies, our "ipseity-for the-other"[12] dies too, thereby becoming impossible. For example, when Mark Aguhar, a "fat trans femme of color icon, revolutionary artist, and self-proclaimed Tumblr calloutqueen," committed suicide, Kai Cheng Thom mourns Mark with these words, "I never knew her, and never will, no matter how much I wanted to. . . . I do grieve a world in which she and I could have met, could have spoken, could have known sisterhood and communion, could have felt the strength of each other's arms."[13] Thom's mourning of Aguhar centers on the possible future where the two could have met, but now this possibility will never occur. Moreover, Thom's survival of this death of the other displays what I have called the existential difference that attends the death of the other. Though Thom and Aguhar had never met, Aguhar had an important impact on Thom's world through their mutual relation to the LGBTQIA community. Thus, even the deaths of others whom we do not know directly can still be a death of the pluralized world for those who survive them. Additionally, Wolterstorff grieves, "Yet Eric is gone, here and now he is gone; now I cannot talk with him, now I cannot see him, now I cannot hug him, now I cannot hear of his plans for the future. That is my sorrow."[14] These possibilities are all now impossible for Wolterstorff.

Second, I read Jonathan Safran Foer's novel *Extremely Loud and Incredibly Close* as a second scenario that describes how this loss of possibilities stirs within a survivor another aspect of this first tonality of the to-come in relation to the death of the other: the impossibility of fixing these fractures in the future. His novel follows the nine-year-old protagonist Oskar Schell, whose father has died in the September 11 attacks in New York City. As Schell mourns the death of his father throughout his own adventures in the novel, Foer concludes the book with a vivid depiction of the tragedy of Schell's situation as Schell comes to grips with a future where his father's presence will forever be absent, that is, with a future where his father's presence is impossibly possible. Foer expresses this by having Schell discover the famous "Falling Man" photos that emerged after 9/11. Schell says:

> Finally, I found the pictures of the falling body.
>> Was it Dad?
>> Maybe.
>> Whoever it was, it was somebody.
>> I ripped the pages out of the book.
>> I reversed the order, so the last one was first and the first was last.
>> When I flipped through them, it looked like the man was floating up through the sky.
>> And if I'd had more pictures, he would've flown through a window, back into the building, and the smoke would've poured into the hole that the plane was about to come out of.
>> Dad would've left his messages backwards, until the machine was empty, and the plane would've flown backward away from him, all the way to Boston.
>> He would've taken the elevator to the street and pressed the button for the top floor.
>> He would've walked backward to the subway, and the subway would've gone backward through the tunnel, back to our stop.
>> Dad would've gone backward through the turnstile, then swiped his Metrocard backward, then walked home backward as he read the *New York Times* from right to left.
>> He would've spit coffee into his mug, unbrushed his teeth, and put hair on his face with a razor.
>> He would've gotten back into bed, the alarm would've rung

> backward, he would've dreamt backward.
> Then he would've gotten up again at the end of the night before the worst day.
> He would've walked backward to my room, whistling "I Am the Walrus" backward.
> He would've gotten into bed with me.
> We would've looked at the stars on my ceiling, which would've pulled back their light from our eyes.
> I'd have said "Nothing" backward.
> He'd have said "Yeah, buddy?" backward.
> I'd have said "Dad?" backward, which would have sounded the same as "Dad" forward.
> He would have told me the story of the Sixth Borough, from the voice in the can at the end to the beginning, from "I love you" to "Once upon a time . . ."
> We would have been safe.[15]

Schell, in this closing monologue, reimagines his future by rewriting his past. The future, after all, makes present only by having-been. Yet the tragedy of this recalibration of his future is that it remains always impossible. This future that Schell wants for himself and that he searches for throughout the narrative will and will have been always impossible because the past in which it would be grounded is impossible now that his father is dead. Like Schell, Didion too desired such a reworking of her past in the future she found herself in without her husband. She writes, "I was trying to work out what time it had been when he died and whether it was that time yet in Los Angeles. (Was there time to go back? Could we have *a different ending* on Pacific time?)."[16] Likewise, Wolterstorff, in a moment reminiscent of Auden's "Stop all the clocks" imperative, wishes to turn back time so that his son could still be alive: "Turn it back. Stop the clock and turn it back, back to that last Friday, that last Saturday. Let him do it over: get up late this time, too late to climb, read a book, wait for his brother. Let him do it right this time."[17] The future to-come in the aftermath of the death of the other is full of such impossible possibilities-to-be or, more precisely, impossible impossibilities.[18] And the present absence of these possibilities in the future leads to a transformation of the survivor's own future.

Accordingly, such a transformation of the survivor's own future can include a transformation of the survivor himself in the future as shown in a third source. Elie Wiesel describes the potential religious overtones of such a transformation in his memoire *Night*. He comments that the death that he witnessed during his time in the concentration camps "consumed [his] faith forever."[19] The deaths of the other in the camps included for Wiesel the death of the Other: "Never shall I forget those moments which murdered my God and my soul and turned my dreams to dust."[20] The death of the other in the past refused to remain past for Wiesel insofar as it consumed his own faith that he would have held as part of his own future possibilities-to-be. Now, however, such a future is impossible for him. While the death of a spouse is not the same experience of the death of the other as Wiesel experienced in the Holocaust, the impact from the grief due to the trauma in even the death of a spouse can have the same effect on the surviving spouse insofar as the death of their spouse can cause them to lose their own faith like Wiesel did. The death of the other in its many modalities can cause a survivor's own religious possibilities-to-be to be altered into impossible possibilities in the aftermath of this death. Through these three scenarios that unpack the first tonality of the to-come in relation to the death of the other, the death of the other is revealed to be not just a death of the world in the present but also "the loss of the future"[21] because the possibilities-to-be for both the survivor and those of the now dead other remain impossible in the impossible to fix, fractured future.

Additionally, the death of the other affects the future by filling the survivor's future with possibilities that arrive only in their absence and are recognized only after the date on which these possibilities would have been actualized. These future possibilities that attend the survivor's future need not be different from the merely impossible possibilities just discussed. Rather, these future possibilities can be considered in their im-possibility in the second tonality of the to-come. For after the future moment comes in which these possibilities would have been actualized had the other not died, this future moment moves into the past without any actualization. In this, these future possibilities are making present as a future that has been but only in the absence of their arrival. This is the existential moment of the specter returning from the past to haunt from the future. In other words, these im-possibilities have rewritten the future of the survivor, thereby also her present. Wolterstorff describes these kinds of im-possibilities when he says that the coming and arrival of future holidays after the death of his son are "[t]he worst days." He continues, "Thanksgiving, Christmas, Easter, Pentecost, birthdays, weddings . . . days meant as festivals of happiness and joy now are days of tears."[22] Similarly, when the actress and comedian Casey Wilson's mother died suddenly, part of Wilson's mourning her mother's death unfolds by Wilson reviewing her mother's datebook or calendar. When looking at these dates, appointments, meetings, and vacations that had been scheduled and planned by her mother in the past for a future time that now will never be for her mother, Wilson comments that her mother was "planning out a future that's just never to be."[23] In looking at these future possibilities, which were to be future possibilities-to-be for her mother, such possibilities are now impossible insofar as, in the first tonality of the to-come, these possibilities have no way of actually occurring. They are impossible possibilities. For Wilson, the world no longer exists in which they could be possible at all. Yet these planned occurrences on her calendar are also impossible in the im-possible tonality because when the particular date for one of those future possibilities passes without the possibility occurring, this occurrence's impossibility now moves into the past and yet returns once again to the present to remind Wilson of the abiding absence of her mother in the coming future. The to-come of these possibilities skip the present and move into the past, and from out of this past they rewrite Wilson's future as further reminders that her mother is gone, lost, absent, *fort*. In these moments, what the survivor mourns is the loss of the dead other's ability to project herself at future possibilities-to-be. Wolterstorff calls such projection the "humanity" of his son: "To be human is to remember, to carry the past along into the present. Even more, to be human is to look ahead, to expect, to envision. To be human is to expect while remembering, to plan while recollecting. . . . Eric was [while alive] bursting with futurity with plans and resolutions. *Humanity in full flower*. Now it's all gone. All the rich future that he held — gone in those tumbling seconds."[24] And the absence of the other's ability to pursue his own possibilities-to-be is an absence that transforms the survivor's relation to her own future because this absence cannot be unified in the presence of any present moment. Such absence haunts through its absence even in the present in that this absence is obdurate and never goes away.

Moreover, the futures of some survivors, especially children who have lost a parent, are often forever transformed on account of the trauma of this loss as a disruption of the survivor's temporality. This fracturing of their future is especially pronounced if the survivor does not work on processing the trauma from this loss. Then, the trauma can become for a child "an adolescent trauma that preoccupies the present and blocks any movement into the future."[25] The death of the other could prevent the survivor from throwing himself at his own further, future possibilities-to-be. Cooper describes her experience of surviving the death of her mother in terms of a "part" or "version" of her dying with her mother. Such is the *mourir à autrui* that Romano describes. Cooper writes, "We grieve a moment in time and place that will never be again, and so, by extension, a version of ourselves that existed in that space."[26] Mourning the death of the other requires coming to terms with the ramifications of the impossibility of the future possibilities-to-be becoming actual. This version of who we might have been merges with the mourning of the dead other because this death has reformulated our own future possibilities-to-be for ourselves. And its impossibility has become an im-possibility that calls for, in turn, a recalibration of the present in the having-been of the dead other that continually returns in the survivor's own future. Didion's own mourning shows that this experience of losing a parent and the mourning of the future without the parent extends also to the death of a significant other in general. For when we mourn, she says, "[W]e mourn, for better or for worse, ourselves. As we were. As we are no longer. As we will one day not be at all."[27]

Moreover, the mourning of the McDermotts and Wolterstorff repeatedly show that the death of a child forever transforms the future of a parent so that everything in the parent's future gets reformulated due to the trauma of this loss. After the death of a child, parents "wear the mask of living but will never be fully alive again."[28] In an extreme account of lifedeath, the parent surviving the death of the other continues living but the future they now make present from out of this past is always haunted by the present absence of their dead child. The survivor's future remains spectral as a lasting living with death. This present absence with the death of a child occurs because the loss of a child "always represents the loss of the future" for the parent on a few levels.[29] First, the parent loses in her child the future that the parent hoped to live through her child. For the parent "wants the child to be and to become not only what she [the parent] *is*, but also what she [the parent] *wanted to be* and could not become in her own life."[30] So the child had represented while alive a possibility-to-be for the parent to achieve the parent's dreams for her own life but vicariously through the child. Now not only is the future of the child impossible, but this impossibility and its absence reflects back on the present of the parent who has now lost possibilities-to-be of her own. Beyond this instance where the parent desires to live in and through her child, second, the loss of the child can also be a failure of the parent to extend her own future through the genetic generativity of the child. For when the child has died so too "a portion of the parent's genetic inheritance, which might have been transmitted to another generation, is now lost forever."[31] In this sense, the child had been but now is no more "the future."[32] Thus, Wolterstorff can write regarding parents, "We do not visualize our future without [our children]."[33] And he describes the tragedy of this loss of his future that continually transforms his present when he discusses conversations with people who ask him how many children that he has. Before the death of his son, he had five children. But after the death of his son, he writes, "What do I say, 'four' or 'five'?"[34] Another father recounts in his survival of his daughter's death, "[S]till every year is marked by how old Amy would have been, where Amy would have been, what she would have been doing."[35] The loss of a child as a death of the other reminds us that the hope people hold for the future is a result of projecting themselves into future possibilities-to-be with those who are significant in their lives. In the absence of the other due to the other's death, the survivor can no longer project themselves into this future. The fractured future without these possibilities-to-be after the death of the other requires a new relation to the future or a new archive of the future in the aftermath of this past death. The impossible possibilities of the future that attend the death of the other come to structure the present of the survivor on account of the absence that attends them in the aftermath of when they would have become actual but cannot now on account of the death of the other. In this, the impossibility of these impossibilities transitions into an im-possibility that transforms the world of the survivor. Thus, surviving the death of the other is a matter of embodying the present that has resulted from the past by "squinting through tears into an unbearable future."[36] For the future that we move toward in surviving the death of the other is a future "unable to escape the grip of a memory laden with grief."[37]

Therefore, a survivor's temporal existence after this event of the death of the other is thoroughly out of joint. The present remains haunted by a past that draws the survivor back to the moment of the inception of this event. And in this haunting, the past continually returns or comes again as if from the future because "the specter is the future, it is always to come, it presents itself only as that which could come or come back" (*SM* 48). Mourning the death of the other concerns, then, the "shared possibilities" with the other that get "de-possibilized" when the other dies, and such de-possibilized, shared possibilities close and open futures for the survivors.[38] Consequently, the present is riddled with the absence of future possibilities once hoped for but now lost or gone with the death of the other. The experience of temporality in surviving the death of the other is thoroughly solicited, fractured, or ruptured by this unexpected and excessive event to the extent that the pluralized world, the with-world, that the survivor still shares after this event will never be the same. The world may still be present, but its presence is felt as and through the absence of the other who has died. So the question remains: what then is a survivor to do now in this spectral present, this spectral moment, if it is so out of joint after the death of the other?

Chapter Eight
The Gift of Mourning in a Present Out of Joint

> Here we touch on what remains no doubt the unavoidable problem of mourning, of the relation between gift and grief, between what should be non-work, the non-work of the gift, and the work of mourning.
>
> — Jacques Derrida, *Given Time: I*

In part 3 of this description of the death of the other, I have been following how the death of the other transforms the temporality of the survivor's world. The idea of the present as a "spectral moment" (*SM* xix) has become an orienting theme in my description. In this final chapter, I turn directly to this spectral moment to argue that the confluence of themes from Derrida regarding the gift, hospitality, and survival can help elucidate what surviving in this moment of the present can become as it is haunted by a past that is not past and a fractured future full of impossible possibilities and im-possible possibilities. I argue that mourning the death of the other is an exercise of responsibility. As Timothy Secret says, "Just as Sisyphus was challenged to *bear* the burden of his rock . . . when we *bear witness* to our admiration for one who has died, we are challenged to *bear* the weight of a heavy responsibility."[1] And this exercise of responsibility to the dead, I argue, helps to open the survivor to the coming of other events, especially, for those events that concern responsibility to the living other. For if, as Derrida argues, acting responsibly entails being willing to give without any expectation of receiving anything in return, then mourning the dead can also help develop responsible action toward the living because mourning prepares a survivor to give without expectation or return. Mourning helps to prepare the survivor to give a Derridean gift. This is what I call the gift of mourning.

I develop this importance of mourning by following Derrida along with Aristotle, Cicero, and Søren Kierkegaard in their engagements with friendship and love to the dead. According to these figures, the love and friendship at the edge or border of life and death with the death of the other give relief to the love and friendship that should be practiced and cultivated with the living. Through these historical engagements with friendship to the dead, I relate mourning to what follows the Derridean logic of the gift. As I have presented in chapter 1, the gift that occurs *sans voir*, *sans savoir*, and *sans avoir* disrupts any economy of exchange by interrupting it in a transformative, evential instant. Such a gift is given unexpectedly, in secret, and im-possibly as it conditions its own possibility. I argue in this final chapter that while mourning is not necessarily a moment in which a survivor can give such a gift, mourning opens a survivor to the possibility, namely the im-possibility, of a gift. More precisely, when we mourn the death of the other, we can open ourselves to the type of giving that lies at the root of Derrida's ethico-political hopes. Mourning opens to the coming of an other friendship and democracy that can have profound implications for our being-with one another in the world. Mourning opens to the im-possible gift because mourning exercises an ethos ready for an event. Mourning welcomes the gift in being ready not to be ready for its surprise, that is, mourning is ready for the coming of something that for all intents and purposes seems impossible. In this, to develop the final fold of the worklessness of mourning, mourning is what I call an instance of *workless* hospitality, and it becomes a chance for the gift.

This gift of mourning through its hospitality to the dead other sheds light on life understood as survival, namely as the living with the other after death in what Derrida has called *survivre* or *survivance*. Being such a survivor pertains to "anyone who is mourning, of all work of mourning . . . regarding the originary guilt of the living as surviving the death of the other" (*AR* 383). The practice of mourning in the spectrality of this present that is out of joint after the death of the other allows the survivor to be transformed into a space of workless hospitality for the dead other out of which the survivor can learn to become such a space also for the living other. To reclaim the present as this place and time for hospitality through mourning, the survivor has to come to terms with the present absence of the past and future in the aftermath of the death of the other. In offering hospitality to the in-breaking of an event of the death of the other, I maintain that mourning's gift to a survivor is that it opens a survivor to the coming of an event so that they can be better prepared for it when it comes unexpectedly, without reason, and im-possibly.

The Gift of Mourning

To begin, the theme of the gift must be recalled. For while mourning is not a gift, mourning can open the survivor to the coming of such a gift through offering hospitality to the dead. Hospitality is, after all, a condition for the coming of any event, which is to say any gift. Derrida carefully aligns the themes of the gift and the event when he says, "There is not an event more eventful than a gift" (DE 93). With this, we must be reminded that a gift occurs according to a threefold logic of the *sans*. The gift occurs unexpectedly, or *sans voir*, for it cannot be seen preemptively on any horizon. The gift occurs without reason, or *sans savoir*, for it does not adhere to the confines of calculative rationality's causal thinking. And the gift occurs im-possibly without being possessed by any sovereign subject, or *sans avoir*, for the gift conditions its own arrival within an economy of exchange.

Derrida's *Politics of Friendship* unfolds how mourning can welcome such a gift through mourning's preparation for a new kind of politics named the democracy to-come. His development of this democracy occurs in and along his engagement with the readings in the history of philosophy of the epigraph — first attributed to Aristotle by Diogenes Laertius in his *Lives of Eminent Philosophers* — "O my friends, there is no friend" (*PF* vii). Derrida explores the meanings of this epigraph by deconstructing the history of meanings of this phrase in the works of Diogenes, Augustine, Cicero, Montaigne, Nietzsche, Blanchot, Heidegger, Nancy, Carl Schmidt, and, naturally, Aristotle himself. Through this history of interpretation, he sees a development of a politics that is ruled by and formed around an economy of exchange. However, in the shadows and cracks of this history he finds glimmers of and hopes for a development of a politics, a democracy to-come, ruled by the logic of the gift under the guise of friendship and what he ultimately names "lovence" (*aimance*) — a becoming love of friendship and a becoming friendship of love.[2] This is another friendship or, perhaps more aptly put, an *other* friendship because it remains other to the canonical tradition of friendship under the hegemony of reciprocity, the fraternal, and brotherhood. Thus, he deconstructs the history of the politics of friendship gathered around this Aristotelian epigraph in order to open this history to an unexpected, eventful, and surprising reconfiguration of the friend and politics. In the end, he seeks lovence as a possible friendship that would be "aneconomic" (*PF* 154) because it would not be grounded upon an economy of exchanging presents in the present. Rather, this friendship would operate according to the logic of *the gift* insofar as it would be grounded upon a giving without reciprocity. Derrida writes, "This logic calls friendship back to non-reciprocity, to dissymmetry or to disproportion, to the impossibility of a return to offered or received hospitality; in short, it calls friendship back to the irreducible precedence of the other" (*PF* 63). In addition to being aneconomic, the lovence operative in a democracy to-come would be unexpected and transformative in its arrival insofar as it would recondition the conditions of possibility for friendship and politics themselves. Adhering to the logic of the gift, the arrival of lovence and a democracy to-come will have been the arrival of an event. And mourning, I argue, can help prepare for this arrival.

Derrida's deconstruction of this politics of friendship suggests such an argument when he writes, "It is indeed through the possibility of loving the deceased that the decision in favor of a certain lovence comes into being" (*PF* 10). Moreover, his own work of mourning his friends and colleagues whom he survived shows that "love and friendship would be nothing other than the passion, the endurance, and the patience of this work [of mourning]" (*WM* 146).³ With this, Derrida maintains that friendship to the dead via mourning is dissymmetrical because regardless of how much is done for the dead, the dead cannot reciprocate. After all, the dead give no recognition of what is given them in our mourning. Consequently, friendship to the dead via mourning is one in which someone loves the dead for nothing, that is, for nothing in return.

Derrida sees this development especially in the works of Aristotle and Cicero. By looking at their works on friendship to the dead, along with a supplement from Derrida's longtime interlocutor, Kierkegaard,⁴ I show how each of these figures maintain that mourning opens the survivor to the coming of the gift event of lovence. Mourning may not be the gift itself, but the gift of mourning can help us keep ourselves and our economies of exchange open to the coming of what we cannot see coming. In this regard, the accounts of mourning from these philosophers show that mourning opens us to the gift event's causality of rupture as what occurs *sans voir*, *sans savoir*, and *sans avoir* because mourning participates in an unexpectedness, a lack of knowing, and a lack of having or possessing on account of the death of the other being such an event. Together these philosophers develop a logic in which mourning is a limit situation that allows us to see how friendship and love is to be practiced in the present with the living. With this, friendship to the dead is emblematic of the affirmation of life that Derridean deconstruction points toward.⁵

We can begin to see how mourning those who have died opens us to a gift event in Aristotle's *Eudemian Ethics*, a text that Derrida draws on extensively in *Politics of Friendship*. Two moments in Aristotle's *Eudemian Ethics* are important in this regard. In the first moment, during the seventh book, Aristotle is continuing his exploration of the friendships of virtue, utility, and pleasure by breaking each of them into two types "one kind based on equality, the other on superiority" (1239a1).⁶ The first type concerns a relationship of equality and reciprocity between friends. In such a friendship, says Aristotle, the parties "are friends" (1239a5). This would be the kind of friendship that the gift would disrupt because the focus is on the equality and reciprocity of those involved. Aristotle discusses this type only briefly before focusing extensively on the second type concerning a relationship of inequality or nonreciprocity. While he insists that this second type remains a type of friendship, the parties involved are not considered friends. So this friendship lies on the fringes of the concept of friendship itself, which is partly why Derrida takes interest in it and why this iteration of friendship lies close to the gift. In this nonreciprocal friendship, "the superior ought to claim either not to return the love or not to return it in the same measure" to the one with whom she is in a friendship (1239a17). This kind of friendship resists the tit-for-tat type of thinking that dominates the reciprocal friendship by not even requiring that love be returned. Though Aristotle immediately mentions the friendship between a human and a god as an instance of this nonreciprocal friendship, friendship to the dead can be included here as well. In this regard, friendship to the dead would be a friendship in which the circle of exchange is no longer the currency. Consequently, friendship to the dead would keep us open to an aneconomy in which reciprocity, the giving and receiving of debts, and repayment are no longer the focus. Such friendship would keep those in relationship open to what operates *sans voir* and *sans savoir*. The second moment in Aristotle's text develops this idea directly.

He ends book 7.4 with a direct praise of friendship to the dead on account of the focus in such a friendship of inequality on the act of loving rather than the passivity of being loved. He writes, "We praise those who persist in their love towards the dead; for they know but are not known" (1239b1). He praises friendship to the dead through mourning because such friendship is motivated by the act of loving itself and not the receiving of love. In this focus on the actualizing of love, that is, the ἐνέργεια of love, rather than the potentiality and passivity of being loved, the love given to the dead is superior to the love received by the dead precisely because the one who loves is not known by the dead. The dead cannot reciprocate by knowing and loving in return the one who loves, yet the one who loves continues in her love without this reciprocity. Once again, mourning keeps those who mourn open to the aneconomy of the gift insofar as it keeps those in relationship open to the giving of something without any intention of receiving back and receiving without any recognition. Such friendship keeps us open to what operates *sans savoir* and *sans avoir*.

Cicero continues the development of this theme in his *De Amicita*. In remembering what Laelius once had to say about friendship, Cicero praises those who mourn the dead because friendship to the dead represents the true origin of friendship, namely in a love that does not calculate. He ponders the origin of friendship by asking whether friendship is born from a desire for reciprocity or from "another cause, older, more beautiful, and emanating more directly from Nature herself" (viii.26).[7] If friendship arises from reciprocity, then "friendship is felt on account of weakness and want so that by the giving and receiving of favors one may get from another and in turn repay what he is unable to procure of himself" (viii.26). In this regard, friendship would be engendered, run, and ruled by circles of economy dealing with presents and the present. If this were the case, then any openness to the coming of the gift remains annulled indefinitely. Cicero disapproves of friendship based on reciprocity, even though it is a common view of friendship, because such friendship "limits friendship to an equal interchange of services and feelings" by basing the friendship on a "petty accounting" that keeps "an exact balance of credits and debits" (xvi.58).

In contrast, the "older" origin of friendship is to be found in love "for it is love [*amor*], from which the word friendship [*amicitia*] is derived" (viii.26). This origin of friendship in love resists any focus on "calculation of how much profit the friendship is likely to afford" (viii.27). Thus, true friendship, "that pure and faultless kind" (vi.22), begins without calculation, reciprocity, or give and take. This aneconomic origin of friendship in love means that friendship springs not "from the hope of gain . . . not for the purpose of demanding repayment"; instead, true friendship's "entire profit is in the love itself" (ix.30–31). True friendship, as Aristotle said, is in the ἐνέργεια of love. This true friendship "is richer and more abundant than that [ruled by the counting of credits and debits]" because true friendship is not concerned with making sure it "pay[s] out more than it has received" (xvi.58). Therefore, when Cicero writes, "Wherefore friends, though absent, are at hand . . . and — harder saying still — though dead, are yet alive; so great is the esteem on the part of their friends. . . . These things make the death of the departed seem fortunate and the life of the survivors worthy of praise" (vii.23),[8] he shows that he praises friendship to the dead out of love for the dead because in this friendship the focus is on *true* friendship grounded in a love that loves excessively, which is to say without economy, reciprocity, and calculation. Such friendship operates *sans voir*, *sans savoir*, and *sans avoir*. And as such, this friendship to the dead through mourning keeps us open to a gift that would disrupt any economy of exchange.

Kierkegaard builds upon these accounts of mourning in Aristotle and Cicero by bringing into relief in his *Works of Love* that loving the dead through mourning is instructive for how life is to be lived daily with the living. For he concludes his chapter from *Works of Love* on loving the dead by saying, "The work of love in recollecting one who is dead is thus a work of the most unselfish, the freest, and the most faithful love. . . . [R]ecollect the one who is dead and just in this way learn to love the living unselfishly, freely, and faithfully."[9] His explanation of mourning as an act of the most unselfish, free, and faithful love shows that this relation to the dead opens to the gift because this friendship driven by love operates *sans voir*, *sans savoir*, and *sans avoir*.

The most direct connection between mourning and the gift occurs through Kierkegaard's description of mourning as an act of unselfish love because here mourning is described in aneconomic terms. He writes, "When one wants to make sure that love is completely unselfish, one can of course remove every possibility of *repayment*. But this is exactly what is removed in the relationship to one who is dead."[10] Loving the dead through remembering them is the most unselfish love because the dead, once again, can in no way provide any repayment. No thank you from the dead; no return love; nothing can be given back from the dead to the one who mourns. All three of these figures, as well as Derrida, make this claim about the dead being unable to reciprocate because the dead are not present in the way that living others are present. While a survivor may hold some expectation that the dead respond, the dead cannot reciprocate in any direct way that someone still living can reciprocate. A survivor may aim to, for example, start a nonprofit in honor of a dead loved one so that the memory of this other is honored. And a survivor may find much solace in such an act and feel that the dead other is being honored well and is proud of the survivor for how they are mourning her. However, the dead other cannot in a way that a living other can say thank you or reciprocate for mourning them well. Even when a survivor is visited by a dead other, as is sometimes reported, such a visitation is importantly different from a physical visit with a living other because such a visitation of the dead would be marked distinctively by an absence of presence that does not occur with living others. So while love of the living can be "reciprocal love,"[11] following an economy of exchange, the love to the dead remains nonreciprocal and, as a result, gift-like. Love of the dead operates without the knowledge of and without the expectation, the horizon, of anything in return. Mourning is an unselfish love that operates *sans voir* and *sans savoir*. And for Kierkegaard, as for Derrida, if love is to be love, it must operate according to this excessive logic where we love for nothing, that is, for no thing in return. For the hope and prospect of repayment in our love of one another "make one unable to see with complete clarity what is love."[12] But in loving the dead, we open ourselves to this excessive love. Mourning opens us to the disruption of an economy of exchange by the causality of rupture from a gift event.

Moreover, the love of the dead operates *sans avoir* for Kierkegaard because of what he calls the freedom and faithfulness operative in this love. Through this love's freedom and faithfulness, mourning operates without any conditions that hold this love to an accounting of credits and debits. This is no love by extortion says Kierkegaard.[13] Whereas the living other can compel us to love him, her, them, or it, Kierkegaard insists that the dead cannot compel us so. He writes: "[I]n connection with other human love there usually is something compelling, daily sight and habit if nothing else, and therefore one cannot definitely see whether it is love that freely holds its object firm or [if] it is the object that in some way compellingly lends a hand. But in relation to the dead, everything becomes clear. Here there is nothing, nothing compelling at all."[14] For the dead are no longer present for us to hold in our expectant grasp of repayment. Quite literally, then, nothing itself compels us to mourn the dead. When we love the dead, we can do it of our own accord. We can do it freely. We can do it for no thing at all. Furthermore, the dead themselves cannot compel us to be faithful or steadfast in our mourning of them. In fact, as experience shows and Kierkegaard describes, loving and mourning become more difficult as time passes because the dead are no longer present to "beckon" and "bind us" to them.[15] So Kierkegaard writes, "When two who are living *hold* together in love, the one *holds* on to the other and the alliance *holds* on to both of them. But no alliance is possible with one who is dead."[16] No holding or having at all. Consequently, mourning operates *sans avoir* and, thereby, is the most faithful.

Kierkegaard concludes that mourning is an important work of love because only when we love the dead are we then practicing or working at love in its fullest, excessive, gift-like expression. Loving the dead guides us in "rightly understanding life: that it is our duty to love the people that we do not see but also those we do see."[17] Moreover, by loving those who we do not see, those no longer present, or the dead, we open ourselves to loving the living with an aneconomic, excessive, and gift-like love. Then we are opening ourselves for the coming of what we could not see coming, of we know not what, of what we cannot control, that is, then we are opening ourselves to the gift event to break in, rupture, and transform the conditions of possibility around us. This journey from Aristotle to Kierkegaard with Derrida regarding the relation of mourning and friendship helps to show why Derrida concludes *Politics of Friendship* by saying, "[T]he great canonical meditations on friendship . . . belong to the experience of mourning" (*PF* 290). And, moreover, that this experience of mourning "reveals and effaces at the same time this 'truth' of friendship" (*PF* 295), namely that mourning welcomes the coming of the *other* friendship, of lovence and its democracy to-come, that follows the lineaments of the gift. In this, mourning itself is welcoming to the gift. As this welcoming, mourning becomes a way of offering hospitality to the death of the other where such death is a figuration of the coming of a gift event.

Workless Hospitality and/as Mourning

Throughout my phenomenology of the death of the other, the theme of worklessness has become more and more insistent. Mourning, I have argued, has to be workless as the negotiation or *différance* of normal mourning and melancholy in order for the other to be mourned in her alterity. And this workless mourning is accompanied by an experience of memory that aims to both remember the other but always as other in this memory so that memory itself becomes workless as the negotiation or the *différance* of *Erinnerung* and *Gedächtnis*. And, now, these two iterations of worklessness in surviving the death of the other are accompanied by one final return of worklessness in and along hospitality.

When Derrida turns, especially in his seminars, in the late 1990s to explore the theme of hospitality, he presents, as his wont, this modality of responsibility in terms of two kinds of hospitality: conditional hospitality and unconditional hospitality. And if his early work, especially *Of Grammatology*, has taught us anything about deconstruction and *différance*, then we cannot take the temptation to lean only towards the unconditional, impossible idea of hospitality that comes to resemble closely his own thinking of the gift. For unconditional hospitality adheres to the logic of the *sans* in the gift. Moreover, I have shown that Derrida insists during his discussion of the gift that the focus cannot solely be on the gift as pure at the exclusion of economy. His thinking on the gift shows that we must give economy a chance by knowing both how the economy works and how this economy precludes a true gift. Moreover, giving economy a chance requires us knowing how the gift disrupts this economy. Yet, and this is the difficulty, the gift cannot be without the economy, and the economy cannot be without the gift. Likewise in the context of hospitality, we must give conditional hospitality a chance by knowing its limitations that preclude a truly open hospitality. Additionally, we give conditional hospitality a chance by knowing how unconditional hospitality disrupts conditional hospitality and how unconditional hospitality relies upon its other in order to exist as the call to keep hospitality radically open. Through the relation of these two hospitalities, they make possible a *relatively* stable and also *relatively* flexible welcoming of the other. Just as laws without justice become cold, cruel, unforgiving, and unwelcoming while justice without laws becomes a utopic place that is no place at all, so too do conditional and unconditional hospitality need to be brought under *différance* and made, thereby, workless. And I am arguing that mourning the death of the other may just be a moment in which such a workless hospitality can be practiced.

Hospitality, in general, opens up "the here-now in all of its urgency and absolute singularity" because hospitality calls for "action now."[18] As such, hospitality is preparation for the event insofar as hospitality is "the condition of the event" (*SM* 82). In this, hospitality in its unconditional mode welcomes the event *come what may*. For as I have shown in chapter 1, the event as gift breaks in and disrupts the status quo either as promise *or* as poison. We do not know which the gift is though because it occurs *sans voir* and *sans savoir*. So the call of come to the event that may-be requires that this call be ready to be hospitable to that which is without horizon and comes as a surprise. Such hospitality means that we must be ready "to host and shelter" or to prepare "for the coming of the *hôte* [as guest]" (*AR* 360) but also "to be ready to not be ready . . . to be surprised" (*AR* 361). In other words, we must be doubly prepared. We must give hospitality a chance by extending hospitality to our expected, invited guests through conditional hospitality. And yet we must recognize that hospitality extends beyond such conditions. Hospitality remains hospitality especially when we are not ready or when being hospitable becomes unconditional. Our hospitality must not merely be conditional but also unconditional. In this liminal space of the negotiation of the two we find a workless hospitality as a space where responsibility to the dead and living other becomes possible.

So, first, to prepare for the coming of the event means that we adhere to the conditions of hospitality. This means that we welcome that which we expect to come. The conditions for the possibility of hospitality are twofold. First, hospitality is conditioned by the sovereignty of the home and the sovereign who owns the home. Without the home as the place in which hospitality can occur, hospitality never gets off the ground and begins (*OH* 51). The owner of the home through her own sovereignty as the "master at home," the "head of house," the self, or *ipse* in charge of the home assures that hospitality becomes possible. For this sovereign self is the one who is "able to receive whomever" he likes in the home (*OH* 53). Second, hospitality is conditioned by the identification with a family insofar as the home is always the home of some family who welcomes others from other familial homes. Derrida says that from the beginning of such conditional hospitality, "the right to hospitality commits a household, a line of descent, a family, a familial or ethnic group [to] receiving a familial or ethnic group" (*OH* 23). With conditional hospitality, the foreigner is welcomed insofar as she belongs to a family or has a recognizable family name. The family name conditions the hospitality extended to her because here hospitality is extended to those who fall under the category of the expected. Only the foreigner *as* family or citizen is welcomed because we expect such a visitation. In fact, we invite this expected visitation. Derrida explores the effect of these conditions on the practice of hospitality by exploring the linguistic connections among the French *hôte*, for host or guest, and the Latin *hostis*, for stranger. Accordingly, through the conditions placed on hospitality, the understood rule or norm of this hospitality is, then, that the host (*hôte*) is head of the household who has welcomed the stranger (*hostis*) as guest (*hôte*). These conditions, as is the wont of conditions in general, are limitations. They limit the expanse of our hospitality insofar as they limit to whom we can extend hospitality. Conditional hospitality shares with the economy of exchange, then, a limitation on the entrance of the other into the same. Such hospitality limits who or what can come. If you are nonfamilial, a foreigner, or a noncitizen, the rules of conditional hospitality dictate that you are unwelcomed, uninvited, and unexpected. So when the other who has no familial name or citizenship comes knocking on the door asking to come inside, we will not have been ready for this surprise. We will not have been ready for this visitation without invitation, for this event, to arrive.

So this conditional hospitality is an economic hospitality that is finite, and the danger that this modality of hospitality runs is that it will cease to be hospitable. Playing on the polysemy of the Latin for stranger, with conditional hospitality, the stranger (*hostis*) who is the nonfamilial, unwelcomed guest (*hôte*) is now treated as the enemy (*hostis*). So conditional hospitality runs the risk of turning into a war of the family against the nonfamilial. Suddenly, hospitality has become its opposite. A paradox develops, then, with conditional hospitality insofar as what guarantees someone's "right to hospitality" (*OH* 23) through belonging to a family and the family's protection becomes at the same time the condition of the impossibility of hospitality. Moreover, the *ipse* in charge of the home through his sovereignty can decide that anyone who encroaches on his "sovereignty as host" can become "an undesirable foreigner" or "a hostile subject" who is set to take the home hostage (*OH* 55). So Derrida writes, "The law of hospitality, the express law that governs the general concept of hospitality, appears as a paradoxical law" (*OH* 25). Therefore, in order to open up conditional hospitality to be hospitable to the other, the foreigner, or the stranger who is without a family, thereby opening hospitality up to be hospitality, the limitation of who or what can be welcomed into the home must be loosened. To remain hospitable, then, conditional hospitality must be in relation with unconditional hospitality.

Unconditional hospitality is a hospitality that welcomes the other *tout court* without any restrictions, conditions, limitations, or bounds. This hospitality extended not to the expected foreigner but to the "absolute other" requires a "break with hospitality in the ordinary sense, with conditional hospitality" (*OH* 25). While conditional hospitality adheres to "the laws (plural) of hospitality" that limit to whom the family can be hospitable, unconditional hospitality adheres to "the law of hospitality" that commands that the other "be offered an unconditional welcome" (*OH* 77). This singular law remains above the laws and outside the laws that confine hospitality. This singular law is, then, "illegal, transgressive, outside the law, like a lawless law, *nomos anomos*" (*OH* 79). This singular law is a call of *Come* to the other, to any other, come what may. This hospitality "requires that I open up my home and I give not only to the foreigner . . . but to the absolute, unknown, anonymous other, and . . . that I let them come, that I let them arrive . . . without asking of them either reciprocity (entering into a pact) or even their names" (*OH* 25). As such, unconditional hospitality adheres to the logic of the gift by breaking with any "debt and economy" (*OH* 83). Unconditional hospitality is akin, then, to the lovence of the democracy to-come. I welcome not just those to whom I owe a warm meal or a cold glass of water, in hopes that I will receive the same in return on my own journeys. I welcome those who can never reciprocate or those whom I am forbidden to welcome. Being ready not to be ready is for Derrida precisely the function of this kind of hospitality that welcomes the coming of such an event. Unconditional hospitality is the way we prepare for the gift event to interrupt the economy of exchange. It requires nothing of us except to be ready not to be ready. To be ready to be surprised by "such an irruption that I would not even be prepared to receive it" (DE 96). To be prepared not to be ready, then, is to welcome the event to come there where we cannot welcome it. There where welcoming the event is im-possible. To welcome the event means that we are not prepared for the event to-come. Saying *yes, yes, come* to the event means to be prepared not to be prepared for its instantaneous irruption into the same.

And yet the danger that unconditional hospitality runs is that it welcomes this other not simply as the *guest*. Without conditions on who I welcome, I could just as easily be welcoming my enemy. The stranger (*hostis*) as guest (*hôte*) could just as easily be my enemy (*hostis*) to whom I am held hostage. In this case, the guest (*hôte*) becomes host (*hôte*) who holds the home hostage. Hospitality becomes "hostipitality" (*AR* 402), then, because welcoming this stranger means I could be welcoming a guest or an enemy. My hospitality could just as easily lead to hostility once again. I welcome the other who comes. Come what may. These are the demands of hospitality without *constricting* principles. Unconditional hospitality is a demand without demand, as a result, because without any principles of order it demands "to let oneself be swept by the coming of the wholly other, the absolutely unforeseeable [*inanticipable*] stranger, the uninvited visitor, the unexpected visitation beyond welcoming apparatuses" (*AR* 361). Consequently, unconditional hospitality is hospitality run amuck or gone mad. The *nomos anomos* of unconditional hospitality is a kind of madness because in this kind of hospitality no one knows who is giving hospitality to whom and no demarcations exist between host and guest, guest and enemy, and host and hostage. As Derrida says in his 1995–96 seminar, "This absolute hospitality is able, then, to open a savage space of pure violence that would cause it to lose even its meaning, its appearance, its phenomenality of hospitality."[19] Unconditional hospitality, then, becomes a kind of impossible possibility. It is a hospitality to difference that transforms into total xenophobia and anarchy.

Consequently, hospitality must be workless. In order to be hospitality and not become hostile toward the other, conditional hospitality must have a threshold or an opening to its outside, namely to the unconditional call of come to the other. Conditional hospitality must run the risk of welcoming the other *come what may* in order to maintain itself as hospitality. Conditional hospitality must run the risk of being taken over by the guest in order to be hospitable. Likewise, unconditional hospitality must keep itself open to the conditions that limit its call of come so that hospitality can be practiced and kept from running mad. The utopic madness of unconditional hospitality needs tempering through conditional hospitality. Hospitality must remain workless as this negotiation between or *différance* of the conditions of hospitality and the unconditional call to come within hospitality. Hospitality can never merely be conditional or unconditional but must always be moving back and forth between the two in order to maintain itself as hospitality and not become hostile. Derrida reflects, "We will always be threatened by this dilemma between, on the one hand, unconditional hospitality that dispenses with law, duty, or even politics, and, on the other, hospitality circumscribed by law and duty. One of them can always corrupt the other, and this capacity for perversion remains irreducible" (*OH* 135). Each side or modality of hospitality "calls forth, involves, or prescribes the other" (*OH* 147; cf. 81). To put this in terms of the *laws* of hospitality within which conditional hospitality operates and the *law* of hospitality through which unconditional hospitality operates, the laws need the law just as much as the law needs the laws. The "unconditional law" needs and requires the laws in order "to become effective, concrete, determined" and avoid the risk of "being abstract, utopian, illusory, and so turning over into its opposite" of xenophobia (*OH* 79). In the opposite direction, the laws of conditional hospitality need the law that says come to whoever or whatever might be coming in order to continue being hospitable. The conditional laws "would cease to be laws of hospitality if they were not guided, given inspiration, given aspiration, required, even, by the law of unconditional hospitality" (*OH* 79). The ongoing ethical *task*, then, is not to choose between these two types of hospitality. Rather, we have to allow these two modalities to play or be brought under such *différance*.

And one setting for pursuing this task is through surviving the death of the other. Surviving the death of the other is, for Derrida, "hospitality as mourning" (*AR* 358). I argue that Derrida turns to mourning the dead other for exploring this idea of workless hospitality because mourning presents itself as a moment where the unconditionality of hospitality calls forth to the conditions that confine hospitality. Unconditional hospitality goes so far as to "say yes to who or what turns up, before any determination ... whether or not the new arrival is the citizen of another country, a human, animal, or divine creature, a living or *dead thing*, male or female" (*OH* 77; emphasis mine). For Derrida, unconditional hospitality consists in receiving the other especially when the other comes without invitation. Consequently, "hospitality destines itself" to death because the death of the other is a paradigmatic "visitation without invitation" (*AR* 360). Hospitality is then, paradigmatically so, "the preparation of welcoming: *from life to death*" (*AR* 361; emphasis his).

Nancy Moules's work with families surviving the death of the other helpfully illuminates this connection among hospitality and mourning. Moules presents grief itself as an "uninvited houseguest" that "arrives without invitation and remains in such a way that it touches all aspects of one's life, family, relationships, and health."[20] The negative effect and affect that the death of the other can have in this context is inversely related, says Moules, to how much "room" is made "for this uninvited houseguest."[21] For if room is not made for the grief that impacts the survivor after the death of the other and the mourning in response to it, then grief as guest becomes the host who holds the rest of the home hostage. Grief that is not housed and welcomed "has a tendency to take over the house, claiming the bathroom as one tries to get ready for work, sneaking into children's rooms and affecting their lives, sneaking into bedrooms of partners. Metaphorically, invited or not, grief sneaks in and becomes a part of the family and household. The more efforts are made to keep it out, the more it makes its presence known."[22] In contrast, if the survivor makes room or is hospitable to this death of the other, then "its presence becomes expected at times, its comings and goings are not surprises, its intrusions not unanticipated. In time, its presence even becomes welcomed as something familiar."[23] Moules's work, and my position here, raises the question concerning the deaths of others who were abusive or oppressive and whose specter is not welcome for the survivor in mourning their death. As difficult as mourning these others may be, Moules's work argues that even these dead others must be offered hospitality so as not to let their specter affect the survivor in a more negative way. The idea here is that the dead other is going to come back through our mourning of them one way or another. Mourning such an other is going to happen, in other words, whether or not the survivor wants it. For the sake of the survivor's own health through this mourning, the survivor might as well mourn the other well so as not to allow the dead other to become host and continue affecting negatively the survivor even after the other is dead. This mourning of the other well is the kind of free act of mourning that Kierkegaard mentions above. If the survivor makes space for them by mourning them, the dead other is less likely to continue to oppress and abuse the survivor in the aftermath of their death as they had done while living. So as difficult as mourning these others may be, the most healing path forward seems to be to offer hospitality even to these others through mourning them well.

While I agree with Moules, then, I would emphasize, however, that the aim with workless hospitality as part of the radically hermeneutical workless mourning is not to make the unfamiliar familiar but to grow accustomed to welcoming the unfamiliar precisely as unfamiliar into the familial home. This is an important difference because I am providing a radical hermeneutic phenomenology of the death of the other that aims not to cover over the difficulty of surviving the death of the other but to meet the mourning of the dead in its difficulty. And this difficulty involves not making the unfamiliar or discomfort in loss familiar or comfortable. By maintaining this difficulty or unfamiliarity in the worklessness of mourning, the death of the other can always remain the absolute visitation without invitation, or, perhaps, the absolute event. For the death of the other visits us without our inviting it. As I have argued, no matter the time frame, the medical diagnosis, or the amount of time left given by the doctor, we are never ready for the other to die. The death of the other understood as an event arrives *sans voir*, without horizon, *sans savoir*, exceeding reason, and *sans avoir*, conditioning its own arrival, thereby surprising us "each time singularly, each time irreplaceably, each time infinitely" (*SQ* 140). It comes without invitation. The death of the other will have come whether invited or not. The spectral present becomes an opportunity to welcome this death and allow transformation of the present through this welcome.

With the death of the other, then, we find the confluence of the theme of worklessness at play in Derrida's thinking insofar as the workless mourning, workless memory, and workless hospitality fold in on each other as inflections of one another. Such interweaving of worklessness occurs in Derrida's work as far back as his discussion of the crypt when he defines the crypt as a matter of "a foreigner in the Self" (*F* xxxi). The crypt is the space of workless mourning because it is the hospitable space for the dead other. Yet he develops this thought further during his seminars on hospitality. For example, in his 1996–97 seminar on hospitality, he writes:

> [O]ne has the impression that the work of mourning and of fidelity will only be possible if the other is separated from the bereaved, out of me, before me or, if not out of me, out of my sight; as if the work of mourning, often presented as an interiorization . . . had a chance to shelter the memory or the I of the other in me only to the extent that the dead other remains in his place out of me — in me, out of me. If mourning is hospitality, a burial in oneself and out of oneself, it is necessary for both burials, and therefore for both hospitalities, to remain quite distinct, separated, split. (*AR* 414–15)

In this dense passage, I maintain that Derrida is arguing that mourning can be mourning in its worklessness only if it is a matter of workless hospitality. The weaving together or negotiation between normal mourning's interiorization and melancholy's incorporation becomes possible and able to be practiced only if mourning is the *différance* of conditional hospitality and unconditional hospitality. The dead other is *sheltered* or given hospitality in the crypt of the psyche as a function of such hospitality. The dead other is welcomed "in his place" as other yet welcomed "in me." The other is welcomed unconditionally in the conditions that are my own. More specifically, workless mourning says in the present *Come* to the death of the other. And in this call, such mourning allows the other to remain in her alterity as both in me and out of me by allowing the dead other to remain as the present absence of a past that will not stay put and a fractured future of possibilities. Through workless mourning, the dead other is welcomed in the temporal conditions of the self but not made to adhere to any linearity of these conditions. The other is welcomed as the disruption of any linear conditions of temporality as I have been arguing in part 3. The workless hospitality of workless mourning carries the other and the pluralized world after the death of the other both in and along the body while maintaining the other in her alterity as a present absence.

Derrida continues in this seminar to align this workless hospitality with the workless memory of workless mourning. For he maintains that this mourning shelters "the memory or the I of the other" by letting "the idealizing memory appropriate the guest/host [*hôte*] dead in oneself, in an operation that is entirely one of substitution" (*AR* 415). Workless mourning as hospitality is made possible through workless memory because the sheltering of the other as other can only occur if the other is remembered (*Gedächtnis*) precisely as other. To live "faithfully" and "authentically" in the present after the death of the other, the other must be remembered; "amnesia" and "oblivion"[24] of the other as other must be resisted. The other can be offered hospitality in me through *Erinnerung*, yet out of me as other through *Gedächtnis* as a result of workless memory. The dead other is remembered as other in a process of "idealizing memory" (*AR* 415). And workless mourning helps to assure that the other is remembered as other insofar as this mourning operates with workless memory. Therefore, the workless hospitality of a workless mourning enacts the worklessness of memory in its two modalities. Workless mourning as surviving the death of the other is, then, an offering of hospitality to the past that haunts the present as a revenant in its repeated return.

Hospitality demands that we welcome — *yes, yes, come* — the coming of the other, the coming of the event when we are not ready for it. When we do not want it to come. There where the other dies we find an event that is most difficult to welcome. For when it comes, *die Welt is fort*. The world is gone, lost, or dead when the other dies. With this death of the pluralized world that accompanies a death of the other, the world itself is no longer the same. And this, as I have argued through my description, means that the event irrupts at the instant the other dies, thereby *giving* a world whose spatiality and temporality has irredeemably changed but for which the survivors are, nonetheless, responsible to carry because, once again, even the dead other whether human, nonhuman animal, or even divine, is a modality of otherness that calls to and, thereby, opens the self to the possibility of responsibility. The world is gone with the death of the other. And in this absence, *ich muß dich tragen*. The survivor is responsible for carrying the other, to mourn the other, along with the world that has been lost with him.

Responsibility and Mourning

Consequently, mourning carries a certain "weight" with it. As Rosner has noted in her memoir on being the daughter of a survivor of the Holocaust, this idea of mourning carrying *weight* is "an appropriately physical as well as metaphorical term" because it carries a "palpable sensation of burden and heaviness" that is missed by the abstract notions of obligation.[25] Just as, existentially speaking, our own being and notion of self carries a weight to which we are responsible for responding and attending to, so too does the death of the other and mourning require our response and our attention as part and parcel of "the incalculable coming of the other"[26] because, once again, as a modality of otherness even the dead other opens us to the possibility of responsibility. The weight of this responsibility suggests that it is not only important but also costly. To extend the *tragen* of Celan's poem, we *carry* this weight as we *carry* with us the others who have died. Accordingly, Shelly Rambo describes the effect of the death of the other as the "wounds" that a survivor carries. But she says that these wounds are best understood not as wounds of death but "wounds of life" because these are the wounds we carry in life on account of the one's we have lost.[27] These wounds are "the afterlife of trauma"[28] because these wounds are the traces that the past event of the death of the other leaves as traces in and on the survivor. Carrying this weighty responsibility helps prepare for a gift event by preparing us and the pluralized world for the in-breaking and transformation of a gift. This is not to say that mourning *will* lead to such a gift event because mourning can, after all, end up being too much for a survivor to the point that mourning spells the end of him or her. Mourning may end in suicide, in the pathology of what Freud calls melancholy, or, as I discuss in a moment, in an act of oppression. However, assuming that a person survives and continues living with her workless mourning, mourning harbors the possibility or the impetus for bettering life with one another in at least two distinctive ways.

First, mourning the other in daily life allows us to be *faithful* in an existential and ethico-political sense to the in-breaking of a gift event.[29] The "fidelity to death" or "faith . . . to whom and to what happens to be dead" (*BS2* 153) that mourning practices helps to cultivate, in turn, a faithfulness to the coming of what we cannot see coming in the name of the event. We become better stewards, in other words, of allowing for the gift to disrupt the various economies of exchange around us insofar as mourning makes us and our pluralized world hospitable to the coming of what we could not see coming by opening ourselves to the surprise of such an event. The unexpectedness of the death of the other and concomitant mourning prepares us "to be ready to not be ready" (*AR* 361), which is precisely the *ethos* or attunement that must be taken when welcoming an event. Such an attunement through mourning to the event can help the survivor see that the goal of mourning is not to move past the past. After all, as I have shown in the previous two chapters, to riff on Faulkner again, the past is never truly passed by as the past death of the other continues to haunt the present from out of the ways it transforms the future. Accordingly, mourning can help the survivor to see that remembering the other in her present absence concerns "ways of reconfiguring relational habits so that they continue to mark the truncated relation, but in a way that opens up new possibilities for engagement."[30] After all, the death of the other arrives as an event that unexpectedly and without reason transforms the spatiality and temporality of the pluralized world. And this means that the death of the other is not only a death of the world but simultaneously an opening and possibility for this world. But this opening and possibility, or the new possibilities after the death of the other, can only become actual by taking up the responsibility to carry the other and the world in the aftermath of death. For only through "carrying the other and his world . . . can [there] possibly be another one and unique world."[31]

And beyond this personal, existential reimagining of new ways to live in response to the death of the other, this faithfulness from mourning occurs through an ethico-political possibility within mourning. Derrida even maintains that no politics can exist "without an organization of the time and space of mourning . . . without an *open hospitality* to the guest as ghost" (*A* 61; emphasis mine). And he frames the entirety of his thinking of politics and the democracy to-come around the themes of justice and the death of the other. For his exploration of the themes of the ghost, spectrality, inheritance, and "others who are not present" is done precisely "in the name of justice. Of justice where it is not yet, not yet there, where it is no longer" (*SM* xviii; cf. *AF* 76fn). Such an explicit thinking of politics in and through mourning is currently happening under the name of agonistic or rebellious mourning.

Athena Athanasiou presents the mourning of "the urban feminist and antinationalist movement Women in Black of Belgrade (Žene u Crnom or ŽuC)" as "agonistic mourning" in the way that their mourning challenges the ethical and political power structures in Belgrade.[32] This movement formed in response to the nationalist military violence in the mid-1990s after the dissolution of Yugoslavia. The group performs nonviolent, public demonstrations while dressed in all black in order to practice solidarity with victims of war violence, especially the violence done to women refugees during wartimes, and the families who have lost loved ones in these contexts. Athanasiou's anthropological work makes a connection among the political protest and dissidence of the mourning practiced by those in ŽuC with the idea of preparing for and being faithful to a gift. Athanasiou maintains that the mourning of this organization restructures temporality for the political body by allowing for the death of the oppressed to haunt the present of the "nation's body and psyche."[33] In this way, the mourning of this group opens the political world of Belgrade to a "historicality" revolving around "an incalculable moment, or a 'flash,' of a new and intensified awareness, which might take the form of a crack, even a revolutionary occasion, into the order of homogeneous, chronological time."[34] Much like the gift itself in Derrida's discussion, the mourning of ŽuC opens the body politic to the in-breaking of an event by calling into question and challenging the economies of exchange in the political life of the nation. Through giving economy a chance by challenging its own national attempts to forget the death of those who had been oppressed and marginalized while living, this agonistic mourning prepares the world for the coming of something new that will disrupt the economy itself. In this way, mourning can transform the loss of the other "into a performative power that leaves traces in the body of politics,"[35] thereby opening the political space itself to be transformed by a gift event.

Such agonistic use of mourning is not to deny the fragility that comes with the gift of mourning, namely that mourning does not always lead to more love and openness of others but can lead to further oppression of people and groups who are not allowed to have a voice. In fact, agonistic mourning understands this fragility of mourning and intentionally aims to push against the further oppression of political powers that seek to silence the dead just as they had been silenced while living. Mourning can be turned against a survivor so as not to allow them to mourn the others who have died. But agonistic or rebellious mourning pushes back against such use of mourning to use mourning's fragility for effecting justice and openness in the midst of political oppression. Rebellious mourning seeks to make effective or put into practice the etymological link between the weight of mourning through the Latin *gravare*, which means "to be burdened," and the French phrase *faire grève* meaning "to strike"[36] in order to use mourning as a way to resist further oppression.

This kind of agonistic mourning, in turn, helps to develop "new grammars of listening"[37] to traumatic events. Drawing from Arendt's work on totalitarianism and the survivors of totalitarianism, Maria del Rosario Acosta López maintains that the trauma engendered by totalitarianism presents us with the task "of listening to what otherwise remains unheard in the testimonies of the survivors, as well as in the reports of the secondary witnesses."[38] By providing a voice to those who died due to totalitarian regimes that sought not only to oppress the living but also the dead by erasing their memory, this new way of listening to survivor stories and giving further voice to their stories is a way to exercise "a responsibility to those who lack the frameworks that would allow them to articulate their own claims, let alone turn their own experiences into a meaningful past."[39] And such remembering of the other through story and eulogy is "one of the truest labours of love there is."[40] By giving voice to these dead others so that their memory is not forgotten in their death nor the oppression that they experienced while living, and perhaps continues after their death, the trauma from their death can be redetermined as to how it "takes up residence inside"[41] the person and community of survivors. Considering that the trauma of the death of the other means that a survivor's relation to past, future, and present has been disrupted due to this event's causality of rupture, giving voice to the dead is a way to, in turn, effect change within the disrupted temporality from this death so that a survivor can help constitute a new present by reimagining the future anew in the aftermath of this death of the other. For Athanasiou, telling the stories of the dead who had been oppressed while they were alive amounts to telling "counter-stories that are rendered invisible in the conventionally 'archived' order of things and 'mark a differential political temper and a critical space.'"[42] ŽuC's public mourning provides "an ethical and political responsiveness to the memory of those whose loss has been expropriated."[43] By giving voice to the death of the other in this way, mourning can make of death "an event that authorizes an afterlife — that is, a continuation of life within the profane web of social interconnectedness in the form of stories told without it."[44] Such would be the life after death *in this life* that I have discussed in conjunction with *survivre* and *survivance*. Through mourning the dead, including those especially whose death has come about due to oppression, surviving can give new life to the stories and lives of those who have been lost. This grammar of listening and telling of stories through agonistic mourning allows the dead other in her present absence to have another life that rewrites the future and present by bringing justice to the oppression that cost the other her own life.

Cindy Milstein develops this performative power of mourning through her idea of "rebellious mourning" particularly through an aesthetic function for mourning. She writes: "Our grief — our feelings, as words or actions, images or practices — can *open up* cracks in the wall of the system. It can also *pry open* spaces of contestation and reconstruction, intervulnerability and strength, empathy and solidarity. It can discomfort the stories told from above that would have us believe we aren't human or deserving of life-affirming lives — or for that matter, life-affirming deaths."[45] Mourning can be a way to fight for truth and justice in the pluralized world because mourning can be a way of "reassert[ing] life and its beauty" by allowing us to "struggle to undo the deadening and deadly structures intent on destroying us."[46] For instance, Benji Hart, an artist and activist in the Chicago area, maintains that mourning "shows that I have not given in, not accepted the current, violent reality as inevitable, nor forfeited belief in my own right to life."[47] Mourning, for Hart, can be used in order to begin to repair the social injustices around racial, sexual, and economic lines in our various communities. The poet Claudia Rankine echoes this sentiment when she describes the national mourning of political movements, such as ŽuC or Black Lives Matter, as "a mode of intervention and interruption"[48] of the public space that allows us to develop a feeling for the Levinasian *other* who looks differently, believes differently, and votes differently. In this way, as Kierkegaard has argued, mourning the dead other we cannot see can help us to see and understand better the other who we can see in our communities. Rankine writes, "Grief, then, for the deceased others might align some of us, for the first time with the living."[49] Much like the mourning of ŽuC, mourning the oppressed and marginalized who are not only overlooked while living but even more so in their death, can help society as a whole, and perhaps even an entire nation, not only to remember the marginalized but to treat better the other in their midst.

Public art aimed at mourning the oppressed is often used for precisely this reason.[50] As the artists Melanie Cervantes and Jesus Barraza write about their own work: "We hope that the visual works that we create . . . interrupt the violence of forgetting that silences and negates our history. The pieces we create can be visual aids for political education and discussion; they can be used as public declarations of grief, and are both figurative and literal signs of a larger public memory project that resists dominant narratives that seek to criminalize and villainize the victims of police and state violence."[51] Such "solidarity art" is meant to be "a tool to continue shaping culture specifically in the way we imagine what justice means in our society" and as "a way to take up public space and stand in solidarity" with the victims and the survivors of the victims.[52] Accordingly, survival, understood as the workless mourning and hospitality that carries the dead other, becomes more than simply an individual act of mourning. With this aesthetic function that can attend mourning, the aesthetic theories of both Kant and Heidegger are instructive for the significance that art can play as part of our workless mourning of the death of the other. For Kant and Heidegger both see in their own ways how art discloses the world to us in addition to disclosing how the world ought to be or can be. In this, Kant argues specifically that beauty serves to show us not only how the world is but also that it is not currently how it ought to be. Furthermore, beauty, says Kant, suggests to us as a kind of inspiration for using our own freedom to transform the world into what it ought to be. In this, the artists who combine their craft with rebellious mourning disclose the injustice of the world by drawing attention to the oppression that happens not only in life but also in death. So this aesthetic function of mourning serves as a way to call out the injustices done to those who had been oppressed while living and who are often forgotten in death. And in calling this out, the art done in response to this in the present can help to rewrite from out of the past death of the other what is possible in the future by helping to prevent such further oppression in life and in death. Mourning, in this way, then, is fertile for being faithful to the coming of an event intent on transforming the pluralized world by breaking into and disrupting the economies of exchange in this world. Mourning the oppressed and marginalized who are not only overlooked while living but even in their death can challenge national attempts to forget their death. By not allowing the dead to be forgotten, mourning can begin to transform and interrupt the economy of national memory by not allowing the past to simply be past. Workless mourning allows the past to haunt the present, thereby allowing the present to be open to the event to-come. So the excessiveness of the event of the death of the other as beyond reason requires such aesthetic expression from the Paul Celans and Anselm Kiefers in the world to assure that the past is not passed but continues to recalibrate future possibilities as the world is reimagined around these possibilities grounded in past atrocities. In being with the dead through such rebellious or agonistic mourning, we become open in the present to the surprise of the living by demanding that the pluralized world be more just and less forgetful of those who have died and who continue to shape who we are individually and collectively.

Accordingly, the second way mourning can improve life results from mourning's ability to remind us of the integral connection between life and death. The relation among life and death has been an important theme in the history of philosophy as far back as Heraclitus's ruminations on φύσις through his experience of the bow. As he writes, "The name of the bow is life [ΒΙΟΣ], but its work is death" (B48). However, as has been my focus throughout my description, rather than following the tradition by focusing on personal death in this connection of life and death, we find with mourning the important relation among life and death in and along the death of *the other*. In this regard, mourning the other helps us to develop a better understanding of who we *are* ontologically as human beings by beginning and ending with our being-with the dead. Along these lines, Ruin maintains that humans have a "basic socio-ontological predicament" insofar as we "live not only with the living but also with the dead."[53] This predicament is ontological because this "*being with* the dead . . . determines human existence down to its basic condition and sense of self."[54] Anthropological studies on the origins of burying the dead as a cultural or communal practice show that the moment "when the human being becomes recognizable before and to itself is . . . inextricably connected to when it sees itself as able to represent the other in and beyond death."[55] Yet this predicament is sociological and political because "we belong to a polis not only of the living but also of the dead."[56] Learning to live means to inhabit the shared space with both the living and the dead and to do so in "a responsible way" because life is always a matter of "life after, as inheritance, ancestry, legacy, and fate."[57] So to Plato's announcement in the *Phaedo* that philosophy is "practice for dying and death" (64a), Ruin adds, "[Philosophy] is also the art of learning how to live with the dead and to share the earth with those who have been."[58] Life is always *survival* in this regard because life is a matter of living on after those we have lost. Life as the unfolding of survival, as *survivance*, involves learning to live through "the other and by death" because life is only ever lived with the other and in the aftermath of death and loss (*SM* xvii). Thus, learning comes "from the other at the edge of life" (*SM* xvii). Mourning is more than simply an individual act done out of respect for the dead or cultural necessity. Through mourning not out of such necessity but out of an intentionality to mourn, mourning can become a free act that can positively shape a survivor or survivors. In this, our relation to the dead via mourning can shape who we *are* individually and collectively. Mourning, then, is originary because the death of the other is part of the warp and woof of life. Survival is a matter of responding through mourning to this lifedeath.[59]

Consequently, how we mourn the other or carry the dead other with us in life is no trivial concern. Mourning carries weight. Carrying the other in our mourning is a weighty responsibility. And realizing this integral relation among life and death allows us the possibility to become better at practicing mourning itself. Rather than letting mourning take over a survivor, the idea I have been developing in this chapter is that the survivor can regain some agency in the mourning process so as to mourn the other well by allowing how the death of the other has transformed their past and future to have positive change on the survivor's present. By mourning the other well, a survivor can begin responding well to the call to responsibility coming from the death of the other. We can improve on *carrying* the other by recognizing how integral such mourning is to life itself. We can *be* better by understanding the weight of this responsibility. And in becoming better at mourning the other, we can become better at preparing the pluralized world for the coming of what we could not see coming. In developing such a hospitality to the in-breaking of a gift event, an ethics of mourning is cut precisely to fit the event. For through mourning we can, perhaps, in the present allow the past to haunt the present in an effort "to rewire the future"[60] and carry the world after the death of the world. Mourning opens us to the politics of friendship under the name of lovence and its accompanying democracy to-come whose logic is the gift. By preparing us for the breaking-in of a new politics of friendship that transforms and repossibilizes the world, mourning develops an ethos of workless hospitality to the gift. The gift of mourning is this keeping us open to the event to-come.

The Afterlife

During her "life after life" [*sur-vie*] or "resurrection"...

— Jacques Derrida, "Living On"

I have tried to stick with the difficulty of what happens to someone who is undergoing mourning in the aftermath of the death of the other. In this radical hermeneutics of the death of the other, I have argued that such death is more than just the loss of the person who dies because this death is at the same time a death of the pluralized world. As such, the death of the other is an event according to my argument because it rises into visibility unexpectedly, without reason, and transformatively. Through aligning the death of the other with these symptoms that befall someone who has undergone an event after its occurring, I have argued that the death of the other is unexpected because it adheres to the causality of rupture through which an event occurs *sans voir*, *sans savoir*, and *sans avoir*. While the moment of death is not always unexpected, the aftermath of how the death affects its survivors remains always unexpected and each time unique. As unexpected, I interpret this occurring of the death of the other further as what Marion calls a saturated phenomenon because while this event may occur according to this causality of rupture on account of the effect of this event on those who undergo it, this event resists any cause-effect explanation for why it has occurred. The death of the other occurs while it occurs and is without why or without reason. It sticks to its happening and asks not why. And, lastly, such a rupture without reason effects a transformation across the shared world so that each time uniquely a death of the other is a death of the pluralized world.

Beyond aligning the death of the other with these symptoms of an event, though, I have offered a description of the aspects of this unexpected, without reason, and transformative event by showing how its occurring recalibrates both the spatiality and temporality of a survivor's world in its wake. I have argued, accordingly, that mourning the death of the other has a material element insofar as the meaningfulness of things, places, and the self get transformed with the death of the other. Such meaningfulness concerns, following Heidegger, the spatiality of the world. And considering that this spatiality gets co-constituted with others during our life, when the other dies the absence of the other gets brought into the present on account of the spatiality of the world that had been co-determined with them. This present absence or absent presence gets carried in and along things such as memorials, the material earth, and even the epigenome of the survivor. Such are the traces of the trauma left on things, places, and the self in the aftermath of the death of the other. Moreover, I have unpacked the retemporalization of this event's causality of rupture by showing how the death of the other transforms a survivor's experience to the past, future, and present in the aftermath of such death. A survivor's lived experience or temporality is no longer linear after the death of the other. The past death will not stay in the past but continues to haunt the survivor in the present by rewriting the survivor's future on account of the future possibilities that are now impossible in the aftermath of the death of the other as well as through the possibilities after this death that remain im-possible or condition their own occurring unexpectedly for the survivor. In the midst of such a present that is out of joint or defined as the spectral moment, I have argued that while the death of the other may be the poison that spells the end of a survivor, if the survivor can live on after the other in this life after death, mourning the other offers the survivor a chance of new yet different life. In this, mourning the death of the other becomes a gift that keeps the survivor and the pluralized world open to the coming of other events, even other deaths of the other, by being ready to be surprised by the causality of rupture that is each time unique when an event befalls us. For the dead other, be it human, nonhuman animal, or divine, remains other whose call to the self is one of responsibility to mourn the dead other. A responsibility that can have individual, existential impact on a survivor as well as an ethico-political impact that extends beyond just the individual.

    Throughout this description, I have been sharpening the phenomenological edge of the *tragen* from the last line of Celan's "Vast Glowing Vault" — "The world is gone, I must carry you" (*Die Welt ist fort, ich muß dich tragen*) — as a rejoinder to Heidegger's claim in *Being and Time* that when the other dies, the survivor is just nearby. Thus, I argue that Celan's poetic attestation to the death of the other exposes the survivor to the ontological transformation of the world as a with-world and the being-with of the survivor through the present absence or absent presence that attends the death of the other. Moreover, I argue that Celan's poem helps us to think through the ethical possibilities-to-be that can remain on account of the death of the other. For, as I argue, the world and the other after the death of the other get carried in the present by survivors in at least five ways: in the objects whose meaning the other helped constitute while living, in material elements of the earth impacted by the death of the other, in the epigenome of the survivor, in a survivor's memories that were co-constituted with the dead other, and in a survivor's future possibilities after the death of the other. Consequently, when the other dies, we are much more than just nearby because the death of the other carries with it an ontological and ethical impetus. Such is the survival or the life after the death of the other.

I argue for this impetus especially through the idea of worklessness that I develop throughout as the worklessness of mourning, memory, and hospitality. I have presented workless mourning as a way of thinking through the idea of the work *without* work of mourning, first, in relation to the norm of mourning and pathology of melancholy in Freud so that mourning becomes not an accomplishment to move beyond but a task that remains on-going. And in the progress made, no end or goal remains in sight. I, then, extend this work *without* work to the memory that attends a survivor's mourning on account of how the past death of the other never remains past because, in part, the other's absence haunts a survivor's transactive memory constituted with the other while living. The responsibility to mourn the other worklessly requires that the other be remembered *as* other and, thereby, as absent even when such absence gets carried by us in the present. Memory in workless mourning becomes, then, workless because carrying the other as other requires that the other be remembered or brought back into presence only as absent. In this, the mourning process is never to end in the *telos* of getting over the loss. Rather, through the back and forth of making progress in mourning, and thereby working at it in remembering the other, and of never coming to a complete end, the other gets remembered so that they remain the other who has died and not merely the other as an idealized picture of who the other had been. Workless mourning mourns the other *as* other and thereby always as the absence of who or what has died. Through such workless mourning and its workless memory, hospitality is offered to the dead other through allowing the conditions of hospitality to be loosened by the unconditional call to be hospitable to the other whether living or dead, whether human, nonhuman animal, or divine. The death of the other will always have been unexpected on account of not just the loss of the other but also what the world had meant to and with this other. If hospitality is only ever offered to what is expected, then the dead other will remain, like Polynices before the end of "Antigone," unmourned. To mourn even the death of the other, a survivor must open herself to the coming of the unexpected death of the other. Such is the workless hospitality offered not just to the living other but also to the dead other.

So if this is what the death of the other can disclose to us, why then is all of this not readily recognized and acknowledged by all who experience such death? From a psychological standpoint, we all deny death,[1] or, as Kierkegaard says, we lack the earnestness to see that we too shall die.[2] From a theological standpoint, the fear and trembling at the heart of faith is fear-filling, and the death of the other, especially when the death occurs at the most unreasonable moment (e.g., at a young age), brings this fear and trembling to the fore. For the death of the other can challenge the deepest held theological beliefs. And when an experience challenges these dogmas or deeply rooted belief systems, more often than not survivors do not want to dwell on it. They do not want to *sink deeper* into the experience. For when we do pay attention to the death of the other, when we have the courage to be vigilant about such death, life becomes messier and harder to control. Life becomes messier and difficult because death shows us the reality of things as always already relational and utterly affected by the shocks and disruptions of contingency, that is, of events. But we do not like the difficult. However, life is never clean, neat, and easy because being itself, as I have shown, is a being-with on account of our relation to things, animals, the earth, one another, God(s), *and*, this means, with death.

For these reasons, vigilance over the death of the other needs exercising. The latent truth in the death of the other does not become manifest, does not show itself to us, unless we are vigilant about what the death of the other can teach us. Such vigilance requires a courage to face the facts of death and to sink deeper in order to see what the death of the other can teach us about the life we live now. Vigilance always treads through darkness — think of a soldier keeping the night watch or mourners keeping vigil — but the hope of vigilance is the light of another day, another day in which we remember the world that has been lost with the other and that we now carry. Vigilance requires sinking into the muck and mire of the darkness, keeping awake in this darkness, and hoping not for a fresh start but for another start in light of what the vigil has taught us. If we can remain awake, we can see lifedeath for what it is: a relational interplay between others, the self, the pluralized world, and, consequently, death. Vigilance over the death of the other discloses reality to us as fraught with events as well as our participation with and responsibility to one another when an event of the death of the other occurs. Such is survival. Such is life after life ends for the other. Such is our resurrection in this afterlife.

Introduction

1. Nicholas Wolterstorff, *Lament for a Son* (Grand Rapids, MI: Eerdmans, 1987), 11.

2. Wolterstorff, *Lament for a Son*, 11.

3. Wolterstorff, *Lament for a Son*, 17; emphasis mine.

4. Jacques Derrida, "Living On" in *Deconstruction and Criticism*, ed. Geoffrey H. Hartman (New York: Continuum, 1979), 127.

5. John D. Caputo, *Radical Hermeneutics: Repetition, Deconstruction, and the Hermeneutic Project* (Bloomington: Indiana University Press, 1987, 1).

6. In drawing on the use of *the event*, I am not confusing or conflating the two ways that this term is used. On the one hand, *the event* can refer to, in a sense, a macrocosmic, large-scale event. Heidegger uses *the event* (*das Ereignis*) in this macrocosmic sense when he talks about the history of being and the ontological difference. On the other hand, *the event* can be used to refer to particular phenomena, in this microcosmic sense, or even to the phenomenality of all phenomena, as Marion uses the term in *Being Given*. In this, Marion draws largely upon Heidegger's own microcosmic use of *the event* in describing the thinghood and worldhood of a being in terms of *das Ereignis* essentially occurring in and along this being. In both the macrocosmic and microcosmic uses of the term *event*, each philosopher focuses on how any event is disruptive of meaning. The difference between the two uses for these philosophers concerns the measure or scope of the disruption. My description treats the death of the other along the lines of the microcosmic kind of event.

7. This notion of degrees of givenness comes from Jean-Luc Marion's important work *Being Given: Toward a Phenomenology of Givenness* but especially as this text has been read by Christina Gschwandtner in *Degrees of Givenness: On Saturation in Jean-Luc Marion* (Bloomington: Indiana University Press, 2014).

8. This group includes, but is not limited to, Martin Heidegger, especially his work from the mid 1930s where he focuses on *das Ereignis* (the event) in conjunction with his career-long task of thinking the truth of being, along with the French reception of Heidegger's work by Gilles Deleuze, Alain Badiou, Jacques Derrida, Jean-Luc Nancy, Marion, Françoise Dastur, and Claude Romano. In addition, John D. Caputo's recent

work has made this topic popular for English speakers interested in Continental philosophy, as has François Raffoul in his *Thinking the Event* (Bloomington: Indiana University Press, 2020).

9. Claude Romano, *Event and World*, trans. Shane Mackinlay (New York: Fordham University Press, 2009), 30–31.

10. Santiago Zabala and Michael Marder, "Introduction: The First Jolts" in *Being Shaken: Ontology and the Event*, ed. Michael Marder and Santiago Zabala (New York: Palgrave MacMillan, 2014), 9.

11. Gert-Jan van der Heiden, *Ontology after Ontotheology: Plurality, Event, and Contingency in Contemporary Philosophy* (Pittsburgh, PA: Duquesne University Press, 2014), 17.

12. Cf. Claude Romano, *Event and Time*, trans. Stephen E. Lewis (New York: Fordham University Press, 2014), 156, where he states that an event "manifests itself as such only after the fact."

13. Here I am drawing on Derrida's account of transcendental violence in his essay "Violence and Metaphysics," where he draws from Husserl to critique Levinas (see *WD* 125).

14. Cf. Robert Sokolowski, *Introduction to Phenomenology* (New York: Cambridge University Press, 2000), 46. Many thanks to Steven Delay for reminding me of Sokolowski's short but precise description of the death of the other.

15. Saint Augustine, *Confessions*, trans. Henry Chadwick (New York: Oxford University Press, 1991), 174. Hannah Arendt and Marion emphasize in their respective commentaries on Augustine's *Confessions* that the death of the other, particularly of Augustine's close friend Nebridius, causes Augustine to pose for the first time the orienting question of his entire *Confessions*: *Questio mihi factus sum* or "I had become to myself a vast problem" (*Confessions*, 57; see Hannah Arendt, *Love and Saint Augustine*, trans. Joanna Vecchiarelli Scott and Judith Chelius Stark (Chicago, IL: University of Chicago Press, 1996), 13, and *ISP* 64).

16. Raffoul, *Thinking the Event*, 15. Raffoul argues convincingly, even if against Marion's own reading of Heidegger, that Heidegger's understanding of phenomenology in both *Being and Time* but especially in *Basic Problems of Phenomenology* is one in which the focus of phenomenology is not on the ontic phenomena but on the ontology of these phenomena. Raffoul concludes that phenomenology is about the being of phenomena where being is the most inapparent amid the apparent, or where the being of phenomena concerns their happening or their eventiality. Consequently, phenomenology as defined by Heidegger and taken up in the post-Husserlian, French appropriations of Heidegger is a phenomenology of the happening or eventiality of phenomena (see Raffoul, *Thinking the Event*, chapter 3, especially 75–83).

17. Raffoul, *Thinking the Event*, 95. Cf. Françoise Dastur, "Phenomenology of the Event: Waiting and Surprise," *Hypatia* 15, no. 4 (2000): 182.

18. Cf. Raffoul, *Thinking the Event*, 22, where he connects hospitality with "an ethics of the event."

19. Van der Heiden, *Ontology after Ontotheology*, 137.

20. Nancy does, however, admit, "In a birth or in a death — examples which are not examples, but more than examples; they are the thing itself — there is the event, some[thing] awaited, something that might have been able to be" (*BSP* 167; brackets are his).

21. "The name of the bow is life [ΒΙΟΣ], but its work is death" (B48). Translations of Heraclitus throughout are from Daniel W. Graham, *The Texts of Early Greek Philosophy: The Complete Fragments and Selected Testimonies of the Major Presocratics* (Cambridge, MA: Cambridge University Press, 2010).

22. See, for example, Richard Polt, "Traumatic Ontology," in *Being Shaken: Ontology and the Event*, ed. Santiago Zabala and Michael Marder (New York: Palgrave MacMillan, 2014), 19–40.

23. See Françoise Dastur, *Death: An Essay on Finitude*, trans. John Llewelyn (Atlantic Highlands, NJ: Athlone, 1996), and *How Are We to Confront Death? An Introduction to Philosophy*, trans. Robert Vallier (New York: Fordham University Press, 2012).

24. Marder and Zabala, "Introduction," 9. Instructive in this regard is Richard Polt's essay "Traumatic Ontology" in *Being Shaken*, where he provides "my birth and my death" as the two paradigmatic examples of events insofar as in my birth and realization of my mortality, being or the real undergoes a transformation that engenders a new interpretation of being's excessiveness (25).

25. Emmanuel Levinas, *God, Death, and Time*, trans. Bettina Bergo (Stanford, CA: Stanford University Press, 2000), 43.

26. In an original interpretation of being-toward-death in Heidegger's *Being and Time*, Hans Ruin shows that while Levinas's and Derrida's criticisms of Heidegger are valid, "it is important to see how Heidegger in his own way . . . opens the door toward an exploration of a peculiar and irreducible intersubjective ontology of *being with the dead*. . . . [The dead in Heidegger's *Being and Time*] continue to inhabit the argument and the overriding question of Dasein's temporality and historicity" (Hans Ruin, *Being with the Dead: Burial Ancestral Politics, and the Roots of Historical Consciousness* [Stanford, CA: Stanford University Press, 2018], 29). This interpretation of Heidegger plays an important role in chapters 3 and 6 below.

27. Emmanuel Levinas, "Ethics as First Philosophy," in *The Levinas Reader*, ed. Seán Hand (Cambridge, MA: Basil Blackwell, 1989), 86.

28. Martin Heidegger, *The History of the Concept of Time: Prolegomena*, trans. Theodore Kisiel (Bloomington: Indiana University Press, 1992), 316–17.

29. Michael Naas, "When It Comes to Mourning," in *Jacques Derrida: Key Concepts*, ed. Claire Colebrook (New York: Routledge, 2015), 117.

30. Ruin, *Being with the Death*, 5; emphasis his.

31. Ruin, *Being with the Death*, 201.

32. Derrida, "Living On," 77.

33. Derrida, "Living On," 111n.

34. As Shelly Rambo discusses in her rereading of Christian religious concepts in this context of Derrida's discussion of *survivre*, the "Christian conception of the afterlife" can now be read "not in terms of an event in the future but as a condition of living amid ongoing violence" (Shelly Rambo, *Resurrecting Wounds: Living in the Afterlife of Trauma* [Waco, TX: Baylor University Press, 2017], 79).

35. Mark C. Taylor, *Last Works: Lessons in Leaving* (New Haven, CT: Yale University Press, 2018), 79.

36. Elizabeth Rosner, *Survivor Café: The Legacy of Trauma and the Labyrinth of Memory* (Berkeley, CA: Counterpoint, 2017), 37; emphasis hers.

37. Kas Saghafi, *The World after the End of the World: A Spectro-Poetics* (Albany, NY: SUNY Press, 2020), 5.

38. Athena Athanasiou, *Agonistic Mourning: Political Dissidence and the Women in Black* (Edinburgh: Edinburgh University Press, 2017).

39. Ruin, *Being with the Dead*, 60.

40. Ruin, *Being with the Dead*, 60. Whereas I put this in terms of being-with, Ruin speaks about "communal existence."

41. Derrida, "Living On," 77.

42. John D. Caputo, *The Prayers and Tears of Jacques Derrida: Religion without Religion* (Bloomington: Indiana University Press, 1997), 180.

43. Raffoul, *Thinking the Event*, 53.

44. Many thanks to Michael Naas for helping me tease out this important difference between my approach in relation to Derrida's reading of Celan.

45. W. H. Auden, "Funeral Blues" in *Another Time* (London: Faber and Faber, 2007), 81–82. I encourage the reader to read Auden's poem in its entirety. It is a powerful poem, but I could not reproduce more of it here due to permission issues.

46. Auden, "Funeral Blues," 81.

47. My further engagement with Auden's "Funeral Blues" occurs below in part 3, specifically in chapter 6 and 7, where I discuss the death of the other's temporal transformation of the world regarding the future.

48. Milstein, *Rebellious Mourning*, 138. On this page, Mari Matsumoto and Sabu Kohso are unpacking the trauma that has attended the nuclear disaster that occurred in Fukushima.

49. Emily Dickinson, "Death sets a thing significant" in *Death Poems*, ed. Russ Kick (San Francisco, CA: Disinformation Books, 2013), 93.

50. Rambo, *Resurrecting Wounds*, 42.

51. Geoffrey Bennington, *Not Half No End: Militantly Melancholic Essays in Memory of Jacques Derrida* (Edinburgh: Edinburgh University Press, 2010), 29.

52. Saghafi, *World after the End*, 93; cf. *WM* 41.

53. Cf. Rambo, *Resurrecting Wounds*, 145, where she writes, "The 'posttraumatic' identifies a way of living with awareness that experiences do not respect lines between past, present, and future."

54. Raffoul, *Thinking the Event*, 14; cf. 91–92.

Chapter One

1. Raffoul, *Thinking the Event*, 233.

2. Interview with Jérôme-Alexandre Nielsberg, "Jacques Derrida — Penseur de l'événement Jacques Derrida," *L'Humanité* 27 (January 2004), https://advance-lexis-com.tamusa.idm.oclc.org/api/document?collection=news&id=urn:contentItem:4CKN-2MF0-TWKN-T25T-00000-00&context=1516831.

3. See, for example, Christophe Bouton, "The Privilege of the Present: Time and the Trace from Heidegger to Derrida," *International Journal of Philosophical Studies* 28, no. 3 (2020): 370–89.

4. John D. Caputo, ed., *Deconstruction in a Nutshell: A Conversation with Jacques Derrida* (New York: Fordham University Press, 1997), 14.

5. Here I am following the translation of *das Ereignis* put forward by Daniella Vallega-Neu and Richard Rojcewicz. In using this translation, I am not conflating *das Ereignis* with the notion of occurrence (i.e., *Vorgang*). With this, the event for Heidegger is not something that happens in the world but names, rather, a deep structure at work in what happens. In other words, the event names not *a* being but being itself in Heidegger's works.

6. Caputo, *Deconstruction in a Nutshell*, 14.

7. See Jussi Backman, "Logocentrism and the Gathering Lo/goj: Heidegger, Derrida, and the Contextual Centers of Meaning," *Research in Phenomenology* 42 (2012): 67–91; Geoffrey Bennington, "Geschlecht pollachos legetai: Translation, Polysemia, Dissemination," *Philosophy Today* 64, no. 2 (2020): 423–39; Adam Knowles, "Toward a Critique of *Walten*: Heidegger, Derrida, and Henological Difference," *Journal of Speculative Philosophy* 27, no. 3 (2013): 265–76; David Farrell Krell, "History, Natality, Ecstasy: Derrida's First Seminar on Heidegger, 1964–1965," *Research in Phenomenology* 46 (2016): 3–34; David Farrell Krell, *Phantoms of the Other: Four Generations of Derrida's* Geschlecht (Albany, NY: SUNY Press, 2015), esp. 14; Adam R. Rosenthal, "On Derrida's *Donner le temps, Volumes I & II*: A New Engagement with Heidegger," *Research in Phenomenology* 52 (2022): 23–47; John Russon, "The Self as Resolution: Heidegger, Derrida, and the Intimacy of the Question of the Meaning of Being," *Research in Phenomenology* 38 (2008): 90–110; Rodrigo Therezo, "'In the Watermark of Some Margin': Heidegger's Other Gesture," *Research in Phenomenology* 51 (2021): 20–36; Daniela Vallega-Neu, "A Strange Proximity: On the Notion of *Walten*

in Derrida and Heidegger," *Epoché: A Journal for the History of Philosophy* 26, no. 2 (2022): 369–87; and Jason Winfree, "Concealing Difference: Derrida and Heidegger's Thinking of Becoming," *Research in Phenomenology* 29, no. 1 (1999): 161–81. Lastly, in charting this difference between Derrida and Heidegger, Françoise Dastur maintains that Derrida does not "sufficiently" think through concealing or absence that takes place as one of the movements of the event for Heidegger ("Heidegger and Derrida: On Play and Difference," *Epoché: A Journal for the History of Philosophy* 3, no. 1/2 [1995]: 15). Per my prefatory remarks, I argue that he likely has thought this through sufficiently but remains suspicious of whether or not a full respect of difference can take place if the starting point is a gift of presence. Hence, Derrida emphasizes absence, dispersion, and dissemination because he thinks this starting and ending point can still be in play with presence and gathering without the force of presence potentially getting the upper hand.

8. François Raffoul, "Sexual Difference and Gathering in Geschlecht III," *Philosophy Today* 64, no. 2 (2020): 336. Raffoul problematizes Derrida's critique of Heidegger's understanding of *Versammlung* in *Geschlecht III* by masterfully showing in Heidegger's reading of Trakl that "gathering is [for Heidegger] the sheltering of difference" (336).

9. Michael Naas, "Violence and Historicity: Derrida's Early Readings of Heidegger," *Research in Phenomenology* 45 (2015): 191. Naas goes to argue that in both Derrida's first seminar on Heidegger in 1964–65 as well as in the essay "Violence and Metaphysics," Derrida sees in Heidegger a thinking of difference in Heidegger's thinking of historicity to the extent that being for Heidegger is not a univocal identity as the ahistorical origin of history but a unity that contains difference and is part of the infinitized, historicizing movement that constitutes history.

10. Dominique Janicaud, *Heidegger in France*, trans. François Raffoul and David Pettigrew (Bloomington: Indiana University Press, 2015), 356.

11. Cf. Other moments in Derrida's *Given Time: II* where he says something similar in his reading of Heidegger: "Giving gives nothing but its giving and *as withdrawal*. This giving as giving that gives nothing but *its withdrawal*" (*DT2* 210; emphasis mine); "[T]he value of the gift [in Heidegger's *On Time and Being*] will be determined *as the withdrawal* of what is given" (*DT2* 222; emphasis mine).

12. Janicaud, *Heidegger in France*, 356; emphasis mine.

13. In addition to *DT2* 119, where Derrida seems to acknowledge that the later Heidegger places greater import on the thematics of withdrawal, see also, Rodrigo Therezo, "From Neutral Dasein to a Gentle Twofold: Sexual Difference in Heidegger and Derrida," *Philosophy Today* 63,no. 2 (2019): 491–511, where he argues that Heidegger's dream in his Trakl essays of the *one Geschlecht* and the ground tone (*Grundton*) of Trakl's poetry shows that Heidegger wants to avoid an originary difference, discord, or divisibility, whereas Derrida's thinking is guided by such an originary difference. Additionally, Krell's reading of Derrida's *Geschlecht* essays convinces me that Derrida remains the more consistent thinker of difference among he and Heidegger (*Phantoms of the Other*, esp. 30, 128–29, and 186–90). Lastly, Ian Alexander Moore argues that Heidegger's thinking of detachment (*Abgeschiedenheit*) in Trakl's poetry, which is the magnet around which Heidegger reads Trakl, remains "metaphysical" because Heidegger too quickly

dismisses in his thinking of detachment the meaning that detachment has in relation to the ideas of dispersion and dissemination. In this, Heidegger runs the risk of searching for a transcendental signified for his understanding of detachment (see *Dialogue on the Threshold: Heidegger and Trakl* [Albany, NY: SUNY Press, 2022], especially 58, 98, 106–7, and 201–10). In contrast, Derrida's work "is nothing if not an attempt to think dissemination rigorously" (107) even if, as Moore points out, Derrida has little engagement with *Abgeschiedenheit* in his reading of Heidegger on Trakl.

14. Cf. Caputo, *Radical Hermeneutics,* 169, cf. 173.

15. Michael Naas, "Violence and Hyperbole: From 'Cogito and the History of Madness' to the *Death Penalty Seminar,*" in *Foucault/Derrida Fifty Years Later: The Futures of Genealogy, Deconstruction, and Politics*, ed. Olivia Custer, Penelope Deutscher, and Samir Haddad (New York: Columbia University Press, 2016), esp. 41 and 58–59. Naas locates such hyperbolic moments in Derrida's reading of Descartes, Foucault, Heidegger, and the history of the death penalty by naming *some* of these moments in Derrida's work: the cogito, the sovereign decision, the decision of the death penalty, the origin of reason, the origin of history, and hypersovereignty.

16. Naas, "Violence and Hyperbole," 51–52.

17. In developing this logic of the *sans*, I follow Derrida's statement about the call of *Come* to an event, "But will I have been able to say to you, *come*, without knowing, without having, without seeing [*sans savoir, sans avoir, sans voir*], in advance what 'come' means to say [*veut dire*]" (Jacques Derrida, *Parages*, trans. John P. Leavey et. al. [Stanford, CA: Stanford University Press, 2010], 15). This call affirms the surprise that befalls when an event comes, thereby opening us to the coming of an event. This call says, "Yes, I welcome the event to surprise me. Come surprise me."

18. Plato, *Parmenides* in *Plato: Complete Works*, ed. John M. Cooper (Indianapolis: Hackett, 1997). Citations appear hereafter following the Stephanus line numbering.

19. Cf. Romano, *Event and Time*, 35, where he comments that this instant "is as if in advance freed from every condition of anteriority and of posteriority, ab-solute in its arising, in no way subordinated to a prior temporal horizon; in its bursting forth from and in itself, it brings with itself its own horizon."

20. Romano, *Event and Time*, 37. An important itinerary for the event's temporality runs from Plato's understanding of "the sudden" in *Parmenides* to Aristotle's notion of movement in his *Physics* to Kierkegaard's understanding of repetition and the decision of faith and up through the work of Heidegger, Derrida, and Romano.

21. Cf. Geoffrey Bennington, *Jacques Derrida* (Chicago, IL: University of Chicago Press, 1993), 190, where he explains similarly that this paradoxical temporality of the aneconomic gift means that the "gift is never (a) present . . . ; it is given in a past which has never been present and will be received in a future which will never be present either."

22. Emmanuel Levinas, "Enigma and Phenomenon," in *Emmanuel Levinas: Basic Philosophical Writings*, ed. Adriaan T. Peperzak, Simon Critchley, and Robert Bernasconi (Bloomington: Indiana University Press, 1996), 72.

23. Cynthia D. Coe, *Levinas and the Trauma of Responsibility: The Ethical Significance of Time* (Bloomington: Indiana University Press, 2018), 2.

24. Levinas, "Enigma and Phenomenon," 75. In this essay, the enigma is Levinas's name for the event, namely the event of the call to responsibility for the other.

25. Levinas, "Enigma and Phenomenon," 72.

26. Emmanuel Levinas, "Ethics as First Philosophy," in *The Levinas Reader*, ed. Seán Hand (Cambridge, MA: Basil Blackwell, 1989), 86. We could, also, likely include our own death, our own birth, and the birth of the other. More will be said about these matters beginning in chapter 2.

27. Cf. Coe, *Levinas and the Trauma of Responsibility*, 59, where she writes, "[D]iachrony introduces the trace of something absent, rather than the overflowing presence of something higher than the ego."

28. Coe, *Levinas and the Trauma of Responsibility*, 21 and 29. Coe is speaking specifically here of diachronic temporality in Levinas. Part of Coe's thesis in her book is that "trauma constitutes the substantive meaning of diachrony, in the wake of the deformalization of time" (21).

29. Bessel van der Kolk, *The Body Keeps the Score: Brain, Mind, and the Body in the Healing of Trauma* (New York: Penguin, 2014), 21. In contrast to this definition of trauma that I am following throughout, see Romano *Event and World*, 109–14, and Romano, *Event and Time* 202–6. Romano argues in his work that trauma is "an event that we cannot make our own" (*Event and World*, 109, and *Event and Time*, 203) because it freezes the person to whom it befalls, making them incapable of appropriating the event into their own further adventure.

30. Cf. Jacques Derrida, "Autoimmunity: Real and Symbolic Suicides," in *Philosophy in a Time of Terror*, ed. Giovanna Borradori (Chicago, IL: University of Chicago Press, 2003), 96, "What is a traumatic event? First of all, any event worthy of this name, even if it is a 'happy' event, has within it something that is traumatizing. An event always inflicts a wound in the everyday course of history, in the ordinary repetition and anticipation of all experience."

31. Jacques Derrida, "On the Gift: A Discussion between Jacques Derrida and Jean-Luc Marion," in *God, the Gift, and Postmodernism*, ed. John D. Caputo and Michael J. Scanlon (Bloomington: Indiana University Press, 1999), 59.

32. The epigraph of *Given Time* reads, "The King takes all my time; I give the rest to Saint-Cyr, to whom I would like to give all" (*GT* 1).

33. Caputo, *Prayers and Tears*, 172.

34. I return to and develop in depth this idea of hospitality in Derrida and its relation to mourning the dead in chapter 8.

Chapter Two

1. Caputo, *Prayers and Tears*, 180.

2. G. W. Leibniz, *Discourse on Metaphysics and Other Essays*, trans. Daniel Garber and Roger Ariew (Indianapolis, IN: Hackett, 1991), 72. In particular, these are from his *Monadology* §§ 31–32.

3. Leibniz, *Discourse on Metaphysics*, 73. *Monadology* §§35–38.

4. Jacques Derrida, "The Principle of Reason: The University in the Eyes of Its Pupils," *Diacritics* 13, no. 3 (1983): 8.

5. Van der Kolk, *Body Keeps the Score*, 45.

6. See Fredrik Westerlund, *Heidegger and the Problem of Phenomena* (New York: Bloomsbury Academic, 2020). One point of this tension in *The Principle of Reason* can be found regarding Heidegger's discussion of the *Abgrund* or groundlessness of being. While this groundlessness of being means for Heidegger, as I discuss in chapter 2, that being is not even self-grounding, a position he takes likely to avoid some onto-theo-logical issues that he says elsewhere should be avoided (see Martin Heidegger, *Identity and Difference*, trans. Joan Stambaugh [New York: Harper & Row, 1969], 42–76), the blooming of the rose in Heidegger's discussion does seem to be grounded on itself, namely on its own blooming.

7. Cf. Derrida, "Principle of Reason," 14.

8. Derrida comments, "What lends itself to calculation is the object, that which is in the figure of the object. What enters into a quantifiable calculation is first objectivated" (*DP2* 151).

9. Naas, "Violence and Hyperbole," 44.

10. The interest of this *Abgrund* in phenomenology moves away from Heidegger's being-historical thinking in order to claim that particular phenomena understood as events can be groundless insofar as their own occurring is their only ground. For examples of phenomena being described as the ground of their own occurring, see *NC* 114; Romano, *Event and World*, 42; and Raffoul, *Thinking the Event*, 10.

11. See Immanuel Kant, *Critique of Pure Reason*, trans. Paul Guyer and Allen W. Wood (New York: Cambridge University Press, 1998), A50/B74.

12. Raffoul, *Thinking the Event*, 69.

13. Raffoul, *Thinking the Event*, 14.

14. Derrida's "Principle of Reason" calls in the end for a new community of thinking, not outside of but, perhaps, adjacent to the university, that focuses on thinking not only according to the principle of reason but also thinking what lies outside of this principle. Moreover, as Derrida argues in part 2 of *Rogues*, reason is divided in itself, reason undergoes *partage*, between thinking the calculable or according to calculation and thinking the incalculable or against calculation (*R* 141–59). Accordingly, this new community of thinking would be a thinking not only according to the first tonality of the principle of

sufficient reason but also a thinking of events. And I suspect that Marion's own study of saturated phenomena and the givenness of all phenomena as events would be required reading for this community.

15. Martin Heidegger, *Four Seminars*, trans. Andrew Mitchell and François Raffoul (Bloomington: Indiana University Press, 2012), 80.

16. Heidegger writes, "What is it that phenomenology is to 'let be seen'? What is it that is to be called 'phenomenon' in a distinctive sense? . . . Manifestly, it is something that does *not* show itself initially and for the most part, something that is *concealed* in contrast to what initially and for the most part does show itself. But, at the same time, it is something that essentially belongs to what initially and for the most part shows itself" (*BT* 33; emphasis his).

17. Marion also regards Heidegger's existential analytic as an attempt to develop such a phenomenology of the inapparent. For Marion's argument on how this attempt fails, see *RG* 77–107.

18. "Incident" is how Marion translates Aristotle's συμβέβηκος, which is traditionally translated as "accident," in conjunction with the German *Zufälligkeit* (*BG* 152 and 355n49). He translates Aristotle's Greek this way to avoid the traditional, metaphysical understanding of an accident's dependence on a substance. Disregarding this metaphysical understanding, we could alternatively call this characteristic of a given phenomenon its "accidentality."

19. Both Shane Mackinlay and Christina Gschwandtner miss this point in their explications of Marion's understanding of the event insofar as their explications begin with book 3 of Marion's *Being Given* without addressing Marion's indexing of givenness to the event in book 1 of *Being Given* (see Shane Mackinlay, *Interpreting Excess: Jean-Luc Marion, Saturated Phenomena, and Hermeneutics* [New York: Fordham University Press, 2009], 79; and Gschwandtner, *Degrees of Givenness*, 27). Though Gschwandtner does not develop this important homology between the event and givenness, she does recognize it in her book (see *Degrees of Givenness*, 23).

20. For example, he claims that every phenomenon has a "hidden eventiality [*événementialité*]" (Jean-Luc Marion, *Givenness and Hermeneutics*, trans. Jean-Pierre LaFouge [Milwaukee, WI: Marquette University Press, 2012], 63; translation modified); every phenomenon has an "originally evential [*événementiel*] character . . . insofar as first it gives itself before showing itself" (*IE* 52; translation modified); the "original phenomenality" of any phenomenon is "governed completely by eventiality" (*IE* 36; translation modified); and a phenomenon's "deployment of the visible" is "the emergence of the event" (Jean-Luc Marion, "Phenomenon and Event," *Graduate Faculty Philosophy Journal* 26, no. 1 [2005]: 151–52).

21. As Gschwandtner argues, Marion may broach this topic of degrees of givenness in his work, but he does not develop it enough, or at least he does not make developing this notion one of his main concerns.

22. In particular, he inverts how Kant uses the categories in the Axioms of Intuition, Anticipations of Perception, Analogies of Experience, and Postulates of Empirical

Thinking in the *Critique of Pure Reason*. Marion admits that this description of the givenness of saturated phenomena that arises through this inversion is prefigured by Kant's own aesthetic ideas in Kant's *Critique of Judgment*. Marion even goes so far as to use Kant's notion of the sublime as an example of a saturated phenomenon from the history of philosophy (see *BG* 219–20).

23. Elie Wiesel, "Does the Holocaust Lie beyond the Reach of Art?," *New York Times*, April 17, 1983, quoted in Rosner, *Survivor Café*, 206.

24. Elie Wiesel, "Trivializing the Holocaust: Semi-Fact and Semi Fiction," *New York Times*, April 1, 1978, quoted in Rosner, *Survivor Café*, 210. Cf. Michael Naas, "Violence and Hyperbole," 54ff, where Naas argues that the excess of an incalculable, hyperbolic moment in Derrida's works is irreducible to history.

25. Raffoul, *Thinking the Event*, 53.

26. Cf. Romano, *Event and World*, 30–31.

27. Romano, *Event and World*, 70.

28. Romano, *Event and World*, 73; cf. 19–20.

29. Quoting *BT* 251, where Heidegger *actually* calls death "the possibility of *the* impossibility of existence [*Existenz*] in general" (emphasis mine), which delimits death to a particular impossibility, namely that of *Existenz*, and not impossibility in general, as Marion's misquotation suggests.

30. For this reason, I disagree with Mackinlay when he writes, "Marion makes no acknowledgement that my being born is the opening of a world in which I play myself out as an event of projecting toward meaning-filled possibilities" (*Interpreting Excess*, 113).

31. Wolterstorff, *Lament for a Son*, 43; emphasis mine.

32. Romano, *Event and World*, 69; cf. 31 and 44.

33. Romano, *Event and World*, 38; cf. Romano, *Event and Time*, 111 and 230.

Chapter Three

1. Marion, "Phenomenon and Event," 153; emphasis mine.

2. Gert-Jan van der Heiden argues that contemporary continental philosophy's concern with the event carries a concomitant concern with how to approach the event. This latter concern is a concern with how to think the event beyond mere theoretical thinking (θεωρία) to a different ethos, attitude, or comportment on how to relate to an event. Considering that the event exceeds the capacities of philosophical concepts and paradigms, "a whole new series of notions is brought into play that should capture how we relate to an event" (*Ontology after Ontotheology*, 19). For example, he lists "hope, promise, oath, fidelity, attestation, conviction, courage, and resoluteness" as such attitudes (19). With this, what

I am calling poetic attestation can be added to this list of comportments to an event that lie beyond theoretical thinking.

3. For example, in *Existence and Existents*, Levinas maintains that anxiety's "object" should not be one's own death but existence itself because only in this way does anxiety point us toward the other. As long as you focus on your own death, says Levinas, you never confront your responsibility for the other (Emmanuel Levinas, *Existence and Existents*, trans. Alphonso Lingis [The Hague: Martinus Nijhoff, 1978]). In *God, Death, and Time*, Levinas explores this idea further when he writes, "The other concerns me as a neighbor. In every death is shown the nearness of the neighbor, and the responsibility of the survivor. . . . It is for the death of the other that I am responsible to the point of including myself in his death" (17 and 43). I argue that Derrida develops these ideas from Levinas by relating them with the event and a distinctive ethical comportment to this event.

4. Paul Celan, *Atemwende* (Frankfurt a. M.: Suhrkamp, 1967), quoted in *SQ* 141.

5. Cf. Dennis Schmidt, "Of Birth, Death, and Unfinished Conversations," in *Gadamer's Hermeneutics and the Art of Conversation*, ed. Andrzej Wiercinski (Piscataway, NJ: Transaction Publishers, 2011), 110–11.

6. Ruin, *Being with the Dead*, 29. In Ruin's further reading of the role of this being-with the dead in Heidegger's *Being and Time*, Ruin creatively and persuasively shows that Heidegger's own understanding of historicity depends on a latent understanding of the historicity of Dasein as being-with the dead. Heidegger does not develop this directly in his text, but Ruin shows that Heidegger's analysis of historicity in chapter 5 of division 2 of *Being and Time* is dependent on this intersubjective ontology of the dead insofar as the historicity of Dasein is, in part, constituted by the "having-been" of Dasein, which includes Dasein's relation with those who have been (see *Being with the Dead*, 29–36, especially 33).

7. Even in a theological setting where Jesus Christ is understood in Christianity as making the ultimate sacrifice for humanity by dying on the cross, thereby securing the salvation of the person from dwelling eternally in Hell, each person must still die his or her own death even after Christ's sacrifice. For Christians, the death that Christ takes away is, then, *not* the human death that Heidegger is describing but the eternal death represented by eternal separation from God. In other words, all people must die their own *finite* death even if such an *eternal* death exists.

8. Heidegger, *History of the Concept of Time*, 317. Dennis Schmidt helpfully comments, "It is not the *cogito sum* that opens up my being to me, but the *sum moribundus* which opens me up to my 'I am'" ("Of Birth, Death, and Unfinished Conversations," 110); cf. Dennis Schmidt, "What We Owe the Dead," in *Heidegger and the Greeks: Interpretive Essays*, ed. Drew A. Hyland and John Panteleimon Manoussakis (Bloomington: Indiana University Press, 2006), 115.

9. Schmidt, "What We Owe the Dead," 118.

10. Romano, *Event and World*, 186.

11. As Schmidt comments, "To say that *a* world dies when someone dies is clear and easy to grasp. To say that *the* world dies, that the whole world is over, is less clear" (Schmidt, "Birth, Death, and Unfinished Conversations," 112; emphasis his).

12. My development of these claims by Derrida in relation to his reading of Celan and the death of the other is inspired by and follows at times Naas's really helpful reading of Derrida's final seminar (see Michael Naas, *The End of the World and Other Teachable Moments: Jacques Derrida's Final Seminar* [New York: Fordham University Press, 2015], 41–61).

13. Cf. Romano, *Event and World*, 116.

14. Leibniz, *Discourse on Metaphysics*, 76. *Monadology* §57. Though Romano develops his own notion of world in a different hermeneutics than Leibniz, for Romano focuses on the world as a collection of possibilities opened first by the event of birth and then by the various adventures of the human, Romano's idea of world remains similar to what Leibniz says here because Romano states, "But there is actually only one and the same world, starting from which our worlds can differ, as so many ways of appropriating one and the same world-in-common starting from dissimilar and singular histories" (*Event and World*, 129).

15. In his collection of essays reflecting on the later Derrida after Derrida's death in 2004, J. Hillis Miller presents an intriguing interpretation of this idea of windowlessness. The particular interpretation of Derrida concerns Derrida's final seminar, *The Beast and the Sovereign II*, in conversation with *A Taste for the Secret* and *The Gift of Death* in an effort to understand the alterity of the other for Derrida in conversation with Levinas's *autrui* and, surprisingly, Heidegger's *das Man*. Miller argues that each other is "enisled" (101) or a "windowless monad" (186) for Derrida because this windowlessness preserves the alterity of the other, including the alterity of our own self, from being appropriated by a constituting *ego*. So the windowlessness of each other describes for Miller the heightened degree of alterity belonging to the other in Derrida's works (see J. Hillis Miller, *For Derrida* [New York: Fordham University Press, 2009], esp. 69, 102, 115, 121–23, 129–32, 153–54, 181, 185–89, 320, and 324). While I do not disagree with Miller's interpretation of this heightened alterity of the other in Derrida's writings, I disagree with using the language of windowless to describe it because such a description can suggest that we have no connection with the other. Miller makes no such claim; in fact, he makes the opposite claim. However, in an effort to avoid this kind of confusing connotation from the adjective *windowless*, when I say that the other is far from windowless, I mean that the other is far from disconnected with the infinite array of other others in Derrida's work.

16. Dastur similarly maintains that in mourning the death of a loved one, what is mourned is "the radical loss of the totality of possibilities which we call *a* world" ("Phenomenology of the Event," 185; emphasis mine).

17. The following two chapters cover such exiled and lost meaning in things, places, and landscapes in the aftermath of the death of the other.

18. Wolterstorff, *Lament for a Son*, 33.

19. Rosner, *Survivor Café*, 134; emphasis mine.

20. Cf. Ana Luszczynska, "Nancy and Derrida: On Ethics and the Same (Infinitely Different) Constitutive Events of Being," *Philosophy and Social Criticism* 35, no. 7 [2009]: 801–21. In particular she maintains that the "most central similarities [between Derrida and Nancy] involve the shared notions of a radically prior being-with that is constitutive of being" (802; cf. 815).

21. Heidegger develops the evential character of such things in the world further in his later work in conjunction with this idea of the with-world. Most notably, things begin to be described as events in their phenomenality in the works "The Thing" (*Bremen and Freiburg Lectures: Insight into That Which Is* and *Basic Principles of Thinking*, trans. Andrew J. Mitchell [Bloomington: Indiana University Press, 2012], 5–20) and "The Origin of the Work of Art" (*Poetry, Language, Thought*, trans. Albert Hofstadter [New York: Harper Perennial, 2013], 15–86). Raffoul develops this line of interpretation helpfully in *Thinking the Event*, 117–27. See also Andrew J. Mitchell, *The Fourfold: Reading the Late Heidegger* (Evanston, IL: Northwestern University Press, 2015).

22. Romano, *Event and World*, 114 and 116.

23. Claude Romano, "Mourir à autrui," *Critique: Revue générale des publications françaises et étrangères* 51 (1995): 817 (my translation); cf. Romano, *Event and World*, 119, when he writes, "[A]nother's death reconfigures all my own possibilities, which implies that my own possibilities were never separable from those of the one whom I mourn."

24. Cf. Rambo, *Resurrecting Wounds*, 40, where she writes of trauma in general, "Perhaps trauma rolls back the curtain of our assumptions about autonomy, exposing this 'fleshy' insight: that we are not immune from the processes of the world but, in fact, profoundly subject to them."

25. Rodolphe Gasché, *Europe, or the Infinite Task: A Study of a Philosophical Concept* (Stanford, CA: Stanford University Press, 2009), 316.

26. Cf. *BSP* 40, where Nancy says, "The 'self,' of the 'self' in general, takes place *with* before taking place as itself and/or as the other" (emphasis mine).

27. Emmanuel Levinas, *Totality and Infinity*, trans. Alphonso Lingis (Pittsburg, PN: Duquesne University Press, 1969), 201.

28. Milstein, *Rebellious Mourning*, 336.

29. See Jacques Derrida "Circumfession," in Geoffrey Bennington, *Jacques Derrida* (Chicago, IL: University of Chicago Press, 1993), period 32; Derrida, "Living on," 115n; Jacques Derrida, *The Post Card: From Socrates to Freud and Beyond*, trans. Alan Bass (Chicago, IL: University of Chicago Press, 1987), esp. 335; and *P* 48, 152, and 321.

30. Though developed, in part, in this chapter, the idea and significance of workless mourning returns throughout parts 2 and 3 below.

31. Cf. Romano, *Event and World*, 225n84, where he writes, "We do not recover from bereavement; at most, we only survive it . . . . [W]e make it ours." My idea is developing with more depth what Romano is only gesturing towards here.

32. Theodore D. George, "The Worklessness of Literature: Blanchot, Hegel, and the Ambiguity of the Poetic Word," *Philosophy Today SPEP Supplement* (2006): 46.

33. Cf. Timothy Secret's use of this same term in *The Politics and Pedagogy of Mourning: On Responsibility in Eulogy* (New York: Bloomsbury Academic, 2015), especially xxiv. Both of our uses find their inspiration from the collection of Derrida's interviews and works in *Negotiations: Interventions and Interviews, 1971–2001*, ed. and trans. Elizabeth Rottenberg (Stanford, CA: Stanford University Press, 2002).

34. Sigmund Freud, *Mourning and Melancholia*, in *The Standard Edition of the Complete Psychological Works of Sigmund Freud*, vol. 14 (1914–16), trans. James Strachey (London: The Hogarth Press, 1986), 244.

35. Freud, *Mourning and Melancholia*, 246.

36. Freud, *Mourning and Melancholia*, 244.

37. Freud, *Mourning and Melancholia*, 245.

38. Freud, *Mourning and Melancholia*, 245.

39. Freud, *Mourning and Melancholia*, 246.

40. For an excellent and detailed account of the relation among Derrida's understanding of melancholy and that of the psychoanalysts Sándor Ferenczi, Nicolas Abraham, and Maria Torok, see Secret, *The Politics and Pedagogy of Mourning*, 141–64. Particularly, Secret argues that Freud, and through him Derrida too, misunderstood Ferenczi's understanding of introjection and normal mourning. Secret argues that introjection is understood by Ferenczi as "a process of investment or cathexis," that is, as the opposite of what Freud calls normal morning (154). Moreover, in the history of Freud's own work, Secret notes that by 1923, six years after "Mourning and Melancholia," in Freud's *The Ego and the Id* his position regarding melancholy has developed so that he sees it playing less of a pathological role for the ego and more of an important structural role as "the precondition of civilization and its concomitant discontent" as well as, perhaps, as Freud writes to Ludwig Binswanger, a *healthy* response to loss (*The Politics and Pedagogy of Mourning*, xviii and 144; cf. 147; cf. Margaret Gibson, "Melancholy Objects," *Mortality* 9, no. 4 [2004]: 292).

41. Celia B. Harris, Ruth Brookman, and Maja O'Connor, "It's Not Who You Lose, It's Who You Are: Identity and Symptom Trajectory in Prolonged Grief," *Current Psychology* 42 (2021): 11223; cf. 11224.

42. Harris, Brookman, and O'Connor, "It's Not Who You Lose," 2.

43. See Nancy J. Moules et al., "Making Room for Grief: Walking Backwards and Living Forward," *Nursing Inquiry* 11, no. 2 (2004): 99–107.

44. Cf. Miller, *For Derrida*, 95.

45. On the association of this saving of the other as other through the crypt as a development of the Hegelian *aufhebung*, see Gregg Lambert, *Return Statements: The Return of Religion in Contemporary Philosophy* (Edinburgh: Edinburgh University Press, 2016), 106.

46. Naas puts this point nicely: "It is this gaze [of the other] that makes all mourning . . . at once necessary and impossible, necessary insofar as the work of mourning involves incorporating the friend, coming to terms with his or her death within ourselves, and impossible insofar as the singularity of the friend, that which must be incorporated, that gaze that first calls us to be responsible, always exceeds our subjectivity and our capacity to make the other — here, the deceased other — our own" (Michael Naas, "History's Remains: Of Memory, Mourning, and the Event," *Research in Phenomenology* 33 [2003]: 79; cf. 93).

47. Cf. Schmidt, "Birth, Death, and Unfinished Conversations," 111; Saitya Brata Das, "(Dis)Figures of Death: Taking the Side of Derrida, Taking the Side of Death," *Derrida Today* 3 (2010): 4–5 and 20.

48. Clayton Crockett develops the kind of ethics of responsibility in conjunction with Derrida's interest in religion in *Derrida after the End of Writing: Political Theology and New Materialism* (New York: Fordham University Press, 2017), 59–73.

49. Derrida's account of the call of responsibility in the death of the other is another instance of what Raffoul calls the "ethicality of ethics" (*The Origins of Responsibility* [Bloomington: Indiana University Press, 2010], 1). Raffoul maintains that Derrida is one figure in philosophy concerned with the ethicality of ethics because Derrida seeks an account of responsibility that is outside of a metaphysical subjectivity and a system of rules that require application to a context or field of study. For Derrida, "the primordial sense of responsibility" is found in "the appropriation of the inappropriable, as inappropriable" (290). The ethicality of ethics is found in this aporetic origin. I am exploring this aporetic origin along the lines of the lack of rules or grounds for our responsibility to the other as well as in the workless mourning of the inappropriable other.

50. See Romano, *Event and World*, 30–31.

51. For Derrida's expansion in these various directions, see *BS1* 110–11, 184, 244–45, 250, and 280 as well as *OH* 77.

52. My thanks to an anonymous reviewer at SUNY for giving me this idea and challenging me to address it.

53. Romano, *Event and Time*, 111.

Chapter Four

1. In this regard, I disagree with Raffoul when he writes, "One might be tempted to say . . . that death is the event *par excellence*, except for the fact that unlike events, which as noted generate time and constitute a world, death closes time and shuts down the world"

(*Thinking the Event*, 95). Parts 2 and 3 of my work indicate how the death of the other both constitutes a world and generates time. Cf. Saghafi, *The World After the End of the World*, xxiii: "The other's death brings to a close the world in the same way that it opens it."

2. Gasché, *Europe, or the Infinite Task*, 316.

3. Christine Valentine, *Bereavement Narratives: Continuing Bonds in the Twenty-First Century* (New York: Routledge, 2008), 114.

4. Valentine, *Bereavement Narratives*, 11.

5. Valentine, *Bereavement Narratives*, 114.

6. Taylor, *Last Works*, 1; cf 81 where he replaces "the end" with "death." While Taylor is speaking about our own death, I show in this chapter that his words apply also to the death of the other.

7. N. J. Moules et. al., "Out of Order: To Debbie and Dave, Chris and Bill, MJ and John," *Journal of Applied Hermeneutics* (2015): 1; emphasis mine.

8. Lori and Brian McDermott, *Learning to Dance in the Rain: A True Story about Life beyond Death* (Bloomington, IN: Balboa Press, 2011), 12.

9. Chimamanda Ngozi Adichie, *Notes on Grief* (New York: Alfred A. Knopf, 2021), 9; emphasis mine; cf. 64.

10. See chapter 1 on the relation of the event to the instant.

11. Joan Didion, *The Year of Magical Thinking* (New York: Vintage Books, 2005), 89; emphasis mine; cf. 3, 77, 136, as well as Taylor, *Last Works*, 175, when he writes, "One moment there is life, the next moment there is death; what disappears in that brief *instant in between*?" (emphasis mine).

12. Didion, *Year of Magical Thinking*, 188; cf. 26–27.

13. Didion, *Year of Magical Thinking*, 189.

14. John Russon, "Haunted by History: Merleau-Ponty, Hegel, and the Phenomenology of Pain," *Journal of Contemporary Thought* 37 (2013): 85.

15. Wolterstorff, *Lament for a Son*, 46.

16. Valentine, *Bereavement Narratives*, 93.

17. Didion, *Year of Magical Thinking*, 17.

18. Didion, *Year of Magical Thinking*, 107; cf. 133.

19. Gabriel García Márquez, *Love in the Time of Cholera*, trans. Edith Grossman (New York: Alfred A. Knopf, 1988), 279; cf. 50.

20. Augustine, *Confessions*, 57.

21. Didion, *Year of Magical Thinking*, 222.

22. Wolterstorff, *Lament for a Son*, 99; emphasis mine.

23. Wolterstorff, *Lament for a Son*, 14.

24. McDermott, *Learning to Dance*, ix, xiii, and 3.

25. McDermott, *Learning to Dance*, 2, 27, 35, 39, and 56.

26. McDermott, *Learning to Dance*, 28.

27. Cf. Wolterstroff, *Lament for a Son*, 11, 17, and 56.

28. Romano, *Event and World*, 121.

29. Dickinson, "Death sets a thing significant," 93. cf. Didion, *Year of Magical Thinking*, 153, where a book of her husband's became a similar site of mourning.

30. The examples of this phenomenon for people who have lost others are innumerable. For some other examples, see Adichie, *Notes on Grief*, 20, 26, 28–29, and 31, where her family realize that in the absence of their father at his place at the dining table at breakfast, his chair by the window, his presence on the sofa napping and reading in the midmorning, his favorite jacket, his collection of maps and sudoku books, and his handwritten notes mean something different now; cf. Valentine, *Bereavement Narratives*, 120.

31. Wolterstorff, *Lament for a Son*, 13.

32. Thomas Attig, *How We Grieve: Relearning the World* (New York: Oxford University Press, 2011), xlvi.

33. Matthew Ratcliffe, "Grief and Phantom Limbs: A Phenomenological Comparison," *The New Yearbook for Phenomenology and Phenomenological Philosophy* 17 (2019): 93.

34. Ratcliffe, "Grief and Phantom Limbs," 85.

35. Moules, "Out of Order," 6.

36. Valentine, *Bereavement Narratives*, 120.

37. Valentine, *Bereavement Narratives*, 87.

38. Valentine, *Bereavement Narratives*, 155.

39. Valentine, *Bereavement Narratives*, 89; cf. 143.

40. Valentine, *Bereavement Narratives*, 146; cf. 159–60.

41. Gibson, "Melancholy Objects," 286.

42. Gibson, "Melancholy Objects," 288; emphasis mine; cf. 289.

43. Valentine, *Bereavement Narratives*, 146.

44. Russon, "Haunted by History," 86. Russon here is talking not about memorials for the dead but of the survivor himself as a site of what I have been calling workless mourning.

45. Valentine, *Bereavement Narratives*, 152.

46. Janet Jacobs, *The Holocaust across Generations: Trauma and Its Inheritance among Descendants of Survivors* (New York: New York University Press, 2016), 105.

47. Jacobs, *Holocaust across Generations*, 114.

48. Jacobs, *Holocaust across Generations*, 124.

49. Jacobs, *Holocaust across Generations*, 124.

50. Valentine, *Bereavement Narratives*, 152.

51. Peggy Kamuf, reading Celan not only through Derrida's work but also through Emily Dickinson's "There came a wind like a bugle" poem, says, in this regard, that we could read Celan's line as "[T]he world is gone 'and still abide the world'" (Peggy Kamuf, "Teleiopoetic World," *SubStance* 43, no. 2 [2014]: 19; cf. 10).

52. Cf. Theodore George, "Grieving as Limit Situation of Memory: Gadamer, Beamer, and Moules on the Infinite Task Posed by the Dead," *Journal of Applied Hermeneutics* (2017): 5.

53. George, "Grieving as Limit Situation of Memory," 5.

Chapter Five

1. The line that I am paraphrasing and will read below concerns Blanchot's notion of the disaster: "The disaster ruins everything, all the while leaving everything intact" (Maurice Blanchot, *The Writing of the Disaster*, trans. Ann Smock [Lincoln: University of Nebraska Press, 1986], 1).

2. He later says that the purpose of his reading is not to say "that there has always already been . . . death or that . . . there will never yet have been . . . death, but rather that if 'science' or 'philosophy' must speak of . . . death, the oppositions positive/negative, more/less, inside/outside, along with the logic of the either/or, of the *and* or of the *is*, no longer suffice" (*LD* 113–14). Derrida maintains this same idea in his eulogy after the death of Sarah Kofman: "The affirmation of life is nothing other than a certain thought of death; it is neither opposition nor indifference to death — indeed one would almost say the opposite if this were not giving in to opposition" (*WM* 175).

3. While I do not cover Derrida's reading of Freud here, Francesco Vitale offers a great reading of this part of Derrida's seminar in *Biodeconstruction: Jacques Derrida and the Life Sciences*, trans. Mauro Senatore (Albany, NY: SUNY Press, 2018), 127–66.

4. Cf. Vitale, *Biodeconstruction*, 18 and 53, where he makes a similar argument.

5. For example, Derrida mentions biology when discussing the general theme of writing in the history of ideas that he will develop more fully: "It is also in this sense that the contemporary biologist speaks of writing and pro-gram in relation to the most elementary processes of information within the living cell" (*OG* 9). And he also mentions it in his discussion of the important notion of trace: "The word trace must refer to itself to a certain number of contemporary discourses whose force I intend to take into account . . . . [N]otably in biology, this notion seems currently to be dominant and irreducible" (*OG* 70).

6. Here Derrida is quoting directly from Jacob's *Logic of the Living*.

7. Michael Naas, "The Inside Story of Derrida's *Of Grammatology*," *Philosophy Today* 64, no. 3 (2020): 739.

8. As Derrida has famously, and infamously, put this idea in *Of Grammatology*, "There is nothing outside of the text" (*OG* 158). Naas helpfully explains that in this phrase Derrida means, "There is no outside the text because there is no inside, no pure inside, no ideal text sealed off from reality or from the world" ("The Inside Story," 739). No text, nothing constituted by textuality, can be pure of a context or contextuality.

9. Julia Cooper, *The Last Word: Reviving the Dying Art of Euology* (Toronto, CA: Coach House Book, 2017), 38.

10. Vitale also draws this connection to cellular biology through the idea first articulated by Jean-Claude Ameisen regarding "cellular suicide as condition of [the] possibility of the living and of its evolution" as well as in relation to autoimmune diseases (*Biodeconstruction*, 176; see the longer discussion on 175–84). Vitale does not make the connection with cancerous cells as I do.

11. Daniel B. Hinshaw, "The Kenosis of the Dying: An Invitation to Healing," in *The Role of Death in Life: A Multidisciplinary Examination of the Relationship between Life and Death*, ed. John Behr and Connor Cunningham (Eugene, OR: Cascade Books, 2015), 161. Derrida notes in his *Life Death* course during his interpretation of life and death in Freud's *Beyond the Pleasure Principle* that Freud himself conjectured that "malignant tumors" consist of such "'narcissistic'" cells (*LD* 275).

12. Didion, *Year of Magical Thinking*, 5. Many thanks to an anonymous reviewer at SUNY for drawing my attention to this Gregorian chant as the source of Didion's words here.

13. Adichie, *Notes on Grief*, 64.

14. Rambo, *Resurrecting Wounds*, 7. cf. Valentine, *Bereavement Narratives*, especially 3–4, 16, 22, 85, 89, 116, and 124, where Valentine explores the interconnection among life and death in the experience of mourning.

15. Cf. Vitale, *Biodeconstruction*, 70–73, where Vitale argues for the importance of reading *Life Death* alongside the recent advancements in epigenetics. Vitale does not make the connection, as I am making here, with the death of the other and mourning in relation to *Life Death* and epigenetics.

16. Speaking in the context of the cultural memory of those who died during the Holocaust, Rosner writes, "We will embody the DNA of the dead" (*Survivor Café*, 33). When Cheryl Strayed, as recounted in her memoir *Wild*, goes on a three-month hike from the Mojave Desert to Oregon along the Pacific Coast Trail to process the grief after her mother's death, she buries her mother's ashes and, in the end, eats some of those ashes as well. Julia Cooper comments that Strayed is an example of the literal "embodiment" of mourning in this experience (Cooper, *Last Words*, 107). Epigenetics shows that the dead other is in us even without such literal consuming of the other.

17. Cf. Ruin, *Being with the Dead*, 131.

18. Rachel Yehuda and Amy Lehrner, "Intergenerational Transmission of Trauama Effects: Putative Role of Epigenetic Mechanisms," *Wold Psychiatry* 17,3 (2018): 246.

19. Louise J. Kaplan, *No Voice Is Ever Wholly Lost* (New York: Simon and Schuster, 1995), 223.

20. Kaplan, *No Voice*, 224.

21. Kaplan, *No Voice*, 225; emphasis mine.

22. See Brian G. Dias and Kerry J. Ressler, "Parental Olfactory Experience Influences Behavior and Neural Structure in Subsequent Generations," *Nature Neuroscience* 17, no. 1 (2014): 89–98. The female mice used in the study had not ever been exposed to the same conditioning as the male mice.

23. For an excellent study on the "transposition" of Holocaust survivors' trauma onto their children and grandchildren see Kaplan, *No Voice*, especially. 221–25, 230–33, and 235; cf. Jacobs, *Holocaust across Generations*.

24. Mary-Frances O'Connor et. al. "Divergent Gene Expression Responses to Complicated Grief and Non-complicated Grief," *Brain, Behavior, and Immunity* 37 (2014): 78–83.

25. Van der Kolk, *Body Keeps the Score*, 2–3; cf. 17, 43, 53, and 82–83.

26. Rachel Yehuda, "Trauma in the Family Tree: Parents' Adverse Experiences Leave Biological Traces in Children," *Scientific American* 327, no. 1 (2022): 50–55. Available online at https://www.scientificamerican.com/article/how-parents-rsquo-trauma-leaves-biological-traces-in-children/.

27. See the work by Maria Yellow Horse Brave Heart on the effect of the historical trauma on Native Americans in their communities: "The Historical Trauma Response among Natives and Its Relationship with Substance Abuse: A Lakota Illustration," *Journal of Psychoactive Drugs* 35, (2003): 7–13; "Wakiksuyapi: Carrying the Historical Trauma of the Lakota," *Tulane Studies in Social Welfare* 21–22 (2000): 245–66; and "The Return to the Sacred Path: Healing the Historical Trauma Response among the Lakota," *Smith College Studies in Social Work* 68 (1998): 287–305. See the studies by Ron Eyerman, *Cultural Trauma: Slavery and the Formation of African American Identity* (Cambridge: Cambridge University Press, 2001) and Joy DeGruy, *Post Traumatic Slave Syndrome: America's Legacy of Enduring Injury and Healing* (Baltimore, MD: Uptone, 2005) on the effect of the US treatment of Black and African Americans on their communities.

28. Jacobs, *Holocaust across Generations*, 91–92.

29. Rosner, *Survivor Café*, 151.

30. Rosner, *Survivor Café*, 38.

31. Rosner, *Survivor Café*, 54.

32. Rosner, *Survivor Café*.

33. Ovid, *Metamorphoses*, trans. David Raeburn (New York: Penguin Books, 2004), 4.103 and 98.

34. Ovid, *Metamorphoses*, 4.125 and 126.

35. Ovid, *Metamorphoses*, 4.157–60; emphasis mine.

36. Rosner, *Survivor Café*, 57.

37. Rosner, *Survivor Café*, 56.

38. Valentine, *Bereavement Narratives*, 85; cf. 116

39. Wolterstorff, *Lament for a Son*, 43.

40. Didion, *Year of Magical Thinking*, 8.

41. McDermott, *Learning to Dance*, 96; emphasis mine.

42. Adichie, *Notes on Grief*, 51; emphasis mine.

43. Joy Netanya Thompson, "To Live and Die Well," *Fuller: Story | Theology | Voice* issue 2: Evangelical (2015): 23–24. Available online at https://fullerstudio.fuller.edu/live-die-well/.

44. Voltaire, *Candide: Or Optimism*, trans. John Butt (New York: Penguin Classics, 1950), 29 and 43. Exceptions to this might be when the deceased was a terrible person who mistreated or even abused those around him or her. In these cases, we might think that the death of such an other engenders a state of affairs that is for the best in the world. Though this might be an exception, such a death would still come unexpectedly and be transformative of the world.

45. Blanchot, *Writing of the Disaster*, 1; emphasis mine.

46. By "the disaster," Caputo comments, "Blanchot means an erosion and hollowing out of the conscious subject, the master of the living present, the knight who confronts death's ominous possibility head on (or flees from it like a slave). Against this active, conscious subject . . . Blanchot thinks in terms of a radical passivity that he calls 'dying' (*le mourir*)" (*Prayers and Tears*, 77–78). Consequently, the disaster must be understood as related to death but more specifically to the syntagm of *my own* death.

47. Wolterstorff, *Lament for a Son*, 51; cf. Simone de Beauvoir, *A Very Easy Death*, trans. Patrick O'Brian (New York: Random House, 1965), 73, where she writes, as her mother enters the final stages of life and is less alive and more a "living corpse," that "when I crossed Paris in a taxi I saw nothing more than a stage with extras walking on it."

48. Adichie, *Notes on Grief*, 12.

49. Rambo, *Resurrecting Wounds*, 15.

50. Cf. Michael Naas, *Miracle and Machine: Jacques Derrida and the Two Sources of Religion, Science, and the Media* (New York: Fordham University Press, 2012), 263–68, 272, and 274.

51. Cf. Rambo, *Resurrecting Wounds*, 142.

52. Augustine, *Confessions*, 61.

53. Rambo, *Resurrecting Wounds*, 7.

54. Moules, "Making Room for Grief," 100; emphasis mine; cf. George, "Grieving as Limit Situation," 4, when he writes, "[G]rieving is not something to get through, get past, or get over, but, rather, becomes an integral part of one's life;" Daniel Ratcliffe, "Grief and Phantom Limbs," 93; and Valentine, *Bereavement Narratives*, 3 and 124–25.

55. Cf. Moules, "Making Room for Grief," 104.

56. Catherine Fullarton, "Grief, Phantoms, and Re-membering Loss," *Journal of Speculative Philosophy* 34, no. 3 (2020): 292.

Chapter Six

1. David Couzens Hoy makes this distinction between *time* as objective time and *temporality* as the lived experience of time that I use throughout part 3 (see *The Time of Our Lives: A Critical History of Temporality* [Cambridge, MA: The MIT Press, 2009]).

2. Cf. William Shakespeare, *Hamlet*, act I, scene 5.

3. Cooper, *Last Word*, 79; cf. 51. Cooper draws on Henri Bergson's notion of the duration of time (*la durée*) in her exploration of the nonlinearity of time and especially of mourning's time (*Last Word*, 51–54). Below, I draw not on Bergson but Heidegger and Derrida.

4. Raffoul, *Thinking the Event*, 92.

5. Cooper, *Last Word*, 9. Thus, she is critical of the stage model of grief because this model seems to suggest that we move linearly through each stage (*Last Word*, 9, 44, and 51). Similarly, Theodore George is also critical of the stage model of grief because he sees mourning as involving us in "a limit situation of memory" and posing, thereby, "an infinite task" that cannot "be reduced to a predefined series of stages and predetermined terminus. Grieving remains unending because, as a limit situation of memory, it can become as necessary for our lives as it is impossible to finish with" ("Grieving as Limit Situation of Memory," 3–4; cf. Moules, "Making Room for Grief," 103; and Valentine, *Bereavement Narratives*, 124–25). For Romano's similar discussion of the nonlinear temporality of mourning, see *Event and Time*, 155–64.

6. Rambo, *Resurrecting Wounds*, 4; cf. 145.

7. C. S. Lewis, *A Grief Observed* (New York: Harper Collins, 2001), 56.

8. Tamsin Jones, "Traumatized Subjects: Continental Philosophy of Religion and the Ethics of Alterity," *Journal of Religion* (2014): 151. While Jones's account of trauma fits nicely here with this description of the death of the other as an event, she does not associate the trauma of the death of the other with this term of art event.

9. Van der Kolk, *Body Keeps the Score*, 21. cf. 206; and Rosner, *Survivor Café*, 74, where she comments that for the survivors of the Holocaust and their descendants, the past mixes with the present with the "trauma intruding into places it doesn't belong."

10. Jones, "Traumatized Subjects," 152.

11. Jones, "Traumatized Subjects," 151.

12. Jones, "Traumatized Subjects," 151.

13. Van der Kolk, *Body Keeps the Score*, 44–45, 69, 178, and 221.

14. Jones, "Traumatized Subjects," 152.

15. Didion, *Year of Magical Thinking*, 4; emphasis mine.

16. McDermott, *Learning to Dance*, 17.

17. Prefigurations of this idea and important touchstones in the history of ideas for this understanding of temporality can be found especially with regard to Aristotle's understanding of φρόνησις, which Sean D. Kirkland explicates as "tragic temporality" (*Aristotle and Tragic Temporality* [Edinburgh: Edinburgh University Press, 2025]), as well as Augustine's understanding of *memoria* as the part of the mind that measures time (*Confessions*, 239–40, 242, and 36).

18. Edmund Husserl, *On the Phenomenology of Internal Time Consciousness (1893–1917)*, trans. John Barnett Brough (Netherlands: Springer, 1991), 77 and 128.

19. Cf. Hoy, *Time of Our Lives*, 51.

20. This is more fully explained by Dan Zahavi, *Husserl's Phenomenology* (Stanford, CA: Stanford University Press, 2003), 84; Dan Zahavi, *Subjectivity and Selfhood: Investigating the First-Person Perspective* (Cambridge, MA: The MIT Press, 2005), 56–57; Dan Zahavi and Shaun Gallagher, *The Phenomenological Mind: An Introduction to Philosophy of Mind and Cognitive Science* (London: Taylor and Francis, 2009), 76–80; and Nicolas de Warren, "The Inquietude of Time and the Instance of Eternity," in *The Oxford Handbook of the History of Phenomenology*, ed. Dan Zahavi (New York: Oxford University Press, 2018), 517.

21. Zahavi defends Husserl against the criticism that Husserl's understanding of time remains a metaphysics of presence by maintaining that the intentionality of retention and, relatedly, protention toward the phase of an object in its absence entails that absence plays a structural role in the simultaneity of the internal time-consciousness structured according to retention, primal presentation, and protention. And this means for Husserl, concludes Zahavi, that "there is no pure self-presence" even for Husserl (Zahavi, *Husserl's Phenomenology*, 97; cf. Zahavi, *Subjectivity and Self-hood*, 69–72). Zahavi's argument brings Husserl's understanding of temporality closer to Derrida's own view that he explores in and through his criticism of Husserl's understanding of time in *Voice and Phenomenon* (see, especially, *VP* 51–59 and 71–74). However, as I maintain, even if Husserl's view provides the possibility for this alternative reading, Husserl is overall more focused on the synchronicity or simultaneous unity of internal time-consciousness than he is in exploring the implications of this structural inclusion of absence within such presence. This relation among presence and absence and its implications for the entirety of philosophy is precisely what Derrida explores in his deconstruction of Husserl in *Voice and Phenomenon*. With this, recall my remarks in chapter 1 regarding the Heidegger-Derrida relation about why Derrida emphasizes absence first and foremost in his thinking.

22. Zahavi and Gallagher, *Phenomenological Mind*, 75; cf. Zahavi, *Husserl's Phenomenology*, 82, and *Subjectivity and Self-Hood*, 56.

23. Cf. Paola Marrati, *Genesis and Trace: Derrida Reading Husserl and Heidegger*, trans. Simon Sparks (Stanford, CA: Stanford University Press, 2005), 70, where she says that while Husserl complicates and makes more complex the structure of time, time for

Husserl has a "'living core,' a now that is and remains necessarily punctual and to which the other phases are attached as a sort of 'comet's tail' of retentions."

24. Martin Heidegger, *The Metaphysical Foundations of Logic*, trans. Michael Heim (Bloomington: Indiana University Press, 1984), 204.

25. De Warren, "Inquietude of Time," 524.

26. Raffoul, *Thinking the Event*, 172.

27. See David Farrell Krell, "History, Natality, Ecstasy," 3–34, and *Ecstasy, Catastrophe: Heidegger from "Being and Time" to the "Black Notebooks"* (Albany, NY: SUNY Press, 2015), 96, where he argues that Derrida's early reading of the unity of ecstatic temporality in Heidegger's *Being and Time* shows that Heidegger does not efface absence with this notion of temporality.

28. Judith Harman, *Trauma and Recovery: The Aftermath of Violence — From Domestic Abuse to Political Terror* (New York: Basic Books, 1992), 37.

29. Jacobs, *Holocaust across Generations*, 49; emphasis mine.

30. Milstein, *Rebellious Mourning*, 347.

31. See Jacobs, *Holocaust across Generations*, 94–98.

32. Van der Kolk, *Body Keeps the Score*, 1; emphasis mine; cf. 143–44.

33. The work by Gillian Bennett and Kate Mary Bennett has shown that what I am calling this haunting of the presence of the dead other in her absence occurs not just immediately after the death of the other but recurs over years after such death up to even twenty years after the death of the other ("The Presence of the Dead: An Empirical Study," *Mortality* 5, no. 2 [2000]: 144–45). Their study further shows that mourning must be understood as something taking place worklessly as I am arguing throughout this book.

34. Rosner, a descendant of survivors of the Holocaust, adds an interesting layer to this haunting when she maintains that even she remains "tethered to *their* past" regarding how her parents' past continues to haunt and both affect and effect her own present (Rosner, *Survivor Café*, 146; emphasis mine; cf. 149).

35. For a more trenchant critique of Heidegger's understanding of temporality in relation to a hermeneutic ontology centered on events, see Romano, *Event and Time*, 126, 138, and 140 in particular. Romano maintains that any event "exceeds every capacity of a subject to gather time into presence by bringing it back to the measure of its own presence" (126).

36. Ruin, *Being with the Dead*, 36–39. Though Ruin does not turn to these texts in Heidegger, he could also use Heidegger's readings of Sophocles's *Antigone* as well as Heidegger's lecture course on Hölderlin's poems "Germanien" and "Der Rhein" to help argue that Heidegger does explore after *Being and Time* some of the significance of the death of the other and mourning for his own project.

37. John Russon offers a reading of Heidegger's anticipatory resoluteness in *Being and Time* that brings Heidegger's notion of temporality closer to Derrida's understanding of *différance* insofar as both, says Russon, are concerned with articulating an understanding

of self-relation that remains always open to further possibilities. Such openness means that Heidegger does not, says Russon, efface absence and difference in his account of temporality's unification (Russon, "Self as Resolution," 90–110). In contrast, Marrati reads many of the same passages as Russon and argues, "Authentic temporality [for Heidegger] is a *unitary* phenomenon" (*Genesis and Trace*, 127; emphasis mine) in which "time is a gathering" (128) whereas temporality for Derrida has no origin that gathers ecstatic temporality together because, for Derrida, temporality carries "the irreducible passivity of the past, and the surprise, equally irreducible and unstable, of the future" (46). Consequently, a "non-self-identity" is at the heart of the present for Derrida on Marrati's reading (73). Krell sums up the ambivalence that Heidegger's philosophy seems to have toward the metaphysics of presence and, thereby the variety of criticisms and defenses of Heidegger, when he writes, "Derrida is also aware of the problematic nature of Heidegger's notion of a history of being as presence, problematic principally because Heidegger sometimes appears to stand outside of such a history and at other times well within it" (*Ecstasy, Catastrophe*, 88).

38. Cf. Michael Naas, *Derrida from Now On* (New York: Fordham University Press, 2008), 190–99. He argues similarly that while spectrality for Derrida, like iterability, is "the condition of every coming to appear" (190), even that of the ghost, the "phantasm" for Derrida is a "metaphysical phenomenality" that aims "to conceal or repress" iterability (199). Also see Kas Saghafi, *Apparitions — Of Derrida's Other* (New York: Fordham University Press, 2010), 76.

39. With this formulation, I am playing with the homophony in French of *ontologie* and Derrida's neologism *hantologie*. Moreover, for an engagement with Derrida's thinking of the ghost and hauntology beyond my limited scope here with regard to how the death of the other transforms our experience of temporality hauntologically but in terms of an engagement with history or historiography as hauntological, see Ethan Kleinberg, *Haunting History: For a Deconstructive Approach to the Past* (Stanford, CA: Stanford University Press, 2017). In short, what I argue for below with regard to surviving the death of the other and temporality is what Kleinberg argues for regarding the ontology of history itself.

40. Levinas, "Enigma and Phenomenon," 72.

41. Cf. Derrida's statement, "Ghosts always pass quickly . . . in an instant without duration, presence without present of a present which, coming back, only haunts" (*MPM* 64).

42. For an excellent account on how the work of Blanchot has influenced Derrida's views on this nonlinear temporality in lived experience, see Caputo, *Prayers and Tears*, 77–87.

43. Auden, "Funeral Blues," 81.

44. Cooper, *Last Word*, 47.

45. Mauro Carbone, "Falling Man: The Time of Trauma, the Time of (Certain) Images," *Research in Phenomenology* 47 (2017): 195.

46. Carbone, "Falling Man," 195 and 199. Carbone is quoting Allen Feldman's notion of "temporal therapy" in his reflections on the 9/11 attacks in "Ground Zero Point One: On the Cinematics of History," *Social Analysis* 46, no. 1 (2002): 30.

47. I engage the depths of the present as this spectral moment of being-with the living and dead others in chapter 8.

48. Rambo, *Resurrecting Wounds*, 37; emphasis mine.

49. Adichie, *Notes on Grief*, 22–23; emphasis mine.

50. G. W. F. Hegel, *Philosophy of Mind*, trans. W. Wallace, A. V. Miller, and Michael Inwood (New York: Oxford University Press, 2007), 186.

51. Hegel, *Philosophy of Mind*, 185 and 187. For Derrida's reading, in part, of this nocturnal pit in Hegel's works, see "The Pit and the Pyramid: Introduction to Hegel's Semiology" in *MP* 69–108.

52. Van der Kolk, *Body Keeps the Score*, 195–96.

53. Secret, *Politics and Pedagogy of Mourning*, 190.

54. Hegel, *Philosophy of Mind*, 200.

55. Hegel, *Philosophy of Mind*, 200; emphasis his.

56. Van der Kolk, *Body Keeps the Score*, 195–96.

57. Gibson, "Melancholy Objects," 289.

58. Daniel M. Wegner, "Transactive Memory: A Contemporary Analysis of the Group Mind," in *Theories of Group Behavior*, ed. Brian Mullen and George R. Goethals (New York: Springer-Verlag, 1987), 186.; cf. Daniel M. Wegner, Paula Raymond, and Ralph Erber, "Transactive Memory in Close Relationships," *Journal of Personality and Social Psychology* 61, no. 6 (1991): 923.

59. Wegner, "Transactive Memory," 199.

60. Wegner, "Transactive Memory," 194.

61. Augustine, *Confessions*, 59; emphasis mine; cf. *ISP* 64, where Marion interprets this loss of self through the death of the other as emblematic of the self's general anonymity or inability to know itself on its own, thereby giving rise to Augustine's famous understanding of the "restless heart" and description of himself being a question unto himself in the *Confessions*.

62. Romano, *Event and World*, 120. Though Romano is not commenting on Augustine here, this statement and surrounding discussion in his text fits nicely with Augustine's own discussion of the death of Nebridius. For his account of *mourir à autrui*, see especially "Mourir à autrui," 821; *Event and World* 115–20; and *Event and Time*, 163.

63. Wegner, "Transactive Memory," 200–201; emphasis mine; cf. Wegner, "Transactive Memory in Close Relationships," 924 and 929.

64. In their recent study on the effect that the death of a partner or parent can have on a survivor, Harris, Brookman, and O'Connor conclude that the grief experienced with the loss of transactive memory is especially significant for children who have lost a parent ("It's Not Who You Lose," 11228).

Chapter Seven

1. Rosner, *Survivor Café*, 160.
2. Raffoul, *Thinking the Event*, 172.
3. Raffoul, *Origins of Responsibility*, 291–93.
4. Caputo, *Prayers and Tears*, 69. Likewise, Caputo writes, "There is no *logos*, no rule or formula — be it metaphysical and teleological, be it theological and eschatological — that could render an account of what is to come, that could determine or foresee its outlines, that could predict its coming or protend its content" (*Prayers and Tears*, 96).
5. Levinas, "Enigma and Phenomenon," 67.
6. Caputo, *Prayers and Tears*, 101 and 129.
7. When Caputo explains this to-come according to "Messianic time" rather than "ordinary time" (*Prayers and Tears*, especially. 79–80), he is explaining, as I am explaining, the im-possible as to-come insofar as such an event *could* arrive but not according to the present. At times in his exposition, however, Caputo seems to conflate the impossible possibility tone of the to-come with the im-possible tone of the to-come (see *Prayers and Tears*, 78, 96, 102, 160, and 245), but I think even these moments of ostensible conflation must be read in light of the distinction between Messianic and ordinary time through which an event can arrive but only unexpectedly and, therefore, not in the present. With this, for example, I think Derrida would say that justice to-come and democracy to-come *can* or *could* occur as im-possible rather than saying more emphatically, as Caputo writes, "[J]ustice is never here . . . the promise is never fulfilled" (*Prayers and Tears*, 231). Thus, I would revise what Caputo says here to say that justice will have come *perhaps* and the promise will have been fulfilled *perhaps*. Ultimately, I think Caputo would agree with this reformulation especially in light of his work on and with the perhaps in *The Insistence of God: A Theology of Perhaps* (Bloomington: Indiana University Press, 2013), especially chapters 1 and 2.
8. Cf. Romano's analysis of the event, temporality, and memory. For he maintains that an event "manifests itself" through a "double character": "To shut down past histories — to open new ones" (*Event and Time*, 230). Memory concerns both of these characters of an event particularly because memory is "fundamentally memory of the possible" (*Event and Time*, 159). Accordingly, memory is not just about a past but also about the future because the past possibilizes a new future or makes possible new possibilities for the future.
9. Sean Gaston, *The Impossible Mourning of Jacques Derrida* (New York: Continuum, 2006), 105.
10. McDermott, *Learning to Dance*, 25; emphasis mine.
11. Romano, *Event and World*, 119, cf. 120.
12. Romano, "Mourir à autrui," 821 (my translation).
13. Milstein, *Rebellious Mourning*, 83.

14. Wolterstorff, *Lament for a Son*, 31.

15. Jonathan Safran Foer, *Extremely Loud and Incredibly Close* (New York: Houghton Mifflin Company, 2005), 325–26. The final pages after this monologue are the photos in reverse order as described by Schell.

16. Didion, *Year of Magical Thinking*, 31; emphasis mine.

17. Wolterstorff, *Lament for a Son*, 23.

18. Cf. Shannon Hayes, "Merleau-Ponty's Melancholy: On Phantom Limbs and Involuntary Memory," *Epoché* 24, no. 1 (2019): 202 and 206, where Hayes explores "phantom futures that have been foreclosed" (208), which correspond to what I am calling here impossible possibilities, that attend the death of the other but in the situation of someone experiencing phantom limb after having one of their limbs amputated. Márquez likens the presence of Dr. Juvenal Urbino to Fermina Daza after his death to the experience that an amputee has in suffering "pains, cramps, itches, in the leg that is no longer there. That is how she felt without him, feeling his presence where he no longer was" (*Love in the Time of Cholera*, 280). Romano also discusses mourning in relation to the experience of phantom limb (*Event and World*, 121).

19. Wiesel, *Night*, 32.

20. Wiesel, *Night*, 32.

21. Taylor, *Last Works*, 127.

22. Wolterstorff, *Lament for a Son*, 61.

23. Ira Glass, "Off Course," *This American Life*, podcast audio, March 20, 2022, https://www.thisamericanlife.org/765/off-course. Many thanks to John Flynn for pointing me to this podcast, specifically the third act of the episode, where Wilson tells a quite hilarious story with her father about the different ways that they mourned her mother's death. Cf. Valentine, *Bereavement Narratives*, 96–97, where survivors of the death of the other express their guilt and sadness for the opportunities that the dead other now no longer has for the other's future.

24. Wolterstorff, *Lament for a Son*, 30; emphasis mine; cf. 21 and 47.

25. Kaplan, *No Voice*, 98.

26. Cooper, *The Last Word*, 105–6.

27. Didion, *Year of Magical Thinking*, 198.

28. Kaplan, *No Voice*, 118.

29. Kaplan, *No Voice*, 123.

30. Kaplan, *No Voice*, 121; emphasis hers.

31. Kaplan, *No Voice*, 122.

32. Kaplan, *No Voice*, 124.

33. Wolterstorff, *Lament for a Son*, 16, cf. 57–58.

34. Wolterstorff, *Lament for a Son*, 62.

35. Kaplan, *No Voice*, 132.

36. Kate Bowler, *Everything Happens for a Reason: And Other Lies I've Loved* (New York: Random House, 2018), 70.

37. Van der Kolk, *The Body Keeps the Score*, 197. Van der Kolk is quoting the work of Lawrence Langer in *Holocaust Testimonies: The Ruins of Memory*.

38. Romano, *Event and Time*, 163.

Chapter Eight

1. Secret, *Politics and Pedagogy of Mourning*, 199; emphasis his.

2. Cf. John D. Caputo, "Who Is Derrida's Zarathustra? Of Fraternity, Friendship, and a Democracy to Come," *Research in Phenomenology* 29, no. 1 (1999): 190.

3. Likewise, Cooper maintains that the practice of eulogy is "to say out loud that a life is not forgotten when it crosses the threshold into death. It means something to those left to mourn it, and the attempt to encapsulate that life in an act of articulation is one of the truest labours of love there is" (*Last Word*, 48).

4. The importance of Kierkegaard for understanding Derrida's *Politics of Friendship* is developed in my article "Oh My Neighbors, There Is No Neighbor," *International Journal of Philosophy and Theology* 90, no. 4–5 (2019): 326–43.

5. This approach overcomes the criticism that friendship to or love of the dead is understood as the only true form of friendship and love, which would entail that friendship or love is not toward the living. M. Jamie Ferreira defends Kierkegaard against such a critique along these same lines (*Love's Grateful Striving: A Commentary on Kierkegaard's "Works of Love"* (New York: Oxford University Press, 2001), 209–27).

6. Aristotle, *The Complete Works of Aristotle* vol. 2, ed. Jonathan Barnes (Princeton, NJ: Princeton University Press, 1995). Citations appear parenthetically according to the Bekker numbering.

7. Cicero, *On Old Age; On Friendship; On Divination*, trans. W. A. Falconer, Loeb Classical Library 154 (Cambridge, MA: Harvard University Press, 1923), 133. Citations appear parenthetically hereafter.

8. The first half of this passage serves as the epigraph to the entirety of Derrida's *Politics of Friendship*. This epigraph remains in the background for the majority of Derrida's text except for the moments where he provides something specific about the *other* friendship for which he hopes.

9. Søren Kierkegaard, *Works of Love*, trans. and ed. Howard V. and Edna H. Hong (Princeton, NJ: Princeton University Press, 1995), 358.

10. Kierkegaard, *Works of Love*, 349; emphasis mine.

11. Kierkegaard, *Works of Love*, 349.
12. Kierkegaard, *Works of Love*, 351.
13. Kierkegaard, *Works of Love*, 351.
14. Kierkegaard, *Works of Love*, 354.
15. Kierkegaard, *Works of Love*, 354.
16. Kierkegaard, *Works of Love*, 355; emphasis mine.
17. Kierkegaard, *Works of Love*, 358. cf. Wolterstroff, *Lament for a Son*, 65.
18. Caputo, *Prayers and Tears*, 124.
19. Jacques Derrida, *Hospitalité I* (Paris: Éditions de Seuil, 2021), 88; translation mine.
20. Moules, "Making Room for Grief," 104.
21. Moules, "Making Room for Grief," 104.
22. Moules, "Making Room for Grief," 104.
23. Moules, "Making Room for Grief," 104.
24. Wolterstroff, *Lament for a Son*, 28.
25. Rosner, *Survivor Café*, 153.
26. Raffoul, *Thinking the Event*, 295. I am drawing explicitly from his careful distinction between traditional responsibility and responsibility understood "as responsiveness" (294). However, Raffoul does not make the connection here between this coming of the other and the death of the other.
27. Rambo, *Resurrecting Wounds*, 12.
28. Rambo, *Resurrecting Wounds*, 14.
29. In using ideas of being faithful to or stewards of the event, I am drawing on the work of Alain Badiou regarding the event especially as this is developed in Alain Badiou, *Saint Paul: The Foundation of Universalism*, trans. Ray Brassier (Stanford, CA: Stanford University Press, 2003).
30. Fullarton, "Grief, Phantoms, and Re-Membering Loss," 291.
31. Gasché, *Europe, or the Infinite Task*, 319. Cf. Judith Herman, *Trauma and Recovery: The Aftermath of Violence — From Domestic Abuse to Political Terror* (New York: Basic Books, 1992), 196, where the victim of trauma must ultimately turn to developing "a new self" by developing new relationships and establishing new beliefs through which "the survivor reclaims her world." Romano articulates his own approach to mourning in similar terms in *Event and World* 114–21 and "Mourir à autrui."
32. Athanasiou, *Agonistic Mourning*, 2.
33. Athanasiou, *Agonistic Mourning*, 181.
34. Athanasiou, *Agonistic Mourning*, 181.
35. Athanasiou, *Agonistic Mourning*, 72.

36. See Milstein, *Rebellious Mourning*, 205.

37. María del Rosario Acosta López, "Totalitarianism as Structural Violence: Toward New Grammars of Listening," in *Logics of Genocide: The Structures of Violence and the Contemporary World* (New York: Routledge, 2020), 174.

38. López, "Totalitarianism as Structural Violence," 174.

39. López, "Totalitarianism as Structural Violence," 182. Cf. Radolph Gasché, *Storytelling: The Destruction of the Inalienable in the Age of the Holocaust* (Albany, NY: SUNY Press, 2018), especially 14, 32–33, and 52, where telling the story of not only one's own survival but of others goes to show that our being-with one another is always a matter of being-through-stories. The work by López and Gasché parallels the work done in psychology in and around victims of trauma where, as Herman argues, healing from trauma requires for the victim and their community both the shared recognition of what happened to the victim and the shared sense of restitution through action in the aftermath of this trauma (*Trauma and Recovery*, especially 70–73, 133, and chapters 8–10; cf. Kaplan, *No Voice*, 154–55; and Valentine, *Bereavement Narratives*, 9 and 17). Herman presents the use of story, both personally and communally, as a way for the survivor to confront the haunting, traumatic past by giving continuity to the survivor's own life before and after the trauma (*Trauma and Recovery*, chapter 9). In this, the danger of the haunting past contains the seeds of a survivor's salvation. Lastly, Ruin discusses this import of story under the category of "historicizing" the dead by offering them "a narrative space that preserves them in memory" (*Being with the Dead*, 164; cf. 166–68).

40. Cooper, *Last Word*, 48.

41. Rosner, *Survivor Café*, 77.

42. Athanasiou, *Agonistic Mourning*, 142. She is quoting the work of Ann Stoler, *Along the Archival Grain: Epistemically Anxieties and Colonial Common Sense* (Princeton, NJ: Princeton University Press, 2010), 7.

43. Athanasiou, *Agonistic Mourning*, 171.

44. Gasché, *Storytelling*, 75; cf. Milstein, *Rebellious Mourning*, 337.

45. Milstein, *Rebellious Mourning*, 8–9; emphasis mine.

46. Milstein, *Rebellious Mourning*, 4.

47. Milstein, *Rebellious Mourning*, 21.

48. Milstein, *Rebellious Mourning*, 38.

49. Milstein, *Rebellious Mourning*, 38.

50. Cf. Maria del Rosario Acosta López, "Memory and Fragility: Art's Resistance to Oblivion (Three Colombian Cases)," *New Centennial Review* 14, no. 1 (2014): 71–98; and Rosner, *Survivor Café*, 164–65.

51. Milstein, *Rebellious Mourning*, 215.

52. Milstein, *Rebellious Mourning*, 218 and 224. The artists speaking in these passages are Oree Originol and Zola.

53. Ruin, *Being with the Dead*, 3.
54. Ruin, *Being with the Dead*, 3.
55. Ruin, *Being with the Dead*, 127. Ruin says that this connection is revealed in what he calls "ossuary hermeneutics" or the "'interpretation of bones'" (114).
56. Ruin, *Being with the Dead*, 7.
57. Ruin, *Being with the Dead*, 201.
58. Ruin, *Being with the Dead*, 14.
59. Cf. Saghafi, *World after the End*, 125 and 127.
60. Rosner, *Survivor Café*, 11.

Conclusion

1. See Ernst Becker, *The Denial of Death* (New York: Free Press Paperbacks, 1973).
2. Søren Kierkegaard, *Three Discourses on Imaginary Occasions*, trans. and ed. Howard V. and Edna H. Hong (Princeton, NJ: Princeton University Press, 1993), 73.

Bibliography

Adichie, Chimamanda Ngozi. *Notes on Grief.* New York: Alfred A. Knopf, 2021.

Arendt, Hannah. *Love and Saint Augustine.* Translated by Joanna Vecchiarelli Scott and Judith Chelius Stark. Chicago, IL: University of Chicago Press, 1996.

Aristotle. *The Complete Works of Aristotle.* Vol. 2. Edited by Jonathan Barnes. Princeton, NJ: Princeton University Press, 1995.

Athanasiou, Athena. *Agonistic Mourning: Political Dissidence and the Women in Black.* Edinburgh: Edinburgh University Press, 2017.

Attig, Thomas. *How We Grieve: Relearning the World.* New York: Oxford University Press, 2011.

Auden, W. H. "Stop All the Clocks." In *Another Time,* 81–82. London: Faber and Faber, 2007.

Augustine. *Confessions.* Translated by Henry Chadwick. New York: Oxford University Press, 1991.

Backman, Jussi. "Logocentrism and the Gathering Lo/goj: Heidegger, Derrida, and the Contextual Centers of Meaning." *Research in Phenomenology* 42 (2012): 67–91.

Badiou, Alain. *Saint Paul: The Foundation of Universalism.* Translated by Ray Brassier. Stanford, CA: Stanford University Press, 2003.

Beauvoir, Simone de. *A Very Easy Death.* Translated by Patrick O'Brian. New York: Random House, 1965.

Bechtol, Harris B. "Oh My Neighbors, There Is No Neighbor." *International Journal of Philosophy and Theology* 90, nos. 4–5 (2019): 326–43.

Becker, Ernst. *The Denial of Death.* New York: Free Press Paperbacks, 1973.

Bennett, Gillian, and Kate Mary Bennett. "The Presence of the Dead: An Empirical Study." *Mortality* 5, no. 2 (2000): 139–57.

Bennington, Geoffrey. "Geschlecht pollachos legetai: Translation, Polysemia, Dissemination." *Philosophy Today* 64, no. 2 (2020): 423–39.

———. *Jacques Derrida.* Chicago, IL: University of Chicago Press, 1993.

———. *Not Half No End: Militantly Melancholic Essays in Memory of Jacques Derrida.* Edinburgh: Edinburgh University Press, 2010.

Bible. New Revised Standard Version.

Blanchot, Maurice. *The Writing of the Disaster.* Translated by Ann Smock. Lincoln: University of Nebraska Press, 1986.

Bouton, Christophe. "The Privilege of the Present: Time and the Trace from Heidegger to Derrida." *International Journal of Philosophical Studies* 28, no. 3 (2020): 370–89.

Bowler, Kate. *Everything Happens for a Reason: And Other Lies I've Loved.* New York: Random House, 2018.

Caputo, John D., ed. *Deconstruction in a Nutshell: A Conversation with Jacques Derrida.* New York: Fordham University Press, 1997.

———. *The Insistence of God: A Theology of Perhaps.* Bloomington: Indiana University Press, 2013.

———. *The Prayers and Tears of Jacques Derrida: Religion without Religion.* Bloomington: Indiana University Press, 1997.

———. *Radical Hermeneutics: Repetition, Deconstruction, and the Hermeneutic Project.* Bloomington: Indiana University Press, 1987.

———. "Who Is Derrida's Zarathustra? Of Fraternity, Friendship, and a Democracy to Come." *Research in Phenomenology* 29, no. 1 (1999): 184–98.

Carbone, Mauro. "Falling Man: The Time of Trauma, the Time of (Certain) Images." *Research in Phenomenology* 47 (2017): 190–203.

Celan, Paul. *Atemwende.* Frankfurt am Main: Suhrkamp, 1967.

Cicero. *On Old Age; On Friendship; On Divination.* Translated by W. A. Falconer. Loeb Classical Library 154. Cambridge, MA: Harvard University Press, 1923.

Coe, Cynthia D. *Levinas and the Trauma of Responsibility: The Ethical Significance of Time.* Bloomington: Indiana University Press, 2018.

Cooper, Julia. *The Last Word: Reviving the Dying Art of Euology.* Toronto, CA: Coach House Book, 2017.

Crockett, Clayton. *Derrida after the End of Writing: Political Theology and New Materialism.* New York: Fordham University Press, 2017.

Das, Saitya Brata. "(Dis)Figures of Death: Taking the Side of Derrida, Taking the Side of Death." *Derrida Today* 3 (2010): 1–20.

Dastur, Françoise. *Death: An Essay on Finitude.* Translated by John Llewelyn. Atlantic Highlands, NJ: Athlone, 1996.

———. "Heidegger and Derrida: On Play and Difference." *Epoché: A Journal for the History of Philosophy* 3, no. 1/2 (1995): 1–23.

———. *How Are We to Confront Death? An Introduction to Philosophy.* Translated by Robert Vallier. New York: Fordham University Press, 2012.

———. "Phenomenology of the Event: Waiting and Surprise." *Hypatia* 15, 4 (2000): 178–89.

DeGruy, Joy. *Post Traumatic Slave Syndrome: America's Legacy of Enduring Injury and Healing.* Baltimore, MD: Uptone, 2005.

Derrida, Jacques. *Acts of Religion*. Edited by Gil Anidjar. New York: Routledge, 2002.

———. *Aporias*. Translated by Thomas Dutoit. Stanford, CA: Stanford University Press, 1993.

———. *Archive Fever*. Translated by Eric Prenowitz. Chicago, IL: University of Chicago Press, 1996.

———. "Autoimmunity: Real and Symbolic Suicides." Translated by Pascale-Anne Brault and Michael Naas. In Giovanna Borradori, *Philosophy in a Time of Terror: Dialogues with Jürgen Habermas and Jacques Derrida*, 85–136. Chicago, IL: University of Chicago Press, 2003.

———. *The Beast and the Sovereign*. Vol. 1. Translated by Geoffrey Bennington. Chicago, IL: University of Chicago Press, 2009.

———. *The Beast and the Sovereign*. Vol. 2. Translated by Geoffrey Bennington. Chicago, IL: University of Chicago Press, 2011.

———. "Une certaine possibilité impossible de dire l'événement." In *Dire l'événement, est-ce possible? Seminaire de Montréal, pour Jacques Derrida*, edited by Gad Soussana, Alexis Nouss, and Jacques Derrida, 79–112. Paris: L'Harmattan, 2001.

———. *Cinders*. Translated by Ned Lukacher. Minneapolis: University of Minnesota Press, 2014.

———. "Circumfession: Fifty-Nine Periods and Paraphrases." Translated by Geoffrey Bennington. In Geoffrey Bennington, *Jacques Derrida*, 3–315. Chicago, IL: University of Chicago Press, 1993.

———. *Death Penalty*. Vol. 1. Translated by Elizabeth Rottenberg. Chicago, IL: University of Chicago Press, 2017.

———. *Donner les temps II*. Edited by Lara Odello, Peter Szendy, and Rodrigo Therezo. Paris: Éditions du Seuil, 2021.

———. *The Ear of the Other: Otobiography, Transference, Translation*. Translated by Peggy Kamuf. New York: Shocken Books, 1985.

———. "Final Words." Translated by Gila Walker. *Critical Inquiry* 33, no. 2 (2007): 462.

———. "*Fors*: The Anglish Words of Nicolas Abraham and Maria Torok." Translated by Barbara Johnson. In Nicolas Abraham and Maria Torok, *The Wolf Man's Magic Word: A Cryptonymy*, translated by Nicholas Rand, xi–xlviii. Minneapolis: University of Minnesota Press, 1986.

———. *Geschlecht III: Sex, Race, Nation, Humanity*. Translated by Katie Chenoweth and Rodrigo Therezo. Chicago, IL: University of Chicago Press, 2020.

———. *The Gift of Death* Second Edition. Translated by David Wills. Chicago, IL: University of Chicago Press, 2008.

———. *Given Time: 1 Counterfeit Money*. Translated by Peggy Kamuf. Chicago, IL: University of Chicago Press, 1992.

———. *Heidegger: The Question of Being and History*. Translated by Geoffrey Bennington. Chicago, IL: University of Chicago Press, 2016.

———. *Hospitalité I*. Paris: Éditions de Seuil, 2021.

———. "Jacques Derrida — Penseur de l'événement Jacques Derrida." *L'Humanité* 27 (January 2004). https://advance-lexis-com.tamusa.idm.oclc.org/api/document?collection=news&id=urn:contentItem:4CKN-2MF0-TWKN-T25T-00000-00&context=1516831.

———. *Learning to Live Finally*. Translated by Pascale-Anne Brault and Michael Naas. Brooklyn, NY: Melville House, 2007.

———. *Life Death*. Translated by Pascale-Anne Brault and Michael Naas. Chicago, IL: University of Chicago Press, 2020.

———. "Living On." Translated by James Hulbert. In *Deconstruction and Criticism*, edited by Geoffrey H. Hartman, 75–176. New York: Continuum, 1979.

———. *Margins of Philosophy*. Translated by Alan Bass. Chicago, IL: University of Chicago Press, 1982.

———. *Memoires for Paul de Man*. Translated by Cecile Lindsay et al. New York: Columbia University Press, 1989.

———. *Negotiations: Interventions and Interviews, 1971–2001*. Edited and translated by Elizabeth Rottenberg. Stanford, CA: Stanford University Press, 2002.

———. *Of Grammatology*. Translated by Gayatri Chakrovorty Spivak. Baltimore, MD: The John Hopkins University Press, 1997.

———. *Of Hospitality: Anne Dufourmantelle Invites Jacques Derrida to Respond*. Translated by Rachel Bowlby. Stanford, CA: Stanford University Press, 2000.

———. "On the Gift: A Discussion between Jacques Derrida and Jean-Luc Marion." In *God, the Gift, and Postmodernism*, edited by John D. Caputo and Michael J. Scanlon, 54–78. Bloomington: Indiana University Press, 1999.

———. *Parages*. Translated by John P. Leavey et al. Stanford, CA: Stanford University Press, 2010.

———. *Points: Interviews 1974–1994*. Translated by Peggy Kamuf et al. Stanford, CA: Stanford University Press, 1995.

———. *The Politics of Friendship*. Translated by George Collins. New York: Verso, 2005.

———. *The Post Card: From Socrates to Freud and Beyond*. Translated by Alan Bass. Chicago, IL: University of Chicago Press, 1987.

———. "The Principle of Reason: The University in the Eyes of Its Pupils." Translated by Catherine Porter and Edward P. Morris. *Diacritics* 13, no. 3 (1983): 2–20.

———. *Rogues: Two Essays on Reason*. Translated by Pascale-Anne Brault and Michael Naas. Stanford, CA: Stanford University Press, 2005.

———. *Sovereignties in Question: The Poetics of Paul Celan*. Edited by Thomas Dutoit and Outi Pasanen. New York: Fordham University Press, 2005.

———. *Specters of Marx*. Translated by Peggy Kamuf. New York: Routledge, 1994.

———. *Voice and Phenomenon: Introduction to the Problem of the Sign in Husserl's Phenomenology*. Translated by Leonard Lawlor. Evanston, IL: Northwestern University Press, 2011.

———. *Without Alibi*. Translated by Peggy Kamuf. Stanford, CA: Stanford University Press, 2002.

———. *The Work of Mourning*. Edited by Pascale-Anne Brault and Michael Naas. Chicago, IL: University of Chicago Press, 2001.

———. *Writing and Difference*. Translated by Alan Bass. Chicago, IL: University of Chicago Press, 1978.

Derrida, Jacques, and Maurizio Ferraris. *A Taste for the Secret*. Translated by Giacomo Donis. Malden, MA: Polity Press, 2001.

Dias, Brian G., and Kerry J. Ressler. "Parental Olfactory Experience Influences Behavior and Neural Structure in Subsequent Generations." *Nature Neuroscience* 17, no. 1 (2014): 89–99.

Dickinson, Emily. "Death Sets a Thing Significant." In *Death Poems*, edited by Russ Kick, 93. San Francisco, CA: Disinformation Books, 2013.

Didion, Joan. *The Year of Magical Thinking*. New York: Vintage Books, 2005.

Eyerman, Ron. *Cultural Trauma: Slavery and the Formation of African American Identity*. Cambridge: Cambridge University Press, 2001.

Feldman, Allen. "Ground Zero Point One: On the Cinematics of History." *Social Analysis* 46, no. 1 (2002): 110–17.

Ferreira, M. Jamie. *Love's Grateful Striving: A Commentary on Kierkegaard's "Works of Love."* New York: Oxford University Press, 2001.

Foer, Jonathan Safran. *Extremely Loud and Incredibly Close*. New York: Houghton Miffli Company, 2005.

Freud, Sigmund. *Mourning and Melancholia*. Translated by James Strachey. In *The Standard Edition of the Complete Psychological Works of Sigmund Freud*, vol. 19 (1914–1916), translated by James Strachey, 14:243–58. London: The Hogarth Press, 1986.

Fullarton, Catherine. "Grief, Phantoms, and Re-membering Loss." *Journal of Speculative Philosophy* 34, no. 3 (2020): 284–96.

Gasché, Rodolphe. *Europe, or the Infinite Task: A Study of a Philosophical Concept.* Stanford, CA: Stanford University Press, 2009.

———. *Storytelling: The Destruction of the Inalienable in the Age of the Holocaust.* Albany, NY: SUNY Press, 2018.

Gaston, Sean. *The Impossible Mourning of Jacques Derrida.* New York: Continuum, 2006.

George, Theodore. "Grieving as Limit Situation of Memory: Gadamer, Beamer, and Moules on the Infinite Task Posed by the Dead." *Journal of Applied Hermeneutics* (2017): 1–6.

———. "The Worklessness of Literature: Blanchot, Hegel, and the Ambiguity of the Poetic Word." *Philosophy Today SPEP Supplement* (2006): 39–47.

Gibson, Margaret. "Melancholy Objects." *Mortality* 9, no. 4 (2004): 285–99.

Glass, Ira. "Off Course." *This American Life.* Podcast audio. March 20, 2022, https://www.thisamericanlife.org/765/off-course.

Graham, Daniel W. *The Texts of Early Greek Philosophy: The Complete Fragments and Selected Testimonies of the Major Presocratics.* Cambridge, MA: Cambridge University Press, 2010.

Gschwandtner, Christina. *Degrees of Givenness: On Saturation in Jean-Luc Marion.* Bloomington: Indiana University Press, 2014.

Harris, Celia B., Ruth Brookman, and Maja O'Connor. "It's Not Who You Lose, It's Who You Are: Identity and Symptom Trajectory in Prolonged Grief." *Current Psychology* 42 (2021): 11223–33.

Hayes, Shannon. "Merleau-Ponty's Melancholy: On Phantom Limbs and Involuntary Memory." *Epoché* 24, no. 1 (2019): 201–19.

Hegel, G. W. F. *Philosophy of Mind.* Translated by W. Wallace, A. V. Miller, and Michael Inwood. New York: Oxford University Press, 2007.

Heidegger, Martin. *Being and Time.* Translated by Joan Stambaugh and Dennis J. Schmidt. Albany, NY: SUNY Press, 2010.

———. *Four Seminars.* Translated by Andrew Mitchell and François Raffoul. Bloomington: Indiana University Press, 2012.

———. *The History of the Concept of Time: Prolegomena.* Translated by Theodore Kisiel. Bloomington: Indiana University Press, 1992.

———. *Identity and Difference.* Translated by Joan Stambaugh. New York: Harper & Row, 1969.

---. *The Metaphysical Foundations of Logic*. Translated by Michael Heim. Bloomington: Indiana University Press, 1984.

---. "The Origin of the Work of Art,." In *Poetry, Language, Thought*, translated by Albert Hofstadter, 15–86. New York: Harper Perennial, 2013.

---. *The Phenomenology of Religious Life*. Translated by Matthias Fritsch and Jennifer Anna Gosetti-Ferencei. Bloomington, IN: Indiana University Press, 1995.

---. *The Principle of Reason*. Translated by Reginald Lilly. Bloomington: Indiana University Press, 1991.

---. "The Thing." In *Bremen and Freiburg Lectures: Insight into That Which Is and Basic Principles of Thinking*, translated by Andrew J. Mitchell, 5–20. Bloomington: Indiana University Press, 2012.

---. *On Time and Being*. Translated by Joan Stambaugh. New York: Harper & Row, 1972.

Herman, Judith. *Trauma and Recovery: The Aftermath of Violence — From Domestic Abuse to Political Terror.* New York: Basic Books, 1992.

Hinshaw, Daniel B. "The Kenosis of the Dying: An Invitation to Healing." In *The Role of Death in Life: A Multidisciplinary Examination of the Relationship between Life and Death*, edited by John Behr and Connor Cunningham, 155–63. Eugene, OR: Cascade Books, 2015.

Hoy, Daniel Couzens. *The Time of Our Lives: A Critical History of Temporality.* Cambridge, MA: The MIT Press, 2009.

Husserl, Edmund. *On the Phenomenology of Internal Time Consciousness (1893–1917)*. Translated by John Barnett Brough. Netherlands: Springer, 1991.

Jacobs, Janet. *The Holocaust across Generations: Trauma and Its Inheritance among Descendants of Survivors*. New York: New York University Press, 2016.

Janicaud, Dominique. *Heidegger in France*. Translated by François Raffoul and David Pettigrew. Bloomington: Indiana University Press, 2015.

Jones, Tamsin. "Traumatized Subjects: Continental Philosophy of Religion and the Ethics of Alterity." *Journal of Religion* (2014): 143–60.

Kamuf, Peggy. "Teleiopoetic World." *SubStance* 43, no. 2 (2014): 10–19.

Kant, Immanuel. *Critique of Pure Reason*. Translated by Paul Guyer and Allen W. Wood. New York: Cambridge University Press, 1998.

Kaplan, Louise J. *No Voice Is Ever Wholly Lost*. New York: Simon and Schuster, 1995.

Kierkegaard, Søren. *Three Discourses on Imaginary Occasions*. Translated and edited by Howard V. and Edna H. Hong. Princeton, NJ: Princeton University Press, 1993.

———. *Works of Love*. Translated and edited by Howard V. and Edna H. Hong. Princeton, NJ: Princeton University Press, 1995.

Kirkland, Sean D. *Aristotle and Tragic Temporality*. Edinburgh: Edinburgh University Press, 2025.

Kleinberg, Ethan. *Haunting History: For a Deconstructive Approach to the Past*. Stanford, CA: Stanford University Press, 2017.

Knowles, Adam. "Toward a Critique of *Walten*: Heidegger, Derrida, and Henological Difference." *Journal of Speculative Philosophy* 27, no. 3 (2013): 265–76.

Krell, David Farrell. *Ecstasy, Catastrophe: Heidegger from "Being and Time" to the "Black Notebooks."* Albany, NY: SUNY Press, 2015.

———. "History, Natality, Ecstasy: Derrida's First Seminar on Heidegger, 1964–1965." *Research in Phenomenology* 46 (2016): 3–34.

———. *Phantoms of the Other: Four Generations of Derrida's "Geschlecht."* Albany, NY: SUNY Press, 2015.

Lambert, Gregg. *Return Statements: The Return of Religion in Contemporary Philosophy*. Edinburgh: Edinburgh University Press, 2016.

Leibniz, G. W. *Discourse on Metaphysics and Other Essays*. Translated by Daniel Garber and Roger Ariew. Indianapolis, IN: Hackett, 1991.

Levinas, Emmanuel. "Enigma and Phenomenon." Translated by Alphonso Lingis. Revised by Robert Bernasconi and Simon Critchley. In *Emmanuel Levinas: Basic Philosophical Writings*, edited by Adriaan T. Peperzak, Simon Critchley, and Robert Bernasconi, 65–78. Bloomington: Indiana University Press, 1996.

———. "Ethics as First Philosophy." Translated by Seán Hand and Michael Temple. In *The Levinas Reader*, edited by Seán Hand, 75–87. Cambridge, MA: Basil Blackwell, 1989.

———. *Existence and Existents*. Translated by Alphonso Lingis. The Hague: Martinus Nijhoff, 1978.

———. *God, Death, and Time*. Translated by Bettina Bergo. Stanford, CA: Stanford University Press, 2000.

———. *Totality and Infinity*. Translated by Alphonso Lingis. Pittsburg, PN: Duquesne University Press, 1969.

Lewis, C. S. *A Grief Observed*. New York: Harper Collins, 2001.

López, Maria del Rosario Acosta. "Memory and Fragility: Art's Resistance to Oblivion (Three Colombian Cases)." *New Centennial Review* 14, no. 1 (2014): 71–98.

———. "Totalitarianism as Structural Violence: Toward New Grammars of Listening." In *Logics of Genocide: The Structures of Violence and the Contemporary World*, 173–86. New York: Routledge, 2020.

Luszczynska, Ana. "Nancy and Derrida: On Ethics and the Same (Infinitely Different) Constitutive Events of Being." *Philosophy and Social Criticism* 35, no. 7 (2009): 801–21.

Mackinlay, Shane. *Interpreting Excess: Jean-Luc Marion, Saturated Phenomena, and Hermeneutics*. New York: Fordham University Press, 2009.

Marion, Jean-Luc. *Being Given: Toward a Phenomenology of Givenness*. Translated by Jeffrey L. Kosky. Stanford, CA: Stanford University Press, 2002.

———. *Givenness and Hermeneutics*. Translated by Jean-Pierre LaFouge. Milwaukee, WI: Marquette University Press, 2012.

———. *God without Being*. Translated by Thomas A. Carlson. Chicago, IL: University of Chicago Press, 1991.

———. *In Excess: Studies of Saturated Phenomena*. Translated by Robyn Horner and Vincent Berraud. New York: Fordham University Press, 2002.

———. *In the Self's Place: The Approach of Saint Augustine*. Translated by Jeffrey L. Kosky. Stanford, CA: Stanford University Press, 2012.

———. *Negative Certainties*. Translated by Stephen Lewis. Chicago, IL: University of Chicago Press, 2015.

———. "Phenomenon and Event." *Graduate Faculty Philosophy Journal* 26, no. 1 (2005): 147–59.

———. *Reduction and Givenness: Investigations of Husserl, Heidegger, and Phenomenology*. Translated by Thomas A. Carlson. Evanston, IL: Northwestern University Press, 1998.

———. *The Visible and the Revealed*. Translated by Christina M. Gschwandtner et al. New York: Fordham University Press, 2008.

Márquez, Gabriel García. *Love in the Time of Cholera*. Translated by Edith Grossman. New York: Alfred A. Knopf, 1988.

Marrati, Paola. *Genesis and Trace: Derrida Reading Husserl and Heidegger*. Translated by Simon Sparks. Stanford, CA: Stanford University Press, 2005.

McDermott, Lori, and Brian McDermott. *Learning to Dance in the Rain: A True Story about Life beyond Death*. Bloomington, IN: Balboa Press, 2011.

Miller, J. Hillis. *For Derrida*. New York: Fordham University Press, 2009.

Milstein, Cindy ed. *Rebellious Mourning: The Collective Work of Grief*. Chico, CA: AK Press, 2017.

Mitchell, Andrew J. *The Fourfold: Reading the Late Heidegger*. Evanston, IL: Northwestern University Press, 2015.

Moore, Ian Alexander. *Dialogue on the Threshold: Heidegger and Trakl*. Albany, NY: SUNY Press, 2022.

Moules, Nancy J., et al. "Making Room for Grief: Walking Backwards and Living Forward." *Nursing Inquiry* 11, no. 2 (2004): 99–107.

———. "Out of Order: To Debbie and Dave, Chris and Bill, MJ and John." *Journal of Applied Hermeneutics* (2015): 1–10.

Naas, Michael. *Derrida from Now On.* New York: Fordham University Press, 2008.

———. *The End of the World and Other Teachable Moments: Jacques Derrida's Final Seminar.* New York: Fordham University Press, 2015.

———. "History's Remains: Of Memory, Mourning, and the Event." *Research in Phenomenology* 33 (2003): 75–96.

———. "The Inside Story of Derrida's *Of Grammatology.*" *Philosophy Today* 64, no. 3 (2020): 727–44.

———. *Miracle and Machine: Jacques Derrida and the Two Sources of Religion, Science, and the Media.* New York: Fordham University Press, 2012.

———. "Violence and Historicity: Derrida's Early Readings of Heidegger." *Research in Phenomenology* 45 (2015): 191–213.

———. "Violence and Hyperbole: From 'Cogito and the History of Madness' to the *Death Penalty Seminar.*" In *Foucault/Derrida Fifty Years Later: The Futures of Genealogy, Deconstruction, and Politics*, edited by Olivia Custer, Penelope Deutscher, and Samir Haddad, 38–60. New York: Columbia University Press, 2016.

———. "When It Comes to Mourning." In *Jacques Derrida: Key Concepts*, edited by Claire Colebrook, 113–21. New York: Routledge, 2015.

Nancy, Jean-Luc. *Being Singular Plural.* Translated by Robert D. Richardson and Anne E. O'Byrne. Stanford, CA: Stanford University Press, 2000.

———. *The Inoperative Community.* Translated by Peter Connor, Lisa Garbus, Michale Holland, et al. Minneapolis: University of Minnesota Press, 1991.

O'Connor, Mary-Frances et al. "Divergent Gene Expression Responses to Complicated Grief and Non-complicated Grief." *Brain, Behavior, and Immunity* 37 (2014): 78–83.

Ovid. *Metamorphoses.* Translated by David Raeburn. New York: Penguin Books, 2004.

Plato. *Plato: Complete Works.* Edited by John M. Cooper. Indianapolis, IN: Hackett, 1997.

Polt, Richard. "Tramaumatic Ontology." In *Being Shaken: Ontology and the Event*, edited by Santiago Zabala and Michael Marder, 19–40. New York: Palgrave MacMillan, 2014.

Raffoul, François. *The Origins of Responsibility.* Bloomington: Indiana University Press, 2010.

———. "Sexual Difference and Gathering in Geschlecht III." *Philosophy Today* 64, no. 2 (2020): 325–41.

———. *Thinking the Event*. Bloomington: Indiana University Press, 2020.

Rambo, Shelly. *Resurrecting Wounds: Living in the Afterlife of Trauma*. Waco, TX: Baylor University Press, 2017.

Ratcliffe, Matthew. "Grief and Phantom Limbs: A Phenomenological Comparison." *New Yearbook for Phenomenology and Phenomenological Philosophy* 17 (2019): 77–96.

Romano, Claude. *Event and Time*. Translated by Stephen E. Lewis. New York: Fordham University Press, 2014.

———. *Event and World*. Translated by Shane Mackinlay. New York: Fordham University Press, 2009.

———. "Mourir à autrui." *Critique: Revue générale des publications françaises et étrangères*. 51 (1995): 803–24.

Rosenthal, Adam R. "On Derrida's *Donner le temps, Volumes I & II*: A New Engagement with Heidegger." *Research in Phenomenology* 52 (2022): 23–47.

Rosner, Elizabeth. *Survivor Café: The Legacy of Trauma and the Labyrinth of Memory*. Berkeley, CA: Counterpoint, 2017.

Ruin, Hans. *Being with the Dead: Burial Ancestral Politics, and the Roots of Historical Consciousness*. Stanford, CA: Stanford University Press, 2018.

Russon, John. "Haunted by History: Merleau-Ponty, Hegel, and the Phenomenology of Pain." *Journal of Contemporary Thought* 37 (2013): 81–94.

———. "The Self as Resolution: Heidegger, Derrida, and the Intimacy of the Question of the Meaning of Being." *Research in Phenomenology* 38 (2008): 90–110.

Saghafi, Kas. *Apparitions — Of Derrida's Other*. New York: Fordham University Press, 2010.

———. *The World after the End of the World: A Spectro-Poetics*. Albany, NY: SUNY Press, 2020.

Schmidt, Dennis. "Of Birth, Death, and Unfinished Conversations." In *Gadamer's Hermeneutics and the Art of Conversation*, edited by Andrzej Wiercinski, 107–14. Piscataway, NJ: Transaction Publishers, 2011.

———. "What We Owe the Dead." In *Heidegger and the Greeks Interpretive Essays*, edited by Drew A. Hyland and John Panteleimon Manoussakis, 111–26. Bloomington: Indiana University Press, 2006.

Secret, Timothy. *The Politics and Pedagogy of Mourning: On Responsibility in Eulogy*. New York: Bloomsbury Academic, 2015.

Sokolowski, Robert. *Introduction to Phenomenology*. New York: Cambridge University Press, 2000.

Stoler, Ann. *Along the Archival Grain: Epistemically Anxieties and Colonial Common Sense*. Princeton, NJ: Princeton University Press, 2010.

Taylor, Mark C. *Last Works: Lessons in Leaving.* New Haven, CT: Yale University Press, 2018.

Therezo, Rodrigo. "From Neutral Dasein to a Gentle Twofold: Sexual Difference in Heidegger and Derrida." *Philosophy Today* 63, no. 2 (2019): 491–511.

———. "'In the Watermark of Some Margin': Heidegger's Other Gesture." *Research in Phenomenology* 51 (2021): 20–36.

Thompson, Joy Netanya. "To Live and Die Well." *Fuller: Story | Theology | Voice*, issue 2: Evangelical (2015): 23–25. Available online: https://fullerstudio.fuller.edu/live-die-well/.

Valentine, Christine. *Bereavement Narratives: Continuing Bonds in the Twenty-First Century.* New York: Routledge, 2008.

Vallega-Neu, Daniela. "A Strange Proximity: On the Notion of *Walten* in Derrida and Heidegger." *Epoché: A Journal for the History of Philosophy* 26, no. 2 (2022): 369–87.

Van der Heiden, Gert-Jan. *Ontology after Ontotheology: Plurality, Event, and Contingency in Contemporary Philosophy.* Pittsburgh, PN: Duquesne University Press, 2014.

Van der Kolk, Bessel. *The Body Keeps the Score: Brain, Mind, and the Body in the Healing of Trauma.* New York: Penguin, 2014.

Vitale, Francesco. *Biodeconstruction: Jacques Derrida and the Life Sciences.* Translated by Mauro Senatore. New York: SUNY Press, 2018.

Voltaire. *Candide: Or Optimism.* Translated by John Butt. New York: Penguin Classics, 1950.

Warren, Nicolas de. "The Inquietude of Time and the Instance of Eternity." In *The Oxford Handbook of the History of Phenomenology*, edited by Dan Zahavi, 511–32. New York: Oxford University Press, 2018.

Wegner, Daniel M. "Transactive Memory: A Contemporary Analysis of the Group Mind." In *Theories of Group Behavior*, edited by Brian Mullen and George R. Goethals, 185–208. New York: Springer-Verlag, 1987.

Wegner, Daniel M., Paula Raymond, and Ralph Erber. "Transactive Memory in Close Relationships." *Journal of Personality and Social Psychology* 61, no. 6 (1991): 923–29.

Westerlund, Fredrik. *Heidegger and the Problem of Phenomena.* New York: Bloomsbury Academic, 2020.

Winfree, Jason. "Concealing Difference: Derrida and Heidegger's Thinking of Becoming." *Research in Phenomenology* 29, no. 1 (1999): 161–81.

Wolterstorff, Nicholas. *Lament for a Son.* Grand Rapids, MI: Eerdmans, 1987.

Yehuda, Rachel. "Trauma in the Family Tree: Parents' Adverse Experiences Leave Biological Traces in Children." *Scientific American* 327, no. 1

(2022), 50–55. Accessible here: https://www.scientificamerican.com/article/how-parents-rsquo-trauma-leaves-biological-traces-in-children/.

Yehuda, Rachel, and Amy Lehrner. "Intergenerational Transmission of Trauama Effects: Putative Role of Epigenetic Mechanisms." *Wold Psychiatry* 17, no. 3 (2018): 243–57.

Yellow Horse Brave Heart, Maria. "The Historical Trauma Response among Natives and Its Relationship with Substance Abuse: A Lakota Illustration." *Journal of Psychoactive Drugs* 35, (2003): 7–13.

———. "The Return to the Sacred Path: Healing the Historical Trauma Response among the Lakota." *Smith College Studies in Social Work* 68 (1998): 287–305.

———. "Wakiksuyapi: Carrying the Historical Trauma of the Lakota." *Tulane Studies in Social Welfare* 21–22 (2000): 245–66.

Zabala, Santiago, and Michael Marder. "Introduction: The First Jolts." In *Being Shaken: Ontology and the Event*, edited by Michael Marder and Santiago Zabala, 1–10. New York: Palgrave MacMillan, 2014.

Zahavi, Dan. *Husserl's Phenomenology.* Stanford, CA: Stanford University Press, 2003.

———. *Subjectivity and Selfhood: Investigating the First-Person Perspective.* Cambridge, MA: The MIT Press, 2005.

Zahavi, Dan, and Shaun Gallagher. *The Phenomenological Mind: An Introduction to Philosophy of Mind and Cognitive Science.* London: Taylor and Francis, 2009.

Index

9/11, 11, 26, 116, 118, 141, 160, 218n46

AI, 146
A death of the world, 2, 7, 14, 15, 66, 75–76, 79, 86, 87, 97, 100, 101, 102, 121, 147, 162, 183
Abgrund (Abyss), 49, 201n6, 201n10
Abraham, 84
Absence, 16, 18, 19, 29, 30, 32, 33, 34, 36, 38, 57, 61, 66, 68, 69, 76, 79, 81, 87, 92, 98, 99, 102, 103, 105, 108, 114, 115, 117, 128, 129, 130, 132, 133, 137, 139, 140, 142, 143, 145, 147, 149, 150, 151, 158, 159, 162, 163, 164, 165, 182, 190, 191, 198n7, 210n30, 216n21, 217n27, 217n33, 218n37; of the world, 75, 80, 87 (*See also* absent presence; present absence)
Absent presence, 38, 66, 93, 102, 107, 132, 138, 142, 144, 173 (*See also* present absence)
Adichie, Chimamanda Ngozi, 97
Afterlife, 11, 17, 120–22, 182, 185, 189, 192, 196n34 (*See also* life after; living on; survival; *survivre, survivance*)
Agonistic mourning, 19, 183–85, 187
Alterity, 7, 13, 18, 37, 40, 43–44, 82–83, 85–86, 138, 142, 143, 144, 145, 174, 181, 205n15 (*See also* otherness)
Aneconomic, 36, 169, 172, 174, 199n21

Aneconomy, 36, 171
Animal, nonhuman, 6–7, 14, 48, 72, 73, 85, 86, 117, 153, 181, 190, 191
Anticipatory resoluteness, 18, 133, 135–37, 140, 143, 217n37
Antigone, 191, 217n36
Anxiety, 9, 70, 83, 135, 153, 155, 204n3
Arche-writing, 28, 139
Archive, 157–8, 164
Arendt, Hannah, 9, 60, 184, 194n15
Aristotle, 47, 133, 168, 169, 170–71, 172, 174, 199n20, 202n18, 216n17
Athanasiou, Athena, 11, 19, 183–85
Attig, Thomas, 210n32
Auden, W.H., 15, 141, 161, 196n47
Augenblick (instant/moment), 136, 137, 141, 143
Authenticity, 10, 149, 150
Avenir, 154, 155, 157

Badiou, Alain, 9, 193n8, 223n29
Backman, Jussi, 197n7
Banality of saturation, 55, 56
Barraza, Jesus, 186
Beauvoir, Simone de, 214n47
Becker, Ernst, 225n1
Befindlichkeit, 83 (*See also* mood/moodedness)
Being-toward-death, 9, 10, 18, 61, 83, 137, 140, 151–53, 155, 195n26
Being-with, 2, 10, 11–12, 15, 18, 69, 77–78, 86, 92, 96, 97, 101, 102, 128, 134, 136, 139, 142, 145, 146, 168, 187, 190, 192, 196n40,

204n6, 206n20, 219n47, 224n39
(*See also* memory-with)
Bennett, Gillian and Kate Mary Bennett, 217n33
Bennington, Geoffrey, 17, 197n7, 199n21
Blanchot, Maurice, 80, 81, 108, 120–23, 169, 211n1, 214n46, 218n42
Bouton, Christophe, 197n3
Bowler, Kate, 222n36
Brookman, Ruth, 219n64

Calculable, 43, 48, 49–51, 56, 57, 59, 201n14 (*See also* calculation; calculative rationality)
Calculation, 14, 36, 47–52, 54, 56, 59–60, 119, 142, 171–72, 201n8, 201n14 (*See also* calculable; calculative rationality)
Caputo, John D., 2, 193n8, 214n46, 220n4, 220n7
Carbone, Mauro, 142,
Calculative rationality, 8, 16, 35, 55, 67, 108, 119, 120, 169 (*See also* calculable; calculation)
Carry, 3, 14, 16, 18, 19, 66, 68, 70, 74, 78, 79–80, 82, 83–84, 87, 88, 93, 101, 102, 103, 104, 105, 106, 108, 113–14, 117, 118–19, 121, 122, 123, 130, 136, 142, 163, 181–83, 188, 190–92 (*See also* carry on; *tragen*)
Carry on, 102, 114, 121 (*See also* carry; *tragen*)
Causality of rupture, 13, 24, 26, 28, 29, 31, 32, 34, 39, 41, 44, 45, 54, 58, 59, 62, 123, 129, 156, 170, 173, 185, 189, 190
Celan, Paul, 14, 16, 18, 65–71, 72, 74, 76, 77–79, 84, 87, 88, 100, 105, 106, 182, 186, 190, 205n12, 211n51
Cervantes, Melanie, 186
Cicero, 168, 169, 170, 171–72

Cinders, 34
Coe, Cynthia D., 200n28
Conditional hospitality, 19, 174–78, 181 (*See also* hospitality; unconditional hospitality; workless hospitality)
Condition for the possibility, 30, 35, 131, 132, 175 (*See also* condition of possibility)
Condition of possibility, 5, 12, 13, 35, 36, 37, 40, 43, 44, 45, 60, 140, 156, 169, 174 (*See also* condition for the possibility)
Constitution, 4, 16, 59, 74, 80, 92–95, 96, 106, 117, 137, 139, 154
Cooper, Julia, 129, 163, 212n16, 215n3, 215n5, 222n3
Crockett, Clayton, 208n48
Crypt, 83–84, 114, 145, 180–81, 208n45

Das, Saitya Brata, 208n47
Dasein, 9, 15, 18, 65, 68–70, 77, 78, 93, 94, 95, 96, 122, 133–37, 139, 140, 142, 150–54, 155, 195n26, 204n6
Dastur, Françoise, 9, 65, 193n8, 198n, 206n16
De-distancing, 16, 95–96, 97, 98, 99, 100, 10–07 *passim*, 114, 117, 118, 120, 121, 123, 127, 137
DeGruy, Joy, 213n27
Demise (*Ableben*), 153
Derrida, Jacques, 2, 5, 7, 8, 9, 12, 15, 19, 23, 42, 51, 76, 77, 78, 91, 107, 114, 121, 127, 128, 133, 140, 149, 154, 167, 168–70, 172, 173, 174–81, 183, 184, 189, 193n8, 194n13, 195n26, 196n34, 198n9, 198n11, 198n13, 199n17, 201n14, 205n15, 207n40, 208n49, 211n2, 211n5, 216n21, 218n41, 220n7, 222n8; and Celan, Paul, 14, 65–75, 77, 79–87, 205n12, 211n51;

and Heidegger, Martin, 18, 23, 29–34, 47, 49, 79, 112, 136–42, 155–57, 217n27, 217n37, 218n39; and Levinas, Emmanuel, 10, 38, 204n3; on event, 12–13, 23–24, 34–37, 39–41, 43, 45, 169; on life/death, 17, 108–13, 119, 122; on memory, 142–45; and post-structuralism, 24–29, 31–34, 111, 212n8
Diachronic temporality, 37, 200n28
Dias, Brian G., 213n22
Dickinson, Emily, 16, 211n51
Didion, Joan, 97, 98, 99, 113, 119, 130, 161, 163
Différance, 17, 19, 24, 28–34, 36, 45, 82, 84, 104, 108, 109, 111, 112, 113, 118, 119, 121, 122, 123, 138, 139, 140, 142, 143, 145, 174, 175, 178, 181, 217n37
Différ*ant* logic, 108–09, 112, 113, 122
Divine, 117, 179, 181, 190, 191 (*See also* God)
DNA, 110, 114, 115, 212n16 (*See also* Genetics)
Dying (*Sterben*), 153–54
Dynamics of *différance*, 28–29, 31, 33, 34, 82

Economy of exchange, 35–37, 39–40, 48, 168, 169, 172, 173, 176, 177
Einheit (unity), 136, 137, 149, 157
Embodied signifier, 117, 118
Epicurus, 68 (*See also* Epicurean problem)
Epicurean problem, 68–69, 137, 152 (*See also* Epicurus)
Epigenetics, 17, 106, 113–16, 119, 212n15, 212n16
Erinnerung, 82, 143–45, 147, 174, 181 (*See also Gedächtnis*; workless memory)
Es gibt, 30, 34, 46, 48

Ethics, 8, 79, 87, 170, 188, 195n18, 208n49; of hospitality, 8 (*See also* workless hospitality)
Event, 2–10, 12–15, 17, 19, 23–29, 31–41, 43–50, 52–63, 65–68, 70–71, 74–75, 77–78, 80, 85, 86, 87, 88, 90, 97, 98, 101, 102, 103, 104, 105, 106, 109, 110, 116, 117, 119–23 *passim*, 127, 128, 129, 130, 131, 138, 140, 141, 144, 149, 154, 155, 156, 157, 158, 164, 165, 167, 168, 169, 170, 173, 174, 175, 176, 177, 180–86 *passim*, 188, 189, 190, 192, 193n6, 193n8, 194n16, 195n20, 195n24, 197n5, 198, 199n17, 199n20, 200n24, 200n29, 200n30, 201n10, 202, 202n19, 202n20, 203n30, 203n2, 204n3, 205n14, 206n21, 208n1, 215n8, 217n35, 220n7, 220n8, 223n29
Eventful temporality, 17, 127
Existenz (existence), 61, 69, 70, 79, 133, 135, 137, 150, 151, 152, 154, 203n29
Existential difference, 6–7, 14, 85–87, 103, 116, 146–47, 159
Eyerman, Ron, 213n27

Facticity, 3, 4, 58, 130
Falling prey, 150 (*See also* inauthentic)
Feldman, Allen, 218n46
Ferraris, Maurizio, 43
Ferreira, M. Jamie, 222n5
Flynn, John, 221n23
Foer, Jonathan Safran, 160
Freud, Sigmund, 5, 14, 18, 80, 81–82, 87, 109, 113–14, 143, 144, 182, 191, 207n40, 211n3, 212n11
Fullarton, Catherine, 215n56

Gallagher, Shaun, 216n20
Gasché, Rodolphe, 224n39

Gaston, Sean, 220n9
Gedächtnis, 143–45, 147, 174, 181 (*See also Erinnerung*)
George, Theodore, 215n5
Genetics, 110–11 (*See also* DNA)
Ghost, 18, 128, 129, 138, 139, 140, 141, 142, 143, 147, 150, 158, 183, 218n38, 218n39, 218n41 (*See also* phantom; revenant; specter)
Gibson, Margaret, 207n40
Gift, 5, 7, 19, 23, 24, 28, 29, 30, 31, 33, 34–41, 43, 47, 61, 84, 93, 101, 122, 123, 155, 167–75 *passim*, 177, 182, 183, 184, 188, 190, 198n, 198n11, 199n21 (*See also* givenness; giving)
Givenness, 4, 7, 9, 13, 46, 52, 53, 54–56, 57, 58, 59–60, 61, 66, 87, 193n7, 202n, 202n19, 202n21, 203n (*See also* gift; giving)
Giving, 4, 28, 34–36, 39, 47, 54, 96, 168, 169, 171, 181, 198n11 (*See also* gift; givenness)
Glass, Ira, 221n23
God, 14, 84, 85, 86, 87, 110, 120, 121, 161, 171, 192, 204n7 (*See also* divine)
Graham, Daniel W., 195n21
Grief, 1, 39, 80, 82, 98, 116, 123, 130, 146, 162, 164, 167, 179, 185, 186, 212n16, 215n5, 219n64
Grund (Ground/Reason), 47, 48–49, 52
Gschwandtner, Christina, 193n7, 202n19, 202n21

Half-mourning, 14, 80
Harris, Celia B., 219n64
Hart, Benji, 185
Haunted time, 139 (*See also* haunting; hauntology)
Haunting, 17, 18, 113, 128, 129, 138–39, 140, 141, 147, 158, 164, 217n33, 217n34, 224n39 (*See also* haunted time; hauntology)
Hauntology, 18, 128, 139–140, 142, 144, 218n39 (*See also* haunted time; haunting)
Hauntological memory, 145, 147 (*See also* memory; memory-with; transactive memory; workless memory)
Hayes, Shannon, 221n18
Hazard, Harmony, 80
Hegel, G.W.F., 3, 142–44, 208n45
Heidegger, Martin, 7, 9–10, 12, 13–14, 15–16, 18–19, 23, 75, 81, 83, 92–96, 101, 102, 108, 128, 131–37, 139, 149–54, 169, 186, 189, 190, 193n6, 193n8, 194n16, 195n26, 197n5, 199n20, 201n6, 201n10, 202n16, 204n6, 206n7, 205n15, 206n21, 217n35, 217n36; and Derrida, Jacques, 29–34, 66, 68–70, 77–79, 112–13, 140–43, 154–55, 157, 198n8, 198n9, 198n13, 216n21, 217n27, 217n37; on Leibniz, 45–52, 58, 67; and Marion, Jean-Luc, 52–54, 61–62, 68, 202n17, 203n29
Heraclitus, 9, 112, 187
Herman, Judith, 224n39
Hermeneutics, 2–3, 5, 7, 8, 14, 78, 113, 189, 205n14 (*See also* radical hermeneutics)
Hermeneutic realism, 113
Hinshaw, Daniel B., 212n11
Holocaust, 11, 57, 77, 115, 116, 117, 138, 162, 182, 212n16, 213n23, 215n9, 217n34
Hongerwinter, 115
Hospitality, 1, 8, 24, 41, 167, 168, 169, 174, 179, 183, 188, 191, 195n18 (*See also* conditional hospitality; unconditional hospitality; workless hospitality)
Hoy, Daniel Couzens, 215n1

Husserl, Edmund, 7, 53, 54, 131–33, 134, 194n13, 216n21, 216n23

Impossible possibility, 18, 40, 156, 159, 178, 220n7
Im-possible possibility, 150, 155–56, 167
In and along, 17, 32, 33, 34, 46, 47, 53, 54, 84, 108, 113, 117, 145, 169, 174, 181, 187, 190, 193n6
Inapparent, 53, 194n16, 202n17
Inauthentic, 133, 134, 153 (*See also* falling prey)
Incalculable, 43, 49–51, 52, 56, 57, 58, 59–60, 182, 184, 201n14
Incorporation, 82, 113–14, 119, 143, 180 (*See also* Gedächtnis; melancholy)
Inscape, 1, 100–01
Instant, 35, 36–37, 38, 39, 40, 41, 62, 63, 68, 97–98, 102, 104, 121, 123, 129, 137, 140–41, 158, 168, 177, 181, 199n19, 209n11, 218n41 (*See also* Augenblick)
Intergenerational transference of trauma, 17, 107, 113, 115, 129
Intentionality, 4, 55, 61, 187, 216n21
Introjection, 82–84, 113–14, 143, 207n40 (*See also* Erinnerung; normal mourning)
Intuition, 54–55, 56, 57–58, 59, 61, 131, 143, 202n22
Isaac, 84

Jacob, François, 109–12, 114, 119
Jacobs, Janet, 210n46
Janicaud, Dominique, 30
Jemeinigkeit (mineness), 69–70, 152
Jones, Tamsin, 215n8

Kamuf, Peggy, 211n51
Kant, Immanuel, 3–4, 51, 54, 55, 56, 57, 58, 59, 131–32, 133, 134, 186, 202n22

Kaplan, Louise J., 213n23
Kiefer, Anselm, 187
Kleinberg, Ethan, 218n39
Knowles, Adam, 197n7
Kohso, Sabn, 196n48
Krell, David Farrell, 198n13, 218n

Laertius, Diogenes, 169
Lamarck, Jean-Baptiste, 114
Lambert, Gregg, 208n45
Leibniz, G.W., 13, 44–47, 73, 75, 205n14
Levinas, Emmanuel, 7, 9, 10, 12, 36, 37, 38, 66, 69, 79, 117, 132, 145, 157, 185, 195n26, 200n24, 204n3, 205n15
Lewis, C.S., 130
Life after, 1, 10–11, 96, 106, 121, 123, 185, 187, 189, 190, 192 (*See also* afterlife; living on; survival; *survivre*, *survivance*)
Life/death, 17, 107, 108, 112, 117, 122 (*See also* lifedeath; life death)
lifedeath, 17, 109, 112–13, 119, 129, 142, 163, 188, 192 (*See also* life/death; life death)
life death, 107, 108, 109, 112, 113, 119, 212n11, 212n15 (*See also* life/death; lifedeath)
Limit-experience, 11
Living on, 10, 11, 17, 98, 102, 107, 121, 187, 189 (*See also* afterlife; life after; survival; *survivre*, *survivance*)
López, Maria del Rosario Acosta, 184, 224n39
Luszczynska, Ana, 206n20

Mackinlay, Shane, 202n19, 203n30
Marder, Michael, 9
Marion, Jean-Luc, 7, 9, 12–14, 44, 46, 52–63, 65, 68, 100, 102, 129, 189, 193n6, 193n7, 193n8, 194n15, 194n16, 202n, 202n17,

202n18, 202n21, 203n, 203n29, 219n61
Márquez, Gabriel García, 99, 221n18
Marrati, Paola, 216n23, 218n
Matsumoto, Mari, 196n48
May-be (*peut*-être), 31, 43, 175
McDermott, Lori and Brian, 97, 100, 119, 130, 158, 163
Memory, 18, 63, 80, 99, 106, 109–10, 114, 117, 128–29, 138, 142–47, 158, 164, 172, 174, 180, 181, 184, 185, 186, 191, 212n16, 215n5, 220n8 (*See also* hauntological memory; memory-with; transactive memory; workless memory)
Memory-with, 18, 145–46 (*See also* memory; hauntological memory; transactive memory; workless memory)
Metaphysics, 2, 31, 32, 45, 46, 65, 109, 140, 216n21, 218n
Miller, J. Hillis, 205n15
Milstein, Cindy, 11, 185
Mitchell, Andrew J., 206n21
Modalities of givenness, 55
Moment. *See under Augenblick*
Montaigne, 169
Mood/Moodedness, 70, 81, 83, 135, 153, 155
Moore, Ian Alexander, 198–99n
Moules, Nancy J., 123, 179–80
Mourir à autrui, 146, 159, 163, 119n62
Mourning, 9, 10, 11, 19, 39, 69, 70, 76–77, 79, 80, 85, 86–87, 91, 92, 96, 97, 100, 102, 103, 105–06, 107, 108, 113, 116, 117, 118–19, 123, 129, 139, 142, 144, 146, 158, 159, 162, 163, 165, 167–74 *passim*, 178, 179, 182, 183, 187–88, 189–90, 205n16, 208n46, 212n14, 212n16, 215n5, 217n36, 221n18, 223n31

Melancholy, 14, 18, 71, 80–83, 84, 87, 103, 104, 113, 130, 143, 144, 145, 174, 180, 182, 191, 207n40 (*See also Gedächtnis*; incorporation)
Memorial, 102–05, 118, 119, 141, 190

Naas, Michael, 33, 198n9, 199n15, 203n24, 205n12, 208n46, 212n8, 218n38
Nancy, Jean-Luc, 4, 7, 9, 24, 77, 78, 80, 81, 96, 145, 169, 193n8, 195n20, 206n20, 206n26
Negotiation, 18, 30, 81, 82, 87, 130, 174, 175, 178, 180
Nietzsche, Friedrich, 3, 47, 169
Normal mourning, 14, 18, 80, 81–84, 104, 113–14, 143, 144, 174, 180, 191, 207n40 (*See also Erinnerung*; introjection)

O'Connor, Maja, 219n64
O'Connor, Mary-Frances, 213n24
Oklahoma City, 26, 103–04, 118–19, 141, 142
Ontology, 3–4, 69, 77, 78, 95, 133, 139, 140, 150, 152, 194n16, 218n39; hermeneutic, 217n35; of presence, 31–32; relational, 77, 78, 97, 195n26, 204n6
Originol, Oree, 224n52
Otherness, 7, 29, 37, 84, 181, 182 (*See also* alterity)
Ovid, 107, 117–18

Partage, 11, 43, 146, 201n14
Perishing (*Verenden*), 10, 153
Phantom, 221n18 (*See also* ghost; revenant; specter)
Plato, 3, 9, 36–37, 47, 187, 199n20
Play of traces. *See under* trace
Plotinian One, 47

Poetic attestation, 14, 66–67, 70, 87, 190, 204n
Polt, Richard, 195n24
Possibility, 5, 13, 43, 44, 48, 59, 60–61, 65, 67, 69, 79, 122, 144, 150, 152, 153, 154, 156, 157, 170, 172, 182, 183, 188, 214n46
Possibility-to-be, 14, 66, 68, 70, 77, 79, 80, 84, 87, 94, 95, 96, 133, 135, 136, 150–54, 158, 159, 161–64, 190
Possible impossibility, 18, 61, 150, 153–54
Poststructuralism, 13, 24, 27, 28, 140
Presence, 6, 16, 29, 30, 32, 33, 34, 36, 37, 38, 63, 68, 69, 76, 79, 80, 81, 82, 87, 92, 99, 102, 114–15, 118, 123, 128, 132–34, 137, 140, 141, 143, 144, 149, 157, 159, 163, 165, 179, 198n, 200n27, 216n21, 217n35, 218n, 218n41
Present absence, 6, 16, 38, 66, 76, 77, 78, 87, 92–93, 98–105, 107, 114, 119, 128, 132, 137, 138, 141, 144, 147, 149, 150, 161, 163, 164, 168, 181, 183, 185, 190, 221n18 (*See also* absent presence)
Present (*cadeaux*), 35–36, 40, 169, 171
Primordial time, 18, 127, 133–36
Principle of sufficient reason, 13, 43–50, 52, 55, 58, 73, 108, 120
Projection, 61, 150, 151, 152, 153, 163
Prolonged grief disorder, 82

Radical hermeneutics, 2–3, 5, 7, 8, 14, 189 (*See also* hermeneutics)
Raffoul, François, 7, 17, 127, 155, 192n, 194n16, 198n8, 206n21, 208n49, 208n1, 223n26
Rambo, Shelly, 182, 196n34, 197n53, 206n24

Rankine, Claudia, 185
Ratcliffe, Matthew, 210n33
Rebellious mourning, 1, 19, 183, 184, 185–86, 187
Relational ontology, 77–78, 97
Ressler, Kerry J., 213n22
Responsibility, 9, 10, 11, 14, 19, 38, 66, 68, 78–80, 83–87, 93, 117, 145, 157, 167, 174–75, 182–84, 188, 190–92, 200n24, 204n3, 208n48, 208n49, 223n26
Revenant, 128, 129, 138, 139, 158, 181
Revenir, 128, 158
Romano, Claude, 5, 7, 9, 60, 63, 70, 77, 78, 85, 96, 145, 146, 159, 163, 193n8, 194n12, 199n20, 200n30, 205n14, 206n23, 207n31, 215n5, 217n35, 219n62, 220n8, 221n18
Rosenthal, Adam R., 197n7
Rosner, Elizabeth, 11, 77, 118, 182, 212n16, 215n9, 217n34
Rousseau, Jean-Jacques, 26
Ruin, Hans, 139, 187, 195n26, 204n6, 217n36, 224n39, 225n55
Russon, John, 210n44, 217n37

Saghafi, Kas, 11, 209n
Sans avoir, 34–35, 39, 40, 168, 169, 170, 171, 172, 173, 180, 189, 199n17
Sans savoir, 34–35, 36, 39, 40, 168, 169, 170, 171, 172, 173, 175, 180, 189, 199n17
Sans voir, 27, 34–35, 36, 40, 168, 169, 170, 171, 172, 173, 175, 180, 189, 199n17
Saturated phenomenon, 14, 46, 52–60, 102, 108, 189, 203n
Schmidt, Carl, 169
Schmidt, Dennis, 204n8, 205n11
Secret, Timothy, 167, 207n40
Shibboleth, 67

248 | Index

Sign, 24, 25, 27, 33, 73, 74, 75, 110, 111, 117 (*See also* signified, signifier, transcendental signified)
Signified, 25, 27, 111 (*See also* sign, signifier, transcendental signified)
Signifier, 25, 27, 111, 117, 118, 140 (*See also* sign, signified, transcendental signified)
Silesius, Angelus, 14, 46, 47, 50, 51, 52, 53, 56, 58, 60, 120, 157
Simmel, Georg, 152
Sisyphus, 167
Sisyphean task/stone, xiii, 82
Sorge (care), 77, 134–37, 142, 150, 152
Sokolowski, Robert, 194n14
Spatiality, 2, 6, 12, 15–16, 91–94, 96, 102, 103, 105, 108, 117, 120, 121, 127, 181, 183, 189–90
Specter, 128, 129, 141, 142, 149, 158, 163, 165, 179 (*See also* ghost; phantom; revenant)
Spectral logic, 140
Spectral moment, 19, 141, 142, 144, 149, 150, 165, 167, 190, 219n47
Stoler, Ann, 224n42
Strauss, Claude-Levi, 26
Stimmung, 135 (*See also* mood/moodedness)
Structuralism, 25
Subjectivity, 3–4, 13, 51, 56, 131, 133, 157, 208n46, 208n49
Sukkoth, 138
Supplement, 33, 109, 110–12, 139
Supplementarity, 25, 111–2, 139–40
Surprise, 4, 5, 12, 13, 23–24, 27, 34, 35, 36, 39–41, 44, 55, 57, 67, 91, 93, 97, 122–23, 129, 157, 168, 175, 176, 177, 182, 190, 199n17, 218n
Survival, 1, 2, 8, 10, 11, 12, 17, 73, 75, 93, 98, 100, 101, 104, 105, 106, 108, 113, 121–23, 131, 138, 140, 142, 157, 159, 164, 167, 168, 186, 187–88, 190, 192, 224n39 (*See also* afterlife; life after; living on; *survivre, survivance*)
Survivre, 10, 11, 12, 168, 185, 196n34 (*See also* afterlife; life after; living on; survival, *survivance*)
Survivance, 10, 168, 185, 187 (*See also* afterlife; life after; living on; survival; *survivre*)
Survivor, 6–7, 11, 14–15, 17–19, 26, 28, 38–39, 41, 48, 50, 57, 59, 60, 62, 63, 66, 68, 74, 75, 79, 80–81, 85–86, 87, 88, 92–93, 96–105 *passim*, 107, 108, 113, 115–17, 119–22, 127–30, 132, 137, 138, 139, 140, 141–42, 144, 145, 146–47, 149–50, 154, 158–65, 167–68, 170, 172, 173, 179, 181–88 *passim*, 189–91, 204n3, 210n44, 215n9, 219n64, 221n23, 224n39
Survivor trees, 108, 113, 117–19
Symptomatology, 5, 23–24, 31; as im-possible, 7, 12, 13, 23, 35, 39, 40, 43, 44, 58, 60, 66, 67, 78, 87, 91, 92, 107, 155, 156–58, 159, 162, 168, 177, 190, 220n7; as secret, 12, 13–14, 23–24, 35, 39, 43–47, 52, 53, 55, 60, 65, 66, 67, 68, 78, 87, 88, 91, 92, 119, 168; as transformative, 5, 10, 12, 14, 23, 35, 65–67, 78, 87, 91, 107, 117, 120, 168, 169, 189, 214n44; as unexpected, 5, 6, 8, 12, 13, 15, 16, 17, 23–24, 26–28, 31–36, 38–41, 43, 44–45, 54, 58–60, 66, 78, 87, 91, 92, 93, 97, 98–99, 101, 103, 107, 122, 128, 130, 141, 156, 165, 168, 169, 170, 176, 177, 182, 183, 189–191, 214n44, 220n7; as without horizon, 5, 12, 27, 31, 41, 55, 59, 62, 175, 180; as without reason, 13, 15, 23, 43–50, 52, 59, 60, 91, 141, 168, 169, 183, 189

Taylor, Mark C., 97, 209n6, 209n11
Temporality, 2, 6, 89, 12, 15, 17, 36–39, 44, 91, 116, 121, 123, 127–42, 144, 147, 149, 150, 151, 152, 154, 156, 163, 165, 167, 181, 183, 185, 189, 190, 195n26, 199n20, 199n21, 215n1, 215n5, 216n17, 216n21, 217n27, 217n35, 217n37, 218n39, 218n42, 220n8; diachronic, 37, 200n28; eventful, 17, 127; synchronic, 37, 132; spectral, 142
Textuality, 110, 212n8
Therezo, Rodrigo, 197n7, 198n13
Thompson, Joy Netanya, 214n43
Thrownness (*Geworfenheit*), 134–35, 136, 150–53, 158
To-come, 18, 19, 36, 154–58, 159, 160, 161, 162, 169, 174, 177, 183, 186, 188, 220n7
Token of mourning, 107, 118, 119
Tout autre est tout autre, 7, 84
Trace, 25, 27, 28, 32, 33–34, 38, 39, 45, 67, 111, 130, 137, 138, 139, 140, 144, 182, 184, 190, 200n27, 211n5
Tragen, 14, 18, 68, 79, 106, 182, 190 (*See also* carry; carry on)
Transactive memory, 18, 128, 145–47, 191, 219n64 (*See also* memory; hauntological memory; memory-with; workless memory)
Transcendental idealism, 131
Transcendental Signified, 25, 27, 31, 32, 33, 36, 111 199n (*See also* sign, signified, signifier)
Transposition, 115, 213n23
Trauma/traumatic, 11, 13, 17, 24, 27, 39, 44, 78, 105, 107, 108, 113, 115–16, 118, 120, 129, 130, 137–39, 144, 162, 163, 182, 184, 185, 190, 200n28, 200n29, 200n30, 206n24, 213n27, 215n8, 223n31, 224n39

Unconditional hospitality, 19, 41, 174–79, 181 (*See also* conditional hospitality; hospitality; workless hospitality)
Unexpected death, 97–102, 103, 191

Valentine, Christine, 212n14, 221n23
Vallega-Neu, Daniela, 197n5
Van der Heiden, Gert-Jan, 203n2
Van der Kolk, Bessel, 39, 116, 130, 138
Vigilance, 192
Vitale, Francesco, 211n3, 212n10, 212n15
Vorhandenheit (objective presence), 94
Voltaire, 120
Vulgar time, 133–34

Warren, Nicolas de, 216n20
Warum (why), 47, 48, 51
Wegner, Daniel M., 145–46
Weil (while), 47, 50, 51
Wesen, 70, 135, 150, 151, 152, 154
Westerlund, Fredrik, 201n6
Windowless, 73, 101, 205n15
Winfree, Jason, 198n
Without why, 14, 32, 46, 50–53, 55, 56, 60, 67, 120, 189
Wolterstorff, Nicholas, 1, 2, 16, 76, 99, 100, 101, 121, 160, 161, 162, 163, 164
Workless hospitality, 19, 168, 174, 175, 178, 180–81, 186, 188, 191 (*See also* conditional hospitality; hospitality; unconditional hospitality)
Workless memory, 18, 129, 144–45, 158, 180, 181, 191 (*See also* memory; hauntological memory; memory-with; transactive memory)

Workless mourning, 3, 7, 14, 15, 18–19, 41, 66, 79–84, 87, 99, 103, 104, 105, 113, 114, 129, 137, 141, 143–45, 158, 174, 180, 181, 182, 186, 191, 208n49, 210n44, 217n33

World, 4; as *Mitwelt* (with-world), 75, 77, 78, 80, 83, 85, 86, 87, 99, 101, 128, 165, 190, 206n21; as pluralized world, 4, 6, 14, 15, 75, 76, 77, 78, 80, 81, 87, 88, 91, 92, 97, 100–07 *passim*, 117, 121, 123, 128, 147, 156, 160, 165, 181, 182, 183, 185, 186, 187, 188, 189, 190, 192; as *Selbstwelt* (self-world), 75; as *Umwelt* (surrounding world), 4, 75, 94, 95

World time, 127, 133, 134, 141–42

World War I, 57

World War II, 115

Yehuda, Rachel, 114, 116

Zabala, Santiago, 10

Zahavi, Dan, 216n20, 216n21

Zola, 224n52

Zuhandenheit (handiness), 94, 95

www.ingramcontent.com/pod-product-compliance
Lightning Source LLC
Chambersburg PA
CBHW022004220426
43663CB00007B/954